JEWS･OF･THE･AMAZON
SELF-EXILE IN EARTHLY PARADISE

3 Noviembre, 1999

a Felisa,
  mi primera agente en
castellano en los Estados
Unidos
    Salud y salud

Ariel

JEWS✦OF✦THE✦AMAZON
SELF-EXILE IN EARTHLY PARADISE

BY ARIEL SEGAL

The Jewish Publication Society
Philadelphia
1999 • 5760

The Jewish Publication Society
1930 Chestnut Street
Philadelphia, PA 19103

Composition by Book Design Studio II
Design by Masters Group Design
Manufactured in the United States of America

99 00 01 02 03 04 05 06 07 08 10 9 8 7 6 5 4 3 2 1

Library of Congress Cataloging-in-Publication Data

Segal Freilich, Ariel, 1965-
   Jews of the Amazon : self-exile in earthly paradise / Ariel
Segal Freilich.
      p.   cm.
   Includes bibliographical references (p.   ) and index.
   ISBN 0-8276-0669-9
   1. Mestizos--Peru--Iquitos--Religion.   2. Christian
Jews--Peru--Iquitos.   3. Jews--Peru--History.   4. Jews--Identity.   5.
Iquitos (Peru)--Ethnic relations.   I. Title.
   F3619.M47 S45 1999
   305.892'408544--dc21

                                                      99-10894
                                                          CIP

To Grandma Rebeca Freilich,
Uncle Abraham, and
Aunt Guta Hirzbein,
who do not need to explain their
Jewish identity;
to Netanel Lorch, z"l;
and
to those who feel Jewish and, therefore, study.

CONTENTS

PREFACE

THREE YEARS HAVE passed since I visited the isolated city of Iquitos in the Peruvian Amazon. Since then, I have been writing, rewriting, and polishing the fascinating history and stories of a community of descendants of native Amazonian women and Jewish men who came to the Amazon jungle from Morocco and Europe during the South American rubber boom in the late nineteenth and early twentieth centuries. The "Jewish *Mestizos*" as I call them, since they are the offspring of mixed marriages between Indians and Jewish white people, consider themselves Jews, celebrate Jewish holidays, and bury the members of their congregation in the Israelite cemetery established by their forefathers. Most of them dream of immigrating to Israel and some of them have realized that dream. All of them have caused me to question aspects of my own Jewish identity that I had taken for granted; and therefore, to examine the ongoing debate of "who is a Jew?" (As anthropologist Virginia Domínguez puts it, it is a controversy that "is about exclusion as much as it is about inclusion. It is about otherness as much as it is about the collective self.")[1]

My encounter with the "Jewish *Mestizos*" developed into much more than the researcher-researched relationship between a historian and his or her living sources of information. The history of their ancestors, the original Jews who lived in Iquitos, is a fascinating topic by itself, but I found that the real subject of my investigation was the same people who were telling me the stories of their grandparents and of their Jewish-Christian Amazonian identity. These are some examples of how the "Jewish *Mestizos*" describe their self-awareness of the dual faith they inherited from their ancestors:

> *I am Catholic, but I take the best from every place. All religions are good because they give you a life within laws and the belief in God. After death, I can go into a good place. . . . I am not completely Jewish because I do not carry out all the customs.*

✦

> *We are Catholics, but we always ask of the Israelite God.*

✦

> *[We] the Jews, belong to a selected race, but unfortunately I am not 100 percent Jewish.*

◆

Are there Christian Jews in Israel?

◆

*I know that I have two legacies and I respect both of them, because
my mother is Catholic. I say that I am Jewish but I am afraid to
say that I am because I do not believe I am a good Jew. More than
fear . . . it is shame, not of being Jewish, but of the opposite; I feel
very proud of my blood, but rather I feel ashamed of saying it
because I do not believe I have the right to assert that I am a Jew.
You need to have more knowledge, to practice.*

◆

*We live in a non-Jewish country. That does not mean we do not
wish to be Jews. . . . I say it again, I feel proud of being Jewish, but
regretfully, we live in a Christian environment. Not regretfully!
Because it is a proud thing for us to be Christians!*

I listen again to the tapes of the interviews that I conducted in Iquitos,
I read again the testimonies of the "Jewish *Mestizos*," and now that I live
in Israel, occasionally I visit the four families who have immigrated to the
Jewish state in the last eight months; the more I witness their giant efforts
to maintain sparks of their Jewish heritage, to integrate, and to be accepted as Jews in the Jewish state, the easier it is for me to imagine the
struggle of those Spanish Jews forced to convert to Catholicism (and
scornfully called "pigs" or *Marranos* by their fellow Spaniards), who left
the Iberian Peninsula in the sixteenth and seventeenth centuries and attempted to return to the faith of their grandparents in tolerant havens
such as Amsterdam, Turkey, the Balkans, North Africa, Dutch Brazil, and
other places far away from the dungeons of the Inquisition.

As their remarks show, the "Jewish *Mestizos*" of Iquitos—like other
Jewish descendants typically classified as *Marranos*—identify strongly with
the Jewish people, despite ambiguities regarding the legitimacy of that
identity. Therefore, when I rationalize my feelings toward this isolated
community in the Amazonian rain forest, and compare them to the original *Marranos* of the Iberian Peninsula, I find profound similarities that
draw me to propose a definition of *Marranism* in terms of its consequences and not of its origins. Hence, I define *Marranism* as a syncretic

identity that incorporates Judaism (or at least, an intense sense of Jewishness), an identity not necessarily associated with the compulsory conversion of Jews to another religion.

Even if the reader were to accept that Iquitos's descendants of Jews fit under the broad rubric of *Marranism*—a case that could be refuted by scholars who consider this phenomenon exclusively linked to compulsory conversion of Jews and the history of the Inquisition—one can still ask: Instead of defining these people as *Marranos,* why not define them as living at the edge of assimilation, and thus fix the limits of my argument according to the concepts of syncretism or religious synthesis? I have several reasons for not wanting to do so. First, I believe that comparing contemporary groups such as the "Jewish *Mestizos*" of Iquitos to the sixteenth- and seventeenth-century *Marranos* gives us a unique opportunity to "scratch" the surface of the *Marranos'* identities when they were free to return to Judaism and profess their original religion in Jewish communities, although their Judaism was in many cases questioned by rabbinical authorities.

Second, the *Iquiteños,* like the descendants of *Conversos* (Jews forced to convert to Christianity), underwent a process of religious synthesis and self-identification with Judaism. As with the "original" *Marranos,* who gradually assimilated aspects of European Catholicism and Judaism, occupying some place in the middle of the spectrum that runs from wholly Christian (devout New Christian) to wholly Jewish (secret or crypto-Jews), the Jewishness of the "Jewish *Mestizos*" increasingly revolved around their sense of Jewish peoplehood (or rather, of being distinct from other Christians), even as they began to lose fragments of barely-understood Jewish lore that they had inherited from their ancestors.

Marranism has become a matter of scholarly inquiry. The historiography on *Marranism* attempts to distinguish between variations of this phenomenon within a spectrum of religious beliefs, spanning traditional Christianity and "pure" crypto-Judaism. In between these two extremes is a whole range of *Marrano* practices, which, according to scholar Brian Pullan, includes "dwellers of a no-man's land between two faiths."[2] This definition can be illustrated with the following description from a "Jewish *Mestizo*":

> *My brother and I observe Shabbat every week. We do not work,*
> *we recite psalms, we do not cook. I do not deviate from what my*

father has transmitted to us. . . . Have you listened to the radio program of the Pentecostal church on Saturdays? They make miracles and people are healed with the name of Jesus. Is that true? What do you think? Because, as you know, the sick person is possessed by the demon. . . .

It is forbidden to listen to the radio on Shabbat. Anyway, I do not turn on the radio. I ask [the maid] to do it. . . . The thing [the command] consists of not turning off the radio during Shabbat. . . .

On Yom Kippur [the Day of Atonement], when you have to blow the trumpet at six o'clock in the afternoon, I make it appear as if the trumpet is making the sounds: Buuuuu . . . Buuuuu . . . Buuuuu. . . . Like I have heard in Lima. We all [my family] make the sounds, and we also fast. [I learned that.] The trumpet is blown at the end because God is with us in the gathering and we are saying farewell. Then we say "Shabbat Shalom."[3]

Can we assert that the identity of the "Jewish *Mestizos*" resembles that of sixteenth- and seventeenth-century *Marranos*? Since we are not able to listen to the testimonies of the original descendants of Spanish and Portuguese *Conversos* or *Marranos*, we should probably content ourselves by comparing their experiences to that of the only *Marrano* community that still persists in our time—the so called "Last Secret Jews" found in the village of Belmonte, in northern Portugal. After almost five hundred years of compulsory conversion to Catholicism and an Inquisition, which enforced the integrity of their conversions, the secret Jews of Belmonte and a few towns near Bragança nonetheless succeeded in keeping a sense of Jewishness and some Jewish rituals.[4]

The Jewish scholar Dan Ross, visiting Belmonte some years ago, described how the *Marranos* he was studying attended church alongside their Catholic neighbors: "The parish priest explained that he sees them for baptisms, weddings, and funerals—occasionally to light a candle for a saint. 'But they never take communion,' he added." Later in the account, Ross wrote: "The current priest shrugged his shoulders. 'They are strange Jews,' he mused. 'Going to church is part of their religion.'"[5]

The following are other descriptions of these Portuguese *Marranos*:

"The 'Jew' in the cafe had been baptized a Catholic. He was married in Belmonte's Catholic Church. When he dies, they will hold his funeral there. He is not circumcised. He eats pork. And he keeps his religion absolutely private."[6]

✦

"With the exception of 'Ascension Day' and recently, Corpus Christi Day, the community does not gather its members for other festivities of total Christian inspiration."[7]

The first account, describing the crypto-Jews of Belmonte, could apply equally well to many of Iquitos's descendants of Jews, but with two major differences: the "Jewish" *Iquiteños* do not always hold funeral rites in the church (sometimes in their houses, instead), and their religion is not necessarily "absolutely private." The second account, by David Augusto Canelo, shows parallelisms between Belmonte's *Marranos* and Iquitos's "Jewish *Mestizos*" regarding the celebration of important Christian holidays, although the Amazonian "Jews" do not gather together to celebrate such occasions. (Some of them perform Catholic rituals individually.)

What is the common thread uniting these descendants of Portuguese crypto-Jews who survived the Inquisition and the descendants of Jews who went to the benevolent Amazon where they could openly practice their customs? If we understand *Marranism* as the syncretic identity of descendants of Jews who embraced (willingly or by force) another religion, and more specifically, Christianity, while maintaining a strong sense of Jewishness, we can consider the "Jewish *Mestizos*" of Iquitos as contemporary *Marranos*. In a broader sense, *Marranism* includes all descendants of Jews who have inherited an identity as Jews in places where historical circumstances have forced them to live between two or more religions. However, Judaism remains their central paradigm, and the Jewish people, their main reference group. These modern-day *Marranos* would include self-proclaimed Jews such as the Mashhadi of Iran, the *Bene Israel* of India, and the Döhnme of Salonika, all of whom have been exposed to non-Christian religions.[8] Common to these groups are "*Marrano* patterns," which Israeli philosopher Yeremiahu Yovel describes as "a split religious identity; a metaphysical skepticism; a quest for alternative salvation through methods that oppose the official doctrine; and opposition between the inner and the outer life, and a tendency toward a dual language and equivocation."[9] These patterns will become obvious for the reader through the voices of the "Jewish *Mestizos*" of Iquitos.

As was pointed out previously, important ritual and cosmological differences exist between Belmonte's community of crypto-Jews and the "Jewish *Mestizos*" of Iquitos. Significantly, the approximately 250 practicing "Jews" of Belmonte preserve their rituals in the privacy of their own homes (including Shabbat services), as their fearful ancestors used to do to hide from the Inquisition's functionaries. Although these contemporary crypto-Jews are baptized, married, and buried by the Catholic Church, they keep certain Jewish traditions as if they were Orthodox Jews: They hold private Jewish ceremonies in their homes after their Christian weddings, they rigorously observe Passover (they prepare the matzah, unleavened bread), and they fast during Yom Kippur and pray their own liturgy with some Hebrew words. Belmonte's Jewish holidays are commemorated within periods based on lunar phases as the Hebrew calendar stipulates. Also, this community celebrates holidays unknown to the nearly 150 Peruvian Amazon "Jews," such as the Fast of Esther (their version of Purim), and the *Natalinho* or "Minor Christmas" (a holiday that precedes Christmas and might be related to their vague remembrance of Hanukkah, a Jewish holiday usually celebrated a few days before Christmas). In Belmonte, they only gather as a community to commemorate the Catholic Thursday of Ascension and Corpus Christi Day (the Christian holidays that their ancestors were forced to attend). Mothers transmit their secret religion to daughters on their eleventh birthday.[10]

Conversely, the "Jewish *Mestizos*" of Iquitos search for their roots through evoking the memory of their ancestors (generally men). They are not strict observers of Jewish rituals and they do not perform Jewish weddings; but often, they do bury many of their members in the Israelite cemetery, reading the *Kaddish* in Spanish, regardless of the nominal Christianity of the deceased. As in most of the Jewish communities of the world, Iquitos's "Jewish *Mestizos*" conduct public worship of Shabbat, Passover, and Yom Kippur, and those who celebrate Christian holidays do it in their homes or churches. In Belmonte, until a few years ago, the oldest member of the community directed the rituals for holidays, based on the principle that the most aged person was the one who knew the most about Judaism. In Iquitos, Víctor Edery Morales, a patriarchal figure—but not the oldest Jewish descendant in the city—has been selected the spiritual guide of the community based on his unquestionable knowledge of Jewish traditions. This is a brief portrayal of Víctor Edery, as he is commonly known, which I registered in my personal diary:

> Don Víctor's house (which includes a bar) is the site where the community gathers to celebrate Shabbat services. He places his thin and fragile hands over cups filled with port wine and bread, blessing with his weak voice the fruits of the vine and the land. He is in charge of the long Shabbat sermons addressed to the worshipers, and his eyes radiate while he explains what Judaism is about, "why it is the true religion." The same eyes very often shed tears when he remembers his father, the "man who taught me what I am, the man who told me not to forget that I am Jewish, the man whose steps guide my life."
>
> Don Víctor assures me that the Messiah will come soon, and "he will open the eyes of everybody to see the true religion: Judaism." He sent five of his twelve children to Israel (some of them returned or moved to other countries); he would like to see the whole community emigrate to Israel or, at least, become faithful believers in the Jewish religion: "The problem is that the *paisanos* [compatriots, fellow men from similar origins] only come when we have a guest from Lima or Israel! They still do not assume their Judaism!"

There are some common features between the communities of Belmonte and Iquitos. In both places, the Jewish descendants consider themselves to be authentic Jews who belong to the "race" and religion of Israel. Both communities consist of nominal Christians, having been registered in churches, and both follow a syncretic religion different from Judaism and Catholicism although having origin in both. In addition, the two communities have survived; however, they are at the edge of extinction due to their isolation from mainstream Jewish communities.

In the Portuguese case, the *Marranos* of Belmonte live in remote regions of the country, far from the large cities and towns where Inquisitorial activities wiped out entire *Marrano* populations by the eighteenth century. The Inquisition was less interested in *Conversos,* who could not provide them with a "lucrative hunt," than they were in those who held important positions and possessed fortunes to contribute to its coffers. Hence, crypto-Jews living in isolated rural villages could maintain a certain communal life and perpetuate Jewish traditions more easily. Ironically, in the nineteenth and twentieth centuries, long after the cessation of the Inquisition, these communities, which were still living apart from the Jewish world, continued to integrate additional Christian notions into their religion. Thus, although isolation enabled the Portuguese *Marranos* to survive, it was at the cost of losing the entirety of their religious customs.

In contrast, the "Jewish *Mestizos*" of Iquitos were able to live openly as Jews because the Inquisition never took root in the isolated Amazon. However, this very isolation made it easy for their descendants to assimilate into the predominantly Christian environment. In this case, isolation did not ensure the survival of Amazonian "Jews," but its long-term effect created conditions for the emergence of a special type of Peruvian "Jews."

This is the story of these special Peruvian "Jews." It is a story of cultural survival, a story constructed through historical records and the testimonies of many people who have related to the Jews who arrived in Iquitos and to their descendants. But especially, the story of the "Jewish *Mestizos*" and the description of the *Marranic* identity demanded a detective work that could uncover the voices of the Amazon landscapes, the odors and flavors of Iquitos, the dreams and longings behind what the protagonists of this book tell, and also the sentimental scholar who is presenting this work. Therefore, this is also the story of a Jewish researcher-protagonist who fluctuates from one side to the other along the borders of his own identity, attempting to write a history of other acrobats who are trying to maintain their balance on the thin and trembling tightrope of their identities.

And so, trying to maintain my balance as a historian and storyteller, I invite the reader to join this journey through the currents of the Amazon River. . . .

ACKNOWLEDGMENTS

M ANY COLLEAGUES ADVISED me to write my acknowledgments as soon as possible; thereby, I would avoid forgetting to thank everyone who deserves my gratitude for helping me to realize this work. I purposely made the "mistake" of ignoring this advice, so that, if I have forgotten to mention someone, it could be attributed more to time running away from me, rather than to my memory (although I confess to being very absent-minded). In any case, I accept responsibility if there are important omissions.

First, I must mention that without the help of someone whom I still do not know personally, this work would still be merely a proposal: Jimmy Stone, a Jewish Peruvian friend who supplied most of the financial aid for my field research while I stayed in Lima and Iquitos. I contacted Mr. Stone via his relatives Isaac and Anita Garazi, who endeavored to help a perfect stranger solely on the basis of their interest in this project. I met the Garazi family during a "Sephardic Week," organized in January 1995 by the Sephardic congregation of Miami. I also want to mention the person who told me about that event and encouraged me to meet people who might help me: Rabbi Abraham Benzaquén. I have spent wonderful Shabbat dinners with his family (his wife Rachel and their five children), learning about Judaism, about myself, and about tolerance, and remembering the "old times" when Rabbi Abraham was my *More* (teacher) in Caracas's Jewish School when none of us imagined that we would meet again in Miami, he as a rabbi, and I as a graduate student still reluctant to become a disciple of my Orthodox teacher.

I also want to thank the faculty members of the history department of the University of Miami for contributing financial aid for this research and for my entire training in the Ph.D. program of Latin American history. I am grateful to every professor who encouraged me to continue with my sometimes bizarre ideas, modifying them and suggesting that I reconsider aspects of my study without abandoning them. In this way they provided me with "wings and roots" so that I was allowed to exercise my creativity while always being reminded of my commitment to the historical discipline.

Thank you, Dr. Robert M. Levine, for your confidence in the student I was, in the researcher I am, and in the writer I hope to be. You provided me with constant guidance throughout the way. I hope to repay your trust in me through this work. Thank you, Dr. Thomas Abercrombie, for your ideas, for your flexible stance toward the sometimes rigid currents of the academic world, and for your friendship. Thank you, Dr. Steve Stein, for surprising me with your interest in my big ideas, which had so little to sustain them when I first met you. You helped put my feet on the ground (although I did not keep them there all the time!). Thank you, Dr. Henry Green, for monitoring my scholarly evolution, for your constant suggestions on how to structure my research and also, how to obtain financial aid. Thank you, Dr. Guido Ruggiero, for your interest in the *Imaginario*, that concept I wanted so much to develop in my work and which I was finally able to touch on, no matter how briefly. Together with Dr. Abercrombie, you provided me with an excellent background on cultural history. Thank you, Dr. Chris Lane for your enthusiastic contribution to this work, especially in historical aspects concerning colonial Latin America.

I wish to thank Dr. Frank C. Stuart for his invaluable friendship and support throughout my professional and personal life. Your lectures, Dr. Stuart, greatly influenced my love of history and your everyday actions as a professor and as a person have become a compass to follow in my search for an enthusiastic way to be a pedagogue.

Now it is time to thank the people responsible for making my field research successful:

Rafael Rodríguez, an amateur historian who was the first person to mention to me the *Judíos Charapas,* the Amazonian Jews. He also sent me several articles about these Jews and later in Lima, he introduced me to the first *Iquiteños* Jewish descendants I encountered. He is the person most responsible for my "discovery" of the Amazonian "Jewish *Mestizos.*"

Rabbi Guillermo Bronstein treated me as an old friend from our very first telephone conversation. When I finally met him in Lima, there was a sense of familiarity and affection that only two old pals can share. He helped me with the logistics for my trip to Iquitos and contributed his knowledge about the Iquitos community and also about Jewish issues that were part of the puzzle of their identity. Rabbi Bronstein, his wife Mónica, and their children hosted me with great kindness during my stay in Lima.

Sandy Barak Cassinelli was my accomplice during the whole adventure of studying the Iquitos "Jews." As a member of the Peruvian Zionist

Federation, she provided me with details about how Iquitos's case had been dealt with in Lima. When I first interviewed her, I never imagined she would become a partner during my research. She proposed that I interview a number of people in Lima and she came with me to those interviews. Sandy suggested ideas to me; she even performed several interviews with visitors in Lima while I was in Iquitos. I will never forget our discussions about Jewish identity, about the communities of Lima and Iquitos, about whether hope is a luxury or a need, and especially, her unforgettable remark: Do you really receive fellowships for such entertaining work? Sandy's husband, Ricky Cassinelli, also contributed to a large extent to my understanding of Peruvian history. I doubt that I could have found as knowledgeable a guide for my visits to Lima's museums. I also want to thank their children, Daniel and Ariela, Sandy's parents, Simón and Eva Barak, and Lucás "Bruno," the dog, for their warmth and hospitality.

Alfredo Rosenzweig is the first person who ever researched the history of the Amazonian Jews in Peru. I thank him for the material he brought to me from Israel and for the interview he granted to Sandy Cassinelli while I was in Iquitos, and later, for the warm conversations we maintain now in Israel. Several scholars helped me to put into the Peruvian national context aspects of this work: León Trahtemberg, author of two books regarding the history of Peruvian Jews, Margarita Guerra, Humberto Rodríguez Pastor, Jorge Trillo Ramos, Genaro García, Javier Gutierrez Neyra, José Barletti Pasquale, Teddy Bendayán Díaz, and my friend Elías Szczytnicky (who I know is going to deny that he is a scholar).

In Iquitos I had the fortune of learning from Father Joaquín García Sánchez the many issues concerning the history, myths, religion, and sociological aspects of the Amazon and Iquitos, which cannot be found in books or manuscripts. Father Joaquín, as everyone calls him in Iquitos, is the founder of the Center of Theological Studies of the Amazon (CETA) and the Amazonian Library. Many workers of CETA provided information for this work, but I would especially like to mention Father José María Arroyo, whose intelligence and sense of humor granted me exceptional moments.

In the *Biblioteca Amazónica* I received a "special guest treatment" by the two wonderful women who have transformed that library into a model location for researchers of Amazonian topics: Alejandra Schindler and

María Iglesias. Thanks to both of them, I obtained a great deal of material that otherwise would have been impossible to find by myself. I also thank María for her friendship. I want to express my gratitude to every functionary who amiably helped me dig in the various archives. I owe a special mention to Raúl López del Aguila, who has organized a highly efficient system for obtaining data in the Oficina de Registros Públicos de Loreto (property records), and the professional competence of his team, headed by engineers Dagoberto Guevara and Pierre Reategui Gonzales.

In the "Jewish" community of Iquitos, Jaime Vásquez Izquierdo and Víctor Edery Morales became my full-time advisers throughout my research. Jaime Vásquez Izquierdo provided me with the complete archives of the *Instituto Cultural Peruano-Israelí de Iquitos* (1960s) and the *Sociedad de Beneficiencia Israelita de Iquitos* (1990s). His sense of history is responsible for the preservation of the written documentation of the Jews and their descendants in Iquitos. Víctor Edery Morales is practically the *hablador* (the storyteller), the oral memory of Iquitos's "Jewish" community.

Other people from Lima and Iquitos whom I wish to thank are Anat Kehati Trahtemberg, Jacky Silberman, Debora Frank, Mariana Pollak, Fony Arcela, David and Niela Kiperstok, Beatriz Rosemberg, Esperanza Alemánt, Anita Hurwitz de Swartzman, Joel Salpak, Jaime and Raquel Brodsky, Izak Wallach and Sonia Wallach, and all of my interviewees in both Jewish communities, my *Iquiteños* friends, Marco Mesía Rodríguez, Ronald Reategui Levy and his family, Alicia Assayag Chávez, Mónica Villena, Cristina Cisneros, Ruth Esther Gómez, Claudia Otero, little Karina, Lenny, all the staff of the Hostel María Antonia, and anyone who helped me as a scholar or as a friend. Special thanks go to "Mascarita" Daniel.

In Lima, I had the opportunity to share my experiences with the members of a great family: Don Lucho, Doña Ina, Luchín, and Jenny Caraza Neida, and all their relatives, including my colleague Antony Johnston, who became part of this family. They keep telling me that they also regard me as part of their family, and so do I.

Readers who might enjoy the excerpts from the personal diary that I wrote in Peru must be thankful to the person who advised me to "keep a separate journal in which you place your night thoughts, unusual fragrances and traces of an imaginary life." Blame it on Katherine Kruger, who will always be "Shira" in my sentimental code.

If the English of this work seems understandable, it is thanks to the best assistant anyone could have, Barbara Drake, a very meticulous and patient worker who also added some creative turns in this work. Barbara is also a personal friend who makes me very happy. I must also mention two of the most important people who helped me accomplish this work: Leny del Granado and Jesús Sánchez. Their patience and good heart was in full measure demonstrated during the five years they put up with my requests.

And if patience is the word, I want to thank especially Dr. Ellen Frankel, editor-in-chief of the Jewish Publication Society. Ellen believed in this book and with her enthusiasm and interest in my work made me believe that we would finally publish it together. She is one of my best friends whom I finally met in Israel after two years of telephone conversations. I also want to thank Christine Sweeney, a great editor who became my friend. Christine revised the manuscript to make sense of its words and meanings, and thereby made it a readable book.

Finally, I would like to thank my parents, Jaime and Alicia, in Venezuela, my brother and sister, Ernesto and Carolina, my two best friends in Miami, Mónica Ayala and Helena de Paula Souza Serber, as well as Eduardo and Luiza Serber, Quelia Quaresma, Christina Ardalan, and other friends, who made my life pleasant during my studies. In the list of my friends, I also include loyal pets such as Spunky and "Tucholsky."

Ariel Segal
June, 1999
Jerusalem

INTRODUCTION

IT WAS AN evening of rationalizations. I was overwhelmed after a full day of research, organizing in my mind flashes of three months' experience among the people I had gone to study, my *paisanos*. These descendants of native Amazonian women and Jewish men who came to the Amazon from Morocco, Gibraltar, England (Manchester), Alsace-Lorraine, and other European posts had inherited a cultural legacy that I was attempting to discern. They were the offspring of mixed marriages, of migratory movements to South America, of entrepreneurial adventures through the rivers of the Amazonian jungle. All of them had defined themselves: "I am a Jew." And now I, another Jew, faced the challenge of scientifically analyzing their history and their identity. Nonetheless, I sometimes felt that my own identity was the one in the spotlight of this investigation, as my subjects reflected light back onto puzzles of my own being.

That evening, inspired by the distant murmurs of the Amazon River, I took out my diary, not my research notebook, from my backpack. I found myself writing:

> Some images and voices from the last weeks are hovering over my
> senses: a Star of David and a cross together in a chain, on a grave-
> stone; an old woman telling the history of her Jewish ancestry. She
> tells me how proud she is of belonging to the chosen people, and
> then she asks me why Jews don't accept Christ as God, as if that it
> is an unquestionable fact. The old lady rigorously observes Shab-
> bat, refraining from cooking and using electricity, reciting psalms

from her Old Testament in Spanish translation, but every Saturday she asks her maid, her *Shabbes Goy*, to turn on the radio to listen to the weekly broadcast of Evangelical Christians. She wants me to confirm something that the Evangelical priest keeps saying in the radio program: Isn't it true that a Jew is more Jewish if he believes in Christ?

More images: one of the leaders of the Jewish community, whose house has become the prayer site for every Shabbat, is raising a pig in his backyard for a future banquet; the girl who learned in a week to recite the *Shalom Aleikhem* prayer in Hebrew because she wants to get ready for her future one-way trip to Israel, lights candles and dances for a saint so that her Zionist dream will materialize; someone who never cared about his Jewish origin asks to be buried in the Jewish cemetery; the president of an Israelite institution suggests a Christmas party, while another member of the institution expresses his excitement about organizing a "fiesta" for Yom Kippur (until he is told that there are "fiestas," holidays, in which Jews do not drink and dance).

Recalling these stories, one is tempted to save them for a novel (in the best of cases) or to put aside the idea of taking these people seriously. For a moment I am tempted to do so. Why make my research harder after I have scoured the city for factual data concerning the original Jews who came to this place? Why add to this history the ongoing travails of their descendants? They are simply Christians who fantasize about something mysterious and mystical for them: Judaism.

Yet I have a conflict with such a conclusion. How can I explain the survival of aspects of these people's Jewish consciousness, living amongst and as Christians? Why is Iquitos the only city in Peru, besides Lima, that still claims an organized Jewish community? Aren't such questions reasons enough to take these people's syncretic religious identity seriously? I think so.

Astonishingly, the descendants of Jews in Iquitos still feel themselves to be Jewish, they still are eager to trace their Jewish roots, as good modern Jews they see anti-Semites everywhere! Culturally, they are *Mestizos*, a blending. They experience a fusion of Jewish, Christian, and Amazonian beliefs and traditions; they dwell within a collage of religions and legacies that seem to contradict one another to the foreign eye, but they experience their legacies as a perfectly harmonious system of life.

They know how to maneuver among contradictions, experiencing a profound religious life that is not at conflict with their values (or lack of them?), such as having children with diverse women. *Machismo* is the rule in this place! (I include women because *machismo* is a mentality they accept submissively.) God is part of their daily life, a power to revere, a subject to pray to, to be frightened of. God is not the occasional ritual of part-time believers, the raft to which secular men cling only in cases of emergency. The Amazonian descendants of Jews talk about God and to God. . . . Doesn't that make them as Jewish as many "biologically pure" and culturally coherent Jews who leave God in the closet where they (we) keep their (our) dusty prayer books, to be used once a year on Yom Kippur, the Day of Atonement?

Who is a Jew? Who is purely Jewish?

Let the first one who can claim that throw the first stone.

When I wrote these thoughts, I neither intended to challenge the Orthodox or any other Jewish mainstream view, nor to disconnect myself from my scientific role as a historian. It was purely an emotional moment, a parenthesis in my attempt to remain objective throughout the investigation. Fighting against myself, I had decided to record these personal recollections in a separate diary that I would keep far away from my sources at the moment of writing. But those moments of weakness in my attempt to remain distant from my subjects repeated again and again until I realized a greater truth: Some historical experiences are impossible to understand on an objective level if we do not allow ourselves to be subjective. Anthropologist Virginia R. Domínguez defends this idea: "If emotional fragility is a condition of fieldwork and a consequent tool of data-gathering, then emotional reactions are the most powerful indicators of the sensitivities of the two worlds that meet/clash in us and through us."[1] Virginia Domínguez also argues that the conscious study of ourselves in the act of studying others is not only *not* inappropriate for social researchers, but "it is, in fact, advantageous."[2] I went to Iquitos as a researcher, historian, and ethnographer, but wherever a person goes, he also carries the baggage of his selfhood—in my case—a selfhood molded by my national and cultural origins. I was born in Venezuela and I lived in my birthland for more than twenty years (I owe Venezuela my basic education and my degree in journalism). I am Jewish, obsessively Jewish (I owe this to my family). Therefore, the scholar who had gone to Iquitos was a Jewish Latin American trained as a historian in the United States, but he also was a fiction writer, a lover of imaginary worlds and fantasy. Therefore, why was I surprised that I would become an object of my own research, allowing myself to enter into the relations and perceptions of Iquitos's Jewish descendants? In my particular case, due to the nature of my research and to my own nature, I would say that more than being advantageous, it was imperative for me to insert myself into this work from time to time and to add some of the immediate reactions registered in my personal diary.

This study is a historical recollection of the presence of Jews in the Peruvian Amazon and its main city, Iquitos, since the 1890s. I will explore the socioeconomic reality and the religious and cultural environment of this odd Jewish home; the history of these immigrants' integration into the regional and national life of their new home; the study of their adaptive strategies and their descendants' endeavors to preserve a sense of peoplehood, of Jewishness, in spite of adverse conditions. This is also a contemporary history of perceptions, interpretations, and relations between Lima's Jews and the current descendants of Jewish immigrants who still live in Iquitos, an attempt to understand the permutations of the manifold identities of successive generations through a historical analysis of their discourses in documents and oral testimonies. Through my studies, I learned that the group of reference invoked by the "Jewish *Mestizos*" of Iquitos is not any community in the Brazilian Amazon, as could be assumed, but, rather, is the Jewish community of Lima.[3] Therefore, I reasoned, the study of the contact between Lima and Iquitos could furnish further clues to piece together the puzzle of both communities' collective identities. After all, if the *Iquiteños*, a group product of white and Indian miscegenation were officially recognized as Jewish, wouldn't this pose serious questions to the identity of Lima's Jewish community? How could the more homogeneous and clannish Jews of Lima, whose identity is intrinsically tied to other mainstream Jewish communities worldwide and to the powerful Peruvian white minority, accept the *Iquiteños* as spiritual brethren?

Lima's Jews were and still are the most immediate point of reference for Iquitos's Jewish descendants; however, the "Jewish *Mestizos*" also identify themselves with any Jewish visitor and with the State of Israel, where some have immigrated throughout the last thirty years. Israelis and Jews like myself who have visited Iquitos and met members of the city's Israelite society become "observed observers." Our presence among these people ignites a passionate exploration of the Jewish elements of their tangled identity that otherwise remain in limbo. In this work, I will put in perspective the case of Iquitos's Jewish descendants vis-à-vis Lima's Jewish community, Israel's rabbinical and political establishments, and different Jewish congregations and individuals, taking into account halakhic (Jewish legalistic) and Peruvian socioeconomic and racial questions.

The syncretic identity of Iquitos's descendants of Jews is full of apparent contradictions, and I emphasize the *apparent* nature of their contradictions since that term typically connotes predicament and conflict for those who experience it. Such is not the case in Iquitos, a city with almost no visible contrasts for a foreign visitor; the city contains some rich men, but this economic discrepancy does not provoke noticeable class tensions because they all share the same habits, clothing, behaviors, and discourses, rich and poor alike. Likewise, *Iquiteños* follow diverse religious denominations but all share a common way of interpreting and displaying religious experiences. Unless a trained or prejudiced foreign eye scrutinizes each person, ferreting out what distinguishes him from others, it is hard to pinpoint what makes an *Iquiteño* define himself as a member of a distinctive ethnic or religious group. Father Joaquín García, director of the Center of Theological Studies of the Amazon (CETA), explains this phenomenon in these terms: "Here is a dilution of identities while people are looking for a regional identity. Socially and culturally the *Iquiteño* is homogeneous. Rituals are the same, beliefs are different."[4]

In this culturally homogeneous city, the descendants of Jews share a syncretic cosmology, fluidly intertwining Christian, Jewish, and Amazonian cultural references, to arrive at a perfectly coherent system of beliefs. I utilize the term "syncretism" as a neutral concept referring to any kind of synthesis of different religious traditions and cosmologies that borrow from each other.[5]

We will approach the intriguing world of the Amazonian "Jewish *Mestizos*" through an objective review of several factors; through the history of Jewish immigrants and their descendants' achievements in the Peruvian Amazon and, more specifically, in Iquitos; through a comparative historical analysis of the "Jewish *Mestizos*" and their counterpart, Lima's Jews; and finally, through an inquiry into how successive generations of the first Jewish immigrants in the region have experienced their syncretic identity. It is in this realm where I will try to scratch the surface of "Jewish" *Iquiteños'* sense of peoplehood, their Jewishness, and their Peruvianism.

✦

During the second half of the twentieth century, historians began to explore identity as a historical subject.[6] The question of identity poses for the researcher specific challenges that can hardly be tackled with traditional historical methods. The analysis of the ways in which ethnic groups experience a sense of peoplehood calls for ambitious objectives, which require the researcher to trace the evolution of the historical consciousness shared by the members of those groups. Applied to contemporary communities, such a study demands that the researcher rely on oral history as a paramount source for understanding people's cultural survival and sense of identity; it also demands that the researcher employ innovative writing techniques that can bridge the distance between our westernized minds and our subjects' natural cosmologies. Ironically, the only way trained, scholarly minds can grasp other people's cultures and histories is by presenting objectifications of the very subjective realities explored by the researcher; therefore, readers are fated to miss an important part of the studied subjects' vision and their spontaneous models of representation before scholars begin to codify these models for their scientific works. This study is unavoidably framed within the western scientific discipline, which requires categories of study borrowed from social sciences such as history, sociology, ethnography, and some other fields. This broad framework enables me to describe not only facts but also interpretations and representations of the past, in ways that can be understood and discussed by colleagues and people who share a common intellectual vocabulary. However, to stick rigorously to conventional academic discourses, maintaining a complete distance from my investigated subjects, would be to neglect an essential component of this study: the *Iquiteños'* emotions and feelings, which can tell us as much about identity as can other objective factors, such as historical considerations, cultural paradigms, and socio-economic realities. Hence, this work calls for two "voices" from the researcher: one, a dispassionate narrative voice, relating historical progressions, variables, and insights; and two, a skeptical voice, questioning from time to time the accuracy of its living sources, its own scientific concepts, and its own perceptions of reality.

I hope that I have succeeded in presenting a model of study through which the two functions of history—history as science and history as art—can be synthesized.[7] Richard Price, author of *Alabi's World*, asserts that "like a good historical novelist, the ethnographic historian tries to penetrate existential worlds different from his own and to evoke their texture, by bridging, but never losing sight of, the cultural and semantic gulf that separates the author from the historical actors and from the historical observers."[8] I will attempt to be a diligent ethnographic historian, making clear the gulf that separates me from the subjects of my study, while also acknowledging the risks of being confused as another historical actor in Iquitos's ever-unfolding drama. By taking into account the following caveats, readers may keep from falling off the precipice of my subjectivity:

1. Although I present direct accounts of my informants, I have selected excerpts according to the topics discussed; therefore, these oral testimonies are implicitly out of the general context of the flowing conversations I held with my interviewees.

2. Oral history is still very controversial among historians, although I hope that the way I have combined it with written primary sources convinces the reader of the importance of oral testimonies in any contemporary historical study.[9] I maintain that throughout the centuries written primary sources were first oral sources, until somebody recorded them on paper; therefore, I find the criticisms made by "purist" defenders of conventional history exclusively based on documentary sources, to be nonessential.

3. Some of my informants became my friends; they were so eager to help me that sometimes their accounts may have been influenced

by their desire to see their own community as if they were outsiders.[10]

4. My theoretical framework for this study is based on my limited knowledge of historiography. (I am a young scholar writing his first historical work.) This framework is also limited by my lack of anthropological training.

5. My interpretation of data is exactly that, *interpretation*. I do not claim to have found all the answers to my questions, but I hope that some of my insights make sense to readers.

6. The structure of this work is based on a consciously planned methodological approach; however, to a large extent it has been influenced by my literary inclinations, or rather, an exaggerated sense of lyrical sentimentalism, considerably conspicuous in the excerpts from my personal diary.

7. This study encompasses many topics, including the history and identity of a peripheral group, the story of a Latin American syncretic community, the nature of Jewishness, the nature of Peruvianism, and a definition of *Marranism;* therefore, it will hardly satisfy the expectations of most specialized readers looking for more detailed analysis of their scholarly fields. However, nonscholarly readers may find this work more fulfilling because it covers various different areas that they do not need to "dissect" in order to categorize this work for an academic index.

By outlining these seven points I am admitting how I have merged academic and literary approaches; although this confession may give rise to serious doubts about my professionalism, it may well be, on the other hand, the intellectual buoy that keeps my professionalism afloat.

The role of the historian leads to the question: Is history an art (and, therefore, akin to humanities and especially to the talent of storytelling)[11] or it is a science (and, therefore, belonging to the realm of social sciences)? This issue, which is at the heart of the current debate over the limits of objectivity and subjectivity in any historical work, is continually present in this book. In these pages, my two voices—that of the scholar and that of the human being—compete with each other in an attempt to present the reader with accurate historical facts, as well as the "accurate inaccuracies" of a sentimental researcher.

The study of the history and identity of Iquitos's descendants of Jews demands professionalism and a sensitivity to the human dimension, those details that would otherwise hinder an academic understanding of this case.

✦

This work is organized into nine chapters. Chapter One provides a brief historical context of the Amazon and Iquitos, the setting where my group of study lives and attempts to preserve its sense of Jewishness. This chapter presents an overview of the penetration, conquest, and "Peruvianization" of part of the Amazon region, beginning with the first explorers who navigated its unpredictable rivers and lost themselves in its enormous jungles, where fantasy and reality merge as do the torrential Amazon River's currents. This chapter will place a special emphasis on Iquitos, the current home of the "Jewish *Mestizos*."

Four degrees south of the equator, Iquitos is the most isolated city in South America and, with Lhasa in Tibet and Timbuktu in the Sahara Desert, it is one of the three most isolated cities in the world. Located 1,200 miles from Lima and roughly 2,300 miles from the Amazonian seacoast in the Brazilian state of Pará, this city, surrounded by the Amazon River and two of its tributaries, is separated from other cities by the vast, unbroken Amazon tropical forest and the towering Andean summits. Neither railroads nor highways arrive in Iquitos. However, the Amazon River connects Iquitos to the Atlantic market network, linking its inhabitants with European and North American trends and fashions.

Although Iquitos is a typical provincial Latin American city, it has unique characteristics. At the end of the eighteenth century, Fritz W. Up De Graff, a European traveler who visited the Upper Amazon Basin, portrayed how close and far were Lima and Iquitos before the invention of the airplane: "It cannot be more than about six hundred miles from Iquitos to Lima [in fact, it is about the double of this distance] as the crow flies. But to reach one from the other, the stretch of country which lies between the two towns is not the route that would be followed by the ordinary sane individual, much less by a body of troops. It means crossing the

Andes by practically untrodden paths, and penetrating a belt of country infested with savage tribes, unmapped, and across [sic] a large part of which the only method of transport is by dugouts. . . . The double journey which had to be undertaken was, of course, about nine thousand miles each way; down the Amazon [River] to Pará [on Brazil's shore]; down the Atlantic coast of the South American continent, round the [Cape] Horn, and up the Pacific coast to Callao, the port of Lima. . . ."[12]

Hence, the isolated Iquitos that belonged to the Atlantic economic and cultural system became the most cosmopolitan city of Peru at the beginning of the twentieth century. Eventually, after the collapse of the rubber economy, Lima made more serious attempts to integrate the Peruvian Amazon and Iquitos into its political, socioeconomic, and cultural life.

Iquitos—like other places around the world that, despite being far from political centers of power, nevertheless became important posts of trade, immigration, and cultural life—defies our notions of what is center and what is periphery in a region where the official history revolves around Lima, Cajamarca, and Cuzco. The Amazonian region is a mystery for those who penetrate its dense jungle, and remains so for the majority of Peruvians who live in the coastal area and in the Andes. In this book, the peripheral Amazon is presented as the center it was—and still is—for those who explored it, visited it, or lived there. In tantalizing glimpses, Iquitos unveils itself as what it is: center and periphery, periphery and center, a place where these concepts revolve endlessly, unaffected by their precise location in history.

Historical research about the Peruvian Amazonian region is in its first stages as a scholarly field, but in Iquitos, we can feel the overwhelming weight of oral tradition in the daily lives of the Amazonian inhabitants. It is for this reason that while the first chapter relies mainly on secondary sources based on records obtained from Iquitos's libraries, *Biblioteca Amazónica* and *Biblioteca Municipal*, as well as Teddy Bendayán Díaz's personal book collection and the library of the University of Miami, it also is complemented with voices of some *Iquiteños* scholars (from interviews) to enrich with their analyses some aspects of the region's history, which I needed to address.

Chapter Two presents an overview of the Jewish presence in Lima and Iquitos, two distant communities that share many of the same concerns about their roots, history, character, and fate. The first Jews to arrive in Peru were crypto-Jews who practiced their Jewish traditions in secrecy. Many of them suffered harassment, trials, and punishments carried out by Lima's Inquisition. Some New Christians (Jewish converts to Christianity), such as Diego de León Pinelo, who became dean of San Marcos University in Lima, appeared in the Inquisition's seventeenth-century index, where they are noted as having been suspected of Judaizing.[13] Diego's oldest brother, Antonio de León Pinelo, was a renowned authority in Lima and wrote *El Paraíso en el Nuevo Mundo,* asserting that the earthly paradise was in the Peruvian Amazon, centered around today's area of Iquitos.

This chapter summarizes in a chronological sequence the history of Peruvian Jews on both sides of the Andean mountain chain, Antonio de León Pinelo's residence in Lima, and his "earthly paradise" in the Amazon. The study of these two separate migratory currents and the parallel but distinct history of each community is based on several books, excerpts from newspaper articles, immigration documents, the original certificate that registered the foundation of the Israelite Society of Iquitos in 1909, Jewish immigrants' documents obtained in the 1940s by Jewish *Limeño* geologist Alfredo Rosenzweig,[14] property records from the enrollment office of Iquitos, parish and civil records, and oral testimonies.

Chapter Three analyzes the syncretic religion of Iquitos's Jewish descendants. First, it describes Iquitos's religious and cosmological context: the weight of Christian influence over its inhabitants, the ways people express their syncretic beliefs, Amazonian mythology and its repercussions in the daily lives of *Iquiteños* and in their rituals and holidays. Thereafter, the voices of the "Jewish *Mestizos*" describe what it is for them to be Jews, what makes them feel different from other citizens of the culturally homogeneous Iquitos, why they feel equal to "pure Jews," and how they internalize Jewish religious conceptions. I will argue that Iquitos's descendants of Jews experience a perfectly coherent system of beliefs, amalgamating Christian, Jewish, and Amazonian supernatural notions to produce a syncretic cosmology.

Chapter Four analyzes how Jewishness (the secular aspects of Jewish identity) is experienced in Lima and Iquitos. While Jewishness in Lima's community revolves around the same certainties and contemporary dilemmas of any Jewish mainstream group in the Diaspora, Iquitos's Jewish descendants have a very peculiar way of relating to these same paradigms that connect Jews with Jewish history and the State of Israel. In particular, *Iquiteños* lavish attention on the most visible link to their ancestors: the Israelite cemetery. The study of this community's Jewishness will be based on an analysis of documents from the different Israelite societies established in Iquitos since 1909, on personal documents of current Jewish descendants, and especially, on their oral testimonies. Of course, some documents housed in the offices of Jewish institutions in Lima, as well as interviews conducted with "Jewish *Mestizos*" who now live in the capital city, will contribute to understanding how Judaism is experienced in both communities.

In Chapter Five, the particular circumstances of the Iquitos community are set in the context of other groups—such as the Mashhadi descendants of Iranian Jews, the Döhnme Jews of Turkey, the *Beta Israel* Jews of Ethiopia, and the *Bene Israel* Jews of India—whose Jewishness is questioned by mainstream Jewish communities and by the Orthodox establishment of the State of Israel. Also, here I compare the religion of the first crypto-Jews who lived in Peru with the religion of the "Jewish *Mestizos*" in order to propose a definition of *Marranism* that goes beyond the period of the European and Latin American Inquisition. Under this approach, the testimonies of the "Jewish *Mestizos*" provide elements to define this community as a group of modern *Marranos* (Christianized Jews)—in this case, *Marranos* due not to the Inquisition, but rather to isolation.

Finally, this chapter analyzes such questions as: How do the State of Israel and Lima's Jewish institutions deal with the legal (halakhic) aspects of the *Iquiteños'* Jewish identities? What can we learn from the experience of *Iquiteños* who have succeeded in immigrating to Israel? How does their case rest within the context of the eternal Jewish debate, "Who is a Jew?" Most of these questions are analyzed in a speculative way because this group of approximately 150 to 200 *Iquiteños* who define themselves as Jews (compared to more than 3,000 Jews in Lima) is not large enough to cause debate in Israeli society, which has absorbed thousands of Ethiopians and Russian immigrants during the 1990s. In this chapter I review literature concerning groups on the fringes of Jewish identity, the "Who is a Jew?" controversy, and the Law of Return, which proclaims the right of every Jew to return to his or her ancestral land. In addition, sources related to the Iquitos case include documents of those "Jewish *Mestizos*" who have immigrated to Israel. This data is kept in the archives of the Zionist Federation of Peru. I also rely on oral testimonies from relatives of those who settled in Israel, personal letters, and interviews with rabbis, Jewish scholars, and Israeli representatives in Lima.

Having contextualized the case of the self-proclaimed "Jewish community" of Iquitos within the framework of other groups whose Judaism has been questioned by the Orthodox establishment of the State of Israel, I take up, in Chapter Six, a historical overview of the encounter between Iquitos's and Lima's Jewish communities and their subsequent estrangement from one another. This has been an ongoing history of many ups and downs, in which indifference and slovenliness have eclipsed the few opportunities that presented themselves for incorporating Iquitos's Jewish descendants into the Peruvian Jewish life. Documents from institutions in both Lima and Iquitos, newspaper articles, and oral accounts furnish the sources for this chapter. The same records are utilized in Chapter Seven to explore and analyze, as much as is possible, the perceptions that each group has of the other.

The quick "Peruvianization" of the Department of Loreto, and, especially, its capital city, created a situation in which Lima became the mainstream reference for all immigrants in the Peruvian Amazon; therefore, any study of the transformation of the Jewish identity of Iquitos's community throughout its one hundred years of presence in the city had to emphasize its relations, perceptions, and discourses regarding Lima's Jewish community and therefore, its case in the framework of Peruvian national, ethnic, religious, and socioeconomic categories.

Chapter Seven therefore aims to discern the racial and socioeconomic factors that shape these discourses. Since we will study a group of *Mestizos* (whose features resemble those of the majority of the country's population) living in Iquitos and claiming to be Jews, it is important to determine what questions race poses in Lima's white mainstream Jewish community. In a nation where race and class paradigms are profound elements rooted in the psyches of its inhabitants, the Jewishness of a group of *Mestizos* (regardless of the obviously non-Jewish elements of Iquitos's Jewish descendants' syncretic identity) challenges the national identity of the Jewish minority of Lima, who are hard-pressed to identify themselves with the majority of Peru's *Mestizo* population.

The two chapters in which I describe and analyze the Jewishness and the perceptions of Lima's and Iquitos's communities conceal important aspects of how my identity has influenced this work. Raised in Caracas, Venezuela, whose Jewish community includes neither Reform nor Conservative movements, I have a tendency to perceive Orthodox Judaism as mainstream. Although I have always been a secular Jew, my enormous respect for Orthodox Judaism (albeit, not for all Orthodox Jews, especially those who emphasize rituals and neglect basic ethical behaviors and tolerance) perhaps causes me to be extremely careful—and some may say, benevolent—in the way I depict the Jewish community of Lima, whose main institutions follow Orthodox guidelines. But I also have strong reservations about and disagreements with the tenets of Orthodox Jews; for this reason, some readers may claim that my sympathies toward Lima's Conservative congregation, toward its rabbi (who happens to be my friend), and toward the "crusade" (or counter-crusade) of Iquitos's "Jewish *Mestizos*" in their endeavor to become full-fledged Jews have caused me to fear offending my readers in Lima and Iquitos. I accept this possibility, and, even though I attempt to be as objective as possible when describing the protagonists of this (hi)story, the reader must keep a third eye open while reading this work.

Chapter Eight concerns myself, the author, within the history of Iquitos's "Jewish *Mestizos*." Prior to including this chapter, I had debated many times whether to write it or to simply dismiss it for the sake of academic propriety; however, after having consulted with fellow scholars and friends (not to mention my pillow), I decided that this chapter was a necessary part of this work. In this chapter I disclose components of my identity (including the "religious experiences" during my training as a scholar), and later I provide an account of my participation in the historical setting of the "Jewish *Mestizo*" community.

Any future social scientist or visitor who approaches these people will undoubtedly register the study of my influence on the perceptions and rites during and after my stay with them. Although I am the main protagonist of this chapter, I am also an "excuse" to extrapolate the means by which any researcher who relies on oral history as a main source for his or her investigation or who deals with contemporary history eventually becomes a subject of his or her object of study. Because I am a Jewish researcher, my presence in Iquitos altered to some degree the natural course of my *paisanos'* history; their questions about my own identity might have given them some clues about their Jewishness as well as given me insight into my own Jewish identity and professionalism. Ethical questions arise when we study a group with whom we identify ourselves.

Numerous subjective sources contribute to this chapter. My personal diary—remembrances of my experience in Iquitos and recollections of my activities in the Jewish community of Lima on behalf of the "Jewish *Mestizos*"—reveals my feelings about translating into scientific vocabulary what is a matter of empathy and emotion. However, I also support my "scholarly subjectivity" by providing references from other social scientists who have been concerned with the same type of questions. Doubts about my stance as a researcher comprise the core of this chapter, which must not be taken too seriously by faithful believers in objectivity and orthodox scholars.

Finally, my conclusions in Chapter 9 emulate the Amazonian ritual enacted by souls agonizing in their final hour. Before this work fades away it will retrace the steps *(recogerá los pasos)* of what was registered throughout its short "life" (enclosed within pages, rather than in time).

The conclusions will release the reader from his reading obligation, but not perhaps from confronting his own identity questions, while continuing to draw insights into the nature of this work.

◆

The question that underlies this work is expressed in the excerpt from my personal diary selected at the beginning of this introduction:

> The astonishing thing regarding all these cases is that the descendants of Jews in Iquitos still feel themselves to be Jewish, that they still are eager to trace back their Jewish roots, that as good modern Jews they see anti-Semites everywhere!

The persistence of a "Jewish fiber" that materializes in a precarious organized community still fighting to preserve the memory of its roots and which maintains a collective identity is a factor that deserves scholarly attention. How have these descendants of Jews maintained a sense of

Jewishness in such a culturally homogeneous society, one asks? How does that Jewishness manifest itself within their syncretic cosmology? Why is Iquitos the only Peruvian city other than Lima where an organized Jewish community still exists? What is the role of racial and socioeconomic factors in the set of relationships and perceptions between the Jewish communities of Lima and Iquitos? How does one explain the survival of a peripheral Jewish community in such an isolated spot in the Amazon? Where do the "Jewish *Mestizos*" fit in the big panorama of the contemporary controversy of "Who is a Jew?"

Answers to these questions are to be found in the study of the particular historical circumstances of the Amazonian region of Peru, and of the political and socioeconomic realities that made Iquitos part of the Atlantic economic system until the 1930s, and later on, part of the Peruvian state. In both periods, Iquitos's Jews had contact with different Jewish communities. Some of the answers to questions raised in this study rely on these historical dynamics; other answers can be found in the idiosyncratic way the Iquitos Jews come to perceive reality, selfhood, and peoplehood; in the possession of a sacred place (the Israelite cemetery built in 1895); in the sense of aristocracy that memories of their forefathers inspire in them; and in the curious combination of a culturally patrilineal dynamic within a de facto "matrifocal society" (in which the absence of a father figure causes the role of the mother to be central).[15] Of course, we must also point out less scientific explanations, such as the Jewish obsession with memory and self-preservation.

Finally, I owe the reader an explanation of why I consider these descendants of Jews to be self-exiled in an "earthly paradise." Iquitos was the imagined center of Antonio de León Pinelo's Garden of Eden. Although its contemporary urban appearance and misery hardly could convince any visitor that the city keeps the paradisiacal atmosphere of its pre-urban history, the surrounding rivers and forest, where nakedness (as in the case of some Indian tribes), silent serpents, and innocence still exist, enliven notions of those times before man and woman tried the forbidden fruit. Moreover, the pure heart of today's *Iquiteños*, their simplicity, their intimate contact and knowledge of nature, the mixture between fantasy and reality that most of them experience, their sentimentalism, their candor, their ability to stay afloat in the existential predicaments that contradictions can cause, their unique sense of identity that does not require them to exclude "otherness," but on the contrary, incorporates this aspect smoothly into their selfhood—all these factors evoke the idea that we have of paradise: a realm of harmony and peaceful state of mind. In this manner, Iquitos can serve as a sort of paradise for those not looking for a modernized piece of heaven. In Antonio de León Pinelo's earthly paradise, any group that attempts to distinguish itself from others (whether they are successful or not) is approaching the dangerous "tree" of the forest of estrangement and exclusion.

My *paisanos*, somehow, self-exile themselves from this paradise by attempting to distinguish themselves from the rest of Iquitos's dwellers by fighting against the natural centrifugal forces that call for cultural homogeneity in the Amazon, and by consciously attempting to put to work the centripetal forces of a mythical-historical consciousness that relates them to the Jewish people. The Jewish descendants of Iquitos endeavor to keep a sense of particularism, which seems like an attempt to exile themselves from the cultural homogeneity that most *Iquiteños* share in Antonio de León Pinelo's earthly paradise.

I

The Amazon and Iquitos: Center or Periphery?

"Oh jungle, spouse of silence, mother of loneliness
and of the mist! What spirit made me a prisoner
of your green prison?" (author's translation [AT])
—José Eustasio Rivera, *La Vorágine*

"LIMA IS PERU" is a phrase that one often hears when talking about political and social realities with people from different Peruvian provinces. Lima's excessively dominant role in Peru is confirmed by history books, by the remarks of journalists, by the framework of current political debates, by the degree of modernization of Lima compared to other departments and cities, and even by the way coastal people (*Costeños*) express themselves about native inhabitants from the Andes (*Serranos*) and from the Amazon (*Charapas*).

The hundreds of miles of Amazonian tropical rain forest that comprise over 63 percent of the landmass of Peru are a distant world for most Peruvians, especially the *Costeños*. The geographical distance between the coast and the jungle is short, but immense topological and climatic differences separate one from the other. The Peruvian Amazon underwent a particular way and rhythm of experiencing the Incas' attempts to dominate its native ethnic groups, the Spanish conquest, ecclesiastical missions, the country's independence, the first decades of the republic, modernization, progress, and national and regional identity. Studies on Amazonian natives, on Spanish colonization, and on European neocolonialism in the region, and of course, on the Amazon's current problems and challenges, have been subjects scarcely registered in most scholarly books concerning Peruvian history (not to mention school textbooks!). Instead, scholars of Peruvian history tend to focus on historical events that occurred in Cuzco, Lima, Cajamarca, and other places where the Incan empire and the Spanish conquerors clashed. The Amazon has not yet become an area of interest for most Peruvian scholars, intellectuals, political leaders, and *Indigenistas*.[1] The Incas, who barely penetrated the high jungle where the Andean mountains and the Amazon rain forest meet, had almost no contact with the people who inhabited the Amazon low jungle, an extensive area that encompasses a territory of more than 6,500 square miles and covers more than 40 percent of South America. The Amazon was a peripheral realm for the Andean culture of the Incas and the coastal civilizations. Likewise, it was a peripheral territory for Francisco Pizarro and his fellow conquerors, a place to send their rivals in search of *El Dorado,* the kingdom of a gilded Indian chief, in hopes of diverting them from the gold mines of Cuzco and Potosí and from the conquistadors' burgeoning political center, La Ciudad de los Reyes (Lima). The Amazon was irrelevant for secular priests who were busy enough with the Christianization of coastal and Andean natives. Likewise, it was an unexplored area too distant and inhospitable for the first Peruvian Republican leaders. However, for groups of wealth seekers, explorers, Jesuit and Franciscan missionaries, powerful *encomenderos* (Spanish colonizers in whose charge the crown "entrusted" Indians, from whom they could collect tribute and labor services), and local governors, the Amazon represented a primary area for their ventures. Later, in the nineteenth century, the region also attracted rubber barons, *regatones* (river navigators who traded between cities and villages in the jungle), adventurers, immigrants, foreign companies, Augustinian and Protestant missionaries, and native inhabitants.

Center or periphery? In the next pages the history of the Peruvian Amazon, and more specifically, of Iquitos, will become central to our understanding of how every periphery is a center in itself.

◆

FROM THE MYTHICAL AMAZON TO PERUVIAN IQUITOS

The first European explorers to launch expeditions through the raging rivers of the Amazon saw its indomitable landscapes and abundant wildlife through mythological lenses. The "discoverers" searched in the Americas for places and peoples described in the accounts of medieval travelers such as Marco Polo, Sir John Mandeville, and other lesser-known adventurers. Once they set foot on the rich earth, some expected to find the lands of the Old Testament: Eden, where God created the earthly paradise; Ararat's mount, where Noah opened the gates of his ark; King Solomon's lands of Ophir and Tarshish; and the land of Arzareth, where according to the apocryphal book of IV Esdras (13:12, 40–70), King Salmanassar of Babylon sent the Ten Lost Tribes of Israel. Other explorers expected to find Plato's Atlantis, as well as the strange races and animals described by Greek and Roman writers such as Pliny, Herodotus, and Homer.[2]

When the first Spanish explorers began to venture forth along mysterious Amazonian routes in search of new cities and gold mines comparable to the ones they had found in Hispaniola, Mexico, and the Andean mountains, they already had formed a strong impression about the wealth of the native American peoples. Hence, the first travelers who attempted to unveil the secrets of the South American jungle had in mind specific objectives while leading their crews. Some looked for *El Dorado*.[3] Others pursued *El País de la Canela* (Cinnamon Forest) and *La Tierra Sin Mal* (Land of No Evil). All were convinced that something of great value was hidden in the jungle.

Medieval travelers' stories describing places covered with gold encouraged many Europeans to embark on long expeditions looking for these splendid lands. Columbus was the first explorer to claim to have found in Hispaniola the biblical land of Ophir, where King Solomon sent his fleets to obtain gold for the construction of the Temple. Later, in the sixteenth and seventeenth centuries, the discovery of mines in Mexico and Peru shifted the location of Ophir in the imaginations of colonizers, chroniclers, and scholars who discussed the precise location of that land. Some theologians, such as Rabbi Menasseh ben Israel, author of *Mikveh Israel* or *The Hope of Israel* (1650), asserted that the Indies had been inhabited in ancient times by some of the Ten Lost Tribes of Israel while other Israelites dispersed to other parts of the world, all of them keeping the Jewish faith and expecting the fulfillment of Isaiah's prophecy of their return to Jerusalem and unification with the other tribes.[4]

European and native American myths intertwined during the first stages of the colonization, before racial and religious *mestizajes* emerged. Hence, the myth of the land of *El Dorado,* or *El Paititi,* a lost Incan city of gold, seems to reflect American versions of the European longing for gold. Travelers Francisco de Orellana and Sir Walter Raleigh epitomized this hunger for wealth. In 1542 Orellana and his Spanish crew became the first Europeans to navigate the Amazon, naming it the Marañon. Years later, when the explorers returned to Spain, the stories they told of furious battles against Amazonian female warriors ignited the European imagination so much that the name of the river was changed from Marañon to Amazonas.[5] In 1544, authorized by the Spanish king to conquer the country of *El Dorado,* Orellana returned to the region, but this time the voyage was unsuccessful. In most history books, nonetheless, Orellana is credited as the pioneer navigator who crossed from west to east on terra firma, the discoverer of the Amazon River, and the first to prove that it could be navigated.

In 1564 Sir Walter Raleigh received permission from Queen Elizabeth I to discover lands not yet possessed by any Christian prince. Years later, in 1596, he embarked on an expedition through the extensive forests between the Amazon and Orinoco Rivers expecting to find Manoa, a golden city described by native Indians of the region, according to stories told by previous explorers. Raleigh was confident that he would be able to localize Manoa, which he called Manao, and as his travel diary attests, he believed that in that Venezuelan Guiana city he also would meet his *Dorado,* the mythical "Golden Man" who was allegedly anointed every day by his subjects with oil and rolled in gold dust.

During the 1640s, the Jesuit scholar Antonio de León Pinelo proposed a theory concerning the origins of the Indians and humanity that added a cosmological element to the mapping of the Amazon. Perhaps, León Pinelo suggested, God created earthly paradise in the Americas, specifically in the Amazon. In León Pinelo's seventeenth-century masterpiece, *El Paraíso en el Nuevo Mundo,* the scholar asserts that Adam and Eve's paradise was located in the Peruvian Amazon, that its center was in the fringes of the Amazon River, specifically in the Pacaya-Samiria reservoir (contiguous to the current city of Iquitos), and that *granadilla,* passion fruit, was the forbidden fruit.[6]

Up until the nineteenth century, the Amazon still was a mythical place for scientists who arrived in the region. In 1869, the French traveler Onffroy de Thorón published a series of notes in which he alleged that the biblical Ophir and Tarshish were actually located between the Peruvian and Brazilian Amazonian forests, near to one of the Amazon River's tributaries, the Yapurá River. De Thorón claimed to have found some evidence to prove that King Solomon's ships had voyaged through tributaries of the Amazon River. He related Amazonian trees that yield valuable wood, monkeys, and *pavos reales* (peacocks) to references from 1 Kings 10:11–22 and 2 Chron. 8:18, 9:21, in which we are told how King Solomon's fleets brought a great number of almug trees (usually regarded as the sandalwood tree), precious stones, gold, silver, ivory, apes, and peacocks from the lands of Tarshish and Ophir. De Thorón also argued that the River Solimoes, a tributary of the Ucayali River and the Río Negro, was named such in honor of the Hebrew king. Finally, he claimed to have found similarities between words in Hebrew and in Quechua (the language of Andean natives of Peru), evidence of the presence of ancient Hebrews in Peru.

In 1908, the Peruvian traveler Hildebrando Fuentes endorsed Onffroy de Thorón's Ophirite theory in his meticulous accounts of the Loreto department (or state, whose capital is Iquitos), *Loreto: Apuntes Geográficos, Históricos, Estadísticos, Políticos y Sociales.* As I read this book, I could not help but notice that the Amazon still caused learned, modern researchers to combine objective observations with the highly imaginative arguments of travelers and theologians who had previously visited the region. How to explain this? I wrote in my diary:

> It seems as if the majesty of the Amazon rain forest generates in its visitors such a sense of wonder that it causes the most objective beholders to fathom its mysteries with traces of both reality and imagination. Perhaps that explains why I can hardly detach my factual findings from my personal discoveries. My heart is being kidnapped from my brain by the charm of the landscapes and the people of this place.

And so, it seems that the Amazon jungle enchanted the hundreds of explorers who looked for the earthly paradise, Ophir, *El Dorado, El País de la Canela, El Paititi,* and *La Tierra Sin Mal* (a fruitful and paradisiacal land blessed by divine grace). But sooner or later, these travelers encountered real peoples, villages, and a new notion of Amazonian geography. Specifically, in what is today's Peruvian Amazon, Spanish conquerors and Catholic missionaries navigated throughout various tributaries of the Amazon River, arriving at Indian villages such as those of the Maynas, the Omaguas, and the Tupis, native peoples never conquered by the Incas.[7] The conquerors pushed the Indians out of their settlements on the principal rivers and established *reducciones* (Hispanic-style resettlements for scattered native peoples), forcing the natives to abandon their traditional lifestyles in the four departments that today comprise the Peruvian Amazon: Loreto, Ucayali, Madre de Dios, and San Martín.

In 1638 Spanish authorities sent the first contingent of Jesuits to this area and they founded a total of eighty towns, where they established a communal system of work and preached the gospels to diverse Amazonian ethnic groups. One of these towns, San Pablo de Nuevo Napeanos (today's Iquitos), was founded in a territory surrounded by three rivers, the Amazon River and its tributaries, the Nanay and Itaya Rivers.[8]

After the signing of the Treaty of San Ildefonso in 1777, which delineated the borders between Spain and Portugal in their South American colonies, Francisco de Requena, the Spanish representative and governor of the province of Maynas (where San Pablo de Nuevo Napeanos was located), wrote letters to the Spanish king requesting that Maynas belong to the Viceroyalty of Peru instead of the Viceroyalty of Granada, which at that time was the administrative body ruling Colombia, Venezuela, and Ecuador.[9] The *Real Cédula of 1802,* a royal edict from the Spanish monarch, granted this request, and Maynas officially became a Peruvian domain.

By 1818 Archbishop Hipólito Rangel had estimated eighty-one inhabitants living in the village of San Pablo de Nuevo Napeanos; only forty-two years later this town became an important city when, due to the arrival of the first steamboats manufactured in England, Peruvian President Ramón Castilla commanded the building of a shipyard in the Malecón of Tarapacá (the water-front promenade), on the shores of the Amazon River, to catapult trading in the Peruvian jungle. Hence, steamboats from Europe and the United States began to dock at the city—now called

Iquitos[10]—entering inland through the mouth of the Amazon River in Bélem do Pará, Brazil, 1,924 nautical miles (some 2,300 land miles) from Iquitos.

Some historians attribute Iquitos's development to Castilla's visionary stance regarding eastern Peru, which foresaw the economic possibilities of that region and encouraged studies for geographical explorations. Castilla's government established the Maritime and Military Department of Loreto in 1861, sending Peruvian troops to the province to deter Brazil's increasing supremacy over the navigation of the Amazon River and its monopoly on trading products from that zone.[11] In any case, Iquitos sprang up from the necessity of establishing a distributing center for rubber and merchandise between the coastal Amazon region in Brazil and the Amazonian hinterland.

In 1861, when Italian historian and naturalist Antonio Raimondi visited the city, he described it as a small *ranchería* (settlement) of Indians. Four years later, Raimondi returned to Iquitos and wrote a new account detailing the astonishing development of the city after the construction of a big shipyard. Hence, the once-tiny settlement lost in the midst of a region founded by Jesuit priests was transformed overnight into the trading post of the Peruvian Amazon.

✦

RUBBER BOOM AND THE COSMOPOLITAN IQUITOS

Up until the end of the nineteenth century, the major income of Peru came from the exportation of *guano* (high-quality fertilizer), but the loss of nitrate territories to Chile after the War of the Pacific (1879–1884) and the inexorable decline of the *guano* economy, turned the eyes of Lima's governments to the new *Dorado* of the Amazon: rubber.

Prior to the 1880s rubber boom in the Amazon, ships loaded with Amazonian products, such as *zarzaparilla* (a medicinal plant), fish, and cotton, embarked to international trading posts. In exchange for these goods the Department of Loreto purchased from Brazil alcoholic beverages such as *aguardiente* (raw sugar cane rum), some European wines and gin, and the famous *cachasa* (the Brazilian *aguardiente*). The structural basis for the future rubber economy had already emerged: the *comerciante fijo* (settled businessman) who provided ships and equipment to *regatones,* who then traveled through the rivers looking for towns and Indian settlements from which to buy products and to sell goods from the cities.[12] The figure of the *patrón* (overseer) who supervised the labor in Indian settlements became more and more deplorable when rubber became the source of wealth in the Amazon, transforming most of these powerful men into cold-blooded masters of enslaved populations in a society where slavery supposedly had been abolished.

While rubber trees had always been abundant in the Amazonian forest, rubber did not became an important commodity in Europe until industrialized countries discovered more practical applications for the product. This economic shift happened after Charles Goodyear devised the process of vulcanization, mixing rubber and sulfur to obtain a stronger, elastic, and cold-hot temperature-resistant product that in 1880 was utilized for the fabrication of tires. The rubber boom together with the "Second Industrial Revolution,"[13] that of the car industry, incorporated the Amazon into the Atlantic economic system and ignited an impulsive, massive migration of peoples from the high jungle (San Martín) to the low one (Loreto, Ucayali, and Madre de Dios). This was a revolution that changed the face of the jungle, bringing about economic, political, social, demographic, and even racial changes in the region. The rubber tree or "crying tree" or "weeping tree" (*cajuacju, cauchu,* or *cauchuc* in native terms) became the reason to cry for thousands of native peoples. Local *caucheros* (rubber barons), sponsored by foreign companies, had reason to smile at this business during the last decades of the nineteenth century and the first years of the twentieth century.[14] The *caucheros'* profits were as huge as the tragedy of the Amazonian Indians: In the region of Putumayo alone, between 1900 and 1912, the production of more than four thousand tons of rubber cost the lives of approximately thirty thousand natives, according to documents written by Roger Casement, the British consul in Iquitos.[15]

The economic boom in the Amazon brought thousands of immigrants to the region. Most of them became settled businessmen who established commercial houses in cities such as Manaus and Bélem do Pará, in Brazil, and Iquitos, in Peru. Many of the Jews who arrived in Iquitos owned commercial houses. Also, many Jews worked as *regatones,* but the role of these traders changed once the rubber lords and their associates from foreign companies (especially the Iquitos Steamship Co., Ltd. and the Booth

Steamship Co., Ltd.) hired overseers who stayed in the jungle administering the exploitation of rubber.[16] Now the *regatón* became the main provider of merchandise from the city to these overseers, offering them alcoholic beverages, food, clothing, guns, rifles, machetes, and other products acquired in urban commercial houses owned largely by immigrants. After finishing their trade, the *regatones* loaded their boats with rubber shipments to export to Europe through Brazilian ports.

Iquitos in Peru, like Manaus in Brazil, was the hub from which representatives of foreign industries administered their businesses in a manner totally oriented to the external market. Despite the fact that the socioeconomic life of the Peruvian Amazon was part of the Atlantic "mercantilist-extractive economy,"[17] Lima had always monitored the commercial activity of the region, regulating the functioning of foreign companies via rules, laws, and concessions given by the governments, and sharing part of the profits of the region's extractive economy dominated by foreign capital. Nevertheless, in the first half of the twentieth century, the Peruvian republic was still far from dictating the political life in Amazonian departments and cities controlled by rubber barons, foreign businessmen, and local governors. The Peruvian Amazon was the most remote area from the center of power.

Hence, Iquitos began to develop rapidly as an international post, and soon it became a cosmopolitan place, blooming with big mansions and stores built in the European style of that epoch, covered with blue glazed tiles and marble from Italy. The emergent rubber bourgeoisie behaved like aristocrats, enjoying their comfortable furniture and French wine and champagne. This upper class enjoyed concerts in the Alhambra theater; they practiced sports in private clubs and traveled occasionally to Europe. Like Manaus's famous Opera Theater, where Caruso performed for sophisticated "rubber audiences," Iquitos also had its cosmopolitan symbol: *La Casa de Hierro* (the Iron House). Designed by the architect A. G. Eiffel in Paris and built in 1900, this theater featured an "Edison" projection machine which "expelled" pictures from a carbide lamp for the first Peruvian film lovers.

The immigrants enjoyed an environment of freedom and prosperity, establishing societies from their native countries and also associations to share their bohemian life.[18]

Documents and old photos and films show how Iquitos had become an international city inhabited by modern urban dwellers, financiers, powerful businessmen, politicians, and bohemians. Christianity was the official religion taught in the schools; pound sterling was the religion of the streets. The city was living its *belle époque,* which would last longer than the prosperity of the rubber exploitation. The aristocratic class enjoyed all kinds of comforts, while most of the native inhabitants of the city lived in impoverished conditions. Joseph Orton Kerbey, who was the United States consul in Pará, Brazil in 1891 and 1892, visited Iquitos more than a decade later, and described the houses of its average inhabitants in the following way:

> The principal part of the town is composed of the Indian huts, made of bamboo on end, tied together with a cord of a vine which is as tough and flexible as twine. The *casas* [*sic*] or houses are always of one story [*sic*] topped with a mass of overhanging palm leaf thatch, which is supported on the corner post independently of the bamboo side or end walls, leaving an open space between the roof and the sides all around for ventilation as well as to allow smoke to escape. The floors are of earth. . . .[19]

During the First World War, due the abrupt collapse of the price of rubber[20] and the rise of other rubber empires such as those of Ceylon, Malaysia, and other British colonies in the Far East (according to several historians and most Amazonian people, English citizens stole seeds of rubber trees to plant them in their colonies), the Peruvian Amazon faced a huge economic crisis that abruptly ended the reign of the high society in cities like Iquitos.[21] The rubber barons left, but many commercial houses survived, especially the biggest: Khan y Cía, Israel y Cía, Arana y Hermanos, Luis F. Morey, and Casa Power. The remaining businessmen learned to trade and to make a profit through other regional products.[22]

The emergence of the airplane industry after Elmer Faucett launched his first flight through the Amazonian jungle in 1923 promised a new era of intercommunication between Iquitos and other Peruvian cities. Although Iquitos was no longer a prosperous and cosmopolitan city, it maintained the commercial spirit of its beginnings for many years. Many foreign banking agencies still operated in the city as late as 1929. Iquitos was no longer the ostentatious home of rubber magnates, but the inhabitants of the city still enjoyed a good life for a few more years.[23]

Between 1914 and 1943, many former immigrants left the Peruvian Amazon and settled in Brazil or their native countries. Some of them decided to "make America" in Lima, where they could exercise their commercial skills and be part of a city in which "big news" happened. Although the Peruvian state and the Catholic Church worked together to integrate the Amazon into the political and religious life of the country, by the 1930s the New York traveler James Ramsey Ullman described Iquitos as a "city without a country" in his book, *The Other Side of the Mountain: An Escape to the Amazon:*

> This vast area of jungle, of which Iquitos is the only important city, is, as has been pointed out, almost completely isolated from the rest of the country and leads an economic life of its own. In consequence the average *Loretaño* feels little bond between himself and the *Costeño*, or inhabitant of the west coast, and is apt to resent the interference of Lima in the conduct of his affairs.[24]

The consciousness of isolation and indifference from the Peruvian leadership in the coast and the highlands explains to a good extent several regionalist and popular uprisings in Iquitos.[25] These incidents were the direct consequence of political and economic realities in a developing city where the promising echoes of central government could barely be discerned while, in the name of a unified homeland, this population was left behind in the margins of progress. Iquitos was a neglected city of Peru, and the projects for a prosperous Amazonian region, a Peruvian national myth proclaimed in political speeches, remained on paper.

President Fernando Belaunde Terry, in his different governments, attempted to bridge the Amazon to the coastal area. In 1943 terrestrial communication was established between the city of Pucallpa and Lima via the construction of a highway. In 1965 Belaunde Terry decreed the whole territory of the Peruvian Amazon a "free-tax zone." The president's aim was to encourage investments in all departments of the region. Between 1965 and 1968, when the region was virtually a free-tax area, the Amazon experienced a surge of relative economic prosperity, especially in Iquitos. Many entrepreneurs came to do business, and thousands of tourists descended upon the city to buy cheap imported products that they could not find in Lima or in other coastal cities. Father José María Arroyo, who has been in Iquitos since 1954, remembers those times:

> On Christmas, for example, people came especially from Lima, and you could not walk in the streets because they were crowded. Even though visitors had to pay airfares to come here, it was cheaper to buy many things here and then go back to Lima. There were some who bought televisions, radios, and other merchandise, to sell to their friends [in Lima]. They even got an extra profit and then came back here to make more business and to enjoy the hotels and cafés. Even "high class prostitutes" were brought to Iquitos, because we had already the other ones . . . the average ones.[26]

This was also the "era of the radio" in the Amazon, and especially in Iquitos; Japanese transistor radios flooded the market. People of all social classes learned about imported products via radio advertising, which encouraged expenditure among the city dwellers and among families who lived in distant villages far from Iquitos's urban areas.

Gradually the economic crises of the nation forced Belaunde Terry's government to impose successive tax increases in some economic sectors in the Amazon until the businessmen in the region lost all their privileges. In the 1970s, most of the newcomers went back to Lima and elsewhere, and Iquitos's economy depended upon its oil and on the cocaine boom of the 1980s.[27]

Traveler Brian Kelly's account of his visit to Iquitos in the 1970s described Iquitos as a more heterogeneous city than any of the Brazilian cities (from the point of view of its diverse ethnic and cultural origins). He claimed that Peru had never really made much progress in "conquering" the jungle and integrating it into the rest of the country.[28]

Thus, why does the isolated *Iquiteño* feel *Peruano* when coming from a cosmopolitan city within a region dominated by foreign entrepreneurs. Historian José Barletti Pasquale asserts: "The *'Peruanidad'* [Peruvianism] of the people of the region, of the Iquitos inhabitants, is not questioned.

There is no historical record or evidence that can make us doubt the possibility that Iquitos people could have not felt part of the Peruvian nation in recent history. Even during the regionalist revolts, you will not find any serious attempt to break administratively with Lima. Those were revolts inspired by the aim of improving social conditions; those were political revolts, not secession wars."29

How does one explain the Peruvian nationalism of the *Iquiteño*? I dare to argue that besides the history of Peru's struggle for the sovereignty of part of the Amazon—highlighted by the policies of administrative demarcation, drawing of maps, establishment of jurisdictions, and appointments from Lima's governments (the empowering of *Limeños* political functionaries including prefects, bishops, and missionaries, the building of the shipyard, the highway to Pucallpa, the Law of Tax Exoneration, etc.)—what makes the Amazonians of Peru feel as though they are part of the nation is today's economic and commercial dependence on Lima and especially, the enormous presence of the Peruvian military in the city.

I base my assumption on my own impression of the militaristic aspect of the city (Peruvian flags, military quarters, weekly marches, and parades) and on my reading of two works. The first one, Mario Vargas Llosa's novel *Pantaleón y las Visitadoras,*30 is the first book in which I read about the existence of a place called Iquitos. Vargas Llosa satirizes the militarizing of Iquitos during the 1970s, describing the story of poor commander Pantaleón, who is assigned the "important mission" of administrating a ship-brothel to keep his troops happy. The second work, James Ramsey Ullman's *The Other Side of the Mountain: An Escape to the Amazon,* provided me with the account of a traveler who visited Iquitos in the 1930s, perceiving the city as a place where officialdom was omnipresent: "The town has the appearance of a military encampment rather than a community of civilians."31 Still today, Iquitos is a military bulwark of Peru, and officials of the armed forces belong to the highest social classes of the city and the whole Amazon region.

There is no doubt that the international conflicts in the area—with Colombia in 1911 and 1932, and especially the more recent military conflicts with Ecuador, which started at the beginning of the twentieth century and peaked in the wars of 1942 and 1981, and the 1995 conflict—

have roused a sense of nationalism in the inhabitants of the Peruvian Amazon, who consider themselves to be Peruvian citizens.

Iquitos belongs to Peru, but its history can be registered in a twofold album in which Europe, Brazil, the United States, and North Africa have an important presence. Geographically, Iquitos is the most isolated city in South America and therefore, peripheral. Historically, the city has always been an urban and bohemian center for trade, business and, more recently, national strategic objectives as Peru defended its sovereignty in the Amazonian region.

◆

THE HOMOGENEOUS IQUITOS: "CENTER OF SYNCRETISMS"

Progress arrived in Iquitos earlier than it did in many other Peruvian cities due to the rubber boom, but the rhythm of progress did not follow the needs of the urban population. By 1905 Iquitos already had electricity and even an urban train; by the 1920s the first city streets had been paved, especially in the commercial area around La Plaza de Armas and Calle Prospero. Private companies, together with the government, developed the basis of the city and built water and sewage systems, public buildings, and hotels.

Although Iquitos is today a declining city far from the prosperous trade center that it was during the rubber boom, the extractive-export economy of the late nineteenth century is still the region's source of wealth. Oil extracted by *Petroperú* (the Peruvian oil company established in 1969), cocaine (during the big cocaine boom in the 1970s), ornamental fish, wood, live animals (especially parrots and monkeys), and essence of *palo de rosa* for perfumes are the main sources of income for the richest people of Loreto, which have led to the rise of a nouveau riche class. But the vast majority of the population makes a living through trade and services: small stores with all types of merchandise, tiny restaurants, and precarious market stands.

Iquitos, the once cosmopolitan city, is now, in its majority, a humble urban area for working people who share an economy of subsistence five days a week, capped by weekends of dancing and drinking. For the roughly 350,000 inhabitants of the city, for tourists, for a few businessmen, for several religious missionaries and cultural visionaries (who have established universities, academies, research institutes, libraries, etc.), and for a few researchers and writers, this apparently peripheral place is their unquestionable center. It could be the wrong impression of a foreign visitor, but Iquitos seems to be a very homogeneous place in spite of the existence of different social classes, characteristic of all Peruvian big cities.

Augustinian Father Joaquín García says that Loreto's capital—unlike most Latin American urban centers—still preserves a peculiar characteristic: "Iquitos is a city with no social or cultural differences in spite of its economic differences," he claims.[32]

Anthropologist Marlene Dobkin de Ríos could not disagree more with Father Joaquín García's view. In her book *Visionary Vine: Hallucinogenic Healing in the Peruvian Amazon,* based on research she had conducted in Iquitos in 1968, she depicts a city divided into distinct social classes: A minority of self-admitted "high-society" (around 12 percent of the population) was composed of businessmen, government officials, army officers, and professionals—many of whom migrated to the jungle from coastal and highland cities. Another segment of the population, the middle-class, constituted about 35 percent of the population and included artisans, clerical personnel, some peddlers, and professionals. More than 50 percent of Iquitos's residents in the 1960s were poor people, many of them living at the edge of starvation and surviving by working in makeshift occupations and at small stands of cooked foods and fruits. Most of these *Iquiteños* still live in the floating slums of Belén or in wooden houses covered by palm roofs that encircle the city.[33]

I believe that Iquitos is neither the socially homogeneous city described by Father Joaquín García, nor a place of enormous contrasts between rich and poor as defined by anthropologist Marlene Dobkin de Ríos. In fact, Father García is well acquainted with the suffering experienced by the poor people of the city following the abrupt development of foreign capitalism in the region (he constantly works in indigent neighborhoods). Likewise, Dobkin de Ríos acknowledges in her book that even middle-class people in the city share beliefs and attitudes "indubitably linked to traditional jungle life."[34] I would argue that what makes Iquitos resemble a classless place is the cultural homogeneity of its diverse population.

Perhaps the lyrical impressions that I recorded in my personal diary on June 27, 1995, succeed in illustrating Iquitos's sense of homogeneity:

I have visited many people and most of them are very humble. The ones who have a good standard of life, even if they have color TV and spacious houses, must contend with their homes being exposed to the heat and insects from outside. It is hard to find hermetic houses, a "bubble" from which one can shelter himself from the street noises, bugs, and landscape. There are almost no houses with windows or seal-proof roofs, like the ones one can see in modern populous cities.

Even when comparing the houses of rich and poor people, one does not perceive big contrasts. Everybody dresses humbly according to the weather and not according to their status. There are no special neighborhoods for wealthier people. One can go to a dirty street without pavement and sidewalks, crossing sandy ways full of holes and rain ponds, expecting to knock at the door of a very poor family and find them watching cable TV and telling you about their recent trips to the United States. I met much poorer persons in better streets. Nothing hints from outside what kind of family you will meet. Generally, middle-class families live in unpainted houses with broken brick walls and incomplete tin roofs.

Nobody is ashamed of their houses (only if you ask for lodging). They allow you to take pictures wherever you want. Poverty is not a reason for dishonor in Iquitos; it is not a calamity; it is just a fact of life that does not hinder happiness.

Of course, there are those who live in extreme poverty, children without parents to sustain and raise them. They live in places such as the Belém Port, the shores of the Nanay River, peripheral areas of the city. Adults send their children to polish shoes and sell snacks in crowded places, close to La Plaza de Armas [main square]. But I insist . . . it is not like in Lima . . . or Caracas [Venezuela], my native city. These children clean the shoes of humble people like themselves, persons who return to empty houses with gritty floors. It is not the picture of the well-dressed man, smoking tobacco, indifferent to the dirty kid who cleans his shoes. You can almost see the men sitting in the cafés as the children they once were, polishing the shoes of grown kids like those who are working for them. I wonder if some of these men are the fathers who abandoned these children.

Maybe an encounter like that has happened many times without the awareness of either . . . father and son, father and daughter.

Maybe . . . because after the tip, when adults and children leave the café, they become the same classless *Mestizo* people in the tropical streets of Iquitos.

Iquitos is a center of many syncretisms: cultural, religious, economic, political, racial, and historical. The city's population seems to live in a realm of indistinguishable customs and cultural references. It is as if the dream of a "land without evil" *(La Tierra Sin Mal)*—spun by countless adventurers, theologians, and inhabitants—has somehow cast a spell over the city, blending all kinds of cultural, social, and ethnic legacies into a bewitching whole.

James Ramsey Ullman's metaphor of a "city without a country"[35] illustrates the paradox of this village metropolis: a peripheral village that is at the same time a metropolis for those who make their fortunes in the Peruvian Amazon. In Iquitos, the sense of center and periphery behaves like a perpetual pendulum, always in motion, unaware of the meaning of such definitions.

2

León Pinelo's Realms: Jews in Lima and Iquitos

"I will explain it to you, Diego. What is important
is that you be aware of the profound decision that
many of us Jews have made. The decision to continue
existing, though it be only through the preservation of
a few rites and traditions." (AT)
—Marcos Aguinis, *La Gesta del Marrano*

"Although the city [Iquitos] is as remote from the
centers of western civilization as any place could
well be, virtually all its business and commerce
is in the hands of Europeans—and not only Europeans,
but Europeans Jews. The list of its principal merchants
reads like the roster of the Zionist organization. . . ."
—James Ramsey Ullman, *The Other Side of the
Mountain: An Escape to the Amazon*

T HE FIRST IMMIGRANTS of Jewish origin were the descendants of New
Christians, who arrived in the Americas from the Iberian Peninsula
after King Ferdinand and Queen Isabella issued the 1492 edict proclaiming Judaism illegal in Spain. During the period of Francisco Pizarro's conquest of the Inca Empire (1531–1535), New Christian descendants of
Conversos or *Marranos* began to settle in the Viceroyalty of Peru and live
under the authority of the Catholic Church. Nevertheless, there were
always those who maintained their Jewish faith in secrecy (crypto-Jews)
until the Peruvian Inquisition—established in 1569—arrested them, put

them on trial, and sentenced them to death if they relapsed into their heresy. The first Peruvian Jews could not carry out their Jewish traditions openly, with the exception of those few martyrs who refused to abandon Jewish "heretical" views; future generations gradually adopted a fully Christian way of life.

One of the most renowned New Christian families in seventeenth-century Peru was the León Pinelo's, three brothers who were descendants of Portuguese Jews. Antonio, Diego, and Juan de Léon Pinelo gained acceptance as outstanding scholars in the Viceroyalty of Peru despite their Jewish origin and Diego's suspicious life as a crypto-Jew. No obvious evidence exists to prove that the León Pinelo brothers kept the observance of their forefathers' faith; however, certainly, like other New Christians, they were constantly scrutinized by Inquisition functionaries. Hence, the first wave of Jewish immigration to Peru was comprised of *Marranos* who eventually assimilated into the Christian society.

Jews reappeared in Peru in the second half of the nineteenth century, when immigrants from Germany established the first organized Jewish community in Lima, thus laying the foundation for the current Hebrew institutions in the capital city. In the 1880s, Jews from Sephardic communities of North Africa and Europe began to penetrate Antonio de León Pinelo's *"El Paraíso en el Nuevo Mundo,"* the Amazon, through Brazil's port city of Bélem do Pará. Thus, Jewish life was introduced into Brazilian Amazon cities such as Bélem do Pára and Manaus, on the shores of the Amazon River, and later, into distant cities of the Amazonian hinterland such as Peruvian Iquitos.

Two additional waves of Jewish immigration occurred after the world wars. Hundreds of Eastern European Jews arrived in Lima and established a well-organized and prosperous community together with Sephardic Jews from Turkey and the Middle East. This generation of immigrants took over the declining societies created by the German Jews, and founded new institutions, including the *Colegio León Pinelo*, a Jewish educational center built in 1946. Students who have graduated from this school are the current leaders of Lima's Jewish community.[1] Meanwhile, in Iquitos, Jewish life began to fade after many immigrants returned to Brazil or their native European cities, leaving behind children with an "empty trunk" (legacy) of material and spiritual Jewish teachings. The descendants of these Jews were to receive a Catholic education, but their ancestors' words would always reverberate in their ears: "You are Jewish."

What kind of life did these immigrants and their offspring in Lima and Iquitos have? What were their occupations, their achievements? How did they organize as a community? What is their history? These are the questions I will attempt to answer in the following pages.

✦

THE FIRST PERUVIAN JEWS: "BROTHERS" OF LEÓN PINELO

The very first Jews to come to Peru were New Christians or *Marranos* who accompanied conqueror Francisco Pizarro.[2] In the beginning of the sixteenth century, many New Christians who had a prominent role in Peruvian colonial commerce were nonetheless suspected of practicing the heresy of Judaism.

The Spanish Inquisition instituted in the Iberian Peninsula in 1478 had sought to establish a Jew-free empire (what centuries later, Europeans would call a *Judenrein* civilization) after the conquest and colonization of the Americas. *Conversos* and Jews were excluded from the Spanish Indies through a series of laws passed over a period of four centuries as Inquisitorial records reveal. Nevertheless, many *Conversos* succeeded in bypassing these prohibitions and settled in the principal cities of the New World. Answering the call of the Spanish Holy Office, King Philip II decreed on January 7, 1569 that the Inquisition be instituted in the Americas. The king hastily inaugurated the Inquisition of Peru (1569) and Mexico (1571). When the administrative organization of the colonies became more complex, royal authorities opened another Holy Office tribunal in Nueva Granada's city of Cartagena (1619) to facilitate the prosecution of heresy. Spain's Inquisition also attempted to convince the king to open a tribunal in Río de la Plata, due to the increasing involvement of "Portuguese people" (Jews)[3] in the province's commerce. Failing to institute their own tribunal, the Municipal Council of Buenos Aires asked that New Christians restrict their commercial activities or risk expulsion, but neither of these requests were executed. One of the main defenders of these merchants was Antonio de León Pinelo, their "secret brother," who, in his *Memorial* (1623), advocated the New Christians' right to engage in commerce without obstacles or difficulties.

Twentieth-century scholars have registered the *procesos* (trials) and *audiencias* (oral inquirings) conducted by Lima's Inquisition from 1569 to 1813 when the Holy Office was abolished.[4] From 1570 to 1620 the Inquisition held sporadic autos-da-fé (public trials and executions). In this period, more than one hundred New Christians accused of attempting to teach Jewish lore to other New Christians were arrested and subjected to torture and humiliation. The Inquisition also held trials in absence, burning effigies of those who escaped. The Inquisitorial punishments of this period are considered to be mild compared to those of other phases during which Lima's Holy Office put more people to death, beginning with the 1639 *Proceso de Complicidad Grande,* the largest auto-da-fé held in the New World. Scholar Cecil Roth estimates that more than sixty "Judaizing" New Christians figured in these trials, of whom seven were abjured *de vehemneti,* forty-four were reconciled, after being sentenced to punishments of varying severity, and eleven were released. Seven crypto-Jews were burned alive, accused of being impenitent heretics.[5] These trials ignited a wave of anti-Jewish rage, which translated into denunciation and detention of suspicious "Judaizing" New Christians.

The Inquisition's theory of a Jewish conspiracy in the New World motivated the Catholic Church's persecution of suspected heretics. After the Dutch conquest of Bahia in Brazil in 1624, the Portuguese suspected that a connection existed between the Dutch armies and crypto-Jews of Brazil and Peru, who were conspiring to get sugar crops and mines in both colonies. In a letter addressed to the Spanish Holy Office in 1622, the inquisitors Francisco Verdugo and Andrés Juan Gaytan stated that the Peruvian city of Potosí was full of Portuguese people who belonged to the Hebrew nation and observed their Jewish rituals. How much of these reports was based on the existence of a real, vibrant Jewish life among New Christians, the descendants of *Conversos,* and how much was paranoia? The answer is hard to discern.

A few cases prove that crypto-Jews put on trial by the Peruvian Inquisition were really practicing Jews. The most remarkable example of Jewish martyrdom was that of Francisco Maldonado da Silva. The son of a Portuguese Jew who had been forgiven for the crime of "Judaizing" by Chile's Inquisition, the renowned surgeon Francisco Maldonado da Silva was imprisoned from 1627 to 1639, when he was burnt alive during the autos-da-fé of *La Complicidad Grande.* There he proclaimed at the *quemadero* (stake) his last words: "This is the doing of the Lord God of Israel, so that I may now look upon Him, face to face." During the long period he was held in the underground dungeons of Lima's Inquisition, Maldonado da Silva made no secret of his religious convictions, defending his adherence to the Jewish faith of his fathers, and refusing to embrace Catholicism and be forgiven. The prisoner defied all the church dogmas in repeated audiences with Peruvian theologians called to shake his beliefs, and furthermore, Maldonado da Silva began to teach Judaism to inmates in neighboring cells.[6] His life and death confirm the presence of other crypto-Jews in Peru and the Americas, crypto-Jews who were never processed by the Inquisition or who simply gave up their faith after being released from their trials.[7]

The recurrent tides of Inquisitorial activities against those accused of "Judaizing" in the Viceroyalty of Peru point out the presence of New Christians conducting a religious life somewhere between Christianity and Judaism. By the nineteenth century, *Marrano* religious practices faded in Peru. *Marranism* was part of a colonial history far removed from the national project of the new Latin American state. The imagined Jew-free Peru of the Spanish empire became an independent country, and the new imagined national community, the Republic of Peru, opened its gates to the first Jewish immigrants, allowing them to practice their religion freely and to establish institutions as a minority.

◆

MODERN JEWS IN LIMA: "LEÓN PINELO'S" PARENTS AND CHILDREN

Peru's various constitutions throughout the nineteenth century proclaimed Roman Apostolic Catholicism the official religion protected by the state,[8] yet, the first republican governments do not seem to have seriously inquired into the religious beliefs of newcomers, in their endeavor to entice the settlement of productive white European (Protestant) immigrants in the country.[9] Many of these immigrants came as representatives of foreign companies, which received concessions to integrate into the developing economy of the nation between 1840 and 1880, during the fertilizer *guano* boom.

Within the framework of these concessions several Jewish business-men established themselves in the capital city. Most of these foreign agents worked for English companies. Some, however, opened jewelry stores and loan houses, traded cotton and offered professional services; a few even worked in agriculture.[10]

The first Jewish immigrants began to arrive in this context of semi-tolerance and encouragement, one which welcomed foreign settlers but made clear to them the Roman Catholic nature of the nation. The Jews were a small group within European migratory currents to Peru.[11] Dozens of Jews settled in Lima before the mid-nineteenth century, but the first records testifying to an important presence of Jews on Peruvian soil date from 1855 onward. Most of these Jews came from Prussia, where they had not been granted full rights as citizens. (Prussia was one of the most con-servative European states following the 1815 Congress of Vienna.) Once in Lima, they began to open stores and commercial houses. In the 1860s, even greater numbers of Prussian Jews arrived together with a few Jews from France, England, and Russia. Some Jewish newcomers stayed in Peru only for a short period of time, eventually settling in Chile. Those who remained in Lima integrated themselves into immigrant societies and clubs organized by members of their native homelands, for example, the "*Club de Gimnasia Germanía*," founded in 1863 in the home of the Ger-man Jewish gentleman Max Bromberg.[12]

Between 1869 and 1870, some Lima Jews debated the possibility of founding an Israelite Society, inspired by other immigrant associations in Peru. By this time, there were already more than eighty Jews in the coun-try, some of them interested in observing Jewish traditions, at least during the High Holidays. They founded the *Sociedad de Beneficiencia Israelita* in 1870, obtaining official recognition in 1873. A letter from Jacobo Herzberg, president of the society's provisional Board of Directors, pub-lished in the Jewish German newspaper *Allgemeine Zeitung Des Juden-thums* on April 1, 1873, described the nature of Jewish life in Lima at that time:

> We live here in the Peruvian Republic, a country in which freedom
> of religion still has not been decreed by law and whose population
> is totally Catholic. The existence of all religions and sects that per-

form their religious services in the confined area of their houses is
tolerated [by the state]. Here [in Lima] reside, approximately, twenty
Jewish families and thirty to forty single young people. We also find,
among the married men, some capable of performing religious services in the case of death or for the Rosh Hashanah and Yom Kippur holidays. A year ago a *mohel* [person who performs ritual
circumcisions] came to Lima, so we do not have to send our children to Europe to receive circumcisions. We also have since 1870
an Israelite Society of Beneficence in order to help our members
in case of extreme poverty or illness and also to provide them with
[Jewish] burial in case of their decease . . . (AT).[13]

Most German Jews did not have a religious background but, rather,
they shared a sense of solidarity with their national group, which gathered
in the *"Club Germanía."* However, an important fact of life prompted the
decision to organize an Israelite society—death. For twenty years Peruvian Jews had paid for the right to bury their deceased relatives in the
Protestant British Cemetery of Lima, the only authorized graveyard for
non-Catholics. In fact, the main purpose of the 1870 founding of the
Sociedad de Beneficiencia Israelita was to establish a Jewish cemetery
in Lima.[14]

The building and maintenance of the Baquijano cemetery was the
main concern of the *Sociedad de Beneficiencia Israelita,* but other communal issues were specified in its statutes: *bikkur holim,* or aid to its sick
members; charity for those in need; and the recording of births, weddings,
and deaths of the society's members in accounts that were considered to
be parallel to the Catholic Church's records. The statutes also emphasized
the goal of imparting Hebrew education to all Peruvian Jews.[15]

While this predominantly German-Jewish society made great advances
in providing health, charity, and burial services for its members, it did not
show the same enthusiasm in the organization of religious life and Jewish
education. Although some founders of the community used to gather in private houses to commemorate the High Holidays, the number of members
interested in religious activities rapidly decreased. The most fervent advocate
of emphasizing the religious duties of the Jewish community was David
Senior de Castro, an immigrant from Danish Saint Thomas who performed

the function of spiritual guide during holidays and rituals. It is said that
De Castro succeeded in bringing a *Sefer Torah* (Torah scroll) to Lima in
1885, a gift from Segismund Jacobi, a leading Peruvian Jewish philanthropist.[16] In 1887 around twenty-seven members of the society celebrated
the Rosh Hashanah and Yom Kippur holidays in a room of the Freemason's
building in Lima. By 1897 only thirteen members attended services for
the High Holidays. At the beginning of the twentieth century, very few
Jews in Lima continued to make financial contributions to the society, and
practically, with the exception of the *ḥevrah kadishah* (burial society), Jewish life in the city was reduced to a few sporadic meetings of the society's
leaders. Why did this community languish and almost disappear until the
1930s when the rise of Nazism in Germany caused the *Sociedad Israelita
de Beneficiencia* to recover its importance in Lima?

Many factors can give us clues concerning the disintegration of the
first Jewish community in the Peruvian capital:

- The first immigrants came mostly from German territories where
  Judaism was undergoing radical transformations with the emergence of the Reform movement.[17] The religious content of Judaism
  was being displaced by a more historical and cultural view of Jewishness. It was easy for many of the German-born Jews to identify
  themselves with other European immigrants who shared similar
  customs, social preferences, languages, and a sense of aristocracy.
  Then, perhaps Jews did not share any special sense of distinction,
  other than a few rituals, that distinguished them from other European immigrants.

- The official Roman Catholicism strongly advocated by the state at
  the end of the nineteenth century could have discouraged the
  establishment of solid religious communities in Peru.

- Many Jews stayed in Lima for a short period of time due to the economic crisis caused by the Peruvian-Chilean War (1879–1883).
  Thus, I believe, a momentum for maintaining religious rites and
  education of the young never took root.

- Most Jewish children were educated in American or Protestant
  schools. They received religious training neither from the school

nor from private teachers in the Jewish community despite what the statutes of the Israelite Society asserted concerning Hebrew education. The high degree of secularism and marriages with non-Jewish women may have weakened links among members of Lima's Jewish community.

At the beginning of the twentieth-century, Sephardic Jews from Turkey and the Middle East arrived in considerable numbers and eventually they became dealers owning prosperous stores. A major current of Ashkenazic Jews from Eastern Europe arrived between the two world wars and became *mercachifles* (peddlers) and traders of products that they acquired in Peruvian provinces. They sold these products to Sephardic store owners in Lima, receiving in exchange merchandise to market back in the countryside.[18] Later on, most of the Ashkenazic Jews opened their own businesses and together with their Sephardic kinsmen joined the existent community of German Jews, which, despite the feeble institutional life that they had preserved during the first two decades of the twentieth century, still maintained a functioning Israelite Society. Hence, there is an important link between the founders of Lima's Jewish institutions and the later wave of immigrants who developed what is today's Jewish community.

During the 1920s Ashkenazic and Sephardic Jews organized their own congregations: *La Sociedad de Beneficiencia Israelita Sefardita* (founded in 1920 and listed in public records in 1925) and *La Unión Israelita del Perú* (established in 1923 and officially registered in 1926) separated themselves from the German speaking Jewish Society (registered in 1938 in public records under the name of the *Sociedad de Beneficiencia Israelita 1870*, thereby honoring the date of its founding). Each congregation developed its own religious and social agenda.[19]

The shadow of the Second World War and restrictions in the 1940s on migratory policies in Peru forced the country's Jewish population to look for common goals and to establish unifying institutions. Although Peru supported the Allies in the war, and the government expropriated the holdings of German and Japanese citizens and expelled some of them, factors such as the arrival of important flows of newcomers to Peru and the government's increasing fears that immigrants might occupy jobs of native Peruvians propelled the country to issue migratory policies restricting the number of new immigrants in the country, limiting licenses to do business with foreigners, and imposing special taxes on newcomers.[20] The effect of such protectionist measures was to have a profound impact on both immigration and the organization of Jews already living in Peru.

After being rejected by the United States and other Latin American countries, many Jews, especially those from Germany, attempted to come to Peru. Although on paper Peru shared the concerns of other nations represented in the 1938 Evian Conference of Refugees, its government did not open its gates to Jewish and exiled immigrants from Germany.[21]

The Second World War catalyzed unity among Lima Jews. The *Comité de Protección,* founded in 1935, summoned the efforts of the three congregations under the leadership of the *Sociedad Israelita 1870,* led by a new generation of Jewish German immigrants. In 1939 the Jewish community built a home for immigrants to help provisional refugees on their way to other Latin American countries, sustaining an average of thirty people every month. Leaders of the three congregations worked together to convince public officials to make their migratory policies more flexible, to condemn the Nazi atrocities in Europe, and to forbid the publication of xenophobic pamphlets and newspaper articles produced by nationalist industrial, commercial, and political sectors.

The need for a unified voice in this turbulent period led the Jews to establish an entity that would represent all Jews in Lima. In 1942, this institution comprised of members of the Ashkenazic, Sephardic, and German congregations tackled the common problems of Peruvian Jews, representing the whole community before the government and international Jewish agencies. In 1944 this *Asociación de Sociedades Israelitas del Perú* invited representatives of Jewish societies from the provinces to a large assembly in Lima. The cooperation between the three congregations also resulted in joint efforts to develop Jewish life in the capital city, by sharing expenses for maintaining the cemetery owned by the *Sociedad 1870,* and for building the Jewish school *Colegio León Pinelo* in 1946, the *bikkur holim* (the sick visitation society, hospital fund), the *hevrah kadishah* (burial society), and the elderly home founded by the Ashkenazic institution. This partnership worked until very recently.[22] Eventually, all Jews of Lima participated in the foundation of the current institutions that carry out Jewish activities in Lima.

Since the 1920s, a considerable number of Jewish immigrants had spread throughout different provinces of Peru and founded Israelite societies in Trujillo (1928), Huancayo (1932), El Callao (1933), and Ica (1944), but the center of their ritual life was Lima. For every ceremony—*brit milah* (ritual of circumcision), Bar Mitzvah, marriages, and funerals—Jews traveled from the provinces to the capital or brought a rabbi to their hometowns to perform the ceremony. After the foundation of the school *Colegio León Pinelo,* parents routinely sent their children to Lima to get a Jewish education. By the mid 1950s, there were almost no Jews in the provinces with the exception of the Amazonian region, which always was a world apart from Lima.

The vast majority of the founders of Lima's Jewish community were *mercachifles,* peddlers, small traders, and owners of stores, immigrants who after years of hard labor and poverty prospered and became rich. The children who graduated from the *Colegio León Pinelo* in its first years inherited the already prosperous properties of their parents and became professionals. Today they are the leaders of Lima's population, the inheritors of a community with solid institutions. They do not have to deal with other Jewish institutions in the provinces as did their forefathers because contemporary Jewish life turns over one single center: Lima. Only a handful of Jews remain in Peruvian departments and cities where there are no synagogues, associations, or rabbis. Lima is Peru; Lima's Jewry is Peru's Jewry.

On the other side of the Andes mountains, the tiny, exotic community of Jewish descendants who live in Iquitos are a curiosity, a footnote in the Jewish history of Peru (in the best of cases, a chapter) because what separates Lima from Iquitos are not only highlands, jungle, and miles . . . but also estrangement and solitude.

✦

JEWS IN LEÓN PINELO'S "PARADISE": MAKING AMERICA IN IQUITOS

The history of the Jews of Iquitos must be traced back to Sephardic communities in Europe and North Africa where Jews thrived in semi-tolerant Moroccan cities such as Tangier, Tetuan, Fez, and Rabat; and British Gibraltar and the city of Manchester. By the eighteenth century, commercial relations between Gibraltar and Moroccan cities linked European and North African traders, among them, Jewish merchants who eventually succeeded in settling in French and British cities and colonies from which Jews had been previously expelled. The presence of European settlers in the port city of Tangier and the Gibraltar Peninsula attracted migrating Jews and other foreigners.

Moroccan Jews were able to rule themselves, establishing in their communities their own assemblies, societies in charge of conducting rituals in synagogues and constituting their own educational system. Through the sponsorship of the *Alliance Israélite Universelle* (AIU) and maintained by the financing of Sir Moses Montefiori, Salomon Munk, and Adolphe Cremiux, schools were founded in cities like Tetuan and Tangier in the 1860s.[23] It was from the well-organized cities of Morocco that most of the Jews who settled in the Amazon came: from Spanish Morocco—Tetuan and Ceuta; French Morocco—Casablanca; Arab Morocco—Fez and Rabat; the international city of Tangier and neighboring villages; as well as British Gibraltar and Manchester; and Alsace-Lorraine. In the last decades of the nineteenth century, Moroccan Jews began to be the target of hostility from Arab leaders, who frequently charged them with usury. Additionally, in cities such as Tangier and Ceuta, French and Spanish diplomats often gave the Jews a hard time, suspecting them of being allies of the sultans. Trapped in the midst of a delicate political situation in a period of increasing nationalism and anti-Zionism and detecting the first signs of economic decline in the North African colonies and protectorates, many Jews crossed the Atlantic to settle in South American countries such as Brazil, Venezuela, and Argentina. Hundreds of these families first arrived in the Amazon, moving from the Brazilian port of Bélem to other cities in the states of Pará and Amazonas. Some Jews began arriving in Peruvian and Colombian in cities such as Iquitos and Leticia.[24]

Beginning in 1820, and prior to the massive late nineteenth-century migrations to Brazil,[25] Moroccan Jews began to set foot in Brazil, seduced by the first rubber *(borracha)* boom. These were the first Jews to settle in the Brazilian hinterland, after having established a center for Jewish life in the port city of Bélem do Pará, where they built an Israelite cemetery and founded two synagogues: *Eschel Abraham* in 1824 and *Shaar Hashamaim* in 1826. Contrary to future migratory trends, these Jews came to Brazil with their families, maintaining the gregarious and domestic way of life they had in Morocco. After working for their fathers in Bélem, some children of these immigrants moved to other cities in the states of Pará and Amazonas looking to expand their fortunes. When the rise in rubber prices drew thousands of foreigners to the Amazon in the 1880s, these newcomers found many Jews already working as *seringueiros* (rubber tappers) and *regatones*. These merchants, descendants of the Moroccan Jews, dwelled in diverse Amazonian cities such as Manaus and eventually, some arrived in Iquitos. These cities were to become the biggest cities of the Amazon during the nineteenth-century rubber boom.[26]

In the late nineteenth-century, the Moroccan Jews who went into the Amazonian hinterland were young men, well-educated entrepreneurs who worked alone or with family members and friends. Many traders sent part of their profits to their native countries to ameliorate the living conditions of those left behind.[27] The jungle was a dangerous world of strange animals, wild rivers, and diseases that threatened the lives of those who penetrated it. However, the dream of making a fortune kept foreigners going. The exotic flora and fauna of the Amazon haunted the imagination of the most adventurous entrepreneurs who, struggling against all odds, made their way to distant places such as Iquitos. Years later, many Jews who returned to Morocco told frightening stories of their encounters with the wild beasts of the Amazonian jungle.

The Jews who arrived in Iquitos in the 1890s expanded the enterprises of their partners in the Brazilian Amazon. In many cases, they were sent to Iquitos by Jewish businessmen who owned commercial houses in Bélem and Manaus and exported goods to companies in Tangier and European cities. These young adventurers saw themselves as temporary inhabitants of the city who would soon return to Brazil, Morocco, or Europe after making their fortunes. Therefore, their only concern as Jews was to build a cemetery in which they could bury the many victims of jungle disease and wreckage on the tributaries of the Amazon River. In 1895, a group of Jews bought a plot of land in Iquitos to build their own cemetery.[28]

In 1895 most of the Amazonian Jews lived in Yurimaguas, the capital of the former province of Alto Amazonía. This city was a strategic spot for commerce because it lies between Iquitos and Pucallpa, the two major cities of the region. Many Jews who later moved to Iquitos originally settled in Yurimaguas.[29] Alfredo Koblentz became the first mayor to rule Yurimaguas, according to public records. There is an accepted story among the "Jewish *Mestizos*" of Iquitos affirming that Koblentz was the first Jew to set foot in the Peruvian Amazon. According to his grandson Mauro Coblentz Lazo, who uses the modern spelling of his grandfather's surname, Alfredo Koblentz traveled with Shalom Benamú to the region by land because—unlike most Amazonian Jews—they entered Peru through the port of El Callao, traveling, therefore, from Lima to Yurimaguas. While Alfredo Koblentz and Shalom Benamú must be credited as being among the first Jews in the Peruvian Amazon, Coblentz Lazo insists that "as far as I know, the first Jew in Iquitos was Hatchwell."[30]

The Jews of Yurimaguas met twice a year, on Rosh Hashanah and Yom Kippur, to pray in the home of one of these pioneering families. Saúl Benamú Gonzales-Pavón, son of the famous mayor Shalom Benamú, remembers:

> *My father never worried about the Judaism of my sister, but he wanted me to be Jewish because I was the oldest son. We were a together a lot and the Yom Kippur was celebrated at home. I listened to them praying but I do not remember so much because I was a kid busy with my child's stuff and games. . . . There was an old man there, Natan Asarrat or Asarraf, an old Jewish man whom my father helped financially. He led the ceremonies. He was practically the rabbi because he was a very learned man.*[31]

Later on, the Jews kept their traditional Yom Kippur observances in Iquitos. Sofía Ruiz de Aguila, the gentile *convivencia* (mistress) of Rafael Toledano (who lives today in Israel), remembers what her "husband" used to do during that holiday:

> *He said to me: "I will not come for a whole day," and the next day, he asked me to buy a cock to slaughter because the Jews, it seems, make a promise that day. He asked me to cut the back of the cock's neck while he met with his* paisanos, *praying for hours, kneeling down from six in the morning until ten in the night during this weird holiday they have that it is like our Easter.*[32]

Eventually, most of the families from Yurimaguas, Pucallpa, Contamana, and other Amazonian towns relocated to the larger center: Iquitos. In the first decade of the twentieth century, many Jews founded commercial houses, which competed with the powerful Wesche & Company, Morey & Company, and the company of Julio Arana. Among them were three prosperous companies: La Casa Khan, La Casa Cohen, and La Casa Israel.[33]

Jewish businesses were thriving in Iquitos and playing an important part in the commercial expansion of the Peruvian Amazon. In his travel accounts, Hildebrando Fuentes registered more than fourteen commercial houses with Jewish names among the fifty-one companies in Iquitos,[34] this in a population of only fifty-two "Israelite" immigrants from a total of 9,439 inhabitants, according to the Iquitos census of 1903. In 1910 Professor Isaac Pisa, a traveling *instituteur* of the *Alliance Israélite Universelle* school in Morocco, visited Iquitos and wrote a report about the Jewish immigrants in the city:

> In Iquitos, there live more than two hundred of our former students [from the *Alliance Israélite Universelle*] from Morocco. Upon arrival, you would think that you were in a Jewish city. In the lettering of the stores on the great street Prospero you can read the names Cohen, Toledano, Benmergui, Delmar, Serfaty, Benassayag, Elaluf, Pinto, etc; exactly as in Morocco. There are more than three hundred Jews in Iquitos, including *Ashkenazim* originally from Alsace. Of the Moroccans, one hundred are from Tangier, some fifty from Tetuan and the rest from coastal cities and from Rabat and Casablanca. In Tangier, they speak of Iquitos as if [it is] a fabulous city with streets of gold. It is typical of [a] Tangerian to make his fortune in Iquitos. That is the vision and the dream of young people. You must know without doubt that the road is long and [the] climate is harsh.
>
> The most valiant, who confide in friends and parents, depart via Lisbon. When they arrive, they try to find the home of a coreligionist. The first years for the immigrant are terrible. They have to adapt to climate, customs, and commerce. However, they have valor and ambition and these give them the strength. The boss will

leave Iquitos for health reasons, and the employee becomes the boss.

They do business with everything imaginable. They install great bazaars with various products: English textiles, French novelties, German hardware, and American machinery. They travel up river by canoe or steamship and exchange merchandise for rubber. It is a hard life. Many times they have to live for months in the canoe. They eat only rice and plantains. They fight off alligators until an Indian comes to buy some goods. Many of the businessmen study the navigation of the rivers of the Amazon for months and obtain pilot's licenses. They are navigators, pilots, importers, and exporters all in one. If one loses his merchandise due to bad luck tens of miles up the Amazon, he will be helped by his coreligionist. That is their life. . . .[35]

This report continues with references to the type of Jewish life that his coreligionists practiced (limited to the observance of Yom Kippur), in which the author pointed out how these men had been sharing their lives with native women, and raising their children as Jews. Professor Pisa also mentioned the existence of a Jewish society and an Israelite cemetery, and he estimated that only a few of these Jews remained in Iquitos: "They come back to Morocco to found a Jewish family, never forgetting what they left in Iquitos. Back in Morocco they live as small businessmen or landlords. . . ."[36]

Alfredo Rosenzweig, author of the first article ever written about Jews in the Peruvian Amazon, does not idealize the lax lifestyle of these Jewish immigrants:

They spread children all around the jungle. Sometimes, when you asked a child rowing a canoe what his name was, he told you that his name was David. 'I am Jewish,' he said and then he told you who his father was. There were very few cases of Jewish couples who came from Morocco, but we must not judge the Jews as if they were the only ones who had many *convivencias* and children. It was a modus vivendi in the jungle. The woman stayed on the farm, and the man traveled and met his women during his trips. It was the custom to not marry and to have children whom the fathers [legally] recognized as their kids; but later, these immigrants left their [Amazonian] families to return to Europe.[37]

In Morocco, Jews had a patrilineal society in which the father was also the head of the household. Conversely, in the Amazon, women were the authority figures in their homes (it was a matrifocal society) but the patrilineal tendency remained, so children received their last names and also, their sense of lineage, from their (often) unknown fathers.

Returning to Pisa's report, the professor of the *Alliance Israélite Universelle* also claimed that Peruvian Indians preferred Jews to other immigrants from Europe or China. The travel diary of Salomón H. Coriat, a Jewish trader who befriended Amazonian Indians, may have been the source of the myth of the special relationship between the Indians and the Jews. In this diary, an Indian relates to Salomón Coriat's crew that white men massacred his village, killing most of his Cashibo Indian fellows because "my father answered them that he would not sell our *jebe* [rubber] and wood to them, because that was for Don Salomón, who came yesterday and would return today . . ." (AT).[38] Obviously, in this story, the Indians did not perceive the Jews to be like other white people.

At the end of my trip to Iquitos, I attempted to summarize in my diary the history of the Jews in that Amazonian city. As usual, I wrote a passage tangling this topic with haunting questions about my role as a historian:

> What is the most important event or aspect of Iquitos's Jews that I should emphasize as a historian? Did anything happen here that is worth registering in Jewish history books?
>
> I find these questions troublesome since they confront me with the fact that the history of the Amazonian Jews is only a footnote, a peripheral aside in the history of all Latin American Jews. Nevertheless, I could say the same of Lima and other cities in the continent . . . and why not? I could also say the same about European and North American Jewish communities! Somehow, the history of the Jews in the Diaspora is a history of what happened to them, and not of how they "made history." At least, from a political-military point of view.

As in anywhere in the world, what is important from a Jewish perspective regarding the presence of Jews and their ancestors in the Peruvian Amazon depends on the eye of the beholder.

For people interested in the economic accomplishments of Jews in Iquitos, there is a large list of thriving individuals and commercial houses that contributed to developing the infrastructure for the trading of rubber and other commodities to and from Iquitos. This history is still visible in the facade of some buildings, like that of the former Cohen commercial house, which still displays an engraved silver plaque bearing the name Cohen as the only visible remainder of this once important company.

For those interested in the participation of Jews in the political and cultural life of the city, probably the most important aspects to highlight are the roles of Jewish men who became mayors of Iquitos (men such as Víctor Israel, Alberto Toledano, and Joaquín Abensur), who were among the founders of the International Center Club of Iquitos, or were members of the Freemasonry (men such as Solomon Joseph, Pierre Schuler, Rene Hirsh, and Marcel Bloch). Also important were those who founded the city's Municipal Council and the Beneficence Society of Iquitos. I might even point out the history of Jewish participation in navigation and aviation in the Peruvian Amazon. (The airport in the city of Yurimaguas has been named after one of the pioneering pilots of the Faucett Airlines: Moisés Benzaquén.)

Perhaps some historians would use the figure of Víctor Israel, founder of the Israelite Society of Iquitos in 1909, mayor of the city on numerous occasions, and one of the most prosperous businessmen in Peruvian history, as the focal point in their account of the Jews in the Amazon. In addition, Víctor Israel is remembered by his peers for having been the first citizen of Iquitos to fly in a commercial airplane from the jungle to San Ramón and later to Lima, in 1929. The first trip made by Faucett Airlines from Iquitos is recorded in a book containing the chronology of Iquitos's major historical events. "What you will not find in any book," Mr. Israel's stepdaughter Josefa Pizarro Vásquez confided to me, "is that he flew because one of his daughters escaped with the pilot and he had to chase her." I suppose that no serious historian would claim to have made a historical breakthrough by revealing Víctor Israel's motivation for becoming the first *Iquiteño* to experience an airplane ride.

Out of all these personalities, perhaps the most fascinating character in the history of Iquitos was the enigmatic Salomón Casés. In his book about his travels in the Amazon forest during the last years of the nineteenth century, adventurer Fritz Up De Graff mentions a Moroccan Jew and ex-British army officer who, being a prominent merchant in Iquitos, organized a "foreign legion" of local traders to protest the abuse of taxation and the corrupt behavior of their self-constituted authorities.

The story tells how the merchants of the most powerful business in Iquitos, Wesche & Company, supplied firearms to Salomón Casés and his army from diverse national backgrounds. Armed and militant, the group marched to the main military base of the city. The Peruvian army did not oppose the revolt, the governor of Iquitos was sent down river in a boat, and Casés's "foreign legion" took charge of the city, reestablishing free trade and abolishing bribery of local authorities, until Lima sent national representatives to govern the city.

This is all I could learn of Salomón Casés and his "foreign legion," as described by Up De Graff. I could find no living source to confirm this story; nor could I find other sources to support it. Apparently, Casés's revolt was very brief and so inconsequential that it did not merit mention in the annals of Iquitos's history. The only detail I can add to this story is the existence of some letters of a Jew named David Cazes, who was the English consul of the city in 1903. One might speculate that he was a relative of Salomón Casés.

The "epic" of Casés and his foreign legion of merchants deserves a biography—in case someone can find detailed sources about the life of this heroic figure—or at least, a novel or a movie script. Maybe he is the only Jewish figure in Peruvian history to actively make history (and not only to have been a subject of historical circumstances). In that case, perhaps Lima's Jewish community should consider changing the name of its school from *Colegio León Pinelo,* to *Colegio Salomón Casés.* Or, an even better idea, perhaps they should build a Jewish school in Iquitos.

Hence, what I personally consider to be the most important aspect of Iquitos's Jewish history would also be shared by Lima's Jews: the history of spiritual survival of the "Jewish *Mestizos.*"[39]

But before tackling what happened to the descendants of the first Jews who came to Iquitos, we must close the circle of that generation's history.

After 1911, when rubber prices began to drop, only the most financially solid commercial houses survived: those of Morey, Power, Israel, and Khan. By 1911, 60 percent of the Jews in Iquitos had returned to Brazil and Europe, around 15 percent had died during their Amazonian venture, and only 25 percent stayed in the region, working in local commerce.[40] In the 1940s a few Jews came to Iquitos from Lima and became prosperous entrepreneurs, but it was not until the 1960s that the Tax Exoneration Law for the Peruvian Amazon, decreed by President Belaunde Terry, encouraged people to come to Iquitos, including dozens of Jews from Lima. Many of these Jewish businessmen employed Iquitos's "Jewish *Mestizos*" during the short period of prosperity that ended in the early 1970s. In the last two decades, the descendants of the wealthy Jews who found in Iquitos their *Dorado* during the rubber boom worked in local commerce and the subsistence economy. A few are relatively successful entrepreneurs in the area of services (ballrooms, restaurants, etc.); some own little stores or work in branches of shops from Lima. A tiny minority of the "Jewish *Mestizos*" is professionals and students. Certainly, the age of the prosperous Jewish entrepreneurs is over. Víctor Israel,[41] Jerome Kahan, the Pinto brothers, the Cohen family, and many other pivotal Jewish figures are today only a part Iquitos's past. Only historians of the city can recognize, via the decorated facades of the enormous buildings these businessmen owned, the vestiges of a once vibrant Jewish presence in Iquitos.

How then has organized Jewish life in Iquitos evolved so differently from that in other parts of the Amazon? Why did the Jews of Iquitos fail to build synagogues and bring Jewish educators and religious leaders to the city, as did the Jews of Manaus and Bélem? We must take into account that Iquitos was isolated, not only from Lima, but also from the Brazilian Amazon, because the city was part of Peru. Brazilian Jews did not see the fate of Iquitos Jews as their responsibility; neither did their coreligionists of Lima because they knew practically nothing about them. Hence, for many Jews, Iquitos served merely as a temporary station in their lives, a place where they could progress economically before returning to Brazil or Europe. That is the reason why, apart from the Jewish cemetery purchased in 1895 and the establishment of an Israelite Society in 1909, the Iquitos Jews did not set the basis for a Jewish community.

Yes, there was an Israelite Society in Iquitos, but its history is very hazy. *La Sociedad de Beneficiencia Israelita de Iquitos*, founded under the presidency of Víctor Israel on January 10, 1909, began with thirty-nine members who, according to its statutes, would provide moral and material support to its members in case of need, disease, or death. The fifty-three articles of the founding document of the *Sociedad Israelita de Iquitos* follow the pattern and goals of Lima's *Sociedad de Beneficiencia Israelita*, founded in 1870. Perhaps the few Jews who had lived in Lima before coming to Iquitos brought with them the idea of creating a society whose main concern was the welfare of its members, although the same pattern can be found in all the first Jewish societies established in Latin America in the early twentieth century. On the other hand, with the exception of organizing the funerals of their members, other foreign societies in Iquitos presented similar objectives. Most of the members of the Israelite Society were wealthy and prominent citizens of Iquitos who, according to the statutes, were to pay one pound sterling to register and a monthly share of two Peruvian *soles*. A meeting was held every month.[42] There are neither references to the Jewish character of the society nor documents describing the administration of the Israelite cemetery, although all of my informants claimed that the founders of this society maintained the cemetery.

Why did these members make no references to the Jewish nature of their organization as did those in Lima? The *Sociedad Israelita de Lima* emphasized in its statutes the goal of promoting Jewish education among the Israelite youth. The Iquitos society did not. This is the first mysterious aspect of this society; it, among some others, will be discussed forthwith. The statutes of the Iquitos *Sociedad Israelita* are in the public records because on November 6, 1945, Salomón Azerrad gave them to a notary office in order to register the institution over which he then presided. According to the notary public, Azerrad verified that his society would follow the same statutes declared by Víctor Israel on April 14, 1928, in another notary's office.[43] The copy delivered by Salomón Azerrad in 1945 remains in the files of the Iquitos Public Records Office, annexed to the registration of the society's 1945 Board of Directors. Remarks added by the notary public, Benjamín Pérez Rangel, raise some questions about the fate of the original documents of the society when it was founded in 1909:

> . . . Mr. Azerrad thanked the presence of these members [of the society] and offered to serve them in gathering existent documents that prove the legality of the society and in case of not finding them, he will attempt to get copies of those documents and will provide them to the local authorities for future members of the society.

Later on, the notary public adds:

> The president of the society [Mr. Azerrad] expressed that the main aim of this meeting was to register *in Public Records the statutes that rule the society until today in order to incorporate it according to the law; what was not done in the past due to inconveniences that are not significant to mention now.*
> Iquitos, November 6, 1945 (AT: the emphasis is mine)[44]

Why did the 1909 Israelite Society fail to register itself in the public records like other foreign societies did? Why were the original documents of 1909 concerning the statutes of the society apparently given to a public notary in 1928 and why couldn't Salomón Azerrad deliver them in 1945? Why didn't Mr. Azerrad finally find those documents? (There are no further documents added to the 1945 registration of the *Sociedad Israelita de Iquitos.* The contents of the 1909 and 1928 sessions were written down by the same public notary, Benjamín Pérez Rangel, who did not clarify from which written source or record he got the information.) Why didn't the Iquitos Jews incorporate their society in the public records until 1945? What were those "inconveniences . . . not significant to mention now" alluded to in the 1945 record? Why do the local newspapers from those years make no mention of the establishment of the *Sociedad de Beneficiencia Israelita?* Why do none of today's Jewish descendants remember their parents and grandparents attending sessions of this society? And why, again, did this society never claim to be a Jewish institution? There are many mysteries inviting conjectures, and that is exactly what I did during my field research while facing these questions: I speculated.

I wrote some thoughts in my research notebook, I discussed these hypotheses with professors and intellectuals, and they all agreed; my hypotheses are probable or at least logical, although not necessarily right:

> Maybe the Jews wanted to keep a low profile in 1909 because most of them came from cities or protectorates where they felt the hostility of the majority of the Moslem population, in the case of Morocco, or the fragile conditions for Jews in a Europe infected by anti-Semitism. Maybe they did not want "to be noisy" in an eminently Catholic city and a country that theoretically did not allow the open practice of other religions. We must take into account that the *Sociedad de Beneficiencia Israelita de Iquitos* was the only foreign society that represented not a country, but a people with a common religion, although most of its members came from Morocco.
>
> Maybe—and this is a notion shared by Jaime Vásquez Izquierdo, secretary of the current *Sociedad Israelita de Iquitos*— the members of the old society were such an elitist group that they did not open the institution to Jews who really needed material support. Certainly, most of the founders of the society were wealthy men who also belonged to many other cosmopolitan groups of the city: "Iquitos Club," *Club de los Trece,* diplomatic circles, political offices, etc. It seems as if the Israelite Society was established by a group of people who were inspired by a sense of responsibility and who shared a common religion to which they did not necessarily profess a spirited devotion.
>
> A few *paisanos* claim to remember that this society accepted only "pure Jews" (children of a Jewish father and mother) in its constituency, but that is not what the statutes reveal. Article 9 specifies that in order to be active members of the society a person is

required only to have good behavior, good health, and be willing to submit himself to the statutes. There is no evidence to conclude that a "certificate of Judaism" was important for the members of the Israelite Society, and eventually, in the 1920s and 1930s, many of its associates became de facto Christians attending Mass and participating in Catholic holidays. (The most revealing case is that of the founder of the society, Víctor Israel, who later became a philanthropist of churches in the city, and was bestowed with honors by Pope Paul VI in 1964.[45])

The reason why the society decided to go public in November of 1945 might be due to an emotional response to the Holocaust in a period when Jews felt the sympathy of the world, especially in Peru, which was allied with the victorious powers of the Second World War. In all the world, the sense of peoplehood was enhanced among Jews (even the most assimilated ones) after learning about the Nazi massacres in Europe.

But there are some other important factors that might explain why the *Sociedad Israelita de Iquitos,* presided by Azerrad, had decided to project itself after thirty-six years of silence since its foundation: In July of 1944 Lima's Jews organized a meeting with representatives of Jews living in the provinces; Iquitos had three delegates: Víctor Israel, Lázaro Fogiel, and Mauricio Gleizer (they all lived in Lima by that time). In November of the same year, the prominent businessman Simón Samolsky, owner of a huge sawmill and a skin trading company in Iquitos, paid for the trip and wages of Rabbi and mohel Moisés Brener in order to perform the circumcision of his son. 1944 is a key year for the Jews of Iquitos because they had the opportunity to taste what it was like to be part of Peruvian Jewry.

The *Sociedad Israelita de Beneficiencia de Iquitos* never organized High Holiday services. Jews met to pray privately in individual homes as they had done before the institution was founded. (In the 1920s they commemorated Yom Kippur in a room of the *La Unión Amazónica,* the Freemasonry building.) Despite the incorporation of the Israelite Society in Public Records in 1945, there are no accounts showing how it functioned afterward.[46] The members of the institution were disorganized and met one another occasionally, only to celebrate the High Holidays. The Jews reorganized themselves in 1966, when, sponsored by the Jews of Lima they created a society of sympathizers of the State of Israel: *El Instituto Cultural Peruano-Israelí de Iquitos.* In the early 1970s, this institute faded after many Jews from Lima and some descendants of Iquitos Jews left the city, in search of a better standard of living in the capital city.

In 1990 a group of *paisanos* who were very young when the *Instituto Cultural Peruano-Israelí de Iquitos* was the only institute to gather descendants of Jews, decided to create a new Israelite Beneficence Society like the one founded by their forefathers. On January 15, 1991 the *Sociedad de Beneficiencia Israelita de Iquitos,* consisting of approximately one hundred members, elected Víctor Edery Morales as its president. (See Appendix 3.) Although this group claims to be recreating the first Israelite Society founded in 1909, their statutes—unlike those of their ancestors—are clearly designed to restore Jewish life among its members, taking care not only of their welfare, but also of the Jewish cemetery, funeral rituals, High Holidays prayers, and even Kabbalat Shabbat every Friday evening.

What do these members consider to be Jewish life? That is the topic of the next chapters.

3

THE RELIGION OF THE "JEWISH *MESTIZOS*"

"I have a curious animal, half kitten, half lamb.
It is a legacy from my father. But it only developed
in my time; formerly it was far more lamb than
kitten. Now it is both in about equal parts. . . .
I never trouble to answer, but confine myself
without further explanation to exhibiting my
possession. . . ."
—Franz Kafka, *The Crossbreed*

"In accordance with their custom, when someone
did wrong, stole or violated the taboo, the *Viracochas*
flogged him and put a crown of *chambira* thorns on
his head. After that—the way they do with big river
paiche so the water inside them will drain out—
they nailed him to two crossed tree trunks and
left him to bleed. They did the wrong thing. Because
after he'd gone, that storyteller came back. He might
have come back so as to go on throwing this world
into even worse confusion than before. They began
saying among themselves: 'It was true. He's the son
of *Tasurinchi*, the breath of *Tasurinchi*, *Tasurinchi*
himself. All three things together, in a word. He came.
He went and has come back again.' And then, they began
doing what he taught them to do and respecting his taboos.

Since that *seripigari* or that god died, if he really
did die, terrible misfortunes befell the people into which
he had been born. . . ."
—Mario Vargas Llosa, *The Storyteller*

THE CONCEPT OF "religion" is a construct never addressed in the Bible.
The elaboration of such a concept grew out of the necessity to distinguish the corporeal world from the realms of faith. As the biblical human
being, the Amazonian native experiences a religion that encompasses all of
his cosmology, his "everything." Nature is omnipresent in the Amazon. Its
overwhelming power engenders such a profound sense of wonder and awe
over its native inhabitants that it leads almost everyone, even the most
mundane person, to be captivated by the jungle's mystery.

Saúl Zuratas ("Mascarita"), one of the characters in Mario Vargas
Llosa's novel *The Storyteller*, provides an illuminating description of the
religious Amazonian Indians: "When you approach them and observe
them with respect, with a little fellow feeling, you realize it's not right to
call them barbarians or backward. Their culture is adequate for their environment and for the conditions they live in. And, what's more, they have a
deep and subtle knowledge of things that we've forgotten. The relationship between man and Nature, for instance. Man and the trees, the birds,
the rivers, the earth, the sky. Man and God as well. We don't even know
what the harmony that exists between man and those things can be, since
we've shattered it forever."[1]

Iquitos has always kept its provincial character and still preserves a
part of its aboriginal religiosity, even though the city "was born" as a result
of modernity and an extractive and "destructive" relation to nature. At
times, modernity seems foreign to the nature of this city, as a playful
remark from my diary suggests:

> I wonder if the motorcycles and *motocars* (motorcycles with a
> coach for passengers) that buzz and zigzag all over the city, pierc-
> ing with their roar the ears of its inhabitants, are a kind of mechan-
> ical wheeled mosquito brought by "civilized" men to prove to
> native Amazonian people that modernity can create inoffensive
> insects that produce neither disease nor itching. If that is the case,

these wingless mosquitoes expel very toxic fumes and produce a type of irritation (not precisely in the skin, but in the soul) that suggests how our civilized world sometimes produces caricatures of those primitive things that we struggle so hard to eradicate.

In spite of progress, one can still find in Iquitos's population a tendency to preserve a special relationship between man and nature. Oral traditions bestow upon the *Iquiteño* a symbolic universe that conditions his way of perceiving and interpreting reality. In the words of anthropologist Marlene Dobkin de Ríos, no matter how much twentieth-century machinery and values of industrial society have entered into jungle life, magical beliefs still flourish in Iquitos, as "man attempts to achieve mastery and control over the unknown by special rituals and ceremonies."[2]

Iquitos has become a niche for the emergence of a very syncretic, popular Christianity molded by the multiple influences of its environment. The beliefs of Indian Amazonian tribes, the doctrines of the Roman Catholic Church (and more recently, those of the Protestant churches), and the already syncretic cultures of thousands of immigrants who transmitted their particular cultural legacies to their descendants, all these inheritances, have made of Iquitos a funnel where diversity converges. Although the vast majority of Iquitos's population is Roman Catholic, the church has been forced to come to terms with the syncretic beliefs and native conceptions of the city's inhabitants as a result of the absence of Christian missionary activities in the region starting with the expulsion of the Jesuits in 1768 and lasting until the arrival of the Augustinians in 1900.

In the midst of this religious blending, Iquitos's Jewish descendants have incorporated some of their ancestors' traditions with Amazonian Catholic rituals and beliefs that the average inhabitants share. A tiny group of "Jewish *Mestizos*" still attempts to conduct a predominantly Jewish life, but they cannot escape the overwhelming influence of the Catholic Church and the jungle: "To be Jewish in a place like this is to be a weird animal," a third generation descendant of Jews, Ronald Reategui Levy, told me. "It is to have a different social behavior than the rest of the people."[3]

In the New and Old Worlds, most of those "weird animals" that the Inquisition converted by force to Christianity were contemptuously named *Marranos*. Eventually, the children and grandchildren of these

New Christians, whose Judaism could not be erased through a decree, embraced religious concepts and rituals from both religions, creating a new religion that was neither Christianity nor Judaism, but something in between. Can it be said that the descendants of Jews in Iquitos experience a similar identity to that of the *Marranos*, whose faith oscillated between Christianity and Judaism? If so, could we catalog the religion of these "Jewish *Mestizos*" as a type of *Marranism* produced by isolation rather than oppression?

The voices of *Iquiteños* will pave the way for us to search for answers to these questions.

✦

Iquitos: A Christian Missionary Station

In the 1820s when Peru declared its independence, along with most Latin American nations, the emergent republic established a new type of relationship with the Vatican, which refused to recognize the new states until 1835, when the pope finally admitted Nueva Granada (today's Colombia) as an independent state and began to send the first papal *nuncios* (messengers) to the capital cities of Latin American nations. The *patronato,* or system of civil patronage over the church, gave the states the right to control ecclesiastical appointments and administrative issues of the church in return for promoting the spread of Roman Catholicism in their countries. The Vatican sent secular priests to the areas previously controlled by missionaries, and thus, these clergymen began to regain power throughout the nineteenth century, becoming silent accomplices of political functionaries, ambitious entrepreneurs, representatives of foreign companies, and powerful *caucheros* (rubber lords).[4] The religious monopolies of the secular priests ended in 1900 when Peruvian President Nicolás de Pierola and representatives of Pope Leon XIII established three apostolic prefectures in the Amazon. This agreement restored the religious orders to the areas where they had previously been active.

Hence, missionaries returned to the Amazon through two paths: education and missions. The organization of prefectures, today known as *Vicariatos Apostólicos,* meant that these lands were considered uncivilized; therefore, it was the task of the missionaries to civilize the "savage" Indians and to integrate them into civilization.[5] Historian José Barletti

Pasquale claims that the region's unchangeable division into apostolic pre-fectures demonstrates that "Iquitos and the whole Peruvian Amazon is—and I am not saying 'was'—is a missionary area! It means that even though we have priests called bishops, they really are not bishops because they are totally dependent on the Vatican. There is no autonomy here like there is in each diocese. It means that we do not have a native clergy, that theo-retically, we are still considered to be living in an uncivilized area that is still a *Tierra de Misión* (land of mission)!"[6]

While the Augustinians arrived at Maynas in 1901, it took them a few years to assume control of the religious life of the area due to a wedlock between the city's political, economic, and ecclesiastical powers.[7] The Augustinians were opposed initially by the secular priests of the region, who claimed that urbanized towns such as Iquitos were already "civilized" and, consequently, were not under the jurisdiction of any religious order because only savage people living in the jungle were overseen by the mis-sionaries.[8] Economic and political opposition waned after the 1910s due to a number of factors: rubber prices decreased, reducing the power of the aristocracy; the trial of rubber barons such as Julio Arana and his English partners became a scandal in England; and Pious X issued the encyclical edict, *Lacrimabili Lamentu,* ordering his priests not to grant absolution to the perpetrators of the Putumayo crimes against Indians.[9] Only then were secular priests no longer important; only then could the Augustinians begin to exercise full power in Iquitos. Hence, the province of Maynas and its main city, Iquitos, became an Augustinian stronghold.

At the beginning of the twentieth century, the traveler Hildebrando Fuentes made a list of the dominant religions of Iquitos, classifying 9,266 inhabitants as Catholics, 72 Chinese immigrants as Confucians, 52 inhab-itants as Israelites, and 48 inhabitants as Protestants. Most of these immi-grants settled in the city.[10] Today, more than 78 percent of the approximately 350,000 inhabitants of Iquitos are Catholics while roughly 20 percent pro-fess other religions. Most of the private schools are Catholic, and the pub-lic ones require the mandatory teaching of religion, which, until the second half of the twentieth century, was exclusively Catholicism.

However, the winds of change have blown through the Peruvian Ama-zon, and gradually American Protestant missionaries have been penetrat-ing the jungle, founding new churches.[11] Since their arrival in the

Peruvian Amazon in the 1930s, Protestant missionaries have viewed themselves as did the first Franciscan and Jesuit priests in the Americas: as "saviors" of pagan cultures. In 1945 the Summer Institute of Linguistics, an organization affiliated with the Wycliffe Bible Translators, began to convert and "civilize" Amazonian Indians, especially in the department of Pucallpa, under the auspices of the Peruvian government. The institute translated the Bible into Shipibo and other indigenous languages, and succeeded to organize Protestant congregations and sects throughout the Amazon.

Two of these Protestant sects still consider the Amazon to be God's chosen paradise and the believers of these sects expect the end of the world in the promised land of the Amazon. *Los Hermanos de la Cruz* have mingled Catholicism, Evangelism, and some native beliefs of the region, especially the notion of the Land of No Evil *(La Tierra Sin Mal),* a belief that we can trace back to native ethnic groups such as the Cocama-Cocamilla. Also, the followers of *La Iglesia Israelita,* founded in 1968 by Ezequiel Atacusi in the Andes, believe themselves to be descendants of the Cocamas, and therefore, they consider the Amazon to be a kind of promised land."[12]

Certainly, the Peruvian Amazon, Maynas, and Iquitos have been and still are *Tierras de Misión* for Catholics, Protestants, Messianic leaders, religious dreamers, and for a group that struggles in its mission to preserve the religious identity of its forefathers: the "Jewish *Mestizos.*"

◆

RITUALS AND BELIEFS IN THE LAND OF NO EVIL

"There is here a dilution of identities while people are looking for a regional one. Socially and culturally the *Iquiteño* is homogeneous. Rituals are the same; beliefs are different."[13] That is the motto that Augustinian Father Joaquín García keeps repeating. Most scholars I met disagreed with this view. They defined the whole Amazon region as a place with diverse ethnic groups and social classes. Nevertheless, they acknowledged that in contrast to many other Peruvian cities, the gap between rich and poor in Iquitos has little effect on the sexual or religious behaviors of the vast majority of its inhabitants. Therefore, I found that the issue of "cultural homogeneity" was an acceptable premise to several intellectuals and scholars.

For example, anthropologist Marlene Dobkin de Ríos asserts in her study about the healing power of *ayahuasca* (a hallucinogenic substance made of jungle vine that grows in the Amazon tropical forests): "Poor people are not the only ones who look to a healer *[shaman]* for help. Men and women of middle-class background, expensively dressed bank administrators and high army officials, as well as the poor, seek in the drink *[ayahuasca]* the last resort in their search to be cured."[14]

Hence, Father Joaquín García is not terribly mistaken when he describes Iquitos as a city where everybody shares a similar way of living: "Many people, influenced by the western rationalism, are going to tell you that they do not believe in myths and beliefs from the jungle," he elaborates. "But they will tell you, 'Once, I saw a dead man walking around,' or, 'a spirit appeared to me.'"[15]

Father Joaquín knows the *Iquiteños'* idiosyncrasies well. During most of the interviews that I carried out in the city, when I questioned interviewees about specific spirits or metaphysical experiences commonly reported in the Peruvian Amazon, a frequent reply was something like, "I do not believe in those things . . . *but once* I was in the jungle and I heard a *Tunchi* [spirit] or maybe it was a soul retracing its steps."

What do such statements tell us of Iquitos? They show the imminent presence of the magical universe of the Amazonian forest in the *Iquiteños'* cosmology. Following a trip to the jungle I wrote in my diary:

> Now I begin to understand the mystery of the jungle. It is an immense green and dark region full of sounds: the singing of birds, the rustling leaves attempting to hold to their trees against the force of the wind, the quiet intrusion of the river's torrents over the shores. . . .
>
> It is easy to get lost in this green and blue mantle. It is easy to react with apprehension to every single noise or sight.
>
> The world of the jungle has its own rules, its fragrances, its oracles. I feel as if at any moment, a jungle creature like those that I was told about in the city would become visible to tell me: "Hey, you! . . . In the city it was easy to ignore me and see me as a myth. Wasn't it so? Here I am, Mr. Tourist!"

What could I expect? The *Chullachaqui* with its dispropor-
tional legs: one bigger than the other, protecting animals and
plants but teasing foreign visitors who intrude in its domains. The
Chullachaqui might guide me to some place deep in the jungle
and vanish before my eyes leaving me there, unable to return . . .
prisoner of the jungle forever. . . . Maybe I will listen to the *Ayaymama* screaming its grievous cries: AYAY MAMA, AYAY MAMA
because it was abandoned by its mother when it was a human
being. Now, transformed into a bird, the *Ayaymama* flies, wails,
expecting to be heard by its mother and to return to the nest. It
seems that the mother has not found it, but people who have listened still suffer tremors while remembering the shrillness of
its cries.

Maybe I'll meet the *Yacumama* (mother-spirit of the water
often associated with the boa constrictor) or *Yacurunas* (spirit of
the river) in the form of a fish or maybe assuming the disguise of a
Christian person, so it can carry me to the bottom of the river and
convert me into one of his own. (Maybe if the *Yacuruna* learns that
I am Jewish, it will assume the disguise of a rabbi!) I would not be
surprised here and now. But the echoes of the jungle remain in the
city. The *Iquiteño's* blood flows like the Amazon and Nanay Rivers.
In every dance there are representations of fish, fishermen,
hunters, Indian tribes, *caucho* workers.

The *Iquiteño* has a special way of talking. Not only his singing
tone, but also the words he uses. He will say that the wind "flows"
or has been "cut off" (when you do not feel it), the same words
referring to river behavior. The river is not "wild," but rather,
"capricious." The weather is like a young woman because it unexpectedly comes and abandons you (the movements of the sun and
clouds). I am a "gringo" no matter that I am a Latin American who
speaks perfect Spanish, and can therefore stop their teasing and
tricks designed to get money from tourists: "So you are a Venezuelan *gringo*, they discover. Because if you are a blond, white person, you are automatically *gringo*."

Because I am a "gringo," many women look at me and display
flirting smiles.

(I must confess that I never felt like such a "sex symbol" in my life!)
But the legend says that people like me can be dangerous. . . .
I could be a *bufeo colorado* (colored dolphin of the Amazon River)
who may kidnap innocent young women. But in the city, the idea
of the *bufeo colorado* is more associated with the notion of making
a woman pregnant and later vanishing, returning to the river. Many
women in the city take their chances, knowing that the river to
which their "*bufeos*" will return is called "the United States"
or "Europe."

Although the belief in *bufeos* transformed into bearded blond men is
not widely shared in Iquitos, other beings and spirits can wander around
the city, coexisting with people of all socioeconomic and intellectual levels.
Tunchis, or whispering spirits, and harmless hobgoblins are frequently
seen or heard by *Iquiteños.* In particular, *Malignos* or "Bad *Tunchis*" dis-
tress the inhabitants of the city with their strident whispers announcing
bad omens. Consequently, some *Iquiteños* organize *veladas* to ask saints to
protect them from these *Tunchis.* A *velada* is a religious gathering to
honor the images of saints through dances, solemn songs, and other ceremonies that reveal the intense veneration of the worshipers.

Sometimes the frightened victim of a *Tunchi* asks a priest to organize
a mass, *misa de honras,* because the spirit of a deceased person is bothering him. Such cases bear evidence of the intertwining of Amazonian
beliefs and Catholicism, resulting in a new form of popular religiosity
accepted and endorsed by the church.

The Amazonian people's myths and beliefs reflect a peculiar relation
to reality and a way of responding to the reality that surrounds them,
argues Father Joaquín García, who believes that this cosmology does not
distort the essential message of the Gospels, although it does conflict with
canonical Catholicism stereotyped throughout the history according to the
Western world's rationale. This explanation coincides with that of Claude
Lévi-Strauss, who, after many years of studying the Amazonian myths
through a structuralist analysis, concluded that myths provide logical models to express and attenuate the contradictions that peoples face within a
culture. Many years have passed since colonial times when the church
endorsed massive campaigns to "extirpate idolatry" against native Spanish

American populations. Nevertheless, somehow Amazonian people have managed to preserve ancient myths despite foreign emissaries' attempts to impose their authority and to indoctrinate Amazonian native inhabitants into their faith and culture.

The Roman Catholic Church, as an institution, has not recognized the syncretic beliefs and rituals produced by the popular Catholicism of the Amazon; however, most of its representatives, the priests who coexist with native culture and guide Catholic life in the region, have come to terms with that reality: "Our philosophy is to respect people's beliefs and to teach, as much as we can, the church's doctrine. Nowadays, you will not find priests who are going to tell someone not to believe in *Tunchis* or *El Maligno*,"[16] emphasizes Father Joaquín García. This tolerant attitude of the same church that for centuries forced native Amazonian ethnic groups to convert or otherwise pay the consequences of disobedience with their lives may be interpreted as a redefinition of how the Catholic priests have chosen to deal with aboriginal beliefs or as a simple acceptance of (or resignation toward) the way Amazonian natives experience their religious conceptions. Perhaps it is a combination of both factors.

Was the church's mission of Christianization (others would say, of self-aggrandizement) defeated in the Amazon? Not necessarily, one might argue, since Catholicism assumes a role of leadership in guiding the people's ritual responses toward all their beliefs, both native and foreign-influenced. Catholic symbols and concepts have expanded to encompass native beliefs. A good example of this process is the belief in *Almas que Recogen Sus Pasos* (Souls Retracing Their Steps), a widespread notion in the Peruvian Amazon. Almost all of my interviewees had stories to tell about seeing the foggy image of a friend or relative roaming around the places he or she used to visit, a few hours before the death of that person: ". . . And he was dying at the hospital when I saw him!" is a common concluding remark following a description of a whole metaphysical experience.

The belief in Souls Retracing Their Steps has its origins in the cosmology of several native Amazonian tribes, who believe that death is the separation of body and soul. (Other native ethnic groups have different theological views of death.) This conviction does not conflict with the Christian belief in the immortality of the soul and the possibility of resurrection. For Father José María Arroyo, there is no contradiction in combining Catholicism with the ancestral beliefs of the jungle Indians, who have inherited a legacy of legends and stories: "Anyway, the believer asks Jesus to fight those bad spirits or they ask saints. By the way, you will find the weirdest saints here in the Amazon. Saint Judas Tadeo . . . people ask him for money. San Hilarion . . . who knows who he was? We even have saints from the high jungle like San Juan, patron of Iquitos, and from Lima, *El Señor de los Milagros*. The real problem here is that the worshipers do not transcend the image of those saints and they kiss them, they hug them. We attempt to discourage that tendency, because that is idolatry . . . but it is too difficult to stop it."[17]

The Augustinian priests in Iquitos have given up strict canonical views of the church, approaching and, thus, having a certain control over some of the native religious manifestations of the average Catholic *Iquiteño.* Priests participate in *veladas* to combat *Malignos;* they organize special masses for those who request them due to their fear of jungle spirits. Even *La Iglesia Matriz* (the main church of Iquitos) holds a yearly *velada* for San Juan, the patron saint of the city, and has given structural support to devotees of *El Señor de los Milagros* (patron saint of Lima), establishing a confraternity.[18]

Like elsewhere in the world, Protestant churches have been more reluctant than the Roman Catholic Church in endorsing popular beliefs, being totally opposed to the *Iquiteños'* worship of saints. Nevertheless, many members of Protestant congregations also practice a syncretic religion, despite the official stance of their churches. These Protestant movements are mainly founded by North American missionaries; therefore, one finds that the music, the sermons, and the prayers in their churches are very similar to those in the United States. Anthropologist Javier Neyra (a Catholic) asserts that one can see "many Protestants attending Catholic processions or visiting the *shaman* [Indian spiritual leader, medium, healer] in the evenings like everybody else does."[19] Neyra estimates that around 25 percent of the *Iquiteños* who go to Protestant churches adopt all their norms; another 25 percent practice rituals from both Catholic and Protestant beliefs; 25 percent belong to Protestant congregations but still keep their ancient rituals; and the other 25 percent are undecided as to whether they want to belong to the Protestant church that they attend.

Again, Father Joaquín García insists on a quintessential feature of Iquitos's religion: a common tendency to experience religion apart from its dogma or messages: "The link between Protestants and their churches is not based on doctrinal reasons, but emotional ones. The people here never follow an official theology. The people live according to their own way of life, what we call popular religiosity. It is the reinterpretation of their beliefs from their own situation. Then, if you ask any Evangelist, he will not be able to tell you the difference between his religion and another one. There is not a doctrinal difference but rather, a difference in the way of experiencing life."[20]

Why do I quote the explanation of an Augustinian priest and a Catholic anthropologist regarding Protestantism in Iquitos? Because I was unable find any Protestant or secular scholar in the city knowledgeable in matters of religion in the Amazon. (Although one of the "Jewish *Mestizos*" would say that it is because "you like the priests. So, what kind of Jew are you?")

When I was in Iquitos, I met a non-*Iquiteño* Jew who had been living in the city for a few years. I read him the excerpt from my diary of my visit to the jungle; later on, while we were comparing opinions about the influence of Catholicism and Protestantism in the Peruvian Amazon, he warned me to be cautious because the fact that most of my main sources of information came from Catholic priests could make me present a one-sided version of the Christian Amazonian religion. After that conversation I wrote in my diary the following:

> Well, my friend X [I prefer not to mention his name] seems to have a big problem with my interpretation of the role of the Catholic Church here in Iquitos. X believes that I am becoming very fond of Father Joaquín [García] and Father Arroyo (that is true; they have been very nice to me); therefore, I am accepting their versions of how Catholicism has mixed with Amazonian beliefs. "They represent an institution that massacred Indians all over Peru," he reminds me. "Don't let them make you believe that they are so tolerant to the Indians of this region." Besides, X alerted me, "what you read to me about your feelings in the jungle, although it is beautifully written, seems to present the native beliefs as if they are less rational than those of any religion. Besides, remember that Jews in European shtetls [Jewish neighborhoods] also had certain

superstitions . . . you know, the evil eye, dybbuks [a dead person's soul embracing the soul of another person], and those things. What makes you think that the belief in *Tunchis* is less rational than a belief in God?" he questioned.

I told him that my intention was not to question these beliefs, but only to write about the universe behind the Amazonian cosmology. I never said that these beliefs are superstitions, even though I felt that some of the stories I listened to were funny. X might be right; these types of beliefs do not belong only to provincial towns, but still I feel that the jungle is a greater source for these myths than is a mall in Miami or a commercial street in Jerusalem. I guess that other landscapes that I haven't visited such as the Andean summits or the Swiss Alps could be as inspiring as the jungle. Anyway, I have to confess that X's remarks might influence the way I will write my work when I leave Iquitos . . . but still, I think, it is important to mention some of Father Joaquín's and Father Arroyo's insights, as well as some of my impressions about the peculiarity of the Amazonian landscape. Also, as I said to X: "Sorry, but although I respect everybody's beliefs, please don't compare God with *Tunchis*."

I had better not reproduce this part of my diary in my work. . . .

But I just did! Why? Because now, as I am writing, I realize that readers will be better able to understand how religion is experienced in Iquitos if they glimpse my own doubts when I was trying to unravel this mystery.

My challenge of presenting an accurate portrayal of popular Christianity in the Amazon is easier than the formidable task that the Protestant and Catholic churches have faced in their endeavor to change the moral attitudes and family values of Iquitos's population. The most important obstacles they faced in the region were the excessive promiscuity of men and the fragility of the marriage institution, which lead to the large number of households run by women.[21]

Polygamy was a traditional feature practiced by Pre-Columbian Amazonian Indians such as the Cocama ethnic group. According to researcher Jaime Regan, these tribes were patrilineal families in which "the lineage is conceived of as a link between fathers and sons. Daughters and sons have the same *blood* as their fathers. The mother belongs to another *blood,* that of her father. This concept adapts to the Spanish system of surnames, which is also patrilineal, because the father's name is the one kept from generation to generation" (AT).[22] The arrival of colonizers who also came from a patrilineal culture and who easily adapted to the jungle's conditions (without having to worry about their Spanish wives in such an isolated spot) encouraged the spread of sexual freedom to the Amazon's cities. In the nineteenth century the rubber lords and their subordinates continued to have multiple love affairs with the native women, populating the jungle with illegitimate children. One of the struggles that missionaries faced when they returned to the Peruvian Amazon in the late nineteenth century was the "war" against polygamy.[23]

Although theirs is a patrilineal society, for the *Iquiteños* the family revolves around the figure of the mother. There is almost no concrete link between fathers and sons, and this is not about isolated cases of single mothers, but rather, a social phenomenon that prevails throughout the ages. As Jaime Regan analyzes it: "After a marriage alliance between a man and a woman, children are born, but the father cannot, due to diverse reasons, sustain his family in a stable way. The women, then, have the responsibility of raising and providing sustenance for the children. When the male children grow up, the mother attempts to get their economic support" (AT).[24] The demands of the rubber and oil industries, as well as other extractive economic activities, caused the men to leave their homes for long periods of time, originating attitudes and behavior patterns that repeated themselves in successive generations.

What could the church do to stop these patterns produced by cultural legacies and historical circumstances? Very little! *Machismo* became a normal and acceptable characteristic in this society in which mothers are the "father figures" of the families (creating a matrifocal society). The lack of stable relationships between couples and the feelings of hopelessness and fatalism that poverty induces in the majority of Iquitos's population contribute to the relaxation of social and behavioral codes of many Amazonian inhabitants, who have spread a culture of pleasure-seeking, of evasion through drinking, gambling, gossiping, and dancing, expecting a better future thanks to the divine intervention of Christ, various saints, and a sprinkling of jungle spirits thrown in for good measure.

The limited social control exercised by the church maintains the majority of people as nominal Catholics by baptizing them, by providing the sacraments, by assisting them during cyclical events such as First Communion, marriage, and *velorios* (funeral rituals), and by organizing the yearly processions for Easter, Christmas mass, and other holidays. Until the 1960s, many *Iquiteños* only registered their marriages and the birthdays of their sons in church records. Birth certificates were utilized as identity documents in civil matters and especially in registering children in public and religious schools. This is why many non-Catholic fathers baptized their children. For many centuries, the state endorsed the church's efforts to keep records because priests were performing an important function of the government: registering the personal information of Peruvian citizens. Many Amazonians were unaware that it is not necessary to have been baptized in order to marry in the Catholic Church. (This includes Jews who married in Iquitos.)

The Augustinian priests succeeded in assuming the role of civil officers. Not only did they recruit most of the population within their official roll, but more importantly, they added Christian content to the bulk of Amazonian beliefs. Today, the majority of Iquitos's citizens do not understand the complex concept of the Christian Trinity, but God, the Holy Spirit, and Jesus Christ have pervaded their cosmology. In the 1980s, researcher Jaime Regan recorded some oral testimonies that reveal how the average Amazonian man reinterprets religious expressions by intertwining Christianity with his own cultural references:

> God is a good old man who many years ago was living on the earth. He himself made all the things that we are now enjoying. Then, later, He withdrew to the sky where He made the sun and the moon, who stayed to live next to Him. There, He is resting.
>
> ✦
>
> During the day, the father of God realized that his wife was pregnant. He got angry: 'You are pregnant because of the demons. It is not my son, but that of somebody else. How can he be my son if I never united with you?' But the woman repeated: "He is your son!"... Then the woman said: "Your son will be born very soon, so it will be better if you prepare a *tambo* [hut]." The man prepared

the *tambo* like a little altar with *pamakari.* God's mother came into it, and inside that *tambito* of the jungle her son was born, our God, over the little herbs of the mount *(uksha, Jui kiwa).* . . .

✦

The soul, after death, goes to wherever the Lord sends it. If it was a good soul, then it goes to heaven; if it was a bad soul it goes with *Satanás* to hell and sometimes they [the souls] are seen (AT).[25]

The Amazon's popular religion is full of versions of a great flood in the jungle, of *Tunchis* and spirits punishing those who are not good Christians, and of saints and angels provoking natural disasters or inciting animals to attack humans because of their sins. Like the story of the Virgin Birth, Catholicism impregnated popular beliefs, molding the ritual lives of the urban dwellers while leaving their original moral attitudes and habits nearly intact.

The native myth of *La Tierra Sin Mal,* the Land of No Evil, represented the peaceful character of many Amazonian tribes and the bounty of this region, which provided an abundance of food and grace to its inhabitants. When Catholicism began to be incorporated into the Amazonian cosmology, this notion of *La Tierra Sin Mal* was transformed into an attitude, rather than a literal place. This attitude reflected a longing for a utopian realm where a *diosito,* little god, would materialize the wishes of the good people, the only place on earth where paradise could be found. Iquitos is a city populated by a profoundly religious people, who wholeheartedly believe in a benevolent but castigating God, as well as spirits, divine destiny, and Jesus Christ. Modernity has reshaped how they express these beliefs, but essentially, beyond nuances of religious devotion, the everyday life of the *Iquiteño* goes on according to the embryonic values of the region: politeness, kindness, friendship, and respect of God, nature, and spirits. Certainly, wedlock loyalty, sexual restraint, and moral coherence between what is believed and what is practiced are not part of those values.

In Vargas Llosa's novel *The Storyteller,* the character Saúl Zuratas, called "Mascarita" by his friends, gives us insight into the native Amazonian definition of God: "Well, I no longer know whether I believe in God or not, pal. One of the problems of our ever-so-powerful culture is that it has made God superfluous. For them [the natives], on the contrary, God is air, water, food, a vital necessity, something without which life wouldn't be possible. They're more spiritual than we are, though you may not believe it."[26] Perhaps Iquitos resembles paradise because it is a Land of both No Evil and No Goodness, where people simply live without bothering with the concept of contradiction.

✦

PAGES BETWEEN THE OLD AND NEW TESTAMENTS

"I am the blank page between the Old Testament and the New," once proclaimed British prime minister Benjamin Disraeli, son of a Christian mother and a Jewish father.

These words hint at Disraeli's acute awareness of his unique role in history. He believed in the Jewishness of Christianity: "For myself, I look upon the church as the only Jewish institution that remains, . . ." he also wrote.[27] This idea has been endorsed by such twentieth-century Catholic figures as Polish Carmelite priest Brother Daniel, who settled in Israel in 1959, maintaining that his religion was Catholic, but "my ethnic origin is and always will be Jewish."[28] Echoes of this thinking can be found in the words of Cardinal Jean-Marie Lustiger, the current archbishop of Paris, who converted to Catholicism without reneging his Jewishness.[29]

The emancipated Disraeli, the converted Brother Daniel, and Cardinal Lustiger, as well as some other intellectuals, have attempted to reclaim the common ground between Christianity and Judaism, which had been shattered by centuries of religious rivalries and anti-Semitism. In the case of these "Jewish Christians," maybe we can speak about a kind of *Marranism;* however, my definition seems timid compared to Elaine Marks's argument that contemporary Europeanized and Christianized Jews living in urban areas "remained crypto-Jews in the same way that many of the Jews who converted to Catholicism in Spain and Portugal in the fifteenth century . . . remained crypto-Jews."[30] In her work *Marrano as Metaphor: The Jewish Presence in French Writing,* Marks includes in her list of "Jewish Christians," or modern crypto-Jews, names such as the famous Heinrich Heine, Karl Marx, Rosa Luxemburg, Sigmund Freud, Hanna Arendt, and "la crème de la crème" of France's Jewry: the novelist Albert Cohen, the cinematographer Claude Lanzman, the philosophers Jacques Derrida, Sara Kofman, and

Alain Finkielkraut (from whom I quote several times in the next chapter) and of course, the Catholic prelate, Cardinal Lustiger.[31]

Theologians and intellectuals proposing a kind of Judeo-Christian synthesis as well as members of Protestant churches such as the Adventists, the Jehovah's Witnesses, and "Jews for Jesus" (congregations that incite their worshipers to accept Jesus' doctrines while returning to the Jewish origins of the first Christians—the acceptance of the Mosaic Law as it is commanded in the Old Testament) have been filling in Disraeli's "blank page" between the Old Testament and the New. However, in Iquitos, that page was marked and transformed into a whole book of Jewish and Christian motifs a long time ago. Unlike theologians or active members of religious groups, the Iquitos "Jewish *Mestizos*" have created a link between the two religions through a natural process of *mestizaje.*

Iquitos's voices of Jewish descendants reveal a religion without doctrine, without theologians or leaders attempting to make sense of their syncretism. It is a *Marranic* religion of acceptance of God according to their Christian education and their vague Jewish heritage. All this natural process of synthesizing Judaism and Christianity is what makes me define the "Jewish *Mestizos*" as modern-day *Marranos.*[32]

The religion of the "Jewish *Mestizos*" is the consequence of a historical dislocation, of a miscegenation that began with the same Jewish immigrants who came to the Peruvian Amazon. These adventurers, who spent most of their time navigating rivers, trading, and traveling to Europe, left the education of their children in the hands of their women. On the most important Jewish holiday, Yom Kippur, Jews gathered to pray together but they did not take their children to the religious ceremonies. Those who kept some rituals in home did not teach their children the meaning of what they were doing. Geologist Alfredo Rosenzweig, who visited the Peruvian Amazon during the late 1940s, remembers how those Jews who strove to educate their sons as Jews sent them to Europe to study in institutions such as the *Alliance Israélite Universelle;* yet, the rest of the immigrants "were very learned Jews but after their burial, Judaism was over. The 'cut' between the first and the second generations was almost total."[33]

Víctor Edery Morales, current president of Iquitos's Israelite Society, confirms Rosenzweig's impression: "It was not customary for the Jews here to teach their children. Maybe their idea was to maintain the customs of their birthlands among them."[34] Iquitos inhabitant Saúl Benamú Gónzales-Pavón comments that ". . . because I was the oldest male son, my father taught me something of his Jewish things, but my little sisters have been Catholics since they were kids."[35]

The children of these Jewish immigrants attended Catholic schools because they had no choice: all education was controlled by the church. The children of Jewish fathers had to be baptized in order to be accepted in these schools where they learned Christian doctrines and had to perform the sacraments.[36] At home, they saw their mothers praying to saints or invoking the name of Jesus, but they also occasionally witnessed their parents performing curious rituals:

> According to the religion of my husband, circumcising our sons meant a lot. . . . I always respected his religion. I do believe in Jesus, but I belong to another religion . . . but that is not a problem because I ask of the same God, the Father, but through His son. (Non-Jewish woman remembering the circumcision of her sons)
>
> ✦
>
> My father observed all the holidays; he used to fast. "Respect me so that I respect you." The priest told him that if he did not submit himself to baptism, he would not marry him. He told us: "I had to assume all that farce because I loved your mother, but I am still a Jew! . . . If you want to maintain your Catholic religion, it is up to you, and when you want to change it, you tell me . . . so. I [like my father did] baptized my children when they were fourteen years old so they could decide . . . because there is a problem, we do not have anyone to influence our race . . . our children are surrounded by Catholics. What can we do? Besides, here it is a problem not to be Catholic. It is the official religion in Peru. It is stated in the constitution!
>
> ✦
>
> My father had a kerosene lamp that he lit on Fridays and he prayed and fasted. He prayed in Hebrew. Since we know that we are Jews, we pray every morning.
>
> ✦
>
> My father performed all the rituals, the fasting, he ate those cookies . . . the Maso [matzah, *the unleavened bread for Passover*]. Before

he died he learned that we had founded the Israelite-Peruvian Institute of Iquitos and I told him while he was in bed before his death. He said to me: "That is the best thing you could have done." Beforehand, he never worried. Mom took us to the church.

✦

My father is of the Hebrew race. We carry out the religion starkly . . . with the "Meyuya" (Mezuzzah) . . . what you put in the gates of the synagogues. We observed every Shabbat religiously. We did not work, we did not light fire, we did not do anything. Friday we cooked for the next day. We did not turn on lights, but of course, you can do it through other persons. We observed Yom Kippur. Nobody keeps it. Nobody is serious here like we are.[37]

For the fourth and fifth generation of Jewish descendants, there was no opportunity to learn rituals from their assimilated parents. However, most of the younger descendants of Jews are discovering Jewish traditions in the house of Víctor Edery, where the community has been celebrating the main Jewish holidays and Kabbalat Shabbat [Friday evening prayer] since 1990. Marco Mesía Rodríguez, a college student, rationalizes what most of these youngsters can scarcely explain:

My father did not have a clear awareness, definitively, of his origin, and that is why he could not transmit that legacy to his children, to me. I studied in a Catholic school, San Agustín, because it was the best for sciences. At home, very occasionally my father mentioned that his father was the son of such, son of such . . . but those were "sparks."[38]

Several "Jewish *Mestizos*" remember that although their parents did not practice Jewish rituals, they maintained an intensely anti-clerical attitude (probably influenced by their European immigrant-friends). A few fathers took measures to avoid having their children be exposed to the Christian sacraments:

My father succeeded in making the teachers from the Catholic school exonerate me from mass.

✦

My father forbade us to pray in the Catholic school Sagrado
Corazón. . . . *My father went to talk to the Mother Superior and
forbade her to take us to the church. He said: It is prohibited for
them to kneel down! He also said to us: Don't marry with a priest
[officiating the ceremony], go to a civil court!*

✦

*It is forbidden to die without being baptized! It is a terrible thing!
My father did not want to baptize us [in Iquitos], but he finally did
it after my brother died. He did not like priests and did not allow
us to go to church, but he realized that one must receive baptism
before dying.*[39]

Many descendants of Jews seem to have preserved their ancestors'
skepticism towards such Catholic customs as confession, the notion of
ecclesiastical hierarchy, and devotion to saints (like sixteenth- and
seventeenth-century *Marranos*).

*The Bible says that there should not be images, and nevertheless,
the church is full of them, although they [the priests] say that you
really are not praying to the image but to what it represents. I go to
church but I do not like that.*

✦

*I do not like that fetishism . . . you can see many Catholics wor-
shiping saints so much that they break parts of the images after
touching and touching their bodies. I consider myself to be a
Catholic, but I feel a humanist identification with the Jews.*

✦

*My sister goes to church only because we do not have a synagogue
and she feels the need to be in a place where you can hear about
God. Remember that in the preaching, usually the priest talks
about the Old Testament.*

✦

*In Judaism, contradictions are like incisions. In other religions,
they are like loose bricks that make the whole wall fall. For
example, in Catholicism, the idea of the trinity, the Immaculate
Conception, the ecclesiastical hierarchy . . . all of that does not have
any foundation in the Bible!*[40]

Very few of the "Jewish *Mestizos*" revere saints. The particular case of twenty-three-year-old Becky Ríos Bensimón is as exceptional as it is fascinating:

> *I pray to Friar Martín. You know . . . to ask to be freed from a dis-*
> *ease, a problem, social and economic things. Every Sunday I light*
> *two candles for him and I dance. I ask him to help make possible*
> *my trip to Israel because I want to join our people there . . . the*
> *Jews. My sister, the one who lives in Israel, told us that in Israel*
> *people fast and do those things, so they must be very close to their*
> *saints and light candles for them.*[41]

Those who retain vague remembrances of their fathers' rituals imprinted in their visual memories still keep some of these traditions, mixing them with elements from their Christian education and Amazonian beliefs:

> *My father used to light candles sometimes. . . . It was inside the*
> *house for nobody to see. We had a three-armed candlestick. Today,*
> *I do not light candles anymore but I pray every evening to God, to*
> *my father, my mother, my brothers and sisters, to their souls.*
>
> ✦
>
> *Do you know the holy candles of Friday? My father taught me that*
> *it is a prayer that is performed, asking pleas to God. We say to the*
> *Jewish God that we are with Him and we want His blessing for the*
> *rest of the week. Three glasses are brought containing water and*
> *oil and over them we put a little candle and we light the candles.*
> *That is part of the Jewish religion. . . . My father used to say*
> *"Uishtam Shalom" and he knelt down. The next day he did not go*
> *out until noon and he fasted the whole day. He stayed until noon in*
> *his bedroom and he prayed in Hebrew. It is a Jewish thing and that*
> *is why we light candles still.*[42]

The concept of kashrut (dietary laws) is only known by those who have been in Lima, but all the "Jewish *Mestizos*" know that *chancho* (swine) is forbidden food according to Judaism. Some eat it, some refrain, but all reveal markedly diverse understandings of this tradition, from the most rational to the most symbolic, including of course, Christianized and fantastic explanations for the prohibition against eating pork:

> I eat chancho *if they put it in front of me. It is forbidden in the Jewish religion because it was a bad meat—cholesterol. In those times, there were wise men who already knew that* chancho *was a harmful meat. Now, the fish without scales, they say, works as the* baja policía *in the rivers . . . you know, like those lowly policemen who take the garbage from the streets! Those fish clean the filth from the rivers and those I do not eat even in jest! . . . because of the Jewish thing, but also because it must not be eaten. There was a time in Iquitos when nobody ate them.*

> ✦

> I eat a little bit of chancho. *It is not eaten because it is not the adequate meat for Christ's supper, the evening when Christ shared with his disciples the last supper.*

> ✦

> Did you read Exodus? *The* paisanos *ate human flesh in prison. . . . The Sephardic Jews were transformed into* chanchos *years ago— I read that in the* Reader's Digest—*that someplace on the earth they were transformed into* chanchos *and that is why it must not be eaten.*[43]

While observance of dietary laws varies considerably, the descendants of Jews have been able to preserve most of the Jewish rituals for burial. The existence of an Israelite cemetery inspires "Jewish *Mestizos*" to maintain their ancestors' customs of burying their deceased brothers. (See Appendix 1.) Most *Iquiteños* "Jews" wish to be buried in the Israelite cemetery when they pass away. They also know that a Jew must be buried under the earth and covered by sand. Even the most assimilated families attempt to preserve whatever vague notions of Jewish burial rituals they still possess.

Jews registered in the *Sociedad Israelita de Iquitos* have the right to be buried in the Jewish cemetery. Many receive a Christian funeral and later are taken to the Israelite burial ground where Víctor Edery, the society's spiritual guide, and Jaime Vázques Izquierdo, conductor of the rituals, read in Spanish the Jewish mourning prayer *(Kaddish)* and say some words of consolation to the families of the deceased. Father José María Arroyo remembers an amusing incident from these burials:

"They were burying Toledano, and the Jews went there with their *kippah* (the little hats) to the Hebrew cemetery. . . . They buried him according to the Jewish ritual with Vásquez Izquierdo and Edery officiating and while they prayed the relatives of Toledano and some Jews made this"—Arroyo crosses himself and bursts into laughter—". . . Yes, they were crossing themselves!"[44]

In some cases, the family of the deceased refuses to bury him or her in the Israelite cemetery. Víctor Edery and Jaime Vásquez Izquierdo do what they can to convince them. In the worst of the cases, they read the *Kaddish* during the funeral, after the Christian rituals are over and before the coffin is brought to the general cemetery. But for many years the descendants of Jews were not organized; therefore, many of them were buried in the Israelite cemetery without the Jewish ceremony.

Syncretism between Christianity and Judaism accompanies many "Jewish *Mestizos*" to their deaths. Some gravestones are inscribed in Hebrew and Spanish. Two gravestones are adorned with the initials R. I. P. (Rest in Peace): one from 1896 (Jayme Cohen) and one from 1899 (Moisés Isaac Nahón). On Cesar Toledano Torres's gravestone there is an immense Star of David, and on the memorial plaque one finds a little cross printed by his wife and son (Toledano Torres passed away in 1992). Several mausoleums in the Christian cemetery contain plaques with Stars of David, possibly requested by the deceased persons or by members of their families. There are even a few burial sites that display the Star of David and the cross together.

The case of Ana Mesía Velasco's burial illustrates how persistent are the vestiges of Judaism for some of these *Iquiteños.* I registered this story in my diary:

> When I was in the airplane, on my way from Lima to Iquitos, I asked some questions about the city to a nice lady who was sitting next to me. I do not remember how we turned our conversation to this . . . but we did: "Did you know that Iquitos was the first

Peruvian city with cable TV?" she said to me. I was surprised. I didn't expect Iquitos to have cable TV. She explained that a Polish businessman came to this city some years ago and he installed the cable company. "Tyminsky is his name," she added.

Tyminsky? That name sounded familiar to me. Wasn't he the one who challenged and almost defeated Polish president Lech Walesa in the last elections? "The same man," the lady smiled.

I forgot the whole issue for many weeks until I saw a big picture of Tyminsky in the Café Express in Iquitos, and Father Arroyo told me that Tyminsky saved that café from going out of business simply because it was his favorite place, so he gave some money to its owner, and there they were, professionals and old visitors of the Café Express still enjoying their conversations and the cheap prices of the sandwiches and the beer. Suddenly I remembered why I hadn't forgotten Tyminsky's name! Because when I was working as a journalist in Caracas [Venezuela], I had to write about the elections in Poland, and the news agencies had reported that some Polish politicians accused him of being Jewish. That is a hurtful accusation in Poland!

If Tyminsky were Jewish, I should find out, because his story might be important for my work. So, I went to TVS, his cable company in Iquitos. Tyminsky was abroad. I was told that he lives now in Canada and travels twice a year to Poland and twice a year to Iquitos. He married a woman from Iquitos, Graciela Pérez Velasco, sister of a popular *shaman* in the city. "No . . . as far as I know he is not Jewish," the attractive secretary in his office told me. "Why don't you come back another day to talk to Pedro Garufi, who is in charge of the company while Mr. Tyminsky is not here?"

She gave me some newspaper articles about TVS and Stan Tyminsky and set an appointment for me with Mr. Garufi. Before returning to TVS, I read those articles and parts of the puzzle began to fall into place. In an interview carried out by the newspaper *Expreso* on December 18, 1990, Stanislaw Tyminsky, "The Polish Fujimori," who had just arrived from Poland after the elections, complained how his political rivals utilized racist slogans to minimize his possibilities of winning the elections. Tyminsky told how he met his wife, to whom the world press called with disdain "a Peruvian Indian": "She was introduced to me by her brother Max, and since then, I am dazzled because she is really an Inca princess with Jewish drops in her blood," Tyminsky declared to the press.

That was the answer! Tyminsky was not Jewish, but his wife from Iquitos was a Jewish descendant. That was enough argument for Polish anti-Semites and xenophobic people to exploit. He was Jewish because he "had a Jewish wife." My Polish grandfather would not have been surprised by this logic, coming from his hostile birthland!

Well, a few days later, Mr. Garufi helped me to put all the pieces of the puzzle together by telling me an interesting story: "A few months ago, the grandmother of Graciela Tyminsky passed away, and my boss called me from Canada asking me to handle her burial. So, I went to the cemetery and I purchased a niche in one of the better mausoleums, just in the middle . . . it was a good spot! When we met in the cemetery for the burial one of the relatives asked me if I could change the place . . . he wanted to bury her under the earth. I felt extremely annoyed. I got a wonderful place, I took care of everything, and now this man wanted me to pay for a more expensive place to bury the old lady.

"I called Tyminsky in Canada and left a message. I would not become involved anymore in that business, and I would let that relative take care of the burial. Stan called me back in the evening and asked me to help them to bury her under the earth: 'It is not a matter of snobbism, it is a religious matter,' he said. So I helped them to do so.

"Weeks later a Jewish friend from Lima to whom I told this story explained that the Jews only bury under the earth (and the more fragile the coffin, the better) and when Tyminsky was back in Iquitos he told me about the Jewish lineage of his wife."

Hence, Ana Mesía Velasco was buried under the earth according to her ancestors' traditions, in the Catholic cemetery of Iquitos in February 1995. A grandson of Ana Mesía Velasco (a sixth generation descendant of a Jewish immigrant who came to Peru) reminded Mr. Garufi about that family tradition.[45]

In the 1990s, the "Jewish *Mestizos*" finally organized a community and succeeded in preserving the burial rituals of their ancestors.[46] A tradition strictly observed at the Israelite cemetery is that of keeping the tomb without a gravestone during the first year after the person's death.

Out of the cemetery, in the realm of the living ones, the "Jewish *Mestizos*" of Iquitos share a vibrant cosmology that intertwines Christianity, Judaism, and their personal notions of the metaphysical and religious worlds. For most, Christmas is a holiday to celebrate with the family; very few refer to it as the commemoration of "the Lord's birth." Many go to church on Easter, but a few refuse to even approach a church for a friend's wedding or a baptism because they want to make it clear that they are Jews.

The concept of the Trinity is in their vocabulary, but they have a hard time explaining it (I am tempted to say "understanding it," but as a Jew, I am not the right person to judge such a thing). Some widows, *convivencias,* and daughters of Jewish immigrants insist that the only difference between them and their husbands and fathers is that Jews pray to God the father, and not the son. Can a Catholic accept that distinction without rejecting the notion of Trinity?

Other expressions seem to reveal that many *Iquiteños* do not fully grasp the concept of the unity of the Trinity:

> *I believe in the same God that everybody else believes in. The Old Testament is the same for everybody. The psalms are the same. I believe in God and Jesus, but in the Evangelical churches Jesus is first. For me that is a contradiction . . . always Jesus, Jesus, Jesus; but I say that God must be first.*

✦

> *The New Testament is more educational; the Old Testament is more symbolic. . . . I do not have a clear concept of Jesus; God is the important thing. Sometimes I address myself to Jesus Christ, but truly, it is to God.*

✦

> *Jesus was a human being like us . . . fond of women like we are. He had many women. A Catholic told me that Jesus had like three*

thousand women. It is what you hear. I believe more or less in
Jesus, but certainly, I do believe in the Holy Ghost.[47]

The notion of who Jesus was moves throughout the whole spectrum of
beliefs that one can find in our times. For most Iquitos's descendants of
Jews, Jesus is God, the Messiah, God incarnated, the son of God, and
God's messenger to the earth. Some have a more Jewish approach: Jesus
could have been a great prophet, a great man, an esoteric and very spiritual figure, but he was a human being! The real messiah has not come yet.
God is unique. Some depict Jesus through historical lenses: he was a revolutionary, a pacifist, one of the most influential men in the history of
humanity whose teachings are beautiful, and he was a *paisano*, actually, a
good *paisano,* because he was a thorough Jew. When asked about Jesus,
some of them stand firmly in their belief about his divinity while the
majority adopts an apologetic stance justifying Jesus' role in their lives:

> *Because I have believed in Jesus, he has helped me, in 80, 90 per-*
> *cent. What do you think about it?*
>
> ✦
>
> *Those who believe in Jesus Christ are not 100 percent Jewish.*
>
> ✦
>
> *I personally believe that the Messiah has already come. I don't*
> *know whether Israel, the Jewish people are blind. I am a Jewish*
> *believer in Christ.*
>
> ✦
>
> *Jesus is God, the father of Israel. He said: "Those who believe me,*
> *follow me" and he went to meet the people of Israel and that is how*
> *the Jewish people were established. That is why we are never aban-*
> *doned, because Jesus is father of Israel. The proof is Israel. Nine*
> *countries tried to attack Israel: Damascus, Syria, Egypt . . . and*
> *they have lost the war against Israel.*
>
> ✦
>
> *Can the Israelites convert believers of Jesus? It is said that they are*
> *more Jewish when Jews believe in Jesus. Thereby, one is a total Jew.*
> *Someone told me [that]; I do not know so much. . . . In the Bible it*
> *is said Emanuel, not Jesus. Can you explain this to me! In the Old*

Testament the word written is not Jesus, but Emanuel. Then, are we more Jewish if we believe in Jesus?

✦

The Jews do not believe in Jesus. Because I have been educated according to the Catholic religion, I honestly believe in Christ, more like a human being sent to the earth, son of God.

✦

I believe in Christ because one has to believe in something.

✦

I never have understood why Jews do not believe in Christ and I haven't dared to ask that.[48]

"I do not understand: why do Jews not talk about Jesus?" was one of the most frequent answers they gave me. (As good Jews, they answer with questions!) Certainly, most of the Jews do not mention Jesus in their holidays, but the few *paisanos* who clearly distinguish the differences between Christianity and Judaism do so frequently. In his Kabbalat Shabbat preaching, Víctor Edery constantly repeats why Jews do not believe in Jesus as God's incarnation. He repeats again and again every Friday evening how wrong the Christians are in their beliefs, and how only the people of Israel follow the real truth because they believe in one, indivisible, abstract God.

The notes of the Israelite Society's October 14, 1991 session record the following events:

> . . . Then, our president [Víctor Edery] lectured about the topic "The Jewish Religion and the Christian Religion." He spoke about the virtues of the Jewish absolute monotheism, about the theory of the Messiah, about the conditions that must happen in the world before his coming, how he will be announced by Elijah the prophet, that the wars will be over; [he referred to] Christ as a false messiah, because after his coming, life, in general, worsened instead of getting better. The increase of wars every time was more terrible, [he referred to] the Hebrew Holocaust as a consequence of the Second World War. He also mentioned similarities between Judaism and Christianity and made a call for the union of Jews and Christians in order to recognize the true God, *Adonay.*[49]

Edery's explicit antagonism toward Christianity is a reflection of his group's attempt to "open the eyes" of the members of the Israelite Society who are too influenced by the Catholic Church. Other members of the society such as Jaime Vásquez Izquierdo, Ronald Reategui Levy, Alicia Assayag Chávez, Marco Mesía Rodríguez, Sara Bendayán Tello, Jacqueline Levy Vidal, and Pedro Reategui Panduro are adamant defenders of the Jewish idea of monotheism in which no human being can be considered to be God: "We are attempting to attract, to teach, to convince, and convert people in order to make them decide between Catholicism and Judaism. There are many who fluctuate," points out Jaime Vásquez Izquierdo.[50]

The stance of this group is remarkably lucid, almost devoid of the overwhelming Christian exposure that they have received, compared to the Catholic notions of most "Jewish *Mestizos.*" Many current members of the Israelite Society come from a Protestant background; some formerly went to Adventist or Evangelical churches, and the youngsters had the opportunity to attend Shabbat and Jewish holiday services since the community organized in 1990. Víctor Edery's followers have rejected their Christian background after deciding to retrace the steps of their ancestors. They wish to be thorough Jews like the first immigrants who, although they had to accept the authority of the church in civil matters and celebrated in secular ways some of the Catholic holidays of the country, kept the most important Jewish traditions and never converted to Catholicism. Edery's group has decided to teach what it understands Judaism to be, reminding the *paisanos* that such things as the Holy Ghost and Jesus the Messiah are foreign concepts for Jews.[51]

Viviana Toledano, a young woman in her twenties, told me that every time she meets Víctor Edery, he preaches to her the same messages of sticking to Judaism that her grandfather, Alberto Toledano, writes to them from Israel. Alberto Toledano was the son of an immigrant who came to the Amazon in the 1920s, and had thirteen children from several *convivencias,* among them Sofía Ruiz del Aguila, with whom he had six children. In his early thirties, Alberto Toledano traveled to Morocco and later settled in Israel, where he married. Occasionally, he sends letters to his *Iquiteños* family. Irene Toledano, daughter of Mr. Toledano and Sofía Ruiz del Aguila, showed me a letter dated January 14, 1992, in which her Jewish father asked her granddaughter Viviana, to tell Milagros (Viviana's sister who lives in Lima) that, "according to our tradition, there are no children who are God and no person can be God. *Baruch Hashem* [the Lord] is unique and one forever. Amen."

> *This was an answer to Milagros, who sent him a Christmas card wishing grandpa a happy holiday celebrating with his family the birth of the Lord, our God Jesus Christ.*[52]

Regardless of the degree of Judaism or Catholicism of this people, all share a sense of chosenness produced by their strong belief in being worshipers of the "Jewish God." In fact, many of them express how they feel especially protected because they are Jews:

> *We, the Jews, are more protected by God than are the Catholics. Because we have the idea of a unique God, we don't believe in saints. See how Israel, such a small country, won the Seven [sic] Days War, and that only can happen when you are enlightened by God.*

✦

> *I am convinced that I have a halo that protects me. I could tell you many cases in which I have came out from dangers. Now that I know that I am Jewish, I feel even more that God has something for me, something that I must do and I still do not have the answer. One of my goals is to go to Egypt or at least Machu Picchu where it is said that you can feel something of esoteric vibrations . . . the light. It is said that Cuzco is considered the center of the world . . . Jerusalem is too far in my imagination. [In fact, Cuzco is the Quechua word for bellybutton, or navel, meaning the center of the world.]*

✦

> *To be Jewish is to be in glory. The Lord helps me when I suffer from anything. I am neither* pitoncita *[seer] nor a witch, but when I say something about someone . . . it happens.*

✦

> *The proof that we are chosen by God is myself. I am never forsaken.*[53]

Most of the "Jews" consider Amazonian beliefs, such as the existence of *Chullachaquis, Tunchis,* and *El Maligno,* to be superstitions and "old-wives' tales." However, it is not necessary to insist on questions regarding these motifs to make them tell about their personal experiences with these Amazonian beings. Their stories are diverse and frightening, from souls riding white horses to spirits behind people like intruder shadows. The "I do not believe in those things, but once it happened to me that . . ." syndrome mentioned by Father Joaquín García eventually came out in almost all my interviews. The most widespread belief among the *Iquiteños* is that of the Soul Retracing Its Steps. "That is a very complex matter," a skeptical interviewee told me. "It is in a process of discussion," said another. A young woman told me that she did not believe in this myth but, anyhow, if she saw those souls she would not be scared by them; an old lady rejected that "superstition," but related a story of a demon penetrating the body of a friend. I met a woman who believes the *Chullachaqui* to be an incarnation of the Devil in one person's body; others assert that *Chullachaquis* play tricks on visitors to the jungle. One man denied believing in those "jungle stories," but finally admitted having a frightening experience once when he witnessed a friend's fight against shadows or spirits: "Then, I prayed to the Lord," he remembered.

What role do these beliefs play in the cosmology of the "Jewish *Mestizos*"? Generally, these beliefs play much the same role as they do among the rest of Iquitos's population. Many "Jewish *Mestizos*" are descended from foreign fathers or grandfathers who dismissed "those myths and legends"; thus, some "Jewish *Mestizos*" inherited the skepticism of their ancestors. Unlike the majority of the population, the poorest people, and the *ribereños* (people who live along the rivers' shores), the urban dwellers of the Peruvian Amazon only talk about spirits and jungle beings on social occasions and when requested to by pushy foreign researchers. Occasionally, motifs related to Judaism or Jews surface in these stories:

> *I don't believe [in souls retracing their steps] but once, my father's soul chased us after his death because we could not make the mass that had to be done fifteen days after his death, that thing the Jews do [she refers to the* Shloshim, *the prayer for the deceased carried out thirty days after the death of the person]. . . . That was my father requiring us to go and visit him in the cemetery. It is not that we believe; it truly happened!*

✦

That of the soul retracing its steps is not contradictory to Judaism,
and much less to reincarnation. God says in His words that no soul
is lost. Then, these persons that became depraved in the earth, they
die. What happens to them? The only way for them to overcome
their past is through reincarnation, to incarnate in another body
in order to enhance their spiritual life through another person. This
is how man has the possibility to be part of the Supreme Being,
through atonement . . . and not through the blood of Jesus Christ or
because the Lord was crucified, neither of those things . . . only
through atonement.

✦

God can oppose everything but evil. He can not oppose the Devil.
For example, Hitler. It was the Devil that brought Hitler and that is
why God could not help the Jews like He does with Israel today.

✦

I have special powers, and I can see souls and spirits. I can heal, I
see the person's aura. Sometimes I prepare amulets for friends.
Once, I prepared a Star of David to protect a Jewish friend. You
prepare it crying prayers for the person for whom these amulets
are destined, so he can be charged with energy.[54]

These stories show how Amazonian beliefs permeate the cosmology of
the "Jewish" *Iquiteños*, but they are far from shaping their syncretic religion. Conversely, the Christian and Jewish notions that are so rooted in
their lives occasionally cause them to add to their interpretations of metaphysical experiences some motifs from their religious backgrounds.
"Everything is possible in the jungle," I was told many times. The following provocative examples of families, descended from Jewish immigrants,
confirm that everything is possible also in the Peruvian jungle's urban center, Iquitos: two sons of the same father follow different paths, Jaime
Delmar becomes a member of the Fraternity of *El Señor de los Milagros*,
and Carlos Delmar settles in Israel, embracing formal Judaism; Víctor
Edery becomes the spiritual guide of the Iquitos "Jewish" community,
while one of his sisters, Becky Edery Morales, converts to Catholicism in
Lima; Teddy Bendayán Díaz defines himself as a humanist Jew while his

wife, Manuela Zagaseta Mesía, also a descendant of Jews, works as principal of the *Corpus Cristi* school of Iquitos; and so similar cases go on and on. These cases of *Marranism,* of families fluctuating between the pages of the Old and the New Testament probably find the classical example in the instance of Víctor Israel, founder of the Israelite Society of Iquitos in 1909, who agreed in his old age, prior to his second marriage, to be baptized in Lima.

Everything is possible coming from Iquitos! And Benjamin Disraeli presumptuously thought himself to be the only page between the Old and the New Testament!

4

JEWISHNESS IN LIMA AND IQUITOS

"The great Unamuno, speaking of Baruch Spinoza,
said that 'just as one feels physical pain in a limb,
a hand or a tooth, and suffers from it, so Spinoza
felt, and suffered, his God.' Of Edelman we can
say that he feels, and suffers, the [Peruvian]
Hebrew Union."
—Isaac Goldemberg, *The Fragmented Life
of Don Jacobo Lerner*

"And they told [Iquitos's Jewish descendants]. They told
with unbridled emotion where their parents came
from, what their fathers' occupations were; they told
us how they struggled to emerge from a sixty-year
silence. Many of them are high functionaries of the
city. They are beloved and respected by everybody. . . .
They were next to us and they talked about Israel
so much, that it seemed like it had been a taboo to
do it during those sixty years."(AT)
—Yaacov Hasson, "Iquitos: Alma Judía en la
Amazonía Peruana." Article published in the
journal *Comunidades Judías de Latín America* in 1966

WHO IS A JEW in Lima? Who is a Jew in Iquitos? Who is a Jew in today's
complex world? There are Orthodox, Conservative, Reform, and

Reconstructionist Jews; "Jews for Jesus"; Jews who practice Buddhism; Jews whose center of identity revolves around Israel although they are not Israelis; Jews obsessed with the "Never Again" legacy of the Holocaust; and Israelis who proclaim themselves to be atheists, agnostics, citizens of a state whose Judaism is perceived as a civilization rather than a religion.

For Orthodox Jews the answer is unequivocal: A Jew is the son or daughter of a Jewish mother. Although many would argue that the observance of Jewish law should be what determines a person's Judaism, rabbinical tradition mandates that even the most rebellious or heretical child of a Jewish mother is and always will be a Jew. For non-Orthodox Jews the question of "Who is a Jew?" invites equivocal answers: A Jew is someone who feels himself to be a Jew, one who practices some Jewish customs, someone who marries a person of Jewish descent whether or not he is accepted as a Jew by Orthodox rabbis, one who is an active member of a Jewish community, a loyal citizen of Israel, or a believer in one God who does not share the beliefs of Christianity, Islam, or other religions.

Orthodox Judaism is defined as halakhic, based on traditional Jewish law. It is a modus vivendi that does not allow feelings or whims to determine Jewish identity. Today it is not a proselytizing religion.[1] Contemporary secular Judaism, on the other hand, is subjective and emotionally oriented; it is considered not only a religion but a culture, a civilization from which members can select aspects to blend with other habits and beliefs, a "global village" way of living in which multiculturalism is a perfectly understandable and welcome notion, despite the neurosis that it can cause.

On the other hand, what is it to be a Peruvian? Is it merely a matter of citizenship or also of heritage? Whether "Peruvianism" is related to racial and religious notions, can the Jews of Lima claim a common national identity with the country's overwhelming *Mestizo* population? Since ethnicity and religion are fundamental to the discourse of Peru's national identity, why would a group of *Mestizos* in Iquitos decide to turn their backs on the religious identity of the majority of the population? Perhaps they have done so simply because echoes of Judaism have become an undeniable part of their polyphonic identity.

Lima is a big city where the hectic urban rhythm and the "noise" produced by machines, multitudes, and material progress relegate religion to specific spaces and times removed from the routine of everyday secular life. The *Limeño* experiences his syncretic identity in the same way that twentieth century *homo urbanus* does in every cosmopolitan environment: by compartmentalizing the multiple—and sometimes—diverse facets of his persona/personality depending upon social and temporal contexts.

Iquitos is a provincial city. Here modernity appears alien when viewed against the natural landscape and the rural character of its inhabitants. Most *Iquiteños* profoundly believe in God and they tend—more than *Limeños*—to accept the metaphysical as an indisputable fact of life. Within this context, secularism means that one is not a priest, a nun, or a *cucufata* (religious fanatic), but rather an ordinary person without clerical status, who constantly prays and looks to God for guidance regardless of his or her behavior.

The inhabitants of Iquitos are able to identify themselves with people of diverse ethnic, religious, or national backgrounds without losing their own sense of distinction. They see compatriots everywhere, as their remarks attest: "We both are *paisanos* from Yurimaguas"; "He is a Jew, one of our *paisanos*"; "Our families grew together, we are *paisanos*"; "There in Lima, we have a *paisano*. . . . I do not remember his name, but he is a *paisano*, from Iquitos"; "He is my best friend, my *paisano*"; "Go and talk to my *paisano*, because I believe he is Jewish. Me? No way! I am as Catholic as the Pope!"; "Do you know that Chinese guy? He is my *paisano*."

Although descendants of Jews use the word *paisano* to greet one another, at the same time they consider themselves *paisanos* of their non-Jewish friends. The term is used and abused to refer to those who were born in the same town or city, as well as to friends, business partners, and inhabitants of Iquitos. Of course, as in any Peruvian locality, some people feel more privileged than others because of their white European ancestry, but racial and class prejudices are relatively temperate in provincial Amazonian cities and towns, compared to the Andean and coastal regions. In Lima, in contrast, the discourse of common people is severely exclusionary, differentiating people on the basis of ethnicity and race—*Cholos, Charapas, Costeños, negros,* white people, *indiecitos* (little Indians); socioeconomic status—*pitucos* (snobs), *cholos* (in this instance, referring to uneducated people); religious categories—Catholics, Jews, Protestants, Messianic believers, etc.; political labels—*fujimoristas* (followers of president Fujimori), *apristas* (those who support the APRA party), *senderistas* (members of the terrorist movement *Sendero Luminoso*), etc. Among *Limeños,* there is a strong tendency to define identity by emphasizing what distinguishes one person from another.

Because modernity calls for unequivocal definitions of our identities, *homo urbanus*—in a higher degree than *homo rural*—entrusts guidance of the different elements of his identity to institutions: religion to the church, national identity to the government, and sexuality to the institution of marriage or, at least, to the consideration of religious, scientific, or paternalistic advisers (confessions, psychoanalysis, family, friends, or TV experts). In Lima more so than in the provinces, popular culture has been more successfully controlled by institutions.[2]

But in the Amazonian heartland, the Catholic Church was not as successful in diluting non-Christian beliefs as it had been in the coastal cities; therefore, even though people in the Andes and the Peruvian Amazon follow the official religious and national rituals forged by the Peruvian state and the church, they are more independent in experiencing and expressing their cosmology. For the *Iquiteño,* an inhabitant rooted in a city founded by immigrants and inherited by their *Mestizo* descendants, nationalism is heard as a distant echo.

To be Jewish in Lima means to live between the universal culture of a Western city and the particular legacy of Jewish culture. Jewish *Limeños* experience the predicament of sharing the values and fashions of the well-to-do and/or white population of the capital city, but also carrying on the exclusionist and defensive patterns that the big city demands. In contrast, to be Jewish in Iquitos means to retain that part of one's identity that is related to something distant and mystical: the Jewish people.

◆

TO BE JEWISH IN LIMA: ORTHODOX GUIDELINES
FOR A SECULAR COMMUNITY

In Lima, a city of more than eight million inhabitants, people of diverse national and religious backgrounds coexist, respecting each other's differences; nevertheless, Lima is essentially a Christian city with colonial and modern churches, monasteries, processions, and its own religious myths such as that of *El Señor de los Milagros,* the miraculous image worshiped in the church of *Las Nazarenas* since 1651.

Founded by Spaniards, Lima inherited the European Catholicism of the conquerors. Eventually, it became a multicultural city when Indians and *Mestizos* were brought to work for their European masters. A syncretic Catholicism developed in the Peruvian capital city with the ongoing migrations of native Andeans to the coast up until the twentieth century; nevertheless the official church has been successful in "Christianizing" the vestiges of the Indian past belonging to the vast majority of *Limeños* by imposing the Roman Church's creed and by controlling "excesses," the pre-Columbian aspects of Peru's popular Christianity.

In contrast to the Christian majority, the religious minorities of Lima have always kept a low profile in national affairs, mindful that the state's constitutional ordinances endorse only Catholicism. Even the native Peruvian descendants of these minorities still experience a kind of "immigrant complex," which has interfered with their cultural identification with this nation of *Mestizos*. Among these minorities, the Jews in Peru, like those in other Latin America countries, have been most actively involved in their nation's society through economic activities.[3] Jewish identity in Lima is determined by the same factors that define the identity of most minorities in today's urban centers: a sense of identification with fellow-members of a group who share common cultural references, and a need to distinguish themselves from others. Many factors shape the identity of Lima's Jews: ethnicity or sense of peoplehood; the practice of rituals; registration in the community's institutions; identification with a common history and with the State of Israel; and the unconscious presence of cultural dynamics shared by other minorities that descended from immigrants: the sense of race or ethnicity, the sense of belonging to a similar socioeconomic class, and the sense of belonging to a same "class" (kinship shared by classmates who attended the same school).[4]

A sense of distinction is a natural consequence of feeling part of a minority that has lived at the edge of exclusion, expulsion, and persecutions throughout the centuries. And as a former center of Inquisitorial activities, which has preserved colonial buildings and monuments belonging to this era, Lima is a city where Jews can still vividly recall the painful history of their ancestors.

In a special assembly of *Unión Israelita del Perú* held on September 20, 1966, president Michel Radzinsky, speaking in the name of the pioneers of Lima's Jewish community, delivered a farewell address to a new generation of leaders who would take over that institution. His words identify the main constituents of Jewish identity in Lima:

> We, members of the old generation, have done everything to main-
> tain our tradition. We have arrived in this country as poor people
> and without families, lacking knowledge of the country's language,
> the Peruvian culture and traditions; for us, this was an unknown
> country. We knew neither its geography nor its literature and so
> we had to establish the basis of our existence and we had to put
> brick over brick in order to build our institutions. None of us was
> an expert in society's tasks, but we felt that we had to organize our-
> selves. We have helped each other to avoid a total assimilation into
> this new environment. We knew that without organization we
> would lose our place in history as we feel we have lost the immi-
> grants who came in colonial times, whose memories only remain in
> the acts of the Inquisition tribunal; and as we feel we have lost
> touch with the many immigrants who came in the 1860s, of whom
> we have only their gravestones in the Bellavista cemetery . . . their
> children being totally unknown to us. That is why we have endeav-
> ored to organize ourselves, establishing cultural and religious insti-
> tutions (AT).[5]

Maintaining tradition and social, cultural, and religious institutions, avoiding total assimilation, and being aware of the fate of Peruvian Jews in the past (historical consciousness) formed the backbone of Lima's Judaism for Radzinsky and his generation. In his speech, the president of the *Unión Israelita* summarized the forty-year efforts of the pioneering members of Lima's Jewish community, emphasizing how they had created a community that inherited the original values and institutions forged in European cities that were later destroyed by the Nazis and Polish anti-Semites:

> . . . We are the "last of the Mohicans" of a generation that has suf-
> fered two world wars and has witnessed how a murderer like Hitler
> annihilated one third of our people. We are the last witnesses of a
> people murdered by the hands of the Nazi fury. Now we must go

and we leave you everything; we leave you our *kehilah* [community] with all the institutions. I know that you know very little of our rich culture; I know that you do not even know our language [Yiddish], our traditions, but I am sure of something: you have Jewish hearts. I am sure that you are as proud as we are of our brothers in Israel, who have created a homeland for a people wandering around the world.

I am sure that every piece of good news from Israel makes you proud and happy, and every piece of bad news from Israel upsets you and makes you feel sad. Starting today, you are the owners of our institutions. Preserve our spiritual treasures that we have inherited from our parents, take care of our school that is a treasure for your children, and be honorable leaders of our *yishuv* [establishment] (AT).[6]

The Holocaust, the State of Israel, "Jewish hearts," the legacy of institutions and the Jewish school—these are the foundations that Radzinsky bequeathed to the generation of Jews to whom he was conferring the responsibility of continuity. In these words spoken by a representative of the older generation to its "grown up children" we can discern a sense of apprehension, as if he was aware of how the successors' sense of identity would weaken and become more dependent on institutions and fictions rather than on values and traditions. And so it is for most contemporary Jews. Judaism is more a reference than an identity, as French scholar Alain Finkielkraut points out when he refers to what he calls "Imaginary Jews": "They are not religious, at least most of them; in vain they cherish Jewish culture, possessing only its sorry relics. They have not performed their apprenticeship to Judaism under the gaze of the Other. Neither ethnic nor denominational definition nor the Sartrian scheme could suit them. They are unwavering Jews, but armchair Jews since, after the Catastrophe, Judaism cannot offer them any content but suffering, and they themselves do not suffer. In order to deny this contradiction they have chosen to pass their time in a novelistic space full of sound and fury that offers them the best role. . . ."[7]

How have Finkielkraut's "Imaginary Jews" or Radzinsky's heirs with "Jewish hearts" experienced their Judaism in Lima? Until the 1930s no synagogue was built in the Peruvian capital city because the majority of secular Jews from Poland, Rumania, and Germany celebrated only the High Holidays, and did so in the homes of those familiar with religious rituals. Sephardic Jews kept more rituals than did the Ashkenazic Jews, but they quickly adapted to the secularism of the incipient Lima Jewry.

Regardless of their ancestry, all of Lima's secular Jews understood that in order to assure the Judaism of their children and to perpetuate their spiritual survival, religion was an indispensable ingredient. Sooner or later, the new generations would no longer share their parent's cultural legacy of language (Yiddish and Judeo-Arabic), songs, literature, and memories of the European shtetl, or the North African and Middle Eastern autonomous Jewish communities. Anticipating this loss, the founders felt the urge to bring Orthodox rabbis to formalize their Judaism (especially in cases of intermarriage) and to guide the religious life of their congregations. This process became the dominant motif in the evolution of twentieth century Jewish Lima, beginning in the years prior to the Second World War.

The first rabbi who came to Lima was Rabbi Moisés Brener. A native Polish Jew, he arrived in Peru in 1934, having been hired by the Ashkenazic congregation to fulfill the functions of *mohel* (specialist in charge of circumcisions), *shohet* (the person who supervises kashrut while animals are slaughtered), and *hazzan* (cantor). Prior to Rabbi Brener's arrival Jewish doctors performed circumcisions; there were no kosher food stores, nor synagogues. Rabbi Brener oversaw the religious rituals of all the Jews in Lima up until 1950, when the Sephardic congregation brought Rabbi Abraham Shalem to take care of their religious life. Not long after, the workload of Rabbis Brener and Shalem was lightened when the German Israelite Society hired the services of Conservative Rabbi Lothar Goldstein in 1957. Prior to these years, Brener alone provided a sense of Jewish legitimacy to the children of Jewish-Gentile parents, carrying out frequent circumcisions in Lima and in the Peruvian provinces. Eventually, a group of more Orthodox Jews seceded from the *Unión Israelita* and established their own synagogues: *Knesset Israel* in 1942 and *Adat Israel* in 1953. In the 1980s the Ashkenazic congregation unified again.

The role of Rabbi Brener in the history of Peruvian Jews remains a matter of controversy.[8] He began to formalize the Judaism of members of the community by circumcising babies and even teenagers,[9] marrying some Jews to non-Jews, and leading the burial ceremonies of some children of non-Jewish mothers.[10] The rabbis who came after Brener had to decide whether or not his marriages had been performed strictly according to halakhah, Jewish law. The current Orthodox rabbis in Lima assume that the first rabbis, such as Brener and Shalem, did perform their religious duties in a proper way, an assumption that allows them to recognize the people they married and their children as Jews without colliding with Jewish law. It is understood that when these earlier rabbis came, leaders of the Jewish institutions instructed them to be flexible; otherwise many Jews would have been left out of the community. As one commentator notes: "What was done was done, and from now on things are going to be done in a kosher (proper Jewish) way, so rabbis make decisions according to the religious behavior of current members whose Jewish origins are questionable. These members cannot be excluded from the community if there is a general consensus in the community regarding the Judaism of those persons."[11]

But while exceptions are made for those Jews "guided" by Lima's earlier rabbis, today's definition of "Who is a Jew?" is different. Today Orthodox rabbis are very strict in their stances, and although their congregations are comprised of a vast majority of secular people, Orthodoxy serves as the official blueprint of the community. The Ashkenazic and Sephardic congregations proclaim themselves to be Orthodox, and their members must accept the rabbi's halakhic decisions. It is a system of discreet accommodation. People must behave according to halakhah during Jewish ceremonies and rituals: food must be kosher in every community event; men and women must sit separately in the synagogue (with the exception of the Conservative synagogue, which follows Orthodox standards only for ceremonies involving the entire Jewish community of Lima); and women are not called to read the Torah or perform prayers. However, the rabbis know that outside the boundaries of their own synagogues, secularism will resume its sway: couples will dance after the Jewish rituals, and worshipers will drive home after Shabbat services and go out for entertainment. Though the institutions remain Orthodox, their members go their own secular ways.[12]

What do these examples tell us about what it means to be a Jew in Lima today? They show that despite their secularism, the people endow their rabbis with the power to determine their legitimacy as Jews. According to León Trahtemberg, the only scholar of Jewish contemporary history in Peru, in the time of the immigrants, the rabbis only carried out ritual and symbolic functions but nobody needed their approval to feel Jewish. The rabbis became rigorous only afterward, when the children of the immigrants, much more ignorant of Jewish religion and tradition, submitted themselves more and more to the rabbis' rulings. Trahtemberg asserts that "if you know religion, the rabbi is only one person more to talk with and ask . . . but if you do not know about religion, he becomes the only knowledgeable person and you subordinate your ideas, sometimes automatically, to what he says. Then, the more that Jews are less learned and religious, the more rabbis get power."[13]

In small communities such as the one of Lima, the rabbi is the person who keeps alive traditional Judaism, who preserves Jewish memory and Jewish law. His knowledge and his presence give him the authority to decide who is a Jew, and to endorse or refuse ambiguous cases where the "purity" of Jewish origin is hard to trace. The rabbi has the last word as to the legitimacy of someone's Jewish ethnicity or peoplehood. The rabbi also has ultimate power to affirm or undermine any Jew's struggle to be recognized as such. When Rabbi Moisés Brener traveled to outlying provinces to perform circumcisions, his doing so convinced several families that they had been converted to Judaism. But several of those children, who now live in Lima and consider themselves Jewish, later learned that circumcision alone, although an essential part of the Jewish covenant with God, is not by itself a ritual of conversion.

Like most secular Jews in the world, the traditions practiced by most members of Lima's Jewish community have little religious content. They do, however, recite traditional prayers during Passover, Kabbalat Shabbat, Rosh Hashanah and Yom Kippur. Although Orthodox Jews would argue that most of these Jews do not observe these rituals according to the authentic spirit of Jewish law, any Peruvian Christian would consider such average Jews very religious.[14]

Rituals, even for people who perform them unaware of their meanings, provide a concrete sense of identity, of collective self, of distinctiveness regarding others. But for contemporary Jews in Lima, most Jewish rituals have lost their religious content and even the romantic or ideological flavor they once had in European, North African, and Eastern Jewish communities where even secular Jews understood their significance. In the concrete world of modern Lima, rituals have been institutionalized. Religious ceremonies have become incentives for family gatherings and special events in the Jewish school. More than ever before, Lima's "Jewish hearts" need institutions and rabbis to preserve these traditional rituals, so that they can be experienced as part of the rich Jewish culture inherited by a younger generation of people who "know it very little." The founders of the *Unión Israelita,* the *Sociedad Sefardita*, and the *Sociedad 1870* were bearers of a vivid Jewish cultural legacy. They had to learn Spanish and the legal and cultural codes of their new home; even those who married non-Jewish women succeeded in maintaining Jewish traditions due to their *yiddishkeit* [profound Jewish identity] or to their Sephardic culture. Amateur historian Rafael Rodríguez suggests that these immigrants kept Jewish homes because of their fathers' influence, due to the male-oriented nature of Judaism combined with the *machismo* of Peru. Therefore, he claims, "the children of those mixed marriages inherited the Jewish legacy of the fathers, heads of families, father figures who imposed the rules and customs in their homes. So their women followed the husbands' way of life; therefore the children grew up in a Jewish environment celebrating all the Jewish holidays."[15]

Regardless of the attempts made by earlier generations of Jews to maintain their traditions, the legacy of Ashkenazic and Sephardic culture has become, even in the best of cases, merely a family relic for the new generations of Peruvian Jews who have adapted to the culture of their birthland. After the native-born Peruvian Jews took over the institutions founded by their parents, they came to consider the process of registering themselves as members of these institutions as a "way to be Jewish." Simply to belong to one of the three congregations provides members with "a Jewish ID," which makes them feel connected to their ancestors, to their people, and to the State of Israel.

The creation of three separate Jewish congregations testifies to their members' loyalty to their distinct ethnic and cultural backgrounds. But thanks to a common Jewish cemetery and the shared goal of aiding Jewish newcomers, the foundation was already laid for establishing a unified representative body for the three congregations: The Association of Peruvian

Jewish Societies, registered in public record in 1944. The Holocaust and the emergence of the State of Israel further catalyzed the cohesion of Lima's Jews. Organizations such as the Peruvian Women's Zionist Organization (WIZO); youth movements such as *Unión Macabi, Hashomer,* and *Betar;* the Zionist Organization of Peru; and *Keren Hayesod* and the *Keren Kayemet Le-Yisrael* (institutions linking Peru's Jewish community with Israel) have provided the institutional framework for Jewish activism.

Jewish communities have found ways to maintain Jewish life in the midst of a dominant culture, not only in Peru but also around the world. Judaism has been "institutionalized," transformed into a political and social micro-world where Jews can carry out administrative functions through their identification with the State of Israel and the Jewish cause of survival. Rather than constituting a way of life or a system of beliefs, Judaism serves as a referential framework for what scholar Eugene B. Borowitz has described as "disproportionately urban, educated, and secularized" Jews.[16] "Jewishness is what I miss," Alain Finkielkraut categorically asserts, "not what defines me, the base burning of an absence, not any triumphant, plentiful instinct."[17]

In Isaac Goldemberg's novel *The Fragmented Life of Don Jacobo Lerner,* one of the characters who moves to the northern Peruvian town of Chiclayo in 1935 shares with his readers:

> It is good to go the synagogue when one believes in those things, but how many times men go to speak of business and women to show off their jewelry? I let Felisa go to church and pray to her saints all she wants, except not in front of the children. I want them to be Jewish. Otherwise, it's the same living here or living in Lima. There is no Jewish atmosphere in Lima. I told Felisa that to go the Hebrew Union every once in a while to dance fox trots, tangos, or rumbas has nothing to do with being Jewish. People go there like they go to a dance hall. But Felisa always asks, don't you miss your people, Samuel?[18]

For Peru's Jews, ethnic identification revolves around institutions that encourage their members to develop moral activism and to enrich themselves culturally. That "rich culture" mentioned by Radzinsky has thus transformed Jewish laws into Jewish values. Borowitz puts it in this way: "[Modern secular Jews believe that] ethics is what really counts and that you don't need Jewish roots to be ethical."[19] Many subscribe to the notion that ethics is the real heart of being Jewish, that the Jewish people are morally and intellectually superior. León Trahtemberg argues that Jews all over the world overestimate Jewish intelligence, an idea that arises from a unique historical perspective: Jews were bereft of their lands and forbidden to participate in the intellectual and socioeconomic life of their societies throughout the centuries, a situation that caused Jews to cultivate their intelligence and abilities based on what they have learned in their widespread travels from their extensive experience with trade and commerce. These were the only professions open to them and they provided them the security of a livelihood when they were forced into yet another exile. This special Jewish expertise gave Jews a kind of superiority complex as being more skillful and more intelligent. "I believe that Peruvian Jews express in many attitudes some of that self-perception of excellence and overestimation of the Jewish intelligence," concludes Trahtemberg.[20]

Yet among today's generation of Peruvian Jews, the rich Jewish culture is scarcely known; nevertheless, the sense of belonging to a special people remains. The messages of the Holocaust and Israel have become pillars of that identity; the motto "Never Again" and the identification with a proud, powerful Jewish people have kindled the spirit of these modern Jews.

In order to be simultaneously Jew and Peruvian while minimizing social and existential predicaments, the Jews of Lima have assumed Judaism as a religion with its cyclical rituals and holidays while passionately identifying with a nation whose culture they scarcely share: Israel. Finkielkraut aggressively challenges Israel's central role in Western Jewish communities: "*Jew* designates the vacant space of a past that has become a tabula rasa. That's why we must free Israel of its charge. Not contest its legitimacy, of course, or renounce the defense of its existence, but refuse it the position of monopoly. Our Jewishness is so weak that the obsession with Israel imprisons us: it shapes our viewpoint and dictates our past."[21] Indeed, much of contemporary secular Jewishness is based on what Eugene Borowitz defines as the "Israelocentricity of the [Diaspora's Jewish] federations."[22]

Since 1946 the *Colegio León Pinelo* has become the axis of Lima's Jewishness. Students who attend this school are exposed to Hebrew, to the Bible, and to Jewish history classes. The school respects Peruvian and Jewish religious holidays (including Israel's Independence Day and commemorations of the Holocaust). Although rabbis teach religion, they have become the equivalent of Peruvian priests: religious leaders to listen to, not to emulate. Secularism, materialism, skepticism, and upper-class values have led Jews to identify themselves with the rich, white minority that rule the overwhelming *Mestizo* majority.

Yet Jews are not a race; in fact, many Sephardic Jews are not what many people would call "whites." Neither are the Jews in Lima a social class; several Jewish families belong to the lower-middle and poor classes. However, according to many interviewees, racial and social class criteria are unconsciously integrated into the leadership of Lima's Jewish community. (This issue will be discussed in further chapters.) In any case, Jewish *Limeños* do not consciously perceive themselves to be members of a different race or particular social class. They see themselves as members of a perfectly coherent Jewish community that endorses the culture of its forefathers and maintains its link with other Jews and the State of Israel.

Today in Lima, many Jews identify themselves as Jews, particularly because they were classmates in the *Colegio León Pinelo.* The school has created a chain or nexus that seems to substitute for the ethnic and cultural bonds that united their parents.

Later on, when we review the history of the relationship between the Jews and their descendants on both sides of the Andes mountains, we will discover more clues that will provide a clearer sense of what it means to be Jewish in Peru and to relate such concepts as race, ethnicity, religion, Jewishness, and Peruvianism.

✦

THE ADMIRABLE LIGHTNESS OF BEING JEWISH IN IQUITOS

In contrast to the situation in Lima, the Jewishness of Iquitos's descendants, the sense of identification they share in varying degrees of intensity with the Jewish people, does not rely entirely upon the Jewish ingredients of their syncretic religion. Rather, the vast majority of "Jewish *Mestizos*" in the Peruvian Amazon experience their religion as a private matter, due to the absence of religious authorities to instruct them and to endorse what they call their Judaism.

Unlike Lima, Iquitos's community never had a rabbi; neither did it boast a synagogue or a Jewish school. The first Israelite Society founded in 1909 did not appoint a person or committee in charge of religious affairs. And the Peruvian-Israeli Cultural Institute established in the 1960s was not a religious institution but merely an association where sympathizers of the State of Israel gathered. Occasionally, some members debated whether this cultural institution should assume religious functions. Jacobo Goldstein, a newcomer from Lima who arrived in Iquitos during the 1960s' period of tax exoneration in the Peruvian Amazon, upon realizing that the exclusive cultural and social character of this institution was missing an opportunity to deepen Jewish life in the city, proposed that it build a synagogue, but this idea never crystallized. In its statutes, the *Instituto Cultural Peruano-Israelí de Iquitos* proclaimed itself an association "without political and religious aims."[23]

If the religion of Iquitos's "Jewish *Mestizos*" was never institutionalized, what gave them a sense of peoplehood? "Collective identities are funny fictions" argues anthropologist Virginia Domínguez,[24] and the study of these "funny fictions" in Iquitos must take into account two sources of inspiration that led a small group of people to consider themselves Jewish: a collective regional history and a sentimental sense of sharing historical and contemporary references such as the Holocaust, the Holy Land, the notion of Jewish peoplehood, and the "chosenness" of the Jews.

The collective identity and historical consciousness shared by the descendants of Jews in Iquitos arise from the Jewish obsession with feeling part of a unique people. In 1967 Werner Levy Navarro, president of the *Instituto Cultural Peruano-Israelí de Iquitos* summarized the history of city's Jewry in a letter addressed to a foreign Jewish institution:

> . . . We have entered into public and institutional life after sixty years of silence, uniting in order to preserve the Jewish traditions that we inherited from our parents, traditions of many, many years [that they brought] when they came to this Amazonian zone, to settle and live in it; [we have taken this step] because we are aware of the more than 180 Jews who came here more than sixty years ago. Many [of these immigrants] have passed away here, and as a testimony, we have an Israelite cemetery with roughly eighty grave-

stones with more than seventy-five years of antiquity, and their inscriptions are written in Hebrew. Other Jews returned to their birth lands: Tangier, Morocco, Casablanca, Spain, etc., but they left descendants . . . we, who now unite under a common historical past. We know that our parents have been loved in this land where they lived and did good deeds for its people who welcomed them.

We are studying their past in detail in order to write a book, striving to present in an organized way the Jewish achievements of our parents in this area. [These Jews] are older than the Jewish groups that came to Peru's capital of Lima; because the first Jews who came to Peru arrived here in Iquitos, and this is proven by the previously mentioned cemetery, and by the Hebrew names of many cities in this land, as well as the diverse institutions founded by Jews [in Iquitos] such as the *Centro Social Internacional*, which is the first and most prominent among other centers that exist in this city (AT).[25]

Similar sentiments have been repeated in other letters addressed by leaders of the current Israelite Society to Jewish institutions and to the Israeli Embassy of Lima in the 1960s and the 1990s. All of these documents reflect a self-perception that combines real facts with historical inaccuracies (for example, the Amazonian region as the first Peruvian land settled by Jews, the numbers of Jewish immigrants who arrived in the region, the belief that their cemetery was built prior to Lima's Israelite cemetery, etc.), with historical confusion (Morocco listed as a city, dates, etc.), and with exaggerations and myths regarding the "Jewish achievements" of their ancestors and their own traditions. But beyond the blurred borders of reality and imagination, there still exists a clear conviction of kinship with their Jewish ancestors and with the whole Jewish people:

I tell my children about their grandfather Manfred [Weisselberger] . . . about how he was persecuted [in Europe], about the race of his people, about being proud of their Jewish race.

✦

I feel Jewish blood, my grandfather's race. I feel more important because of my father's race. I live with him (my parents are divorced). Besides that, here 99 percent of the people are Catholics, so we are different.

✦

I am very lucky to bear this last name [Levy]. The Jew, despite Hitler's slaughter, belongs to a race that has risked and has developed a lot. It is a powerful, intelligent race. . . . Why not be proud?

✦

To be Jewish is to have the blood, the features, the feelings, a very nationalistic feeling. I love very much my race. I do not think that I have lost my Jewish identity because I accepted the Gospels.

✦

I do not have a religious link to Judaism, but I want everybody to know of my Jewish origins. I am a history professor, and I feel a humanistic identification with the Jews, especially after the Second World War, also with David Ben-Gurion and Israel. The Jews are a superior people, very ethical people.[26]

While conducting my interviews, I could not help wondering why most of the "Jewish *Mestizos*" shared such an idealized view of the Jews when the examples of their own ancestors contradicted the ethical, family-oriented ideal they so admire. Their answers hint at a desire to be as prosperous as their grandparents and as successful as many Jews of the world are. Clearly, they would prefer to overlook their own bitter experiences as abandoned children:

Although our grandparents and our parents were not very ethical persons, they were successful men. Besides that, as a people there has been a [Jewish] ethic, historically speaking. The Jew is proud because he comes from a working people.

✦

The Jew is more ethical. We know it because of our studies, not because of our practical experiences.[27]

Ironically, one young man drew on anti-Semitic stereotypes to explain his love for his people:

> *To be Jewish is the brightest thing that I have been able to attain. I like being a Jew. I have [King] David's blood. Blood calls you to unite with the people. See how many Jews condemned the Holocaust although they were not Germans! [These are the exact unclear words of the interviewee.] The Holocaust is a discrimination that Hitler began because the Jews have economic power.*
>
> *It is the truth. Jews dominate the world. The Jews are big, they are intelligent. It is God's grace. . . . God made us superior.*[28]

Another descendant of Jews was told that he belonged to Ben Hur's lineage:

> *Mr. Mafluf, a Jew himself, told me once that my last name, Abensur, could come from Ben Hur because it seems that the real name of his tribe was Aben and Sur, and maybe it is because we belong to the tribe that went to the South (Sur). . . . Perhaps when Ben Hur left the country, when he became a nomad, he augmented his last name like the Chinese people do. . . .*
>
> *Mr. Mafluf told me that the Abensur family has always been a family of merchants. Ben Hur was a merchant. . . .*
>
> *I am 100 percent Christian, but I am proud of my father and it flatters the personal ego to know where one comes from. It would be interesting to know that one comes from Ben Hur's tribe.*[29]

Jewish blood, Jewish race, pride of belonging to the Jewish people and bearing a Jewish last name—a sense of lineage and peoplehood—is part of the historical consciousness of these descendants of Jews, regardless of their age and whether or not they knew their parents and grandparents. Such feelings are a natural consequence of Iquitos's mentality. Father José María Arroyo claims that as a city developed by immigrants, Iquitos stirred its inhabitants to search for their ancestors. "Everybody here, until very recently, was looking for their ancestors, their roots, traces of nobility."[30]

The most active members of Iquitos's current *Sociedad Israelita* criticize those who only show up at meetings when Jewish visitors come, claiming that they are only seeking acknowledgment from legitimized Jews. What kind of acknowledgment? I asked again and again, and the answer escaped my own understanding: to boast that one belongs to the Jewish people. "Traces of nobility" is how Father Arroyo described it. In Iquitos, the notions of Jewish blood, race, and lineage are related to long-ings for prosperity, reputation, and socioeconomic status. The Jews were successful businessmen; they were renowned leaders and respected pub-lic figures; they were part of a foreign aristocracy that once enchanted the native population of the city.

To be a Jew in Iquitos is a privilege and a hope. It implies that one is part of a minority that once thrived in the region, and with this implication comes the possibility that one can recapture that glorious past. The descendants of Jews intertwine the achievements of their ancestors with an idealized view of Jewish people worldwide and throughout history. Some claim to feel linked to the Jews rather than to Jewish religion, while others cannot separate the two aspects relating the excellence of the Jews to God's promise to make them His chosen people. León Delmar Ruiz's interpretation of why the small State of Israel defeated many Arab coun-tries throughout the Middle East conflict reveals the thread of this connection:

> We have taken the land to Damascus and we had to withdraw and return it to them because of the United States. Israel put its flag over La Plaza de Armas of Damascus [reference to the main square of Damascus since all Peruvian main squares are called La Plaza de Armas]. We have destroyed them [los hemos hecho polilla] because God helps us. . . . God is Jewish. He has not neglected His land, His people.[31]

What else can be more representative of the mixture between the local and the universal in Iquitos than León Delmar Ruiz's description of Israeli soldiers raising their flags in La Plaza de Armas (the Peruvian town square) of Damascus!

This sense of peoplehood is one of the inspirations that encourage many descendants of Jews to join the Israelite Society, the association that attempts to restore the connection between them and their Jewish ances-tors. A few members of this society regard Judaism as something more than peoplehood, and they want to restore Jewish traditions among the

"Jewish *Mestizos.*" The statutes of the *Sociedad de Beneficiencia Israelita de Iquitos* proclaim the religious and fraternal character of the institution, inviting all its members to partake in Jewish traditions based on the Torah, the Book of Prophets, the Talmud, and Jewish values.[32] Among its goals, the society encourages members to develop an ethical life according to the values of the ancient Jewish culture and it advocates the fight against any manifestation of anti-Semitism in the city.[33]

On paper, the current Israelite Society of Iquitos presents itself as an Orthodox institution. When candidates apply for membership, they must fill out a form in which they explain the reasons for their request, "proving" through civil documents their Jewish ancestry. Candidates are allowed to write their own applications in order to explain their personal motivations, and all new members must claim that they are ready to learn and practice Jewish traditions. When they are accepted, the spiritual guide of the society explains to them the "fundamental principles of Judaism: being regarded as a people chosen by God, *absolute* Monotheism, believing in a Unique God, waiting for the Messiah, observing Shabbat, and other aspects."[34]

On paper, it seems as though the "Jewish *Mestizos*" of Iquitos are involved in an Orthodox institution, but in practice things are very different. Most of them limit their compliance with Jewish traditions to the celebration of the Jewish New Year (Rosh Hashanah), the Day of Atonement (Yom Kippur), and occasionally, Passover (Pesaḥ). Shabbat means attending Friday evening ceremonies to "receive the Shabbat" (Kabbalat Shabbat); other than that, Jews in Iquitos do not observe Jewish laws applicable to that twenty-four-hour period. They even formerly held meetings on Saturdays, although they switched to Sundays when one member pointed out that it was a contradiction. Nor do they observe kashrut (dietary laws).

Also on paper, the nature of the current Israelite Society of Iquitos is very different from that of the members' ancestors, who never intended to found a religious institution. However, most "Jewish *Mestizos*" register in the society because it makes them feel part of a community, because they want to be buried in the Israelite cemetery, and because they want to leave open the possibility of one day settling in Israel. In many aspects, the present *Sociedad de Beneficiencia Israelita de Iquitos* is a mirror of the first Jewish congregation of Peru, the *Sociedad de Beneficiencia Israelita de*

Lima, founded in 1870. Like this society, Iquitos's "Jewish" community states that its interests lie in observing religious holidays and helping co-religionists with financial, health, and emotional problems. Both societies largely turned over the issue of burial services to their respective Israelite cemeteries and talked about "Jewish or Hebrew education" without accomplishing important steps in this matter. By 1918, the members of Lima's Jewish Society barely bothered to show up at meetings and services for religious holidays, with the exception of Rosh Hashanah and Yom Kippur. The same process is happening today in Iquitos where absenteeism and indifference worry the leaders of the society. The average number of people who come to Kabbalat Shabbat is between eight and twenty members.

As in Lima, Iquitos's Israelite Society provides its members with a sense of common identity; however, most of its members do not feel that their institution legitimizes their Jewishness. They know that without rabbis and aid from Lima's Jews their identity is in limbo. Víctor Edery Morales, founder and first president of the society, says proudly that Iquitos's Jewry is the only organized community in Peru apart from that in Lima and this is why those registered in the *Sociedad Israelita de Iquitos* are recognized in Lima as Jews. However, contrary to Víctor Edery's assertion, those who have moved to Lima soon discovered that Jewishness is questioned by its Jewish institutions.

There is in Iquitos a "Jewish" institution, but not an institutionalized Judaism. The desire to be buried in the Israelite cemetery and the potential option to make *aliyah* (immigration to Israel) are what draw most descendants of Jews to the society. The cemetery is the only property that the community owns; the roughly forty visible gravestones belonging to Jewish immigrants and their descendants generate the most intense feelings of identification that "Jewish *Mestizos*" express for their ancestors:

> *There is something mystical in the Jewish cemetery. One goes sometimes to the cemetery as though one is looking for a mystery to discern.*

✦

> *Every time I go to the cemetery [the Christian one], I visit the Israelite cemetery. I visit all the Jews: the Cohens, the Bendayáns;*

I go around there. I feel as though in the midst of all that I would
be attempting to get into the good graces of those souls.

◆

I love my father. Every Monday I go to the cemetery . . . [to visit
him]. I would like to be buried next to my father in the Jewish
cemetery. I believe I have that right.[35]

Many descendants of Jews want to be buried in the Israelite cemetery, but sometimes their Christian families decide upon mausoleums in
the general cemetery. Occasionally, the *Sociedad Israelita de Iquitos* has
refused to assign a lot to a member because the person neither complied
with his or her duties nor attended the meetings or ceremonies carried
out by the community. Among members there are passionate debates
regarding the issue of who has the right to be buried in the Jewish cemetery. Who is entitled to that privilege, they ask? Those who pay their dues
to the community? Those who can prove Jewish ancestry? Those who pay
for it, even if they can offer no proof that they are descendants of Jews?

Like the "Who is a Jew?" debate currently raging in Israel and among
the world Jewry, Iquitos has its own ongoing controversy: Who is a Jew
after death? In my personal diary I wrote comments on the Israelite
Society session of July 2, 1995:

> The *paisanos* hold a bitter debate on the case of Edwin Pizarro
> Panduro, a young man who had died tragically a few months pre
> vious to my arrival and had been buried in the Jewish cemetery
> under the authorization of the president Víctor Edery Morales:
>
> Some members of the society questioned this decision based
> on the fact that Edwin Pizarro was not a member of the institution.
>
> Víctor Edery defended his decision, claiming that Edwin
> Pizarro came from a Jewish family and that his sister was a mem
> ber of the society. When Mrs. Pizarro burst into his house, sobbing
> that the family could not afford to pay for a burial in the Christian
> cemetery, he decided to organize the burial ritual in the Israelite
> Cemetery: "If I did not do right, may God punish me!" Edery fin
> ished his defense. "It is part of being president and spiritual guide
> to make this kind of decisions."

The society members continued their debate, airing their many points of view: Who has the right to be buried in the Jewish cemetery? Members of the society? Only those who comply with the statutes (paying their dues)? Any Jew, any person in trouble? Should the criteria be taken into account according to religious or human basis?

There was not a clear outcome in that session, but for me, the conclusions were clear: "These people are immersed in the same type of debate that Jews all around the world discuss: "Who is a Jew?" However, in Iquitos's case, death rather than birth seems to be the event that triggers that question.

In a community bereft of buildings in which to institutionalize its activities, such a passion for belonging is understandable. The cemetery is the only relic of these people's ancestors; it is the tangible link with their parents and grandparents, or as Víctor Edery puts it, "It is our Wailing Wall." Such is the pride for this place that several interviewees told me that Iquitos's Israelite cemetery is the oldest Jewish cemetery in Peru (a notion that is easy to refute simply by visiting the Jewish cemetery in Lima).

Like the cemetery, Israel is another symbol that links the "Jewish *Mestizos*" to other Jews. In the discourse of the *Iquiteños,* Israel is an intriguing, mythical place that evokes feelings of pride. During the Six-Day War (1967), the community sent money to help Israel's cause. Later, members of the Israeli-Peruvian Institute would gather to view movies about the big deeds of the small state, seeing for the first time biblical places such as Jerusalem's Old City. The magic of Israel has lured some descendants of Jews to immigrate (make *aliyah*) throughout the last thirty years; for those who stay behind, Israel awakens a sense of patriotism:

> Israel is the Jewish homeland and if it needs us, if Israel asks for my body for war, I'll give it. I have a brother in Israel [Carlos Delmar], and I tell my children that you are both—Peruvians but also Israelis.[36]

The Israel of León Delmar Ruiz, that nation protected by God, which defeated so many Arab countries by "raising its flag over the Plaza de

Armas of Damascus," is the same mythical Israel that stirs up the hearts of some Iquitos "Jews":

> *I didn't know that there were Jews outside Israel. I believed that all [Jews], after the Second World War, went to Israel. I would like to know the land of Ari Ben Canaan [a character in Leon Uris's novel Exodus], [to know that land] for which so many [Jews] died. I would go to Mount Sinai, although it would be dangerous.*

✦

> *According to the Pentateuch, Israel is the Promised Land of return for all descendants of Jews, even the ones with a single drop of Jewish blood in their veins, and I feel myself a [Jewish] descendant. It was in the land of Israel that religion was given by God to Moses. It is the place where Abraham, Isaac, and Jacob were; it is a land of people who have suffered and undergone hardships, but who have thrived.*[37]

Israel is a holy land the *Iquiteños* say, a superpower, a place of prosperous working people, inhabited by very nationalistic, religious citizens, full of idealistic persons, a very modern country (or city, some call it!). But together with these notions, more realistic views emerge every once in a while. This shift comes about because they have listened to other stories about Israel told by *Iquiteños* who have migrated there and come to visit them (including two sons of Víctor Edery who fought in the 1973 Yom Kippur War and returned to Iquitos in the 1980s). As a result, some members of the community are aware that Israel is a place where daily life is very tense, people must work very hard (forget daily *siestas!*), children are very independent and leave home very young (to go to the army), and where there are even some *chancherías* (pig sties)!

Nevertheless, the mythical Israel overpowers any down-to-earth issues related to the Jewish state, so many Jews still dream of the day when they will be able to settle there. This is one of their primary reasons for maintaining a link with the *Sociedad Israelita de Iquitos*. The Holocaust and anti-Semitism are also mentioned by many "Jewish *Mestizos*," who have learned about the persecution of the Jewish people throughout the ages. The recent showing of Steven Spielberg's movie *Schindler's List* in Iquitos has kindled their sense of identification with the major Jewish tragedy in history. Many of them want to know more about it,[38] and some remember their parents' and grandparents' remarks about the dangers of being Jewish during those times:

> *My father used to say me: "If you lived in Germany, Hitler would have executed you by shooting you, because he did so to fourth-generation Jewish descendants.*
>
> ✦
>
> *We used to joke, "We are Jews but God forbid the Germans should know it because of what happened during the Second World War ... the extermination of Jews.*[39]

Iquitos was never home to anti-Semitism. This can be verified by all of the history records, which reveal the major role that Jews played in the life of the city; by talking to scholars and old inhabitants of the area; by reading the reports of visitors; and by speaking with present descendants of Jews, who acknowledge that Iquitos has always been a place of co-existence and understanding among members of all creeds. But perhaps because *Iquiteños* live in a region where people tend to give free rein to their imagination or maybe because today's secular Jewishness is incomplete without the addition of real or imaginary anti-Semites, a few "Jewish *Mestizos*" have stories to tell:

> *I have seen anti-Semitism in the college of education. A nun expelled Jaime Vásquez Izquierdo because he is Jewish. . . . In fact, I remember the professor [Jaime Vásquez Izquierdo] telling me once, when I asked him if I could attend the Shabbat services with the Jews, that to be Jewish is a blessing and a curse because we are always persecuted.*
>
> ✦
>
> *The Jews were scorned here a long time ago. People spit on them; they hated Jews.*[40]

The community of Iquitos knows that there is no anti-Semitism there, but because modern Jews rely so much on others they feel the need to stress the potential dangers of being Jewish and to question whether any misunderstanding between the community and public institutions of the city are signs of prejudice. For example, on April 7, 1967, the president of the Department of Loreto's Superior Court of Justice received a letter from Alberto Portocarrero Vargas denouncing Werner Levy Navarro, president of the *Instituto Cultural Peruano-Israelí de Iquitos*, because, he claimed, a judge should not be president of a Jewish institution whose members participated in commercial activities. The letter concluded by urging the president of the Superior Court to put a stop to a situation in which a judge was the president of "an institution of Jewish merchants." On June 20, the Superior Court rejected Portocarrero's complaint, endorsing the good work of Judge Werner Levy Navarro. Several ex-members of the *Instituto Cultural Peruano-Israelí de Iquitos* remember this episode as an anti-Semitic event. However, Werner Levy Navarro himself interprets Portocarrero's charge as part of a campaign waged against him due to personal problems between the two men.[41]

Another case perceived to be a consequence of anti-Semitism is related to the Jewish cemetery. Since 1990 the members of the *Sociedad Israelita* have been requesting that Iquitos's Public Beneficence Society give them copies of the original document confirming the sale of a parcel of the Christian cemetery to the Jews in 1895. The society wants this document as proof because the Public Beneficence Society had plans to demolish these gravesites in order to extend the general cemetery.

I was told that the Beneficence Society did not want to release these documents because it wanted to destroy the Israelite cemetery with the complicity of Iquitos's priests. But the truth, which the Israelite society members did not know, is that the Israelite cemetery was built before the Christian one, and the *Sociedad de Beneficiencia de Iquitos* was founded in 1898, three years after the first Jews acquired the lot for their cemetery, probably from a private owner. Therefore, there has not been any deliberate attempt to hide that information, as several "Jewish *Mestizos*" had thought. Moreover, the very leader of Iquitos's Augustinian priests, Father Joaquín García, declared in 1986 that the Israelite cemetery is a "National Patrimony," guaranteeing that it can not be demolished. Still the myth of an anti-Semitic conspiracy to demolish the cemetery persists.

Although Iquitos's history of tolerance refutes any contention that anti-Semitism constitutes a threat in the city, the statutes of the *Sociedad de Beneficiencia de Iquitos* nonetheless proclaim that it will help any member who is the victim of anti-Semitic outbursts. Occasionally, in some sessions, members of the society recall the sufferings of the Jewish people throughout history, especially during the Holocaust.

The Star of David is another way that *Iquiteños* express their Jewishness. Several "Jewish *Mestizos*" proudly exhibit their Stars of David on chains that hang outside their shirts; others have carved the sign in the walls of their homes, on doors, and even on a ramp. Some Jews who are buried in Christian mausoleums boast Stars of David on their gravestones. One living inhabitant even has a natural Star of David in the palm of his hand . . . and he shows it proudly.

Iquitos's descendants of Jews maintain a sense of peoplehood, which although vague, is nevertheless persistent. They share some of the common elements of Jewishness in their historical consciousness; in their (written and oral) discourses; in their strong feelings for Israel, the Jewish cemetery, and the Israelite Society; in the inhabitants' Hebrew surnames and their children's Hebrew first names (Moshe, Uri, Netanel, Sara, Jacobo, Abraham, Yared, Shulamit, etc.); and in their obsessions with the Holocaust, anti-Semitism, and the Star of David. These elements attest to a sense of Jewishness which, though certainly very different from that found in Lima, Miami, Jerusalem, or Paris, is nevertheless real.

I will allow my diary to end this chapter:

> The *paisanos* do not know contradictions but the opposite; they deal with them with the same semblance of repose that the intersection between the turbulent Nanay and Amazon Rivers seems to show. The *paisanos* allow themselves to float over the different cultural legacies that move them like river currents. The nonrational is accepted as a mystery, which must be allowed to remain as such.
>
> It is not unusual to hear them say something absolutely clearly in their statements, and to later hear them say exactly the opposite. Some of them believe that their Jewish ancestry makes them more special than the rest of the people. Several *paisanos* feel closer to God than their Christian brothers when they go to church because the priest mentions the people of Israel . . . and they are part of them.

The *paisanos* are clear regarding their Jewishness, and their lucidity is such that they are aware of their unavoidable confusion on matters of Judaism simply because they have had scarce access to Jewish sources. Their problems in the community are very similar to those of the big Jewish congregations in the world: What name should be given to the Jewish institution? What is it to be Jewish? Who should be buried in the Israelite cemetery? Who should be admitted in the community? Should they help members who do not pay their dues? . . . Even, as do most Jews, they see anti-Semites everywhere!

They are obviously acculturated to their environment, not subtly like most of the Jews in the world are (including myself). They do not deceive themselves and they do not improvise answers when asked about their Jewishness. They assume their syncretism without rationalizing, without intellectual exercises. It reminds me of Milan Kundera's novel, *The Unbearable Lightness of Being.* In my case, I have met a group of people who share an "admirable lightness of being Jewish," leaving us, the ones who dwell in the heaviness of analyzing everything, far away from their "light lightness."

Ronald Reategui Levy and one of his children next to the door of their home in Iquitos. Reategui built the house and carved the door, which contains a Star of David (top); the inscription *"Beth Levy,"* Hebrew for "House of Levy" (middle); and a *menorah*, the symbol of the State of Israel (below).

Gravestones in the Israelite cemetery in Iquitos sometimes contain both Jewish and Christian religious symbols, evidence of the syncretic beliefs of the "Jewish Mestizos."

A view from inside the Israelite cemetery of Iquitos, built by Jewish immigrants in 1895. The wall separates the Jewish burial site from the Christian cemetery.

The facade of the Cohen commercial house, one of the most prosperous businesses during the Amazonian rubber boom from the 1880s to the 1920s. Today the building is divided into small stores that belog to local businessmen, but the sign with the name Cohen remains.

Siblings Linda (left), Jacobo (center), and Heysen (right) Carique Kohn in their apartment in Beer Sheba, Israel. They immigrated to Israel in 1997. Their parents and two sisters still live in Iquitos.

A view of the Amazon River from Iquitos.

Ariel Segal, the author, during a visit to the Amazon River. The children with him are from an Amazonian tribe that lives near Iquitos.

Jaime Vásquez Izquierdo, the general secretary of the Israelite Society of Iquitos and the former cantor of the community. A skilled musician, he is playing the melody of a song his mother sang to him when he was a child.

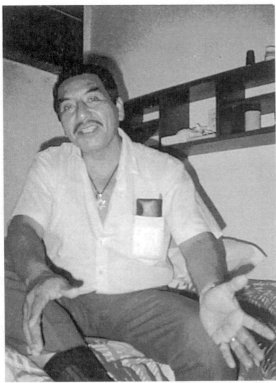

Enrique Mesía Ochoa, a member and cantor of the Israelite Society of Iquitos.

The service of Kabbalat Shabbat in one of the rooms in the house of Víctor Edery Morales. Edery's wife, Diolinda López de Edery (left), is blessing the Shabbat candles while Edery, the spiritual guide of the community (center) and Jaime Vásquez Izquierdo (right) looks on.

During the service of Kabbalat Shabbat, Víctor Edery Morales recites *Kiddush*, the blessing of the wine. Edery, the spiritual guide of the Israelite Society, holds his hands in this fashion while blessing the wine because his father used to hold his hands above Edery's head when he blessed him as a child.

The main church of Iquitos, *La Iglesia Matriz*. Located in the front of La Plaza de Armas, the main square of Iquitos, it is where most of Iquitos's residents, including many "Jewish *Mestizos*," perform and register their baptisms. It belongs to the Augustinians and was built at the beginning of the twentieth century.

5

The "Jewish *Mestizos*": A "*Marranic*" Remnant of Israel

"I did not know there were white Jews
before I came to Israel."
—Menashe, a Jewish Ethiopian immigrant
whom I met on Kibbutz Maagan Michael in 1988

"We all were born [in dispersion] due to an accident
designed by *Elohim,* our God. He sent us and spread
us throughout the world but He, at the same time,
gives us a hope, a promise to gather us from the East
and from the West. He will say to the East: 'Release
them now!' and to the West he says: 'Let them go,'
and the prophecy will be totally fulfilled. We are
pilgrims in other places of the world. We are only
temporarily in dispersion, and our origins were born in
Israel and we belong to Israel. That is what you must
not forget, Sara, and what you must teach to your
children . . . to have an identity, because there is nothing
more terrible than not knowing who we are or not being
anything or anybody. But if you have an identity, you
have a 'why,' a reason why you are here [in the world]
and why you do what you do. . . .
Sara, teach your kids to be Jewish and make them
forget all those things that they learned in the school.

Focus on what you are, on your identity and stop
going from Judaism to Christianity and from Christianity
to Judaism. . . ." (AT)
—Tape sent from Israel by Miriam Bendayán
to her sister Sara Bendayán Tello and her family in Iquitos
(Israel, June 12, 1992). Sara and her family established
themselves in Israel in 1997.

T HE DESCENDANTS OF Jews who today live in Iquitos consider themselves to be remnants of the biblical "Children of Israel" whose covenant
with God grants them the right to return to the ancient holy land.

From the year 70 C.E., when the ancient Kingdom of Israel was
destroyed by the Romans, until the establishment of the modern Jewish
state in 1948, the question "Who is a Jew?" was chiefly a matter of debate
between rabbis and spiritual leaders of communities that claimed to be
Jewish. History presents several cases of controversy and schisms among
Jews,[1] but the unquestionable written commandments of the Torah, which
God delivered to the Hebrews on Mount Sinai, endured as indisputable
guidelines for the vast majority of Jews until the age of Enlightenment.
The emergence of Conservative and Reform Judaism, furnishing modern
interpretations of halakhah (Jewish Law) that loosened the stringent
observance of precepts and rituals practiced during *galut* (exile), generated a Judaism that is predominantly ethics-oriented and therefore, unacceptable to Orthodox Jews.[2]

The conflict between these three mainstream Jewish movements, as
well as the "discovery" of several groups on the fringes of Jewish identity,
have transcended the scope of intellectual rivalry, historical analysis, and
amazement, becoming an essential question for any Jew who settles in
Israel. An Orthodox minority, politically powerful, determines who is a
Jew in the democratic State of Israel; this monolithic authority has given
rise to considerable disagreement and questioning. The "Who is a Jew?"
controversy surpasses even the legal and religious scope of discussion in
Israel. It is a burning question for several dispersed communities that have
developed "*Marranic*" identities shaped by any of several combinations of
religions—Christianity and Judaism, Islam and Judaism, Hinduism and
Judaism, African or Native American forms of popular Christianity and

Judaism. Ultimately, the question is relevant to descendants of Jews in remote lands who have inherited any kind of syncretic legacy.

Where does the case of Iquitos's "Jewish *Mestizos*" fit in the big panorama of Jewish dispersion and redemption in contemporary history? This question underlies the rest of this chapter.

✦

THE CONTROVERSY OF "WHO IS A JEW?"

The prophet Isaiah predicted the problem: "And it shall come to pass in that day, that the Lord will set His hand again the second time, to recover the remnant of His people.

And He will set up an ensign for the nations, and will assemble the dispersed of Israel, and gather together the scattered of Judah, from the four corners of the earth" (Isa. 11:12).

Approximately 2,500 years after Isaiah's prophecy of the return of the children of Israel "from the four corners of the earth" to the land of their ancestors, groups claiming to be remnants of Israel ask for the right to be considered Jews by their mainstream coreligionists and by the State of Israel, whose Law of Return encourages the "ingathering of the exiles" *(kibbutz galuyot)*. Some of these groups successfully meet the Orthodox requirements of Jewish lineage, while others are forced to convert in order to be acknowledged as *Shear Israel* (Remnant of Israel). Groups on the borderline between Judaism and other religions barely survive, waiting for acceptance or aid from mainstream Jewish communities and the State of Israel.

The Law of Return, passed by the Knesset (Israeli Parliament) on July 5, 1950, two years after the State of Israel officially came into being, proclaims that every Jew has the right to immigrate to the country. The 1952 citizenship law endorsed this policy, granting automatic citizenship to any Jew who immigrated to Israel. However, since neither law defines the word "Jew" it was inevitable that once the Jewish state had overcome the initial years of struggle, questions and controversy would arise: Who is a Jew? What does it mean to be an Israeli citizen? How can one distinguish religion from nationality in a Jewish state that considers itself a secular and democratic nation? Prime Minister David Ben-Gurion had to contemplate such questions when a government crisis exploded on June 22,

135

1958, following the cabinet's decision that the label "Jew" would be entered on the identity cards of any Israeli who declared in good faith that he or she was a Jew and did not belong to any other religion, as well as for any children whose parents declared that their children were Jewish. This decision was unacceptable to the Orthodox establishment.[3]

After many years of stormy controversies, on March 19, 1970, the Supreme Court passed an amendment conceding the Orthodox interpretation of Judaism, which defines a Jew as anyone born to a Jewish mother or who has converted to Judaism and is not a member of another religion. This provision also recognizes the right of non-Jewish spouses, children, and grandchildren of Jews to immigrate to Israel on the basis of the Law of Return in order to avoid breakups of these families. According to this amendment, any person who can prove that he or she has a Jewish father or mother, grandfather or grandmother can benefit from the Law of Return, receiving financial and, if needed, social aid from the state (housing, free Hebrew classes, loans, medical insurance, etc.); however, that person is not classified as being "of the Jewish religion" in the national population register maintained by the Ministry of the Interior.

What are the repercussions of being a non-Jewish Israeli? Christian and Moslem citizens of Israel do not experience problems, because marriages and divorces are performed by the religious authorities of their own communities. Any person who professes beliefs in another religion can look to his or her community's spiritual guide for advice and services. However, those descendants of Jews whose identity cards identify them as Israelis but leave an empty space next to the category of religion cannot be married, divorced, or buried by rabbis because only Orthodox rabbis perform these rituals in Israel. Hence, in a secular society that gives Orthodox Jewish religious courts exclusive jurisdiction in matters of marriage and divorce, the "non-Jewish Jews" (descendants of Jewish grandparents or fathers, but not of mothers), must convert according to the rigorous and lengthy processes of Orthodox Judaism.[4]

✦

REMNANTS OF ISRAEL: OLD AND NEW TRIBES

In most of the individual cases presented to the Israeli Supreme Court contesting the ruling of the Chief Rabbinate, the Orthodox point of view has prevailed. The Orthodox have established their hegemony over the issue of "Who is a Jew?" and the majority of secular Israelis have accepted this hegemony; however, over the past fifty years, the religious establishment has been forced to assume more realistic stances toward certain groups of Jewish origin.[5] During the first years of Israel's independence, diverse communities immigrated to Israel and their Judaism was questioned and debated by religious and political institutions. Among these groups, we find the seven thousand members of India's *Bene Israel* (Children of Israel) from Bombay; a few dozen Samaritans; between eight and ten thousand Karaites or *Karaim* (Readers of the Scripture); and other groups. Eventually, all these groups reached compromises with the Orthodox leaders of Israel and a kind of *status quo* allows them to be Israeli citizens with full rights and, moreover, "Jewish" citizens of the state. In the 1980s, the Ethiopian *Beta Israel* (the House of Israel) also had difficulties with Israel's Orthodox Rabbinate, but they have been recognized as Jews from the lost tribe of Dan. (See Appendix 4 for a summary of each one of these communities' [hi]stories.)

These cases show how various compromises have been worked out from time to time to provide partial solutions to the question of "Who is a Jew?"[6] Of course, the Israeli Supreme Court, the government, Parliament, and prominent national figures have all played important roles in these cases. The Orthodox establishment has loosened its position gradually and subtly when confronted with groups whose Jewish origins are debatable, and especially when dealing with immigrants from Russia and other ex-Soviet nations who are registered as Jews with complete rights and the privileges granted by the Law of Return.[7] Only in certain instances have both the authorities and the general population reached a consensus on the non-Jewishness of some groups.[8]

People who are converted to Judaism by Orthodox rabbis and decide to immigrate to Israel have the same status of Jews by birth, but it is not common to find entire groups willing to accept such conversion. Among such cases, there are three "new tribes of Israel." One comes from Italy and the other two come from Latin America.

In 1952, seventy inhabitants of the tiny Italian village of San Nicandro settled in a village in Galilee after being converted to Judaism. This astounding conversion happened despite the fact that none of them had seen or communicated with a Jew until the 1940s. San Nicandro's "New Jews" followed their self-taught seer, Donato Manduzio, who, one night in 1930, had a vision. Manduzio received a message from God commanding him to lead the whole village to "return to its Old Testament roots," and so they did, inspired by the prophecies of their master.[9]

Many of the Indian Jews of Mexico or, as scholar Seymour Liebman calls them, "the *Mestizo* Jews of Mexico,"[10] have also converted to Judaism. The case of this group from a few towns in the states of Hidalgo and Veragua, and especially from the village of Venta Prieta, came to the attention of Mexican Jews in the 1930s, when Mexico City newspapers reported a clash between Catholics and a self-proclaimed sect of "Israelites." Jewish leaders from the capital investigated and found a community that gathered in a one-room adobe synagogue in front of a Holy Ark to worship "the God of the Jewish people," reciting a mixture of Catholic, Protestant, and Jewish prayers. Mexican Jews began visiting the village and delivered books and presents (Shabbat candlesticks, prayer shawls) to these exotic "Jews." The indigenous Mexican members of Venta Prieta's synagogue asserted that they were descendants of Spanish crypto-Jews who had dispersed throughout colonial New Spain. In the 1940s North American newspapers and magazines such as *Jewish Frontier* and *Life*, published articles about this community of "Indian Jews," enticing many tourists to the village.

In 1950 Israeli anthropologist Raphael Patai published the first study on the fifty practicing Jews of Venta Prieta, based on a three-month field research that he conducted in 1948. The scholar described a small congregation of Christians who claimed to be descendants of *Marranos* (and there were a few who even claimed to come from the Lost Tribes of Israel!), when the reality proved that they had split from a Christian church that began to stress the doctrines of the Hebrew Bible over the ones of the New Testament. Although they did not openly profess Christian beliefs and strove to follow Jewish rituals, they still kneeled in the synagogue, sang some Christian hymns, and showed no interest in the new State of Israel.[11] Patai returned to the village in 1964 and found that the incipient Jewish community of Venta Prieta had abandoned some of the unquestionably Christian practices that he had witnessed sixteen years before. Now, the members of the congregation had learned some prayers in Hebrew and many expressed a fervent desire to settle in the Jewish state.

The "loss of their isolation" led them to request Mexico City's Jews to recognize their Jewishness. However, the religious establishment of Mexican Jewry did not recognize their Judaism, and in the best of cases viewed them as an exotic group that wanted to convert to Judaism. Seymour Liebman interprets the group's claim of *Marrano* ancestry as a means of affirming an identity after the convoluted process of coming from Catholicism to Protestantism, and, finally, switching to Judaism. Liebman quotes some lines of Octavio Paz's *The Labyrinth of Solitude:* "Our lies reflect both what we lack and what we desire, both what we are not and what we would like to be."[12]

Liebman also quotes from a personal interview with Dr. Robert Ravicz, an anthropologist who studied Venta Prieta: "He has confirmed that, rather than telling the truth, these "*Mestizo* Jews" tell tourists what they think the tourists want to hear."[13] I share Raphael Patai's view of their identity: "For the purposes of this [his] study, it was of little importance whether they really believed they were descendants of Spanish *Marranos,* or only made up the story out of an easily understandable desire to gain prestige through relating themselves to New Christians who had been part of the proud conquistador army of New Spain."[14] Whether the "Jews" of Venta Prieta come from an old tribe, from Jewish ancestors, or are simply a "new tribe" in the midst of the Jewish people, does not change the fact that they feel themselves to be a remnant of Israel, who will share the same fate conferred upon all Hebrews' descendants.

In 1987 Rabbi Eliahu Avichail, head of *Amishav,* an organization whose goal is to seek out remnants of Israel around the world,[15] traveled to Mexico and converted one hundred Jews according to the strict rules of Jewish Law. Rabbi Avichail, himself, is related to the most remarkable case of contemporary mass conversion to Judaism, which happened in the country where the "Jewish *Mestizos*" live—Peru.

Scholars have not yet formally studied this story, but documents testify that in December of 1989, Rabbi Avichail from Jerusalem, Rabbi Mordechai Orya from a religious court of Haifa, Rabbi Yaacov Kraus of the Ashkenazic congregation of Lima, and Rabbi Abraham Benhamú of the Sephardic congregation of Lima converted 55 *Mestizos* belonging to a group called *Bene Moshe* (The Children of Moses), which had begun its long journey to Judaism in the 1960s. The converted families from the cities of Cajamarca, Trujillo, and Lima settled in Eilon More, a Jewish settlement on the West Bank. In July 1991, another 102 members of their community joined them on Israeli land.

Who are these people and how did they succeed in convincing Orthodox rabbis to take their case seriously?

The origins of *Bene Moshe* can be traced to 1954, when Segundo Villanueva Correa, a Protestant believer, joined a group of vegetarian Seventh Day Adventists from the city of Cajamarca who observed Shabbat. Segundo Villanueva made a friend, José Goldenstein, a Jew who introduced him to some Jewish prayers and traditions. In the early 1960s, Villanueva became a member of the Christian group *Movimiento de Reforma* and later, challenged his members to abandon some Christian beliefs and to focus on the Hebrew Bible. Villanueva then met José Aguilar Velasquez, another devoted Adventist who belonged to the group *Israel del Nuevo Pacto* in the city of Trujillo. Intrigued by what they saw as contradictions between Christian doctrine and the teachings of the Old Hebrew Bible, both men created a study group to delve into the Hebrew Bible. The *Israel del Nuevo Pacto* began as a branch of the Christian Saturday Keepers' congregations, an alliance they maintained until 1967, when they decided to celebrate Jewish holidays. That year, they established the religious settlement of "Hebrón" in the Peruvian Amazon. Demetrio Guerra Torres, one of the members of the congregation, describes this enterprise:

> It was approved unanimously to go to the Amazonian jungle, exactly after the 100-Hour War of Israel [Six-Day War]. We were nineteen *hermanos* [brothers] and we went with enough provisions, tools, medicines, etc. We knew that our future would be successful, so we requested allotments of land through the Ministry of Agriculture: allotments were bestowed upon us to cultivate and raise crops of coffee, cacao, sugar cane, yucca, oranges, sweet and sour lemons, cherimoya, etc. We were delighted to cultivate the land and enjoy its fruits, celebrating the holidays the Lord had commanded to Moses, his servant, on Mount Sinai (Lev. 23). We observed Rosh Hodesh (the beginning of the Jewish Month), our leaders being Mr. Segundo and Mr. Alvaro Villanueva . . . (AT).[16]

In 1968 Segundo Villanueva, Alvaro Villanueva, and Demetrio Guerra traveled to Lima to hold an interview with Rabbi Abraham Benhamú of Lima's Sephardic congregation. They wanted to learn Jewish beliefs concerning the Messiah, and they expressed their wish to delve into more Jewish practices. Rabbi Benhamú suggested that they learn Hebrew in order to understand Jewish lore in depth. Several followers of Segundo Villanueva left the Amazonian settlement of "Hebrón" and created the *El Milagro* congregation in the city of Trujillo, in the Province of Cajamarca. They began to learn Hebrew with the few books given to them by Lima's Jewish community; they studied the Hebrew Bible; they strictly observed Shabbat, the Jewish holidays, purity laws, and kashrut. In 1971 many members of *El Milagro* went to Lima and asked Dr. Rubén Kogan to circumcise them, which he did. By 1973 the congregation had abandoned all traces of Christian beliefs and traditions, rejecting the dogma of the Trinity and Jesus' divinity. In 1983 they made the first contacts with Israeli rabbis, presenting their case through letters and asking to be converted and admitted to the Jewish state.

The big breakthrough came on February 15, 1987, when David Kiperstok and his wife Niela, Jews from Lima who had immigrated to Israel, visited members of *Bene Moshe* who lived in the city of Cajamarca. Kiperstok, a man moved by curiosity and altruism, decided to help these people: "The last night of our visit, the third night, they called us [him and his wife] to the *bimah* [pulpit] of their synagogue to thank us for our visit and after praying and singing Hebrew songs, they asked us: 'Please, don't forget us.'"[17]

Once Kiperstok returned to Israel, he decided to meet with Rabbi Avichail after having read a letter in Cajamarca that the congregation had received from the head of the *Amishav* organization. Kiperstok showed pictures to Avichail and told him about the genuine wish of these people to convert to Judaism and immigrate to Israel. Avichail expressed concerns: The Peruvian group was not precisely a remnant of Israel, but he promised to find out more about them. On August 9, 1988, Jonathan Segal, an Orthodox Jew who lived in Israel, was sent to Cajamarca to stay with this community for a few days. In Segal's report about the *Bene Moshe* community he expressed his opinion that their motivations were genuine and recommended that Rabbi Avichail help them. On March 5, 1989, Kiperstok visited Peru and traveled to Trujillo to spend some days with the new "Jewish" congregation. He brought good news: The process of conversion and *aliyah* for *Bene Moshe* was being discussed by Israel's Chief Rabbinate.

A program was drawn up to teach the members Judaism and to prepare them for exams. Those who passed the exams went through the final stage of the plan. Rabbi Eliahu Avichail, together with Rabbis Orya, Benhamú, and Kraus, performed the conversions. The *mikveh* (ritual immersion) was carried out on a winter day in the Moche River (not to be confused with *Moshe!*) and all couples from the congregation were remarried according to Jewish law. (In such marriages, the rabbis write a *ketubbah,* a document that is signed by them and some witnesses. Every Jew who wants to marry in a religious court must show the rabbi the *ketubbah* of his or her parents.) In 1989 the first contingent of *Bene Moshe* members left for Israel, and remaining members were encouraged to continue their studies in order to be converted in the near future. In 1991 a second group joined the first and since then, the rest of the congregation has been immigrating gradually to Israel.[18]

Thus, a "new tribe" was founded in Peru, and its story sounds like a fairy tale to those who believe in prophecies predicting the ingathering of the exiles.[19]

But what about that remnant of Israel, on the other side of the Peruvian Andes mountains, who live in that land of dreams, the Amazon, where the same members of *Bene Moshe* once founded the settlement of "Hebrón"? The "Jewish *Mestizos*" do not have to convince anyone of their Jewish origins; it is unquestionable that their forefathers were Jews. Yet, it is also unquestionable that, according to the prevailing interpretation of Jewish Law, they cannot be regarded fully as Jews. Therefore, Orthodox Judaism requires their full conversion.

The Iquitos "Jews" consider themselves a remnant of Israel, as many of their oral testimonies certify. And they are considered as such by the Jewish religious courts in charge of legitimizing the Jewishness of those who do not have a *Yiddishe Mamma* (Jewish mother, in Yiddish)—but only if they return to Judaism on *their* terms.

✦

THE FIRST AND THE LAST *MARRANOS* OF PERU

Where do the "Jewish *Mestizos*" of Iquitos belong?

To a certain extent, the descendants of Jews in Iquitos are poised between the two extremes: On the one hand, they do not need to argue as do other groups, that they are linked to the Jewish people in order to prove their Jewish lineage; on the other hand, they are asked to convert to Judaism (beyond symbolic rituals), like other groups that come from vastly different religious backgrounds.

This situation resembles the "long way home" that many sixteenth- and seventeenth-century *Marranos* had to travel in order to be recognized as Jews by rabbinic authorities in Central and Eastern Europe and North African Jewish communities. *Marranos* would have undergone the same travail (rather than "travel") in the Viceroyalty of Peru, had they the possibility of fleeing the Americas and asking for refuge in any European Jewish community living in relative freedom.

The first crypto-Jews in Peru lived a Roman Catholic life without feeling themselves to be Christians, identifying instead with the Jewish people; nonetheless, they could not appreciate Judaism in its comprehensive whole because as second and third generations of *Marranos* in the New World, they gradually lost the knowledge transmitted in secrecy from generation to generation, practicing only a few Jewish rituals whose meanings became increasingly foreign to them. Nevertheless, they still retained what Cecil Roth defines as "a vivid realization of the brotherhood of Israel and their own identity with the great mass of their people wherever they might be found."[20] This sense of common identity eventually was lost in the nineteenth century by the time the Peruvian Inquisition was abolished. The descendants of Jews who had come to the Americas gradually assimilated to the Christian environment of the new Latin American republics.

What were the main characteristics of the religion of the *Marranos?* Inquisitorial records of the Holy Office in Mexico, Lima, and Cartagena in the New World have yielded some of the most common features of the secret Judaism practiced by the *Marranos* in the Americas. Many crypto-Jews accepted the veracity of the Law of Moses over the Law of Jesus (despite their ignorance of Mosaic Law); they expected deliverance from a future Messiah (not Christ); they did not worship images; and they secretly celebrated Shabbat through the quintessential *Marrano* ritual of lighting Shabbat candles on Friday evenings (the minimum was two but many women lit three: one for her husband, one for the offspring, and the third for herself). *Marranos* also kept some rituals of three Jewish holidays: Yom Kippur, Pesaḥ (Passover), and Purim (commemoration of the Persian Jews' survival in ancient times). Purim is a happy holiday, but the *Marranos* used to celebrate it only by fasting as did Queen Esther in Persia in order to save her people. For crypto-Jews, the story of Queen Esther was an inspiring example of Jewish survival over the tyranny of Persian minister Haman, the perfect symbol of what the Inquisition represented to them. In summary, secrecy was the main feature of their mutable Judaism.[21]

The first Jewish custom to disappear was circumcision. Kosher dietary rules followed (although many descendants of *Marranos* kept the custom of not eating swine). Bit by bit, worshipers forgot the Hebrew liturgy with the exception of the *Shema* prayer: "Hear O Israel, the Lord *(Adonai)* our God, the Lord *(Adonai)* is One." Eventually, the religion was reduced to a few misshapen ceremonies for the three holidays, the weekly lighting of the Shabbat candles, and burial rites. Historian Seymour Liebman asserts that very few *Marranos* adopted the practice of confession, many spit out the communion's host after exiting the church, and in several cases, *Marranos* manifested their hostility toward Catholicism by hitting images of Jesus and Christian saints or by keeping those figures with their faces toward the wall, except when they had Christian guests.[22]

Gradually *Marranos* intermingled Jewish and Christian customs, and although crypto-Jews considered themselves to be proud descendants of "the Jewish race" (some of them knew by heart their lineage), they began to lose their sense of peoplehood, abandoning such practices as Jewish charity until they submitted to the church's formalities: baptism, wedding, funeral, and confession—never revealing their Jewish origin! I argue that the voices of the "Jewish *Mestizos*" sound like echoes of these *Marranos*.

Then, where in the whole spectrum of groups that can be considered to be remnants of Israel, can we locate the last *Marranos* of Peru? Who are these Amazonian people who today claim a Jewish identity? In his "Survey of Minorities in Israel," *Seker Hamiyutim Be Israel* (1972), sociologist Erik Cohen classified the following groups as communities marginal to mainstream Judaism: the *Bene Israel* from India, the Karaites, the

Ethiopian Jews, and the Samaritans.[23] Cohen listed other sects as emergent movements. Finally, he categorized other communities such as the Black Hebrews, *Mestizo* Jews (descendants of Mexican *Marranos*), *Marranos,* and the community of San Nicandro, Italy, as converted groups.[24]

The "Jewish *Mestizos*" are not descendants of *Marranos,* although they do not escape the phenomenon of *Marranism,* a modern *Marranism* representing the synthesis of Judaism with other religious systems and cultures, not the result of compulsory conversion to another religion. As a phenomenon, *Marranism* need not be exclusively associated with the Spanish Inquisition. One case in point: The Moslem *Marranos* of Mashhad, a major city in eastern Iran, practiced Orthodox Judaism until 1839, when they were forced to become Moslems. Until the twentieth century, Mashhadis remained secret Jews praying in underground synagogues and only marrying among themselves. Yet, because of their exposure to Islam, this group of approximately ten thousand souls acquired a more casual attitude toward religion than other Orthodox Jews. Many Mashhadi "Jews" left Iran and settled around the world in secluded communities, representing a kind of "Diaspora within the Jewish Diaspora," maintaining an exclusive sense of identity derived from the memories and traditions of their birth land. As scholar Dan Ross asserts, unlike other *Marrano* groups, "the 'Jewishness' of Mashhadis has never been in doubt."[25]

However, my definition of *Marranism* goes beyond the notion that all *Marrano* groups are necessarily the products of a compulsory conversion of Jews to another religion. *Marranism* can result from the natural assimilation of a religious system that coexists without totally eclipsing a group's original Jewish heritage. Such has been the case of the Döhnme Jews of Turkey and the *Bene Israel* of Bombay.

The Döhnme Jews were until very recently an exceptional community of ten thousand to fifteen thousand secret Jews whose ancestors embraced the Jewish false Messiah Shabbatai Zevi, in the seventeenth century. After his conversion to Islam, in 1666, the Döhnme Jews also began living outwardly as Moslems while retaining some Jewish observances. Eventually, their descendants left Salonika (today Thessaloníki, Greece) and immigrated to Bulgaria, the Balkan states, Western Europe, America, and Palestine, looking for recognition among the Jews. Today, these *Marranos* have all but faded from the Jewish landscape.[26]

The Indian *Bene Israel* of Bombay, consisting of roughly four thousand members, is a racially mixed community, which has blended Hindu customs, morals, and behaviors with Jewish rituals, the practice of polygamy, and a religion of faith and piety, while selectively observing some Jewish laws. Its outlook, however, is profoundly Hindu, as Dan Ross maintains: "The *Bene Israel,* in fact, share this most Indian of obsessions [status]—to the point of internalizing the caste system."27

The Mashhadis, the Döhnme Jews, and *Bene Israel* are all descendants of Jews who at one point proclaimed themselves to be Jewish (the Döhnme Jews have finally assimilated to Islam in the last decade). While their historical experiences differ greatly, all of these groups see themselves as remnants of Israel with a share in the historical future of the Jewish people. These groups, like Iquitos's "Jewish *Mestizos,*" may be classified as "*Marranos* without Inquisition."

Hence, as modern-day *Marranos,* the "Jewish *Mestizos*" are neither a lost tribe nor a "new one." Rather, they are authentic descendants of Jews, a pedigree that most of them can prove. But this fact does not count for the Orthodox establishment because their ancestors were Jewish males. In traditional Judaism, Jewishness is matrilineal. Then, what happens to those "Jewish *Mestizos*" who decide to live in Israel? Let us examine the cases of several immigrants.

Since the late 1960s, the few descendants of Jews who have emigrated from Iquitos to Israel have received the benefits of the Law of Return.28 These *olim* (immigrants) receive an identity card on which they are categorized as Israeli citizens, but the entry for religion is left blank. According to the Law of Return, they have the right to receive automatic citizenship because their fathers or grandfathers were Jews, but according to halakhah they are not Jews; therefore, Orthodox rabbis do not marry them or circumcise their children unless they successfully complete a strict course of conversion. Several *Iquiteños* have converted to Judaism in Israel.

Immigrants from Iquitos have never been treated as members of a whole group returning to Judaism. No program encourages their *aliyah* (immigration) and helps them to settle and convert in Israel, unlike the communities of *Bene Israel, Bene Moshe,* Jews from the ex-Soviet Union, and others. Due to the small numbers of immigrants from the "Jewish" community of Iquitos, they come as individuals. The way they prove their

Jewish ancestry is by exhibiting pictures of their fathers' and grandfathers' tombstones in the Jewish cemetery, which they attach to civil documents certifying their kinship with their ancestors. The lack of religious documents such as *ketubbot* (marriage certificates) in a place where there never were rabbis or even Jewish women to marry led Israeli functionaries to request photographs of the tombstones, an unusual documentation to confirm Jewish lineage. But what happens to those whose grandfathers died in places other than Iquitos? What happens to those who have neither religious documents nor these pictures, and yet want to settle in Israel? These persons have still managed to cling to the Law of Return by presenting detailed accounts of their cases through civil documents and letters from "pure Jews" from Lima certifying that they had known these people's ancestors. For many years (especially in the 1960s and 1970s), these procedures worked because functionaries of the Ministry of Absorption were interested in encouraging the *aliyah* of every single Jew or potential Jew. After all, the immigration cases from Iquitos were only a few dozen.

But things changed for these "Jewish *Mestizos*" in the late 1980s. Many of them—the youngsters—represent the third or fourth generation of those Jews who first came to the Peruvian Amazon. Although they can claim to be descendants of Jewish great-grandparents, that does not entitle them to the benefits of the Law of Return. Even for those who can prove that they have Jewish grandparents, the situation has now become more complex. As a result of the massive migrations of Russian and Ethiopian Jews in recent years, the standards governing applications to immigrate under the Law of Return have been tightened. For *Iquiteños*, it is now an indispensable requirement to send a clear photograph of one's ancestors' tombstones in the Israelite cemetery in order to be accepted as an *oleh* (immigrant) with full rights. This new development has forced those descendants of Jews interested in *aliyah* to ask for help from Lima's institutions and rabbis.

The encounter between the communities of Iquitos and Lima forms the subject of the following chapters.

6

WHEN LIMA MET IQUITOS

"Our small delegation [from Lima] was received with
amazing affection. Dozens of Jews were waiting for us.
They held our hands and were smiling. With that smile
full of friendship and excitement they said loudly their
names: Levy! Bendayán! Benzaquén! Edery!
Samolsky! And they added, *Shalom U'brakha* [peace
and blessings to you]!"(AT)
—Yaacov Hasson, "Iquitos: Alma Judía en la Amazonía Peruana,"
Comunidades Judías de Latin América (Edición de 1972–75)

"They did not do too much to preserve their Judaism.
They could have established a [Jewish] school, but
it is also true that we in Lima did not do justice by
them. Our efforts to preserve them as Jews were
minimal. For the majority of us [Lima's Jews]
their question [of the Amazonian 'Jews'] does not
belong to us; it is as if they were in another country."
—Alfredo Rosenzweig, Jewish geologist who
lived in Iquitos for two years (1948–1949),
during an interview in Lima on July 7, 1995

WHEN I DECIDED to embark on this project (to penetrate the heart of
this community set on the banks of the Amazon River), I thought
that the history and fate of Iquitos's Jewish community was common
knowledge among Lima's Jews. But I was mistaken.

Lima's ignorance of its Amazonian brother was not due to a lack of published information. The 1950s *Enciclopedia Judaica Castellana* contains an account of the thriving past of the Jews in the Amazonian region within the section regarding Peru's Jewry; in a Jewish periodical in the 1960s, geologist Alfredo Rosenzweig had written a detailed article about the Amazonian Jews; two Latin American scholars had referred to this Jewish community in their books (mostly based on Rosenzweig's article).[1] Prior to my trip to Peru, I read these works and several letters sent to me by Jews in Lima, delving into some events that I supposed were known by the majority of Peruvian Jews. I was wrong. For instance, almost none of Lima's Jews know that Rabbi Moisés Brener traveled from Lima to Iquitos in 1944; nor that Yaacov Hasson, director of the Human Relations Office for Lima's Jewish community, inaugurated a Peruvian-Israeli institute in that Amazonian city during the 1960s; nor that Rabbi Guillermo Bronstein of Lima's Conservative congregation "1870" met Iquitos's "Jewish *Mestizos*" in 1992; nor that an Israeli ambassador also visited them some months afterwards. I mistakenly assumed that I would be able to talk with the capital city's Jews about their "brothers" in the Peruvian Amazon, but I could not have been more wrong.

For these urban Jews in the capital city, Iquitos's Jewish descendants were barely remote figments of the imagination. Most of the Jews in Lima had no inkling that descendants of Jews lived in the Peruvian Amazon. Even those who had heard or read "something, someplace," thought this was an episode belonging to the distant past. Others had even visited Iquitos and regretted not having been aware of the existence of a Jewish cemetery, of Shabbat services, of people with Jewish last names. Only a handful of Lima's Jews had a clear picture of these "Jewish *Mestizos*," either because they had been actively involved in communications between the two communities or because they had relatives in Iquitos or had formerly traveled to the city on business. During my investigations I also found several families from the Jewish community of Iquitos who had migrated to Lima. These people, obviously, knew much about their hometown and its past.

During my first weeks in Lima, before I traveled to Iquitos, I was amazed at the paltry knowledge these Jews had of the events in Jewish history that had taken place on the other side of the Andean mountains. I wrote in my diary:

Jews in Latin American nations have a tendency to reminisce about the places in their countries where there was a Jewish presence. These recollections provide a sense of legitimacy to Jewish communities in search of acknowledgment and a historical stature that may endorse their often comfortable socioeconomic status. Hence, several Latin American Jewish intellectuals have produced articles and books recording everything demonstrable, possible, or wished-for that involves Jewish protagonism in the national epics and historical events (or myths) of their countries.

Examples of this tendency to incorporate Jews into the history of Latin American nations can be recognized in Argentina's idealized stories about the Jewish *gauchos,* and in Brazil's scholarly debates on the number and influence of crypto-Jews who created the economic basis of the country (for instance, whether Jews developed the sugar and wood trades, whether almost half of Brazil's seventeenth-century population consisted of Jewish descendants). In Colombia, Jews express pride that native writer Jorge Isaacs, author of the Latin American romantic novel par excellence, *María,* came from a Jewish family. In Venezuela, the Jewish community has published several works and articles highlighting Curaçao's Jews, who received Simón Bolívar during his exile on that island, and the history of the "glorious" Jewish community of Coro, the capital city of the state of Falcón, where one still can visit the remains of the first Jewish cemetery in the country.

In all of these cases, Jews show interest in keeping alive the memory and achievements of Jewish communities or individuals who assimilated into the Christian society, in order to link their achievements to their country's national history. I find this tendency throughout Latin America, even in Peru, where some *Limeño* Jews with intellectual inquisitiveness claim that Diego de Almagro and some of the first conquerors were Jews and that the civil war during Pizarro's age was a conflict between Old and New Christians. However, I find scarce interest in integrating the history of the Jews of Iquitos into the historical consciousness of Lima's Jews (despite the efforts of a few intellectuals who wrote about the Amazonian Jews). I wonder why. . . . Could it be because the presence of a still-ongoing history becomes controversial rather than anecdotal? . . . Recalling cases such as philosopher Baruch Spinoza's excommunication from the Amsterdam Jewish community in the seventeenth century (today Spinoza represents a thoroughly Jewish figure, especially for secular Jews) and taking into account the way many Jews proudly include in their "Jewish lists" celebrities such as Benjamin Disraeli, Karl Marx, and Charlie Chaplin (all of them sons of Jewish fathers and non-Jewish mothers) in order to highlight the importance of Jews in Western civilization, I am tempted to think that contemporary Jews only feel comfortable accepting the Judaism of such people when they are past history, not a living history. However, I do not have a clear explanation for why the history of Jews in the Peruvian Amazon is so foreign to Lima's Jews.

At that moment I did not have an answer; and I am still uncertain whether I have since gained one. Perhaps Jewish *Limeños'* unawareness of the "Jewish *Mestizos*" is merely a symptom of the coastal city's centralism, of the rhythm of our times that alienates city dwellers from "trivial" things that happen far from their surroundings. Perhaps the answer I seek is implicit in the sequence of contacts between the Jews of Iquitos and Lima, contacts that reflect a history of proximity and estrangement and of egos and alter egos tottering between parallel and crossed roads.

✦

THE FIRST ENCOUNTERS BETWEEN *LIMEÑOS* AND AMAZONIAN JEWS (1930S TO 1950S)

In the 1930s the Jews of Lima were fascinated to learn that there were Jews in the Peruvian Amazon. An article published in 1932 in the Jewish weekly magazine *Nosotros* revealed the presence of Sephardic Jews in Iquitos: "Israelite traders, representatives of the principal European nationalities, are established in our first river port; a few years after its foundation, [these Jews] contributed to expand commerce in Loreto [and] to urbanize the city of Iquitos, taking with them the seeds of civilization to the most remote zones of the complicated net of rivers of our Oriental region" (AT).[2] Two years later, in March 1934, *Nosotros* published a second article announcing the death of Salomón Brechman in Iquitos, who had left a fortune not claimed by anybody in that city; therefore, the editors of *Nosotros* considered it their duty to "make public knowledge [of this news] for all the community, in case there might be a possibility that a relative of Mr. Brechman lives among us, and he or she could claim the right to inherit [the fortune]" (AT).[3]

Several letters attest how Jews in Iquitos contributed to the Jewish national cause in Palestine during the 1930s and to aid European Jewish refugees arriving in Peru in the early 1940s.[4]

Since the 1930s, merchants from Lima have "discovered" the economic benefits of trading wood and skins from Iquitos. Benjamín Samolsky, a Jewish immigrant from Rumania, was one of the few Jews who selected Iquitos as the center of his business operations. Samolsky owned a sawmill and a commercial house that specialized in selling skins. Soon, he became one of the richest and most successful citizens of the city.

The year 1944 is especially important in the histories of the Jewish communities of Lima and Iquitos. On March 23, 1944, the *Sociedad Israelita de Iquitos* sent 16,700 *soles oro* to Lima's Jewish institutions, the most generous contribution that they had ever made. On July 17, 1944, members of this society sent a letter to Jacobo Franco, president of the body that represents all Jewish congregations in Lima, asking him to help them obtain from the Peruvian government legal recognition of Iquitos's Israelite Society.[5] On July 28 and 29, the same Jacobo Franco summoned representatives from every Jewish organization in the provinces to a meeting in Lima. Three delegates represented the Amazonian Jews.[6] Four months later, in November 1944, Rabbi Brener landed in Iquitos to perform the circumcision of Benjamín Samolsky's son, Simón. According to León Trahtemberg, the arrival of the first rabbi who ever visited an Amazonian city was a great event for Jewish *Iquiteños:* ". . . His stay was very cherished and it was the perfect occasion for a welcome party in which *'Hatikvah'* [Israel's national anthem] was sung and the people sang Jewish songs. When he learned that the community lacked a *sefer torah* [Torah scroll], Rabbi Brener suggested that someone put forward a donation to acquire it. This project, regretfully, never materialized" (AT).[7]

The events that happened in 1944 seem to indicate an ongoing relationship between Lima's and Iquitos' Jews; however, when geologist

Alfredo Rosenzweig arrived in Iquitos four years later, he was surprised to find Jews in the Amazonian region. Thrilled by this encounter, Rosenzweig decided to gather information about his fellow Jews. He asked Herman Weisselberger, a businessman from Lima who had settled in Iquitos, to look for the birth and death certificates of Jewish immigrants in the region, as well as the original statutes of the *Sociedad Israelita de Iquitos.* Weisselberger obtained twenty-nine death certificates from the *Registro Civil de Maynas.* Rosenzweig conducted some interviews but he did not publish his article about Jews in the Amazon until June 1967.[8] Of particular interest is that Alfredo Rosenzweig's account of the history of the Jews in the Peruvian Amazon mentions nothing of the contacts in 1944 between Lima and Iquitos.

Until Rosenzweig's work was published, Jewish *Limeños* paid little heed to stories of Jews in the Amazon—despite the fact that Jewish merchants traveled frequently to Iquitos; despite the business activities of some Ashkenazic Jews from Lima who had spent most of their lives in Iquitos; despite Rabbi Brener's presence in the Amazonian city during his second visit in 1959 when he carried out the circumcision of Herman Weisselberger's son, Beny; despite all these uninterrupted contacts between Jews in the two regions.

It took twenty more years, after the first highly visible encounters between the two communities in the 1940s, before Iquitos finally received recognition as the only organized Jewish community in Peru's provinces.

✦

Sharing the Euphoria of Good Times (1960s)

On December 20, 1966, on the front page of Iquitos's newspaper *El Oriente,* an unusual announcement was published:

> *El Instituto Cultural Peruano-Israelí de Iquitos* announces: In spite of its recent foundation, [the institution] has already had direct contact with the Israeli Embassy in Lima and with important associations [of Lima], such as *Hebraica* [a sport and cultural club] and the Sephardic association, [two] organizations of a cultural nature.
>
> Also, a news magazine in the Jewish community of Colombia just published an ample report regarding the Hebrew Association

of this city, something that we are delighted to inform our readers about in our attempt to convey the ideals [of the institute] to the people who dream and think (AT).[9]

The Jews of Iquitos and their descendants had organized again, and this time they were proud to announce to everybody the "birth" of their organization. They had even obtained the recognition of Jewish institutions in Lima, Colombia, and the State of Israel. How had this happened? The explanation is related to factors in Peruvian history. In 1965, President Belaunde Terry issued a decree of tax exoneration for the Peruvian Amazon in order to boost the region's economic potential. The new business opportunities offered to businessmen by the Amazonian region, especially Iquitos, seduced thousands of *Limeños*, including Jewish traders. Hence, Jews from Lima encountered their Amazonian "lost brothers" and decided to organize a Jewish institution.

On August 4, 1966, Rubén Braidman, a member of the *Instituto Cultural Peruano-Israelí de Lima* (ICPI), visited Iquitos and met more than forty descendants of Amazon-born Jews in the *Club Iquitos.* Braidman told them about the institution over which he presided in Lima. This association encouraged cultural links with the State of Israel. Descendants of Jews expressed their desire to create a similar institute and, sponsored by Braidman, they wrote a letter to Netanel Lorch, Israel's ambassador to Peru, introducing themselves as members of the Iquitos ICPI. On November 18, 1966, Rubén Braidman, Dr. Salomón Pardo, and Professor Yaacov Hasson traveled from Lima to Iquitos to participate in the official founding of the new Jewish institution.[10]

The three-day visit was a big event. News of the visit by Lima's Jewish delegation to Iquitos was constantly broadcast on the radio during its stay. For many "Jews" living in cities and villages on the Amazon's shores, the radio was the only means of communication with Iquitos. On Friday evening, November 18, 1966, the three delegates witnessed the inauguration ceremonies of the institution. Werner Levy Navarro, a renowned judge of the superior court of the city, and Willy Benzaquén Nájar, a prestigious lawyer, took an oath promising to make that organization the center of "return" for those Iquitos descendants of Jews searching for their Jewish roots. Of all the elected candidates to participate in ICPI's Board of

Directors only two members were Jews from Lima who had recently settled in the Iquitos.

The next day, Yaacov Hasson, acting as cultural attaché of the Israeli Embassy in Lima, lectured about Israel's kibbutzim (cooperative settlements) in the *Universidad Nacional de la Amazonía Peruana,* where a local military band played the national anthems of Peru and Israel. That evening there was a cocktail party (including *canutillos de jamonada,* small flour pipes stuffed with ham![11]) in the *Hotel de Turistas* for all descendants of Jews, as well as prominent citizens of the city, celebrating the inauguration of the new institute. Several descendants of Jews navigated through currents of the Amazon River, from distant towns in the jungle, to participate in the event. On Sunday, the three guests visited the Israelite cemetery of Iquitos and then returned to Lima.

Hence, Lima's Jewish institutions began an active campaign to make their members aware of the existence of this community and encouraged the rebirth of Iquitos's Jewish organized life. On December 8, 1966, Dr. Salomón Pardo presented a report covering the Lima delegation's trip to Iquitos, in which he proposed to help the community in its objectives of acquiring books and information concerning Judaism, of maintaining its Israelite cemetery, of legalizing the Jewish status of those who would request it (Pardo suggested members contact Rabbi Lothar Goldstein of the Conservative congregation "1870" for this purpose).[12] Lectures about the life of the Amazonian ICPI's members and their Jewish ancestors were organized in places such as the *Club Hebraica.*[13] Alfredo Rosenzweig published his article about the history of the Jews in the Peruvian Amazon and the Israeli Embassy sent books, journals, films, and radio tapes of Jewish history for the Iquitos community.[14] The Jewish community of Lima had organized plans with Eliahu Kehati, the principal of the *Colegio León Pinelo,* in order to send one of its teachers to Iquitos during the vacation season. (In February 1967, Claudio Kaiser visited the Amazonian city for a few days and lectured to an audience that barely understood his lessons.[15]) Meanwhile, *Club Hebraica* encouraged its "distant brothers" to organize a soccer team so they could expand their contact through athletic competitions.

Letters to and from Lima, filed in the archives of Iquitos's ICPI, suggest that the members of the Amazonian community had high expectations of their *Limeño* brothers. The euphoria of the 1966 encounter gradually evaporated as the *Limeños* gave them limited feedback. The "Jewish *Mestizos*" succeeded in renting an apartment for their meetings; they met weekly and registered their decisions in a *Libro de Actas* (records notebook); they organized prayers for the High Holidays and Passover. (In one of the first meetings the president of the IPCI, Werner Levy Navarro, suggested that Christmas be celebrated as "a universal holiday." The request was denied because the institution did not have a place to hold the party.[16]) The Institute's board of directors advocated the restoration of the Israelite cemetery, and, again, they requested that Lima send them financial aid and advisers to oversee its reconstruction; although a pair of Jewish engineers went to Iquitos to assess the cemetery's conditions, the burial ground was never restored. Finally, in January 1968, Jaime Gomberoff, president of the representative association of Lima's three congregations, told the dispirited "Jews" of Iquitos that they should organize themselves better and obtain more money from their own members because the capacity of Lima's Jewish community to provide financial aid was very limited.[17]

From the very beginning, the Peruvian-Israelite Institute created expectations among its members that could never be realized. Only a handful of its more than seventy associates regularly paid their dues.[18] However, in spite of its economic difficulties, the Jewish community in Iquitos collected money for the State of Israel during the Six-Day War of June 1967. The Israeli embassy received a check of 25,050 *soles* as a small contribution to "the distant homeland" during the harsh days of the conflict.[19]

The news of Israel's impressive triumph during the Six-Day War caused as much enthusiasm among the Iquitos community as it did throughout all the Jewish communities of the world. For a few months, Iquitos forgot its educational and financial needs, and in a letter addressed to the Israeli ambassador in Lima, requested that the embassy supply it with simple items, such as short films and tapes about the war, maps of Israel, and "pictures of Dr. Theodore Herlst [Herzl], founder of the Zionist 'idealism' [*sic*] of Israel; of Dr. Jaim Weisman [Haim Weitzman], first president of Israel; Dr. Isaac ben Shazar [a confused appellation referring to two successive presidents; Izhak Ben Zvi and Zalman Shazar]; Dr. David Ben-Gurión [the Prime Minister would have been flattered to be

called Doctor] and General Moshé Dayán; and more pictures of prominent men who will be part of our Gallery of Illustrious Men."[20] These
modest requests were quickly granted.

What Lima found harder to deliver was money for the many needs of
the "Jewish *Mestizos.*" Eventually the relationship between the Jewish
institutions of the Peruvian capital city and the Amazonian Jews became
limited to a few epistolary communications and official communiqués.
Projects once envisioned by Lima and Iquitos, such as the building of a
little Jewish school and a synagogue in the Amazonian city, and sending
children to study in the *Colegio León Pinelo,* remained on paper or in the
memory of ex-members of the *Instituto Cultural Peruano-Israelí de
Iquitos.*[21] One of the few agreements to be partially realized was Lima's
promise to help those interested in immigrating to Israel. In August 1970,
Iquitos sent to Lima a list of thirteen candidates who were ready to make
aliyah, many of them non-Jewish youngsters. Although no records exist
concerning what happened to these candidates, I learned through oral history that at least three of them succeeded in going to Israel.[22]

By 1970 the heart of the *Instituto Cultural Peruano-Israelí de Iquitos*
had "beat its last palpitations." Taxes gradually began to be introduced in
the Amazonian region, causing an exodus of profit-seeking *Limeños.* The
majority of Jewish businessmen who had revived Jewish life in Iquitos
returned to the capital city; some "Jewish *Mestizos*" also left their birthplace, looking for prosperity in Lima. Divisions among members of ICPI's
board of directors increased; the "tasty flavor of prestige" separated
friends (my interviewees called it "power struggles," but I am inclined to
believe that a sense of prestige or pride of one's "aristocratic lineage" are
better definitions of what caused animosity among some associates of
ICPI); the organization was running out of money; Lima was losing interest in Iquitos altogether. Even the visit of Israeli ambassador Moshe Yuval
on February 9, 1971 could not halt the decline of the institution. Although
Yuval, who was invited to Iquitos by local political figures to inaugurate
an exhibition about Israel, met many members of ICPI, by the end of that
year the organization had stopped holding meetings.

I have pointed out some of the factors that led to the demise of ICPI;
however, according to some of its former members, the association was
doomed from its very founding. Why? Willy Benzaquén Nájar, first vice-

president of ICPI now working in a law firm in Lima, provides a categorical answer:

> *I regret very much that our association did not have a religious component. We spoke about that on a number of occasions, but we did not know what path to take. . . . We took advantage of the visit of these people [the Lima delegation] in the 1960s to tell them our concerns and we told them about the religious aspect. . . .*
>
> *My feeling—I am going to be very honest— is that they [Lima's Jews] abandoned me to my own fortune in the religious aspect. We did not know how to make it by ourselves, and, although I know it sounds unfair to put all the blame on Lima (because we were not precisely diligent in the institute), they came to establish a cultural institution, neglecting the religious aspect. . . . In my opinion, to be Jewish means to carry out the Jewish religion; that is why I had doubts about a [Jewish] cultural institution. . . .*
>
> *Sometimes I wonder if these people came to Iquitos as tourists and then created an institution because they saw some Jews right there . . . before their eyes. These are doubts I have always had.*[23]

Certainly, the Peruvian-Israelite institution established in Iquitos did not attribute any importance to Jewish religion. Jaime Vásquez Izquierdo subscribes to the notion that the institution did not last:

> *because it was really an association of sympathizers of the State of Israel, so there were many non-Jewish members, and most of the members of the board of directors just wanted to keep contact with the Jewish leaders of Lima and Israel. It was not a Jewish organization!*[24]

Some of Iquitos's "Jewish *Mestizos*" requested books about Judaism (religion, Jewish traditions, theology) and they received books about anti-Semitism, the history of Israel, and the Soviet Jews. They asked for Jewish education, but they received information about Israel, contemporary magazines updating them on secular topics about a state whose Jewish character they did not know. Lima did not attend to the main needs of the "Jewish

Mestizos" and although the Iquitos community was not consistent in its pursuit of learning about Judaism, as Willy Benzaquén Nájar expresses it, "Lima is the place that holds up the foundations of Peru's Judaism."[25]

In his report to Lima's Jewish institutions, concerning the founding of the ICPI in Iquitos, Dr. Salomón Pardo wrote on December 6, 1966: "They [Iquitos's "Jews"] do not want this contact to end; they want a constant relationship with the Sephardic Society and the Israeli Embassy."[26] This intuition of having experienced only a temporary acceptance from Lima was adequately expressed by Pardo. Iquitos's "Jewish *Mestizos"* seem to have always felt estranged from Lima's Jews, a feeling that proved to be justified.

✦

THE FORGOTTEN BROTHERS (1970S AND 1980S)

In his article "Iquitos: Alma Judía en la Amazonía Peruana" (published in the 1970s in the periodical *Comunidades Judías de Latin América*), Yaacov Hasson wrote:

> Sixty years have passed, maybe enough time to erase any Jewish vestige in the zone [Peruvian Amazon]. And so it was believed. Therefore, while the blooming Jewish community of Lima hid under its shell, a group of forgotten brothers settled in the Amazonian region, they had children who learned to love [the department of] Loreto's land and who followed their fathers' footsteps (AT).[27]

Hasson was right. Lima had forgotten the *Iquiteños* before his visit in 1966, and especially by the time his article was published. During the 1970s, very few Jews in the capital city did anything for their "forgotten brothers" in the Peruvian Amazon.

Jewish life continued in Iquitos, thanks to the efforts of a few families who kept the traditions of the High Holidays. The Edery family in particular was successful in maintaining a certain Jewish "spark" after sending five of their twelve children to Israel.[28] As Ronald Benzaquén Pinedo puts it:

> *Don Víctor Edery is like a lamp that does not want to extinguish the flame, and the name of that flame is Judaism. He is using customs, not love, and custom is stronger than love.*[29]

Such was Jewish life in Iquitos until the 1990s. Meanwhile, what happened to those "Jewish *Mestizos*" who settled in Lima?

In the 1960s, Rabbi Lothar Goldstein of the Conservative *Sociedad de Beneficiencia Israelita 1870* led a study group of five people, among them three "Jewish *Mestizos*" from Iquitos who had settled in Lima. Initially, Rabbi Goldstein's students (all of them sons of non-Jewish mothers) attended the classes as the first requirement for conversion; eventually they continued attending classes for seven years. Ronald Benzaquén Pinedo, an *Iquiteño* pilot for a Peruvian airline company who now lives in Lima, recalls:

> *Rabbi Goldstein had a plan for us, although he never told us. He probably thought "I will transform these* Marranos *into Jews." [This is an* Iquiteño *imagining a rabbi thinking about himself and his* paisanos *as* Marranos!*] He showed interest in Iquitos; he asked me to bring him pictures of Iquitos and I believe he even traveled there once. Together with me in the course was my brother Jaime and Roger Foinquinos Ruiz (you know, the one you met in Iquitos). . . . He [Rabbi Goldstein] was the only rabbi, I remember, who cared for half-Jewish people like us* [Iquiteños].[30]

In 1966, when Rabbi Goldstein went to the United States, the "disciples" he left behind were interested in integrating with the Jewish community of the capital city. Ronald Benzaquén Pinedo explains why the people he calls the "*Marrano* disciples of Lothar Goldstein" did not succeed in maintaining the unique case of Iquitos's "Jews" on Lima's agenda:

> *We were discouraged by the way other rabbis saw us. [They saw us] as non-Jews; we also were busy in our jobs. I visited Iquitos in 1970 and I married a non-Jewish woman. . . . That was the end of my return to Judaism. My brother also married a non-Jewish woman. The only one who went back to Iquitos was Roger Foinquinos [Ruiz].*[31]

I am unable to determine the exact number of Jewish descendants who migrated from Iquitos to the capital city after 1970 because there are no statistical studies regarding birthplaces of the contemporary Jewish population in Peru. But what I can do is to provide examples of what some descendants of Iquitos's Jews told me regarding their travails with Lima's Jewish institutions and leaders.

The following voices—and names of persons mentioned in these stories—will not be identified to spare individuals from being denounced:

I was always segregated from my cousin's Jewish friends when I lived in Lima in the 1970s. My cousin is a complete Jew (his father married in Lima and then came to Iquitos), but because I was not a "complete Jew," I felt rejection from my cousins' friends.

✦

I could not register my children in the Colegio León Pinelo *because I just could not afford it. I regret so much that now they are not Jews!*

✦

I succeeded in registering my children in the Jewish school, in spite of the opposition of the community, because I had influential friends in Israel. You know, because of my job—and because I was influential in Peruvian politics. . . . So, a telephone call from Israel solved the whole situation.

✦

When I attended the meetings for parents of kids in the Colegio León Pinelo *many "pure Jewish" parents who were not rich complained about how their children were discriminated against by those kids who had lots of money.*

✦

When I studied in the León Pinelo [School], *I felt discriminated against because I was not a "pure Jew" and because the only thing that made me a Jew before them was my last name. My classmates did not consider me Jewish. But there was discrimination also among themselves as to who did not have "that car," or "that clothing." I felt a little resentment . . . for the Jews we are not Jewish, and for non-Jews we are Jewish! Do you understand this?*

✦

We buried our father in Iquitos because we were told by a rabbi that my father was not Jewish because his mother was a Gentile, so he could not be buried in the Israelite cemetery [in Lima]. I think

that the real reason our request was denied is that my father was not
a wealthy man; therefore, he never contributed to Jewish institutions.
But . . . anyway, thank God we have our cemetery in Iquitos.

✦

When my father passed away in Lima (he had moved here years
ago), I went to talk to Rabbi X, and he presented a series of hurdles
to burying my father in the Israelite cemetery [of Lima]. I
explained that my father was never circumcised because there were
no rabbis in Iquitos, but he expressed his wish to be buried among
Jews: "Rabbi," I said to him, "it took me a lot of striving to be what
I am now, because I never had a Jewish education in Iquitos. I
worked hard to learn what I know of Judaism, to convert to
Judaism, and now you are going to tell me that you cannot bury
my father as a Jew because he was not circumcised! . . . I will cross
that door and I am going to abandon Judaism." That is what I told
him, and my friend Y, who was born in Iquitos but whose parents
were both Jews, told Rabbi X: "If you do not bury his father in the
Israelite cemetery, you will lose two Jews, because I will abandon
Judaism too." Then, the rabbi decided to help us.[32]

These are examples of stories told to me by "Jewish *Mestizos*" who
moved to Lima. I cannot attest to the truthfulness of these stories, but
certainly they reveal that Iquitos's descendants of Jews have experienced a
sense of indifference, discrimination, and unfairness from their "older
brothers" of Lima.

Beyond these people's perceptions lie several widely acknowledged
characteristics of the stance of Lima's Jewish community toward the question of "half-Jewish" people. We know that the Jewish institutions of Lima
do not have discriminatory policies and that they attempt to negotiate with
two realities: on one hand, the increasing number of children of "mixed
marriages" and youngsters marrying non-Jewish spouses and, on the other
hand, the reality of the strict stance of the Orthodox rabbis of the
Sephardic and the Ashkenazic congregations. We know that the vast
majority of *Limeño* Jews have a secular conception of Judaism, which, in
principle, does not exclude the idea of accepting every person who
genuinely expresses his or her wish to belong to the Jewish people. However, they accept and respect the decisions of the rabbis who are in charge

of religious issues. We know that, with the exception of the Conservative congregation (which includes many converted members), the Orthodox rabbis of Lima perform no conversions unless they receive instructions from the Rabbinate of Israel. With regard to Iquitos's Jewish descendants, the Orthodox rabbis of Lima simply do not consider them Jews because they are not such according to Jewish law.

To what extent do economic factors play a role in Lima's exclusion of the *Iquiteños?* We know, according to statistical studies carried out in 1988, that approximately 65 percent of Lima's Jews belonged to the middle and upper classes of the capital city, 23 percent required scholarships or discounts in order to register their children in the *Colegio León Pinelo*, and 12 percent received financial aid from the Jewish community for their subsistence. These statistics reveal that the Jewish community does help a good number of its poorest members and that few children are rejected by the Jewish school because one of their parents is not Jewish. However, there is a very important aspect underlying this data: The vast majority of mixed marriage couples do not send their children to the *Colegio León Pinelo*.[33] Why?

Perhaps the answer can be found in the stories of Iquitos's "Jewish *Mestizos.*" Perhaps these parents prefer to spare their children from the social pressure of a community in which Orthodox paradigms of Judaism determine the "Jewish status" of its secular members. Perhaps these parents hesitate to immerse their children in a clannish community in which it is too difficult to be "half-Jewish" and command full rights (membership in Jewish institutions, burial privileges at the Israelite cemetery, full participation in religious ceremonies, etc.). It is at this point that socioeconomic status begins to play a determining role in the acceptance of "half-Jewish" persons.[34]

The impoverished "Jewish *Mestizos,*" then, had to struggle to find acceptance in a community impregnated by the values of the nouveau riche upper economic classes of Lima. The Amazonian "Jews" had to integrate themselves into a community that was decreasing in number due to the migration of hundreds of Jews to the United States, Israel, and other Latin American countries, as Peru struggled against terrorism (committed, for example, by the "Shining Path," and the *Tupac Amaru*), inflation, and social convulsions.[35] The Jewish community was dwindling, and its religious and political leaders adopted more defensive, clannish attitudes toward foreign sympathizers, rather than opening up the community to potential new members, something that Orthodox rabbis would have never allowed. Most of Iquitos's descendants of Jews bear a strong physical resemblance to average Peruvian *Mestizos;* therefore, the predominantly white Jews of Lima have found it difficult to identify with them as members of a same people. Eventually, most of Iquitos's "Jews" in Lima adopted the Christian religion of their spouses' families.

Lima provided little direction for whatever remained of the Jewish identity of these "modern *Marranos,*" so the few who still wanted to return to Judaism began to send letters to functionaries of the *Federación Sionista del Perú* in Lima. In 1985 Ronald Reategui Levy, a young Jewish descendant, restored epistolary communication with Lima and opened the gates for several of his *paisanos* to make *aliyah.*[36] Due to personal problems he himself was unable to travel to Israel, but he paved the way to new connections between Iquitos and Lima. Meanwhile, a small group of former members of the *Instituto Cultural Peruano-Israelí de Iquitos* began to fantasize about an idea: What if they organized themselves again?

When I learned how the *Sociedad de Beneficiencia Israelita de Iquitos* had been reestablished, I wrote in my diary in Iquitos:

> After conducting many interviews, after reviewing the archives of the Israelite Society of Iquitos, after striving to find "that one event" that sparked the resolve of a few men to struggle again to maintain themselves as Jews, I simply am unable to explain the rebirth of a Jewish society in this city. The scholar has been defeated, and I can only agree with what my friend, the amateur historian Rafael Rodríguez said to me in Lima before coming to this place: "Maybe it is that Jewish flame that does not want to be extinguished." The most scientific insight I can add to this explanation is related to the science of medicine: "Yes," as the medieval scholar Ibn Verga wrote, "probably Judaism is really one of those incurable diseases."

✦

A STREETCAR NAMED DESIRE (1990s)

It was 1990 and Debora Frank, an activist member of the *Federación Sionista del Perú* in Lima continued to receive letters from Ronald Reategui Levy and a few people of Iquitos asking her to help them make *aliyah.* Occasionally,

Iquiteños showed up in Debora Frank's office to find out what possibility they had of immigrating to Israel. Some were youngsters studying or working in Lima; others had come to the capital city to visit relatives.[37]

The *Federación Sionista del Perú* took Iquitos seriously due to an awareness that Jewish descendants had organized an institution to revive Judaism in the Amazonian city and to encourage its members to settle in Israel. What trigger, the federation wondered, drove such a group to institute a religious and Zionist community in such an isolated place? One may argue that the revival of Jewish religious sentiment in Iquitos was Ronald Reategui Levy's inspiration; however, if we examine the man's life more closely, we find that this young technician of *Petroperú* (Peru's national oil company) spent most of his time in the oil fields adjacent to Iquitos.

Nostalgia seems to be what motivated the "Jewish *Mestizos.*" Jaime Vásquez Izquierdo remembers the origins of the present-day *Sociedad Israelita de Iquitos.*

> *We had been calling each other "paisanos" since we were kids; we kept going to celebrate Rosh Hashanah and Yom Kippur in Don Víctor Edery's home. Many times we met in the Plaza de Armas [main square] and we talked about Judaism, news from Israel, our ancestors, the times of the* Instituto [Cultural] Peruano-Israelí [de Iquitos]. . . . *So, one day, Don Víctor, [Roger] Foinquinos [Ruiz], and I decided: Why not organize ourselves as a community? And so we did!*[38]

Debora Frank believes that the precedent of Cajamarca's *Bene Moshe* massive conversion to Judaism and their *aliyah* influenced Iquitos's descendants of Jews to return to their roots, and persuaded Lima's Jewry to aid another group in the fringe of Jewish identity; however, in Lima and Iquitos almost nobody knows about the *Bene Moshe* case.

The initiative of the first generation of Jewish descendants, together with the enthusiasm of younger descendants of Jews who wanted to immigrate to Israel because of idealism or socioeconomic reasons, led to the foundation of the *Sociedad de Beneficiencia Israelita de Iquitos* on January 15, 1991. The society was inaugurated during a meeting in Víctor Edery's house; the "old patriarch" was appointed provisional president and Jaime

Vásquez Izquierdo was asked to keep minutes of the sessions until a future board of directors was established. This time, with neither Jewish *Limeño* visitors nor ceremonies, the thirty-three members pledged to pay dues to maintain the Israelite cemetery. They also began a campaign to bring Rabbis Guillermo Bronstein and Yaacov Kraus from Lima to guide them in their crusade to acquire a legitimate Jewish identity. In this way, they could become eligible candidates to immigrate to Israel under the Law of Return, once they had undergone a future conversion.[39]

Henceforth, the society's board of directors began to meet every week in Víctor Edery's house, organizing committees to work for the Israelite cemetery of the city, to recruit Jewish descendants, to get money to bring rabbis to Iquitos, and to write letters to Jewish institutions in Lima introducing their recently established "Jewish" institution. On April 11, 1991 big news was revealed to the society's members: Conservative rabbi Guillermo Bronstein would come from Lima to Iquitos in a few days![40]

On April 14, Rabbi Bronstein landed in Iquitos, where for two days he held meetings with the "Jewish *Mestizos*." Bronstein proposed that the community write statutes for their institution and that they celebrate the main Jewish holidays of Rosh Hashanah, Yom Kippur, Pesaḥ (Passover), and Shabbat every Friday evening. (According to many *Iquiteño* Jews, they had already been celebrating all these holidays before Rabbi Bronstein's visit.) The rabbi also suggested that members of the community organize cultural activities, sponsor lectures about Judaism, and study Jewish holidays, rituals, and principles. Lima would send them books for these purposes.[41]

Rabbi Bronstein's presence in Iquitos encouraged more descendants of Jews to join the *Sociedad Israelita*. By June, the institution had grown from thirty-three to eight-one members. Leaders of the *Sociedad Israelita* welcomed new members, exposing to them some principles of the Jewish religion, the institution's objectives, and "the character, advantages, and dangers of anti-Semitism included in being Jewish."[42] Although the current leaders of the *Sociedad de Beneficiencia Israelita de Iquitos* assured me that from the very beginning their institution had a religious character, it is in later documents that one finds the first written references to Shabbat ceremonies and Jewish burial rituals (such as the reciting of the *Kaddish* mourner's prayer). We also find formal statements made by members pledging to follow the "Jewish religious rules," in records following Rabbi

Bronstein's visit. Definitely, the rabbi's proposals were taken seriously. In June 1991 the society proclaimed that those interested in immigrating to Israel had to fulfill their (financial) duties to the institution for a period of six months "at least."[43] In July, the first draft of the society's statutes was presented, and the first election of the board of directors was held.

At the end of July 1991, the "Jewish *Mestizos*" were unexpectedly visited by an important Israeli visitor, Dror Fogel, mayor of the Israeli city of Ramat Ishai. Fogel had come to Lima due to personal reasons and, once in Peru, he decided to travel to the countryside. He was told about the beauty of the Amazonian landscapes and about the organized community of Jewish descendants of Iquitos. Thus, he traveled to the Amazon. Before an audience of approximately one hundred "Jewish *Mestizos*," Dror Fogel lectured about the State of Israel and promised to spread the news of the existence of a "Jewish community in the city of Iquitos, on the shores of the Amazon River, [comprised of] descendants of Jews who migrated to Peru during the rubber boom period."[44]

According to the "Jewish *Mestizos*," before he left Iquitos Dror Fogel promised the city's "Jews" that he would do as much as he could to organize their massive immigration to Israel, inviting them to settle in Ramat Ishai, a developing Israeli city. Some interviewees recall the Israeli mayor talking about sending some "Hercules" airplanes to bring them to Israel (although it should not be a surprise if this is an exaggerated interpretation of what the visitor offered them!).[45] Later in that month, the community learned that Víctor Edery's daughter, Rachel Edery Shomron, and Miriam Bendayán Vásquez had been invited to the radio network *Kol Yisrael*, in Jerusalem, to tell about the "Jews" of their birthplace.[46]

During the society's October 14, 1991 session, Víctor Edery told fellow members that Debora Frank had traveled to Israel to meet with immigration authorities "in order to (among other issues) deal with the issue of our *aliyah*" and to discuss with Mayor Dror Fogel [in Ramat Ishai] the possible settlement of Iquitos's Jews in his city.[47] Víctor Edery's story was somewhat an exaggeration of the truth. Certainly, Debora Frank traveled to Israel and met Dror Fogel, but that was only a short meeting during a trip she made for sightseeing purposes.[48]

Since August 1991 the *Sociedad Israelita* has established statutes. The society defined itself as a religious institution open to "any person wishing to participate in the Jewish faith, the practice of Jewish traditions based on the Torah, the Hebrew prophets, and the Talmud."[49] The members appointed a spiritual guide (Víctor Edery) until a rabbi came to lead the community and plans were made to build a synagogue. By November 1991, the *Sociedad Israelita* had ninety members, and Víctor Edery's sons, Yared and Víctor Jr., who had been living in Israel, began teaching Hebrew to some members. (This attempt only lasted a few weeks.) On December 11, the community celebrated the visit of Debora Frank, who spent several days in Iquitos investigating the situation of the "Jewish *Mestizos*," explaining to them the requirements for *aliyah* and preparing a report for the Zionist Federation regarding the possibility of helping this community immigrate to Israel. In her report to Lima's *Federación Sionista* she wrote:

> We could learn that this community that calls itself "Israelite" or "Jewish" is not such, according to Jewish law; however, among them there is an amazing feeling of belonging [to the Jewish people]. . . . For nearly twenty years they have had practically no contact with Lima. Therefore, they were disconnected from Judaism and its traditions, but they kept calling themselves Jews. It is very interesting to see their will to return to Judaism, and they promise to do everything possible to do this. There are many among them who are fourth generation [descended from Jewish immigrants] and they cannot make *aliyah;* but nevertheless, they want to learn Hebrew and learn about Judaism . . . (AT).[50]

The Zionist Federation representative explained all the requirements that had to be fulfilled to immigrate to Israel. This included providing birth and death certificates of their parents and grandparents in order to prove family ties with Jewish ancestors. Frank elaborated on the urgency of the *Iquiteños'* case in her report:

> Our goal was to provide them with information about *aliyah* and to explain, in general terms, that Iquitos's ['Jewish'] community has no future in the short range, because many of them are third and even fourth generation and therefore they do not fall under [Israel's] Law of Return. Besides this, the community continually grows

smaller and has less and less knowledge of Judaism and Israel. That is why I was very clear in telling them that *their last train is departing* and they had better take it, or they will stay here until it will be too late (AT).[51]

Debora Frank's report concludes with positive remarks about Iquitos's "Jewish *Mestizos*," and encourages Lima to help this community, which is already organized and has a list of candidates ready to go to Israel (approximately twenty people). She notes that most of the *tareas* (homework) that Rabbi Bronstein had assigned the community (attending regular Shabbat services and lectures and drawing up statutes) were being carried out by its members. She adds: "They are not doing [all these things] out of necessity, but instead due to conviction (at least the majority of them). It is not easy to live as a Jew in such a difficult environment . . ." (AT).[52]

But that "departing train," that "streetcar named desire," seemed unreachable to many "Jewish" *Iquiteños*. They could not prove that they were descendants of Jews because the Orthodox establishment in Israel would not accept records from a place where there had never been rabbis. Even third, fourth, and fifth generations of Jewish descendants who could send pictures of their fathers' and grandfathers' gravestones in the Israelite cemetery, thus being able to prove that their deceased ancestors were indeed Jews, were not considered Jews by Israeli functionaries who had to work their cases according to the immigration principles of the Law of Return. Many of the ancestors (fathers and grandfathers) of the "Jewish *Mestizos*" were buried in areas far from Iquitos, and their birth and death certificates had been lost in dusty folders in the civil offices of little towns unable to preserve old documents. As Ronald Reategui Levy claims: "Israel requires things [documents] that are impossible to find in Amazonian towns because, simply, there are no records preserved here."[53] Regarding the requirements for conversion to Judaism, the words of Fernando Levy Martínez epitomize the perplexed state of many Jewish descendants:

> *If you want to be a Mormon, an Adventist, you do not have so many requirements; but in order to be a "pure Jew" you have to undergo very demanding requirements; For example, if you want to be Evangelist or Adventist, you only have to accept Christ; but*

to be Jewish, my God, you have to fulfill one million requirements
that sometimes you cannot comply with even if you want to. It is
easier to be a Christian![54]

Indeed, the Peruvian Amazon was and still is a difficult place to be a Jew.

Debora Frank left Iquitos's *Sociedad Israelita* with a "bubbling" series of projects for its community. By February 1992, the numbers of members registered in the society surpassed one hundred. (See Appendix 3.) That month, the Israeli ambassador in Lima, Yuval Metzer, visited Iquitos to receive an *Honoris Causa* degree from the *Universidad Nacional de la Amazonía Peruana*. Yuval Metzer met with members of the *Sociedad Israelita* on February 9th, during a ceremony in which attendants organized an homage to the recently deceased ex-Prime Minister of Israel, Menachem Begin. The guest of honor lectured about Israel's history, the life of Begin, and the Law of Return, inviting the Iquitos community to visit and stay in the Jewish state.[55] In following sessions, the community discussed establishing a plan to circumcise all of its members. They agreed to consult with Lima. Another concern was establishing a synagogue (Edery's bar was a less-than-ideal place to pray during Shabbat and the major holidays), but in spite of several promises from *Iquiteños* and *Limeños,* this project never materialized.[56]

The community continued along its slow path to learn the tenets of Judaism. Each session, a member lectured about one aspect of Jewish culture or religion. The *Sociedad Israelita* maintained epistolary relations with most of Lima's Jewish institutions and also with congregations in Argentina and New York. In January 1993, the new board of directors sent a letter to Rabbi Bronstein to accelerate their planned conversion to Judaism.[57] Rabbi Bronstein promised to analyze their progress in a meeting with Debora Frank and members of the Zionist Federation, and he sent basic books concerning Jewish topics, to hasten the first phase of a possible conversion.[58]

Letters continued going back and forth between Lima and Iquitos through June 6, 1993, when Rabbi Bronstein wrote a letter drawing up the conditions for the conversion:

> In regard to the possible conversion [of the Israelite Society's members] I reiterate: a) It will be performed only on those who

pledge to make *aliyah;* b) It must be performed according to every single item required by halakhah (Jewish law); c) [The conversion] must include *brit milah* [circumcision] of all males, and that must be performed by a Jewish and circumcised *mohel* (or a medical doctor trained in that kind of surgery). The cases of those who are already circumcised will be analyzed individually; d) The final ritual ceremony of conversion must be performed by a *bet din* (rabbinical tribunal); therefore, two other rabbis will accompany the signer of this letter [Rabbi Bronstein] to Iquitos. These rabbis must be brought (for a period of two days) from abroad. In the right time, I will personally explain the reason [for this procedure]; e) This conversion will be accepted in any *non*-Orthodox community and it will help those who wish to go to Israel. However, I must make it clear that Israel's Rabbinate will *not* necessarily recognize this conversion; f) Regarding the financial aspect of this conversion, I hope that the costs will be as low as you can afford. I think that two trips for a period of three days (two nights) will be enough time to prepare you before the conversion. Every candidate must assume the responsibility of getting himself or herself ready, of studying the material [books] and complying with all the assigned tasks [exams]. The first trip will allow me to provide an introduction and to organize a plan for your studies. Between the first and second trip, you must send papers to me in Lima that I will evaluate. In the second trip, approximately six months after these papers are returned, I will conduct an oral exam. On my third trip I will be accompanied by the two other rabbis, when *all* the male candidates have been circumcised and *all* men and women are ready for the exam in front of the *bet din* and for the final ritualistic ceremony [of conversion] (AT).[59]

During the following months, members of the *Federación Sionista del Perú* in Lima requested books from Jewish publishing houses in Argentina, in order to send them to Iquitos.[60] Rabbi Guillermo Bronstein drew up the final plan for the *Iquiteños'* conversion, requiring all the candidates to immigrate to Israel. He was very cautious not to set precedents that could cause problems for other Peruvian rabbis in the future; and therefore,

Orthodox conversion was mandatory for those who received Conservative conversion in Iquitos, once they settled in Israel. Rabbi Bronstein presented a realistic plan that took into account the strict rules for conversion to Judaism, and the realities of maintaining a proper Jewish life in a city like Iquitos. (Rabbi Bronstein's explanation of how the *Federación Sionista*'s 1993 project of converting Iquitos's Jewish descendants would deal with all these difficulties and his accompanying punctilious halakhic details are quoted in their totality in Appendix 5.)

During his second trip to Iquitos, on November 29, 1993, Rabbi Bronstein detailed the plan to the members of the "Jewish *Mestizos*" interested in making *aliyah*. The plan appeared to be working. On January 6, 1994, the *Sociedad Israelita* agreed to establish a "Hebrew School" in order to prepare its members for writing papers for Rabbi Bronstein and to convey the basics of Jewish education to many *paisanos* who, according to the institution's board of directors, possessed "tiny and diffuse knowledge [of Judaism], which is full of inaccuracies, and is reflected in their behavior, which shows an *incorrect pride* in their Hebrew ancestry. . . ."[61] A few months later, on April 5th, members of the *Sociedad Israelita* sent the first papers to Rabbi Bronstein. The next month, seven other members sent their papers. On July, they received their grades.

The conversion candidates seemed well on their way to catching that "streetcar named desire," which led to Israel through the trolley tracks of Judaism; however, political and personal problems among members of the society soon led to dissociation. Sessions were held less and less often, fewer members attended, and Shabbat services were attended by a mere dozen descendants of Jews. Justifiably, Rabbi Bronstein and other friends of the *Iquiteños* "Jews" halted their impetus to help the community, which was not complying with the agreement.

Then, I appeared . . . first as a distant voice, and later, in person. From the moment Rabbi Bronstein told members of the *Sociedad Israelita* that a Jewish researcher from Miami would come to visit them, the community came back to life. On January 29, 1995, the *Sociedad Israelita* held a session to look for lodgings for the "Jewish visitor."[62] My visit to Iquitos on June 8th of that year revived Jewish activities in Iquitos, especially Shabbat services, which more people began to attend after meeting me during the interviews. After more than six months of delay, the community held elections on July 2nd, selecting a new board of directors.[63]

As an intruding researcher, I am to blame for many of the recent strategies set up between Lima and Iquitos. In Chapter Eight I will discuss my role as a protagonist in these affairs, addressing important issues regarding the struggle between the professional and the human being, issues faced by each historian who deals with ongoing historical events that involve him in the fate of the subjects of his study.

7

Inter- and Intra-Views

"... The Jewish community of Lima never accepted
her [Saúl Zuratas's mother] even though to please
Don Salomón [Saúl's father] she had gone through
the ritual of lustral bath and received instruction from
the rabbi in order to fulfill all the rites necessary for
conversion. In fact—and Saúl winked a shrewd eye
at me—the community didn't accept her not so much
because she was a *goy* as because she was a little
Creole from Talara [the province], a simple woman with
no education, who could barely read. 'Because the
Jews of Lima turned into a bunch of bourgeois, pal.'"
—Mario Vargas Llosa, *The Storyteller*

"We are not pure Jews. We come from generations
of Catholics. But the Jewish spark remains in us.
When I married I told my wife about my origins,
and when the children grew up I revealed the
genealogy to them. My daughter wants to visit
Israel. I myself would like to settle there, but
what would I do? I'm too old to enter—how do you
call it?—a kibbutz. But my daughter could marry a Jew."
"The Jews in Israel are not all religious" [I told him].
"Why not? Well, I understand."
—Isaac Bashevis Singer, "Shabbat in Portugal"

PERU IS A predominantly *Mestizo* society, whose powerful white minority dominates the nation's political and economic spheres. (This tendency has not altered even during the two terms of President Alberto Fujimori, son of Japanese immigrants.)[1] The hegemony of Creoles (white people born in the Spanish Americas) and descendants of European immigrants has been manifest in Latin America since colonial times; this has been specially true in the mid-nineteenth century, when the Creole elite, inspired by racial theories based on "Social Darwinism," purposefully engineered massive campaigns of European immigration to "whiten" their societies.[2] At the beginning of the twentieth century, Latin American thinkers challenged traditional theories of white racial superiority by proposing romantic utopias wherein a *crisol de razas* (blending of races) would flourish in the continent,[3] or by declaring pride in being descendants of pre-Columbian native Americans.

In Peru the *Indigenista* movement gained strength in the 1920s and 1930s, calling for a return to the Incan communal socioeconomic system, which, according to left-wing thinkers, was a "socialist empire."[4] The traditionally subordinate Indians and *Mestizos* suddenly became icons of Peruvian nationalism. Since the 1920s, when President Augusto Leguía adopted an *Indigenista* rhetoric, established the *Patronato de la Raza Indígena* under the jurisdiction of Lima's archbishopric, and declared June 24th "Indian Day," the ruling white classes of Peru publicly have praised the Incan heritage (or "blood") of "all Peruvians."

However, Peru's official discourse does not necessarily reflect the nation's racial reality. In his work *Buscando un Inca,* Peruvian scholar Alberto Flores Galindo argues that "in Peru nobody would define himself as a racist. Nevertheless, racial categories not only mark, but also condition our social perception" (AT).[5] Accordingly, despite the lofty tones of national discourse, the white minority of Peru displays not-so-subtle attitudes of discrimination and marginalization toward the majority *Mestizo* population. As some Peruvian scholars note, racism is not only related to an interpretation of Peruvian history or related to political projects, but is also part of the trivial life. Many white *Limeño* children have internalized discriminatory attitudes toward *Cholitos* [urban Andean *Indios* and their *Mestizos* descendants], learned at home by watching how their parents treated their maids.[6] By 1908, 19 percent of Lima's population worked as maids, most of them Indians, *Mestizos,* and a few "yellows" (Asian immigrants).[7] Generations of *Limeños* have grown up with a hierarchical conception of society according to class and racial categories in which *Mestizos* and *Cholos* are perceived as uneducated, inferior people.

The Jews of Lima—a white minority within a white minority that gradually adapted to and adopted most of the ruling classes' notions, codes of behavior, and perceptions—hardly can identify themselves with the majority *Mestizo* population. What happened, then, when they "discovered" a group of Amazonian *Mestizos* claiming to belong to the same people? How did they assimilate the challenge of seeing as "brothers" people who looked like most average Peruvians? What can we conclude from the complex set of perceptions that belong to the two racially different "Jewish" groups of Lima and Iquitos that could shed light on the questions of what it means to be a Jew, and what it means to be a Peruvian?

In this chapter I will explore how Jews from Lima and Iquitos regard each other as revealed by their discourses about "that community of brothers on the other side of the Andes mountains." In addition, by examining the self-perception of Iquitos's descendants of Jews—those voices of selfhood echoing whispers of peoplehood—we can gain clues about Peruvian racial attitudes and realities, as well as peculiar interpretations of Judaism, all of which have influenced the views of those protagonists who ask themselves, "Who is a Peruvian Jew?"

◆

THE EXOTIC JEWS OF IQUITOS: A VIEW FROM LIMA

Although the Jewish immigrants who first settled in the Peruvian Amazon were regarded as "exotic" by Lima's Jews, these European and North African immigrants were still considered members of the "Jewish family": "The Jewish colony of Iquitos enjoyed and enjoys (and are worthy of) the affection and esteem from all social circles of our first Amazonian port," reported a Jewish weekly newspaper in Lima in 1932. ". . . It is because the Jew knows how to adapt easily to the environment in which he is immersed. Due to his intelligence and the decency of his procedures, he causes himself to be esteemed in high spheres and because of his understanding and refined character, he becomes popular" (AT).[8]

Rather than providing insight into how Lima's Jews regarded their Amazonian "brothers," this article, written for Lima's Jewish publication *Nosotros,* describes how Jews saw other Jews (as intelligent, honest, "decent", and "refined") and more significantly, how Lima's Jewish community perceived the way non-Jewish Peruvians related to Jews (they respected and liked them). What made the Amazonian Jews seem exotic to their urban compatriots were the unusual occupations they engaged in as navigators and owners of trading steamships, and their remarkable cosmopolitanism: They frequently traveled to the European port of Le Havre, and they could savor what *Nosotros* described as "the bubbling taste of champagne, exquisite perfumes, gum, or the most recent book published in Paris, Berlin, London, or in Madrid" (AT).[9]

An interesting aspect of the *Nosotros* report on Jews in the department of Loreto is the use of the term "race" to describe the Jewish people. (In the 1930s, "race" was indiscriminately used by Peruvian scholars, politicians, journalists, and everyday people to describe any minority, foreigner, ethnic, or religious group): ". . . Iquitos's Israelites are worthy descendants of that admirable *race* that becomes more vigorous the more they are persecuted, of that *race* that has in European history a legitimate and outstanding representative, Disraeli, that Jewish man who had such a powerful mentality that he deposed the hitherto untamed prejudices of the rancid English aristocracy, in order to build up worldwide the power of the British Empire" (AT).[10]

Here one finds Jews in general described as an "admirable race," while the Amazonian Jews in particular are compared to a successful British aristocrat (ironically, himself a "questionable" Jew who converted to Anglicanism) and described as part of a people, race, and lineage that connects them to Lima's Jews. The Peruvian racial discourse of the 1920s and 1930s, by transforming the Jews into a race different from other immigrant groups and, of course, different from the *Mestizo* population of the Amazonian region, allowed Lima's Jews to identify with their distant "brothers" in the jungle. However, in selecting Benjamin Disraeli as the "legitimate representative of these Jews," the author of this article seems to have foreseen that descendants of these exotic Jews would have to fill "blank pages between the Old and the New Testaments" in order to define their identities.

As time went by, the Amazonian descendants of those Jews no longer served *Limeños* as a mirror of the Jewish people. After the *Instituto Cultural Peruano-Israelí de Iquitos* was established in December 1966, Salomón Pardo, a member of Lima's Jewish community delegation who attended the event, returned to the capital city and described Iquitos's descendants of Jews as a people with "an exaggerated [sense of] Jewish pride" despite the isolation of the area and more than half a century of abandonment. He defined the community in these terms:

> There are two opinions [among them]: a) A first group, in which the Ashkenazic Jews are included, think that there should be a religious center because there are enough elements to constitute it and because [Amazonian descendants of Jews] had been complying with some religious holidays, which is a proof to endorse their thesis; and b) A second group, to which the majority belongs, agree unanimously to establish religious services after they learn more about our ritualistic traditions (through our recent contact and aid). They call themselves "social Christians" and they do not reject at all returning to the faith of their ancestors. But they suggest that their children begin to receive a Jewish education, starting in early childhood, so adults will eventually learn from themselves (AT).[11]

Salomón Pardo proposed to help them because he firmly believed "in their rooted and proud Judaism, a fact that can be proved through the tendency they have to marry among themselves" (AT).[12] Pardo's assertion appears unfounded. When I looked at the marriage certificates of the Peruvian-Israelite Cultural Institution's board of directors, I found that almost none of them had married descendants of Jews; furthermore, the vast majority of these "Jewish *Mestizos*" married in the Catholic Church.[13]

Thus, by the 1960s Lima's Jews viewed these children of immigrant Jews as "exotic" because of the "exaggerated Jewish pride of these socially oriented Christians." By that time, the Other had become a real Other, not a mirror of themselves. These were truly foreign "Jews" as Yaacov Hasson depicted them in his flowery article, "Iquitos: Alma Judía en la Amazonía Peruana": "When we arrived at the *Hotel de Turistas* in Iquitos, we could notice in their faces the anxiety and affection that they professed to us [to the delegation of Jewish *Limeños*]. Sun and nature were not able to erase that ancient Jewish stock; they had stayed in Loreto's lands, and now they revived, like a hidden murmur of intimacy and pride, the Jewish spirituality" (AT).[14] Yaacov Hasson's description reveals as much about the emotions of Iquitos's Jewish descendants anxiously awaiting the *Limeños,* as it does about the Jewish *Limeños* ethnocentric, but affectionate view, of their "forgotten brothers who belonged to a common stock."

In May 1976, during the period of greatest estrangement between the two communities, the Jewish weekly journal *Nuestro Mundo* published an article about Iquitos's Jews and their descendants. The article was in the form of an interview with Nessim Scialom, a Jewish *Limeño* who had just visited Iquitos and wanted to share what he had learned about the once-prosperous Jewish community of that Amazonian city. Nessim Scialom emphasized the presence of Ashkenazic families still living in Iquitos (the Datzinger, Weil, and Meckler families); he mentioned the most renowned Jews in the history of the city ("the great capitalists and former mayors Víctor Israel and Alberto Toledano"); and he provided a few names of Jews and their descendants buried in the Israelite cemetery of Iquitos. Scialom's praise focused on the figures of two brothers, Oscar and Raul Hirsh, who arrived in Iquitos after the Second World War and became successful businessmen. According to Scialom, the Hirsh brothers were diligent in maintaining the lawn of the Israelite cemetery, together with a few coreligionists. The article concludes: "To finish this piece, we want to send our regards and a message of congratulation to Oscar and Raul Hirsh due to their devoted labor of years working in such a noble task (part of their family tradition) of preserving that cemetery, a truly Jewish relic in Peru" (AT).[15] When I interviewed Oscar Hirsh on June 30, 1995, I showed him the article and he laughed:

> Yes . . . yes, I read it years ago. That is not true. The man [Nissim Scialom] came to visit and asked my brother to take him to the Israelite cemetery, and that is all that he did. We have never been in charge of that cemetery. I myself am not Jewish [he officially converted to Catholicism] but I help the community when they ask me for money, and my brother was buried in the general cemetery. . . . I requested to be incinerated when I pass away, so my ashes

*can be thrown into the Amazon River. . . . We just showed the city
and the cemetery to this man [Scialom].*[16]

The view from Lima became increasingly ethnocentric; Iquitos was a part of Peruvian Jewish history, although the most important aspect of this history was the presence of *Limeño* Jews who resided in Iquitos. In a sense, one may argue that for Lima, the "new Jewish aristocrats of the Amazonian region," the inheritors of Víctor Israel's and Alberto Toledano's past glories, were the Ashkenazic Jews who came from the capital city to Iquitos only after the Second World War. When Jewish *Limeños* recall their visits to Iquitos they usually tell how they met Jacobo Goldstein, Simón Samolsky, David Seinfeld, Zeev and Kalman Abramovitz, Manfred and Joseph Weisselberger, Raul and Oscar Hirsh (regardless of their conversion to Catholicism), and other Ashkenazic Jews, who often married non-Jewish native *Iquiteñas,* as had the descendants of Sephardic Jews. The "Jewish *Mestizos*" are increasingly perceived as an exotic group that claims to be Jewish without knowing what Judaism is all about. They are regarded more as *Mestizos* than as Jews, which in contemporary Peruvian "vocabulary" means a separated social class or religious group having little contact with modernity, people who perhaps share a common past but certainly not a common historical destiny with Lima's Jewry. Although the word "race" is seldom uttered by contemporary white *Limeños,* the concept is latent in their view of *Mestizos.* Debora Frank's description of these "Jewish *Mestizos,*" in her report to the *Federación Sionista del Perú* in January 1992 hints at this unconscious tendency to correlate ethnic background and class:

> Iquitos is a city [that can be visited from Lima via] an hour trip by airplane: It is not easy to arrive by car; there are no highways in good shape [in fact, there are no highways to Iquitos at all!]. Besides this, there are risks of terrorist attacks along the way. In Iquitos the subversive movement is not very perceptible, but further away in the hinterland there is [terrorism].
>
> The economic situation of the zone is, in general, problematic. The people who live close to the big cities have the minimum needed to live, housing and food, but they feel complete. . . . You see neither economic apogee nor modernism. (By the way, I was in

a five star hotel, but it lacked some normal services like air conditioning, which only worked during certain hours. . . . With the tem-
perature being 35 [Celsius], this is very important! Water cannot
be drunk and immediately after cleaning [the room], one can see
insects everywhere.) In other words, living standards are very low,
but they do not feel it.

The ["Jewish"] community was in a latent state for many years.
They have not had major contact with Lima's community since the
1960s and 1970s; recently they realized that, but, meanwhile,
mixed marriages happened in vast numbers. Not only did time
affect their marriage patterns, but also the quality and quantity of
information about Judaism, which deteriorated. [All these] led to
the problems they are undergoing now.

The interesting thing about them, as a community, is that in
spite of not being updated, they maintain themselves as an elite
and still call themselves "Jews," treasuring the little they preserve
and transmitting it to the whole family in the best way they can.
They have very little notion of Jewish culture, religion and, in general, they know very little about Israel. However, even though it
may seem incredible, they identify strongly with the little they
know and they read the same books [about Judaism], which have
been in the family for years . . . (AT).[17]

Debora Frank's report not only shows an attitude of wonderment, but
also of compassion for a people who "feel complete" despite the uncom-
fortable quality of their lives. This lack of comfort is also the reality for the
vast majority of Peruvian people, the *Mestizos*. Although some Peruvian Jews
genuinely wish to help the Iquitos community, Lima's ethnocentric milieu
conditions their view. The Judaism of Iquitos's Jewish descendants is mea-
sured according to the Judaism of average Jewish *Limeños;* however, who
measures the Judaism of Lima's community? The Jews of the capital city
consider themselves to be different from *Mestizos* and also from their main
national group of reference: the white, upper- and middle-class *Limeños*.
Therefore, the notion that a group of Jews feels absolutely comfortable
not only as Jews but also as members of the majority of Peru's population
(that "non-distinctive distinction") baffles them. Syncretism is a foreign,

exotic concept for Latin American Jews, who acculturate to their societies cautiously (always preserving an intact sense of distinction, even though, in some cases, it might be a groundless Jewish identity, as Alain Finkielkraut, author of *The Imaginary Jew,* would argue[18]).

The "exotic Jews" of Iquitos inspire wonder, compassion, and ambivalent feelings of admiration and distrust among the few Jewish *Limeños* who know about their struggle to maintain a Jewish identity: One can listen to remarks about the "Jewish *Mestizos*," such as "There must be a Jewish feeling among them!"[19] or simply, listen to commonplace reactions such as "Are there really Indian Jews? That is cool!"

The *Iquiteños'* spiritual leader, Víctor Edery, is aware of Lima's perception of his *paisanos:*

> In Lima they know that we are real Jews, but, surely, there are many who see us as the Jews of Abyssinia [Ethiopia]. I guess that there are those [in Lima] who feel superior, purely Jewish, but not all of them think this way.[20]

I found no one in Lima who compared Iquitos's descendants of Jews to Ethiopian Jews. Surprisingly, the sole figure who called them a "lost tribe" was Dror Fogel, the Israeli mayor of Ramat Ishai. In November 1991, Yared Edery López, one of Víctor Edery's sons who lived in Israel, received a call from the Israeli radio network *Kol Yisrael* (The Voice of Israel) in Jerusalem, asking him about his community, "that lost Jewish tribe" in the Amazon:

> One of my sisters was there in the studio, in front of the interviewer, and he posed questions to her and to me. He asked me if I could see the Amazon River from my house, if there were crocodiles and those types of questions.[21]

(Rachel Edery Shomron, who was in the studio during the program, clarifies that these were a few of several relevant questions about the exotic Jews in the Amazon asked by the journalist during the program.)

The isolation of Iquitos's "Jews" from their mainstream Jewish counterparts in the capital city has caused the Jews of Lima to perceive them as an exotic group somehow linked to them, but not exactly part of them. The *Mestizo* features of Iquitos's Jewish descendants make it difficult for the white Jews of Lima to identify with them; after all, they live in a country in which race and social class still play an important role in the people's psyche.[22] Of course, the Jews of Lima are Peruvians who identify themselves with their birthland, but they are also members of a clannish people who bestow upon their rabbis the responsibility of determining who is a Jew. The delicate balance between national and ethnic-religious identities makes Jewish *Limeños* oscillate between tolerance and empathy for the "Jewish *Mestizos*" but also prejudice and dogmatism toward the unorthodoxy that the Iquitos case presents. Usually, they treat their exotic *paisanos* from Iquitos with thoughtfulness, but they do not summon them to integrate with the community.

The relationship between the communities of Lima and Iquitos is ambivalent and complex. It is not an open conflict between two groups that claim to be authentic Jews, as has happened between the Baghdadi Jews of Bombay and the members of *Bene Israel*, who have settled in that Indian city. (For many years the Baghdadi did not accept the Jewishness of the *Bene Israel* Jews.)[23] Conversely, the Jews of Lima show enormous sympathy to Iquitos's descendants of Jews. Nevertheless, the community's reticence to fully integrate them into their school, their congregations, and their institutions shows that there are subtle, deeply held prejudices regarding a group whose features and surrounding culture are more akin to the vast majority of Peruvians.

The approach of Lima's Jewry to Iquitos's "Jewish *Mestizos*" can be likened to the case of the Jewish communities of Shanghai and Kaifeng in China during the first decades of the twentieth century. Jews settled in Kaifeng sometime during the twelfth century. Hundreds of years of isolation pushed the impoverished descendants of these Jews to the brink of total assimilation. Therefore, encouraged by British and American rabbis and Jewish philanthropists, a group of people from the organized Jewish community of Shanghai created the Society for the Rescue of the Chinese Jews in 1901. There were unsuccessful attempts at building a Jewish school in Kaifeng, and at studying the culture and history of that community; the challenge of restoring Judaism to a community that had already internalized the Chinese Confucian culture proved impossible to overcome. After two decades of somnolence, the Society for the Rescue of the Chinese Jews in Shanghai bestirred itself and made new attempts to "rescue" the Kaifeng Jews in the 1920s, but only their history remained.[24]

Like those of Shanghai and Kaifeng, Lima's and Iquitos's Jewish communities present a history of approximation and withdrawal between Jews and remnants of Israel who are united and separated by their Peruvianism.

◆

THE EXOTIC JEWS OF LIMA AND ISRAEL: A VIEW FROM IQUITOS

To the descendants of Jews who live in Iquitos, other Jews—the Jews of Lima, Israelis, in other words, the Jewish people—are foreign, a mystery, the center with which to identify, but, nevertheless, strangers. Few of these *Iquiteños* have visited Lima; certainly, Israel remains a mythical place, almost extraterrestrial. When speaking of the larger Jewish world, their conversation revolves around the names of Rabbi Bronstein, the Israeli ambassador to Peru, or the Jews who sporadically visit the city (like this researcher who came from Miami to spend several weeks with them in 1995). In fact, the Jewish *paisanos* have had startlingly little contact with mainstream Jewry. Then why should anybody be surprised that many *Iquiteños* believe that *all* Jews, in Lima, in Israel, in the whole world, observe religious traditions?

A "Jewish *Mestizo*," who has lived in Lima since the late 1970s is neither the first nor the last *Iquiteño* "Jew" to be shocked to learn of widespread Jewish secularism:

> Before I came to Lima, I thought that all the Jews were a very religious people, maybe because I idealized that I was the son of a Jew. Eventually I realized that many Jews do not perform religious practices and that, for example, Shabbat is something theoretical to them. They open their stores during that holy day and they keep thinking in the Baalistic [reference to the Middle Eastern ancient god Baal] vein of idolizing money. . . . I am very radical about this: to be Jewish is to comply with Jewish religion. Either we are or we are not Jews, but we cannot take a middle ground. If I were totally Jewish, I would be a religious, observant Jew. I would not admit

185

the possibility of being a secular Jew. Do you understand? The
problem is that now I realize that there are Jews who do not look
like Jews, and non-Jews who look like Jews.[25]

Sara Bendayán García, an *Iquiteña* who has visited Lima several times, agrees with this view: "Why in Lima do they [the Jews] not comply with Jewish precepts if they all are Jews? For me, they are not Jews. The bottom line is to comply with the Commandments!"[26] Meanwhile, Ramón Coriat asserts that, in Lima, the Jewish religion is followed properly: "See how they read the prayer books from right to left there, while here in Iquitos we have to read from left to right!"[27] (For this gentleman the fact that the *Limeños* read Hebrew is enough to prove the intensity of their religious convictions.)

The younger generations of descendants of Jews in Iquitos, who never had contact with Lima, idealize other Jews: They see Jews as a very ethical and united people, modern yet attached to their traditions and to their ancient culture. *Iquiteños* presume that Lima, Israel, or any Jewish community would receive them with open arms. They express such naive sentiments as:

> *I guess they [Lima's Jews] are warm people; they would teach us*
> *many things"; "The Jews are an extremely smart, united, and thriv-*
> *ing people; that is why they are rich"; "The young Israelis are mod-*
> *ern people, but they also have strong religious convictions";*
> *"I imagine Jews to be very clannish, but they would always receive*
> *people like me in their houses as equals. The Jews never*
> *discriminate!*[28]

However, those who have lived in Lima or have sent their children there to study in universities disagree, pointing out that the clannish community of the capital city discriminated against them.

The State of Israel's synthesis of holiness and modernity amazes these isolated "Jews." They speak about the Holy Land, the spiritual Israel, God's nation, pausing to marvel at its state of development. On November 16, 1991, Elías Bensimón Puyó lectured at the *Sociedad Israelita de*

Iquitos about his first trip to Israel, which he visited when one of his daughters made *aliyah:*

> He told how the non-stop flight lasts eighteen hours. He expressed that, once in Israel, he found a beautiful country, excellent communications, blooming commerce; the most important cities, among many others, are Tiberias, Haifa, Heilat [Eilat]; the population consists of Jews, Arabs, and other groups; another important city is Nazareth. The day after his [Elías Bensimón's] arrival, he found himself missing nothing [in Iquitos], and his health was good due to the nice weather. In Israel there are also universities, technological colleges, and nicely preserved zoos where many animals, including some native to the Amazonian jungle (such as the partridge), are protected and well assisted. There are submarine environments with transparent walls, through which the Israeli and any person of the population can appreciate large amounts of fish, common and ornamental. Regarding flight traffic, they have many commercial airplanes with a minimum of fifty flights every day. One can also appreciate large waves of tourists . . . (AT).[29]

Exotic Jews live in Israel, people who go to universities and colleges, who have zoos, a huge aquarium, and important cities! (Elías Bensimón mentioned not Jerusalem and Tel Aviv, but Jesus' Nazareth and Peter's Tiberias!) Most "Jewish *Mestizos*" who have relatives or who have lived temporarily in the Peruvian capital, in Israel, or in big cities, understand and accept variety within the Jewish people. However, their comments focus on those archetypes and themes utilized by activist Jews anywhere when addressing Jewish audiences. For example, in a letter to Sandy Barak Cassinelli (of the *Federación Sionista del Perú*), Alicia Assayag Chávez wrote: "Reading the history of our people, I draw out from it the teachings of [our] strength, perseverance, tenacity, and hope. . . . And after 1,814 years, from 133 to 1947 C.E., the *paisanos* [Jews] succeeded in recovering our land, that our Lord *Adonai* promised to Jacob [the patriarch]" (AT).[30] The martyrdom of the Holocaust and the glories of the State of Israel are frequent themes in the letters and documents of the *Sociedad de Beneficiencia Israelita de Iquitos*, preserving archetypal notions that transcend the boundaries of time and historical fact.

The idea that nearly all Jews are wealthy is widespread and very much admired by the "Jewish *Mestizos*": "Lima's Jews are rich as Iquitos's Jews once were . . . and [they] are also honest and hard-working people."[31] Despite the irony of their own poverty, their idealized portraits of "aristocratic pure Jews" in Lima endure, making them feel proud of their lineage, of "their blood and race." Although "race" is a word that has vanished from the everyday vocabulary of *Limeños*, it remains in that of *Iquiteños*. The term "race," used and abused throughout the years by politicians and scholars, remains a powerful construct among Amazonian inhabitants. In the view of Iquitos's descendants of Jews, race and peoplehood are similar conceptions. Although "Jewish *Mestizos*" are perfectly aware of the physical differences between them and the white Jews of Lima, they nevertheless consider themselves as belonging to the same "race." According to them, what distinguishes a Jewish *Limeño* from a Jewish *Iquiteño* is the "degree of Jewish purity." This is the matter to be discussed in the following pages.

✦

"Pure Jews," "Half Jews," "Quarter Jews": Labels and Levels of Meaning

Discrimination is not such a strong factor in Iquitos compared to other Peruvian cities where racial categories and social class play a determinant role in the way people of different ethnic groups interact with each other. Probably, this is why the *Iquiteño* utilizes the word "race" indiscriminately. The inhabitants of this predominantly *Mestizo* city, where cultural homogeneity is widespread, do not merge their conception of ethnicity with that of class when they use the term "race." Instead, in Iquitos, race is mainly a matter of lineage, of ancestry.

The "Jewish *Mestizos*," therefore, frequently discuss their degree of Judaism using racial categories:

> Samolsky [a Rumanian Jew who came from Lima in the 1940s] used to say that he was a "pure Jew," and that we were Mestizos of the third, fourth, or fifth generation; therefore, we did not have

"pure Hebrew blood." That is why we quarreled a lot [vivíamos encontrados]. "I am the only Jew of first generation here," Samolsky used to say, and so he boasted all the time.

✦

You are Jewish from all points of view [addressing the researcher]. . . . You are biologically Jewish, and, although I am not 100 percent Jewish, I feel I am linked with the race of my father.

✦

God had separated Abraham from the Chaldeans and his [Abraham's] descendants, giving Isaac a purpose, and God gave him the law. That is why Jews must preserve their race, like the gypsy who does not mix his race. We must not allow the race to be spoiled, and that is the reason why I will not allow my children to marry non-Jews. Our race is already too mixed!

✦

There is no such thing as a "pure Jew." Throughout the ages, diverse races have mixed since the time of Abraham when the Hebrews were tribes. . . . If the Limeño *Jews see themselves as "pure Jews," it is a matter we are not concerned about because a "pure Jew" is the one who proves that he has a truthful devotion to our religion.*[32]

Iquiteño Jews who live in Lima and have been accepted as members of the capital city's Jewish institutions also draw upon this concept of race:

I am 50 percent Jewish because my father was Jewish and my mother was not. However, when I married and my wife converted, it changed things, so our children are 100 percent Jewish. There are no reasons to doubt our Judaism.

✦

You are blond, Ariel [addressing the researcher]. You look like an Aryan. By any chance do you think Isaiah, Samuel, or Moses had your appearance? I am 75 percent Jewish because three of my four grandparents were Jews. There is no such thing as a "pure Jew," but in this community [Lima] as in almost all the Jewish

communities of the world there is this wrong idea that there are
"uncontaminated pure Jews." Maybe a bunch of Orthodox families
are really "pure Jewish," because they never mixed with other
people, but most of us are as mixed as the paisanos *of Iquitos.*[33]

Those *Limeños* who question the Jewishness of Iquitos's descendants of Jews do not overtly use the word "race" in their arguments against accepting them as members of the Jewish people; instead, they express their doubts in terms of religion, of Jewish law. However, when a non-Orthodox Jewish *Limeño* rejects the idea that Peruvian *Mestizos* can be Jews, he is perhaps concealing a subtle form of discrimination behind the label of "religion." After all, most contemporary Jews, including those in Lima, define themselves as non-religious, regarding Judaism as a matter of feeling and identification.

For centuries, the issue of race in Peru had been intertwined, in subtle ways, with the issue of religion; however, it was not until the 1990 presidential election that race and religion were paired together in the nation's spotlight.[34] During that campaign, some opponents of candidate Alberto Fujimori claimed that his Japanese origin was the cause for the massive support he received from Evangelical Christian voters in a predominantly Catholic country. Ethnicity and religion were exploited for electoral purposes.

Similarly, in a country where the popular Catholicism of the provinces is seen as belonging to the *Cholo, Charapa,* or *Mestizo* traditions, it should be no surprise that Lima's mainstream Judaism would link ethnic characteristics to a "popular Amazonian Judaism" that they perceive as exotic.

✦

Echoes of Jewish Peoplehood through Discourses of Selfhood and *"Imaginario"*

Up until now, I have discussed how the descendants of Amazonian Jews have fabricated and deepened their identity as an "imagined community." Within their history and ethnography they have included religious concepts and rituals, a sense of lineage, the existence of an Israelite cemetery, the community's relation to the State of Israel, its understanding of the Holocaust, a series of inconstant encounters with Lima's Jewry, and the prevalent notion of being a remnant of Israel. However, what has also shaped their unique collective identity is a very peculiar "mythical-historical consciousness."[35] I will discuss two aspects of this consciousness, which can provide us with additional clues to help us explore the syncretic psyche of the "Jewish *Mestizos*": First, I will refer to the "Jewish obsession syndrome," a kind of recessive gene carried by some Jewish descendants, no matter how assimilated they may be. Second, I will examine the role the Imaginary *(El Imaginario)* plays in how the *Iquiteños* conceive of Judaism.

The cases of Ronald Reategui Levy and Alicia Assayag Chávez from Iquitos illustrate what I call the "Jewish obsession syndrome." Although this attitude can be explained on historical and sociological grounds, I insist as a historian, who is also a storyteller, that these stories result from a hereditary syndrome that the Jewish medieval philosopher Ibn Verga defined as "that incurable disease called Judaism." Both of these individuals have been writing to Lima for more than five years, asking for help in settling in the Promised Land with full Israeli citizenship and the subsequent financial aid provided by the Law of Return. In addition, both adamantly long to become part of the Jewish people.

As previously mentioned, Ronald Reategui Levy is one of the main parties responsible for the renewal of relations between the Lima and Iquitos communities. In the late 1980s, he asked Debora Frank and Israeli functionaries in Lima send him a Tanakh (Hebrew Bible), a *siddur* (prayer book), books of Hebrew grammar, dictionaries, and the *Kuzari* (a book written by the Spanish Jewish medieval philosopher and poet Judah ha-Levi); he also asked for information about Israel.[36] In many letters, the young man described his situation: The grandson of a Jewish immigrant who had come to the Amazon, he was proud of being a Jewish descendant, and he wished to settle in Israel before it was too late. "I am twenty-eight years old," he wrote, "and a single man who could settle down very soon, and to be honest, I think that if I marry a *goy* [non-Jewish] woman I will die of shame, because I am worried about my future children."[37]

By March 1988 Ronald Reategui Levy's worst fears had come to pass. Yet despite the fact that he married an *Iquiteña*, he still was requesting help for legitimizing his marriage according to the Jewish religion.[38] In 1989 the couple had a son whom they named Uri. When Manuel Harmon, a Conservative rabbi, came to Iquitos six months later as a tourist, Ronald dragged him to a hospital, and asked him to bless the six-month-old baby while a doctor performed the circumcision. In the meantime, Ronald had succeeded in sending his brother Ramón to Israel (Ramón currently lives in the city of Eilat), preferring to remain in Iquitos himself in order to tend to his sick mother, paying for her treatments with the excellent income he earned from his job in *Petroperú,* the Peruvian oil company. Still, he postponed his plan to go to Israel. By the 1990s, after he had been promoted in the company and had a family to sustain, Ronald Reategui Levy wanted guarantees that he could make a comparable living in Israel: "If I can be assured that I will have a job once I arrive in Israel I will depart tomorrow!"[39]

My diary tells the rest of the story:

> It is June 1995. I meet Ronald Reategui Levy in a café. He tells me about his wife; his two sons, Uri and Netanel; his job; his dream of immigrating to the Holy Land; his problems finding somebody to help him to realize that dream; his readiness to leave if he can work in oil fields or in agriculture ("You have to see my garden; I make hybrid plants"); his house ("You have to see it, especially my front door"). Finally, he tells me how he has improved his Hebrew. Trained to be skeptical, I begin to ask him questions in Hebrew, and he answers me in good Hebrew! "How did your learn?" I ask him. He replies: "I learned the Hebrew letters thanks to Yared Edery López and a few classes I attended in Lima (I lived there a few months); the vocabulary I picked up with my Hebrew Bible and a dictionary. You know, the nights in the oil fields are long, and the workers gather to drink and talk. I spend hours in my room, reading the Bible with my dictionary. I have being doing that for more than seven years."
>
> It takes me a while to realize that he is not exaggerating, that he really speaks Hebrew, that he really read the *Kuzari,* a book that even many secular Jews have never heard about. So I decide to go to his house. What does he want to show me? Yes, his garden. Yes, his fishpond. Yes, his wife and children, and the front door. What is so special about it? When you go to a humble tin-roofed house on the perimeter of Iquitos, a green zone of small-scattered houses where everybody is a farmer, and you see a wooden door with a

huge, carved Star of David, a *menorah* (the seven-armed Jewish candlestick), and the Hebrew words *"Beth Levy"* (House of Levy), there are reasons to feel a tug at the heart. I am really in front of a Jewish house in the middle of the Amazonian jungle. . . . I am before something that makes me feel very small; I thought I was coming from a universe to a little town, but I have just traveled from the little town of my big aspirations to the huge universe where the star of that door is located. . . .

The case of Alicia Assayag Chávez, granddaughter of immigrant León Assayag Nahón, who in a civil court did not acknowledge his own son Arturo before returning to Morocco, also illustrates how proud some individuals can feel about their Jewish roots. Like Ronald Reategui Levy, Alicia Assayag Chávez has been asking Lima's institutions to help her immigrate to Israel together with her two daughters and her husband. Because she had no written proof that her grandfather was León Assayag Nahón, the Israeli immigration authorities denied her application. In various letters addressed to Debora Frank and Sandy Barak Cassinelli, members of the *Federación Sionista del Perú,* Alicia Assayag Chávez explained again and again who her grandfather was. She was able to prove that her father, Arturo Assayag, was a member of the *Instituto Cultural Peruano-Israelí de Iquitos* in the 1960s; she sent pictures of a gravestone in Iquitos's Israelite cemetery with a similar family name (Isidro Saadia Assayac, buried in 1912) to show how there were Jews with the same last name in Iquitos; and she sent photocopies of pages from a book about the Jews of Morocco to demonstrate that her last name was very common within the Jewish communities of that country. Debora Frank and Sandy Barak Cassinelli sent her case file to Israel, but her request that she be granted the right to immigrate within the framework of the Law of Return was rejected.

On June 23, 1993, Sandy Barak Cassinelli wrote a letter to Abraham Azancot, president of a Jewish congregation in Tangier, to request his aid in finding documents belonging to León Assayag Nahón that could help demonstrate his presence in the Amazon.[40] While waiting for an answer, Alicia Assayag Chávez knocked at other doors and even wrote a letter to an Elías Assayag from Manaus, to find out whether their two families were linked. (Most of the Jews who came to Iquitos stopped and spent some time in that Brazilian Amazon city.) Finally, on August 4, 1993, Elías Assa-yag answered her letter, explaining the origin of their last name and ex-plaining who his ancestors were. Unfortunately, he had never met any León Assayag Nahón.[41] Alicia Assayag Chávez continued to search for clues that would help her solve the mystery of her identity, always dreaming that she would one day be able to settle in Israel:

> . . . I will never give up hope. That is why I keep looking and look-ing for documentary proof of my Jewish ancestors in archives and libraries, interviewing elderly paisanos. I must tell you that I have re-viewed documents in the municipal library of the prefecture, and in diverse private libraries in Iquitos, checking books, newspapers from the beginning of the [twentieth] century. May God give me strength to keep going in search of proof of my Jewish background. . . .[42]

In her relentless search for answers Alicia Assayag Chávez even resorted to non-traditional strategies, such as visiting a priest:

> I went to see Father Joaquín [García] and to ask him to write a let-ter to any priest in Morocco who could find out the name of my father there. He told me he knew a priest in Tangier, a Spanish city. Perfect! I said, that is the place where my grandfather was born, and so, Father Joaquín tried to help me.[43]

On February 18, 1994, Father Ramón Lourido, from the general vicar-ship of the archbishopric of Tangier, replied to Father Joaquín García's letter, explaining that even though he was not the best person to locate León Assayag Nahón's birth certificate, he had contacted the leader of the city's 250-member Jewry, Mr. Azancot, to try to find it. However, the priest added that "he said that they [the Jewish community] had nothing partic-ular about Iquitos; instead, they have a lot [of information] about immi-gration to the American continent."[44] In his letter, Father Lourido also provided Father Joaquín García with the names of several books about Moroccan Jews, and he mentioned that a Catalonian friend who resided in Tangier confirmed that he had been a friend of one León Assayag many years ago, and that this man's son now lived in Caracas, Venezuela. In

1995, Sandy Barak Cassinelli attempted again to obtain information from Mr. Azancot in Tangier; she is still waiting for his reply.[45]

Where is Alicia Assayag Chávez now? In my diary, I record my impressions:

> Alicia Assayag Chávez, a nice, very sensitive woman, has been struggling for many years to learn about Judaism and settle in Israel. She still lives in Iquitos, but travels twice a year to Lima to visit her two daughters (who are registered in Hebrew classes in the *Colegio León Pinelo*). She is a very active member of Iquitos's Israelite Society, she daydreams constantly about Israel, and she feels profoundly Jewish and rejects any Christian notion or ritual: "There is only one God, no three in one, no saints, nothing of that. . . . We are an ancient people and we must remain together and gather in Israel from the four corners of the world. The Jewish people have suffered a lot. I have suffered a lot too, so I am not afraid of belonging to our people. Our community in Iquitos is too precarious, but we do what we can. Although during Shabbat services we all feel happy, we cannot be totally happy until we celebrate Shabbat in the holy land." This is the way she talks, and she cries while she tells her stories, her travails, and hopes. Some people in Lima told me that she was too exaggerated, too obsessive, because of the way she mentions God all the time and her fantasies. But I did not see it that way. She is a hypersensitive woman, a little weepy and maybe a little bit nuts, but don't you need to be a little bit crazy to feel Jewish in Iquitos? I am positive that, without a little bit of that "madness" which maintains the mental health of this people, whatever Judaism remains here would have vanished a long time ago.

In his essay entitled "The Real Cause of My Grandmother's Death," Israeli writer Amos Oz claims that "Lies are real. Not factual, not genuine, but real they still are. . . ." And he continues, "So are dreams. So are inventions, and nightmares and fantasies and pain and fear and desire. Macbeth is real, and so are the Emperor's new clothes, no less than Jacob's ladder and Ivan Karamazov's demon and the continent of Atlantis and even the part-woman part-fish sirens who seduce sailors out at sea; they, too, are real [as are *bufeos colorados, Tunchis,* and Souls Retracing Their Steps, I would add], because they all affect or have affected the world, just as the obsession of cleanliness and terror of microbes brought about my grandmother's death. The terror, not the microbes." (Although his grandmother officially died of a heart attack, Oz maintains that she died of cleanliness or terror of contamination, starting from the moment when she had decreed from the balcony of her home in Jerusalem, in 1933, that "the Levant is full of microbes.")[46]

Similarly, the titanic efforts of some "Jewish *Mestizos*" to observe a Jewish life result from having decreed that their Judaism is real. So just as Amos Oz's grandmother died from an obsession with cleanliness, so too these "Jewish *Mestizos*" rejoice and suffer because they are infected by a syndrome of Jewish obsession.

In my diary, I recorded brief biographical sketches of informants whose voices deserve to be listened to, whose dreams are worthy of being recorded on paper:

> Don Víctor Edery Morales, a seventy-five-year-old son of a Moroccan immigrant, is the leader of the *Sociedad de Beneficiencia Israelita de Iquitos* and its spiritual guide. "He is the flame that refuses to be extinguished," as one *Iquiteño* defined it, the burning bush witnessed by Moses, a Jewish poet may say.
>
> Don Víctor's bedroom serves as an idiosyncratic model of the blending between his Jewish historical consciousness and his Amazonian cultural paradigms: tottering tin-plated shelves are filled with all kind of books about Christianity, Islam, Buddhism, Taoism ("a Jew must learn about other religions," he insists), metaphysics, and, of course, about kabbalah, Jewish history, and Jewish rituals. Among the books, one can see a poster of the ancient walled city of Jerusalem and a postcard of former Israeli Prime Minister David Ben-Gurion next to a bunch of pictures of his family in Israel, Montreal, Miami, and Iquitos, and, old photographs of his father. Hanging on the wall is a silver "*Shalom,*" next to a *menorah,* which barely conceals the poster of a very voluptuous, unabashed woman. All over the wall, a gallery of sex symbols keeps company with the

woman who "poses for the *menorah*." On a wooden table, which functions as his desk, Don Víctor keeps plastic bags containing the Hebrew Bible, prayer shawls, an ornamented and colorful Moroccan *kippah* (skull cap), and Hebrew prayer books covered with pictures of beautiful women: "You know, I use this to cover the books and protect them from the dust." I make a joke about the pictures, and he explains with a smile showing his broken teeth: "These posters and pictures remind me of when I was a *chibolito* [very young person] and I had women like these."

The sacred and the profane mixes together in this bedroom, which epitomizes the *paisanos'* smooth way of balancing what, to the foreign eye, seems contradictory or, rather, unsuitable. Don Víctor spends a couple of hours proudly showing me each possession: books and pictures, gifts from Israel, and objects from the Amazon. He explains everything as if he were lecturing an audience: "This is a picture of David Ben-Gurion, the hero of Israel's independence, and these are pictures of my sons Yared and Víctor when they fought in the 'Yom Kippur War' in Israel. . . . This is my mother, my daughter in Israel and that?. . . That is a woman that I liked; she lives nearby!"

Why does he not spend his last years in Israel? Don Víctor Edery meditates and at a leisurely pace answers: "I have a mission in Iquitos; besides, I want to be buried next to my father in the Israelite cemetery."

Jaime Vásquez Izquierdo, a music teacher and history professor, also believes that his role is to stay in Iquitos because "I am already sixty years old, and I can help the youngsters to learn about Judaism and go to Israel . . . although sometimes I still dream of settling in the Holy Land."

Don Jaime Vásquez Izquierdo is, no doubt, the most learned person in the community. An intellectual, he is the author of two books, *Cordero de Dios* (Parts I and II), stories about his childhood that he prefers to call "reminiscence literature." He is a quiet, placid man whose humble house seems to be a kind of public library (his students come all the time to borrow books or sit and read about history, music, religion, literature . . . you name it!).

Don Jaime plays the violin for me: he plays two Sephardic songs that he remembers his mother singing to him when he was a kid. I can identify the melody of one of the songs. He has also developed the voice of an opera singer, and now that he learned some Hebrew prayers, it is a pleasure to listen to him in the Shabbat service on Friday evening. He organized the "Hebrew School" for those interested in studying to convert to Judaism (following Rabbi Bronstein's plan) and he is teaching himself Hebrew. Out of all the "Jewish *Mestizos*" I am meeting, Don Jaime is the most consistent in his enthusiasm and obsession to be Jewish.

Why be Jewish? I ask him several times during our frequent meetings in his house or in Ari's Burger [the "McDonalds" of Iquitos]: "I just cannot explain it! I have experienced many phases in my life. I was an atheist, a communist, an existentialist, an *aprista* (supporter of Haya de la Torre's political party: APRA) . . . but nevertheless, I always considered myself to be Jewish. My Judaism never was lost; it was like an underlying structure . . . always there, in one way or another. I have arrived at the conclusion that you cannot stop being Jewish even if you try!" Don Jaime recalls frequently what he calls his "romantic Judaism" in the 1960s, even before the establishment of the *Instituto Cultural Peruano-Israelí de Iquitos:* "Moisés Bendayán Casique and I were daydreaming all the time about Israel. We spoke about Jerusalem, Masada; we discussed the exile, the possibility of settling in Israel. He was a poet, a bohemian. I was a romantic . . . maybe I am still a romantic!"

A twenty-five-year-old student of economy, Marco Mesía Rodríguez, also gives me that "I just cannot explain it!" answer when I ask him why he is so adamantly convinced that he wants to be Jewish: "I just don't feel Christian; I just feel Jewish! I have read many books about Judaism; I would like to settle in Israel when I finish my studies in the university. Maybe it all began when I decided to write a paper about immigrants in the Amazon and I found the name of my great-grandfather, Toribio Mesía, in history books. He came from Morocco, like most of the Jews during the rubber-boom period. Then I began to inquire more about the history of the Jews in Iquitos. One day, I learned that there was a

Jewish community and I decided that I wanted to feel part of something, that I was lacking something in my life . . . a sense of belonging. So I went to Don Víctor Edery's house for Shabbat and I loved it; I felt it like part of my faith.

You know? . . . I often cannot go to Shabbat because I have classes on Friday evening, and many times I listen to the professor talking about inflation, interest rates, and all those concepts and I think, my God, what am I doing here? I should be in Shabbat!"

Behind all the historical, socioeconomic, and cultural factors that shape the identity of Iquitos's descendants of Jews lies a determinant emotional element that includes an intellectual component conditioning the way "Jewish *Mestizos*" conceive of references from Jewish history and culture.

Scholars have coined the term *"Imaginario"* to describe their own ways of interpreting this concept,[47] but I understand the Imaginary as a symbolic repertoire that plays a role in the mythical-historical consciousness of any group or individual. To create this repertoire, groups reconstruct collective notions of peoplehood upon which to superimpose their own ancient and modern historical, religious, and cultural paradigms, local and foreign (universal) archetypes, and fantastic conceptions.[48] Hence, the members of the group consider other people's traditions, beliefs, symbols, myths, and stories as part of their own historical consciousness. I will provide some examples:

Enrique Mesía Ochoa likes "to play being Jewish" with his four-year-old daughter:

> We play that we are Jews. I put a towel over her head, like a turban, and I tell her: "You are Jewish." "Am I a Jew?" she asks me. "So what is my name?" and I tell her, "Your name is Avadalalara" and she asks, "What is your name, Daddy?" "I am the Jewish Balam."[49]

This instance shows how Enrique Mesía Ochoa blends Turkish and Arab characteristics with his Jewish notions. The turban and invented Arab names (even the non-Hebrew biblical character Balam) have become part of his Jewish historical consciousness. Also, Enrique Mesía Ochoa has some natural lines that form a Star of David in the palm of his left hand, hinting that magic realism is not only an invention of talented Latin American writers, but also an intrinsic feature of the continent. He interprets that Star of David as a sign proving his *"Berraco" [Marrano]* origin. (It took me a while to figure out that he believes himself to be descended from *Marranos*, a term he confuses with *berracos*); therefore, Mesía Ochoa believes that all descendants of Spanish Jews who came to the region have, more or less, the same sign in their palms. He claims that other people in his family have the Star of David in the palm of their hands, although not so conspicuously.)

This fantastic notion about *Marranos* recalls Israel Bento Mass's belief that Jews do not eat *chancho* (pork) because some time in the past they were transformed into *Marranos* (swine). Again, fantastic interpretations of historical events influence the historical consciousness of the "Jewish *Mestizos.*" As shown by the last two examples, the Iquitos descendants of Jews mix their historical notions about *Marranism* with fantastic interpretations of reality.

Another example of what I call *Imaginario* can be discerned in the words of Pedro Reategui Panduro, explaining during a Shabbat service why the Jews must use a *kippah* (skullcap) in the synagogue:

> The kippah *reminds us that Judaism has been one of the most humiliated religions in the world. I read in a book that, in the times of the Inquisition, the Jews were forced to walk in the streets with a huge hat as a symbol of extreme humility, to point them out as members of a low stratum in society. Therefore, maybe unconsciously, the Jew keeps using the* kippah. *It is a tradition that comes from the medieval times. Beforehand, only the high priest utilized the* kippah, *but now, Jews wear it to remember those moments of hardship, so we must be humble persons. Judaism is not arrogant; it is not a religion that intends to be the only religion. Judaism invites us to be tolerant. . . . Indeed, the fact that other religions considered themselves to be more saintly, more pure, led to things like the killing of six million people during the Holocaust.*[50]

This explanation combines highly personal interpretations of historical facts from different epochs with what he has learned in books about

Judaism and Jewish history. It is true that priests in biblical times covered their heads, but, then, so did every Jew. It is true that Jews accused of being *judaizantes* (those who taught their heretical religion to New Christians) were forced to wear *sanbenitos* (the habit of the penitents); this outfit sometimes included a large, sharp-ended hat, but certainly this is not the reason why Jews should cover their heads (not only in the synagogue but everywhere). Although one could argue that European Christianity created a fertile ground for the emergence of anti-Semitism, which ultimately led to the massive collaboration and indifference of millions of people during the Holocaust, religion was not the essence of the ideology behind Nazism.

Based on the little he knows about the Holocaust, Ramón Coriat argues that Jewish law forbids anyone to tattoo the arms (he relates Jewish law to the numbers that Nazis stamped on the arms of concentration camp prisoners).

A woman admits that she has dreamed of Israel's *pyramids* since she was a child; a man attributes characteristics of the Amazonian descendants of Jews to Jesus: "He was like us, he had many women." An old man "reveals" to the community that the Pope is Jewish and "that proves that there are Jews all around the world, like the prophecy says." A woman believes that the Jews are descendants of Ben Hur: "Didn't you see it in the movies?" León Delmar Rengifo describes Israel's "*Seven* [Six] Day War" as a fight between the Jewish state and a bunch of ancient and modern countries such as Assyria, Egypt, and Jordan, emphasizing how Jews arrived at the Plaza de Armas [main square] of Damascus and put up a flag.

The imagination of the "Jewish *Mestizos*" is prolific; the imagination of the scholar who conducted this research and wrote this book is also fertile. In the next chapter, readers will understand that "highly personal interpretations" of history can also be a "problem-solution" for scholars who learn to see their objects of investigation as subjects. After all, this is much more than a historical study. It is a human story.

8

THE RESEARCHER AS PROTAGONIST

"'[The storytellers] are a tangible proof that storytelling
can be something more than entertainment,' it
occurred to me to say to him. 'Something
primordial, something that the very existence
of a people may depend on. Maybe that's what
impressed me so. One doesn't always know
why one is moved by things, *Mascarita.* They
strike some secret chords, and that's that.'"
—Mario Vargas Llosa, *The Storyteller*

"There was a time when I thought you came
from the nothingness, from a silly little
town, toward the perfect, this civilized [urban-
modern] existence. Now, I have discovered
that I am the one going from the authentic nothingness
toward the real wholeness, looking for you." (AT)
—Alicia Freilich, *Cláper*

I WENT TO Iquitos as a historian, an ethnographer, a social scientist, some-
one who would keep a distance from the subjects of his investigation.
Sometimes I thought I was the right man for the job. I am a Jewish Latin
American, raised in the Jewish community in Caracas, Venezuela, consist-
ing of thirty thousand souls, mainstream compared to the three thousand
Jews of Lima, although peripheral when compared to other cities where I

have lived: Jerusalem, Philadelphia, and Miami. Other factors, as well, made me seemingly well-suited to accomplish my research. I lived in Israel for more than a year, where, with members of Kibbutz Maagan Michael, I had the opportunity to visit frequently Ethiopian immigrants who had recently settled in the town of Binyamina. I had also experienced myself what it is like to be a newcomer in Israel.

Was I the right candidate for this project? I was a historian with an M.A. in Jewish studies. My years of study at Gratz College in Philadelphia and at the University of Miami gave me the professional tools necessary to research and write this work. Equally important, perhaps, I have an insider's understanding of Jewish obsessions and that Jewish sense and "non-sense" of humor that can affect objective studies such as this one. I also know Latin America's slippery sense of reality and fantasy because I am Venezuelan. I know what it is to live in a Latin American capital, but I am equally comfortable in small cities and little towns in the country-side. I even have some familiarity with rural life, having worked in citrus orchards during my six months on the kibbutz.

My professional background and my familiarity with Latin American Jewish institutions, then, led me to believe that I was perfect for this research study. That is, until I arrived in Iquitos. Once in this remote Ama-zonian city, my work interviewing the city's descendants of Jews eventu-ally led to my becoming an honorary member of the community. This posed a quandary since it made it impossible for me to write an objective account of the history and identity of Iquitos's "Jews." My emotions became involved and I began to question the identity of Lima's Jews. Even more problematic for an objective historian, I began to feel insecure about my own Jewishness. I succumbed to the *Iquiteños'* requests to organize lectures for them about Judaism, to participate in the Shabbat services, and to teach them to recite prayers. I found myself asserting that I would return to Iquitos and assist them in their endeavor of immigrating to Israel.

These experiences transformed me into an admirer rather than an examiner of the community that I was studying. As I mentioned in a pre-vious chapter, the most telling moment in my metamorphosis came when I wrote in my personal diary what I felt upon beholding the door to Ronald Reategui Levy's home, carved with a *menorah*, a Star of David, and the Hebrew words, *"Beth Levy"* (House of Levy):

I am really in front of a Jewish house in the middle of the Amazonian jungle. . . . I am before something that makes me feel very small, I thought I was coming from a universe to a little town; in reality I have just arrived from the little town of my big aspirations to the huge universe in which the star [of David] of that door is located. . . .

I began to review my diary and I saw that it was a mistake to record my emotional reactions on the same pages as my objective findings. My "Messiah complex," that urge to help others, particularly the lost and the down-hearted, had defeated my professionalism. In this drama of the Amazon, I had become a protagonist, molding the identity and shaping the history of Iquitos's "Jewish *Mestizos*." It was too late to regret my involvement: I was now as much a subject as my study's original subjects. At the time, I had no idea how I would write an objective ethnohistory of what I was researching.

The clues began to present themselves when I departed the jungle. Back in Lima, as I interviewed other Jews and lectured to them about what I had witnessed in Iquitos (this exchange was part of a deal with one of my sponsors), I began to realize that my own identity could provide some insights into understanding the Jewishness of *Limeños*, of *Iquiteños*, and, by and large, of contemporary Jews. I also realized that when I talked to non-Jews about the Iquitos community, I referred to them not only as "they," but also as "we."[1] I saw that my involvement in my subject's community affairs was not the all-important matter I had thought it to be; ultimately, questions of my own identity would be implicit in my codification of their constructions and their discourses. Therefore, recognizing these truths, I decided to embrace my role as a Jewish Latin American researcher/storyteller and, explicitly, to analyze it. This decision is the origin of this chapter, which, of course, has led me to the work of other researchers who have confronted similar questions: Should the researcher limit him- or herself to giving an unenthusiastic account of the ongoing history and the vibrant identity of a people, or should he or she also provide sincere descriptions of how that history and identity are experienced by others? Isn't recognizing our own subjectivity the key to objectivity, even as we attempt to be as objective as we can? If so, why not allow readers to grasp our perplexity, together with the actual data we present? The development of historical and anthropological studies of still-existing communities has definitely reached a crucial moment, in which heeding the scholar's self-critical voice has become essential if the scholar intends to provide an honest, accurate representation of the way his subjects' historical consciousness manifests itself.[2]

Any piece of a people's history, especially contemporary and oral history, has as much to tell about that people as it does about the historian who writes it; therefore, as a soul retracing his steps in the Amazon, I will also attempt to track the main protagonists' steps of this story.

◆

THE RELIGION OF THE SCHOLAR

Since I have been describing and analyzing the "Jewish *Mestizos*" from a scholarly pedestal, this ivory tower where I stroll about peering down on the world of historical fact, trying to convince myself and my readers of the accuracy and wisdom of my work, I must begin by providing some insights about the institutional framework that empowered me with the right to conduct my research and to receive my credentials as a historian.

My study of the "Jewish *Mestizos*," and the acceptance of what I initially wrote about them, gave me entrance to a close circle of people all around the world who call themselves scholars, professors, or doctors. (I have problems accepting this last label because my father and my brother are medical doctors; therefore, since my childhood I have always identified doctors with white robes and stethoscopes.) If I graduated as a historian from a university, it is because my professors decided that, in spite of my literary excesses, I had produced a work that fulfilled the minimum requirements demanded by our scholarly profession. History for historians is an academic discipline; however, it is a scientific practice that relies on words rather than machines. For this reason, it should be viewed as an art. It can be a wonderful personal experience for those who consecrate themselves to its application; it is a way of making a living (although seldom a profitable one), and it is also a particular school of thought that instructs its disciples in a set of beliefs. These "religious instructions" that I call "Academicism" comprise part of the identity of the scholar.

When I left Peru, the last notes that I wrote in my personal diary were about what I called "the religion of the scholar." I jotted down some of the sharp and ironical views of my own profession out of frustration with having had to translate vivid recollections full of emotions into the sometimes tedious language that my discipline traditionally has imposed. This was my last small rebellion before settling down to write as a serious scholar. Therefore, I deliberately attempted to shatter the myths of what I regarded as the doctrines of academia, which I had to follow rigorously in order to be accepted in the congregation of scholars. I never thought that I would dare to include my diary pages on the "religion of the scholar" in this book, but I have changed my mind because I think that this concept can help readers understand my identity vis-à-vis one of the "Jewish *Mestizos.*" My notion of the "religion of the scholar" explains my dilemmas as a historian who is also a storyteller, a dialectic that informs the entire work.

Before I went to Iquitos I promised myself that I would do my best in observing the precepts of my scholarly discipline. After witnessing the religion of the "Jewish *Mestizos,*" I could not avoid the temptation to compare scholars and *paisanos,* both worshipers of realities that they perceive as their truth:

> Tonight I leave Peru. I will miss the people I met in Lima and Iquitos, and to them I owe an explanation. Don't be deceived by my disguise as a scholar, my friends. Knowledge, grants, and degrees do not make someone a good person, and that lesson I learned from you. During these months I observed how most of the people who met me easily allowed themselves to admire me because I am a doctor, and they suppose, wrongly, that doctors always say intelligent things. Not me, nor most of the scholars I have met.
>
> I came here to observe and analyze the history, beliefs, rituals, supernatural conceptions, and cosmological views that Iquitos's "Jewish *Mestizos*" share, but I should have spent more time describing to them the set of beliefs that I learned in the "church" where I come from. It is called "The University" and like Iquitos's Israelite Society and the different houses of worship attended by some of its members, my *templo del saber* (temple of knowledge) is also a institution that promulgates its rituals and tenets.
>
> The members of my congregation of scholars would be very upset by this perception, but I see them as clergymen transmitting

a tradition that descends from generation to generation, and in my view, this tradition seems a lot like a religion. How would I describe the religion of the Academy to my *Iquiteño* friends? Here is a description using a vocabulary that is familiar to them:

The main churches are comprised of a type of priest called "scholars" or "professors." These priests meet during cyclic synods called "congresses" or "conferences" in which they exercise all their wisdom by reading insightful lectures and attempting to prove that they are closer to truth than are other priests. Even when scholars acknowledge that they do not have answers to all the questions they discuss, the most radical believers in the scientific method defend every single argument in their search for the truth, as if they are fighting for their own lives.

Scholars elaborate an entire theology to support their faith; they sustain their reasoning by relying on excerpts from what they call "primary sources" (more or less what you would call the "primal source of life"). Or they quote the sayings of their favorite apostles or of those who are more convenient to cite. Unlike religious zealots from some denominations, like yours, scholars allow themselves to doubt, but not to the extent that they could become apostates by being considered ignorant, rather than humble seekers of truth. This leads me to express a major difference between this and your religion, which worships nature and God.

Academicism is a religion of hubris, of exhibitionism and self-aggrandizement. In your religion you humble yourselves by expressing a sometimes exaggerated gratitude to God (even though He often does not deliver what you implore of Him). You also ask, usually unsuccessfully, for the wisdom to forgive others and for solidarity with the weakest and poorest. I am aware of the gap between what your leaders preach and what you all do, but at least the concept of humility is the essence of your religion. This is not the case with the religion of the scholar. Doctors long for recognition and prestige. They want to be known and liked in their congregations, as does any cardinal, mufti, or American rabbi. They like people to read their works, comment on their ideas, invite them to lecture, grant them awards. The long but mystical experience of writing soon transforms itself into a more immediate urge for tangible rewards. They hunt honors and patrons.

Of course, there are modest scholars who practice this religion selectively, cherishing the more human side of their training: the joy of sharing what impassions them, a genuine dedication to the art of teaching; but I am stressing here what this religion recommends to its followers. For example, take the case of a scholar applying for a job. He is advised to write a letter presenting himself as a heroic figure, as "the only person who fits the position." The scholar must idolize himself or herself, even though he or she knows that everybody else plays the same game. The scholar must also request letters of recommendation overestimating his or her contributions to the religion (a kind of indulgence that makes scholars feel like heavenly creatures), and strive to write more and more articles that must be published in "sacred books" called journals.

The more the scholar publishes, the more he or she is acknowledged by fellow coreligionists. The fact that one's name is printed in a book makes it easier to open the gates of the heaven, thus ascending by transcendental levels. Publications, as do prayers and penitence in your case, pave the way for the advancement of the scholar's being. These publications are attached to a document called a c.v., whose purpose is to convince other scholars how elevated are the intellect and spirit of the members of the congregation.

Like your identity, the identity of the scholar is very syncretic. There are Jewish, Christian, Moslem, Buddhist scholars; there are Marxist, Existentialist, Structuralist scholars; they can belong to different denominations: economics, history, sociology, philosophy . . . even religious studies that do not include their own!

I wrote more things about "the religion of the scholar." I described many of its rituals (such as comprehensive exams, the dissertation defense, graduation); I emphasized the human nature of the supreme tribunal that judges candidates for hierarchical posts, in contrast with the celestial tribunal of Christianity and Judaism. I compared the black gown and hats worn during academic events with priestly garments, and I traced the ironic parallels between traditional religions and some tenets from the academic world:

> We believe in the sanctity of the sabbatical year, in the almighty certainty of historical evidences, in the aura of some pioneering scholars (ask the followers of Marx, Lévi-Strauss, Gramsci, and others). We believe in the grace of the originality of our projects instead of the original sin of Adam and Eve; we believe in the resurrection of theories, in the immortality of one's own name, and in the invisible forces of history that cannot be seen, but certainly, according to fellow scholars, are experienced by whole societies.
>
> Average Amazonian persons relate to supernatural beings; they describe stories with *Tunchis* and Souls Retracing Their Steps and they entrust their devotion to God. Average scholars also relate to invisible and untouchable entities, such as models of analysis, theories, concepts. Both self-proclaimed religious persons and scholars rely on abstract conceptions and visions in order to put order in their worlds.

My Jewishness, my scholarly training, and my literary inclinations are all part of my background. All these components of my syncretic identity influenced the way that I gradually became a protagonist in the history of the "Jewish *Mestizos.*"

◆

REVIEWING THE WORKS OF UNORTHODOX SCHOLARS

Four works became my point of departure to get familiar with "secular scholars" who merge in their works different scholarly disciplines in which the story (history) provides an occasion for the author to examine processes of researching and telling. These books were: John Lukacs's *Confessions of an Original Sinner,* Paul Rabinow's *Reflections on Fieldwork in Morocco,* Smadar Lavie's *The Poetics of Military Occupation: Mzeina Allegories of Bedouin Identity Under Israeli and Egyptian Rule,* and especially, Virginia Domínguez's *People as Subject, People as Object: Selfhood and Peoplehood in Contemporary Israel,* an anthropological work that inspired me to allow myself as an emotional scholar to constantly remember and express how I was learning about the "Jewish *Mestizo*" identity.

Yet, these four books are only a small part of a vast body of scholarly literature that I perused, in which scholars bring to their scientific craft the tools of self-scrutiny, self-doubt, and confessional techniques.[3] Thus, I decided that I, too, should adopt a "secular" approach in order to present the ethnohistory of a group whose identity led me to question my own Jewishness. In an article that I wrote at the request of members of Lima's Jewish community, I expressed this idea more fully:

> It would be easy to arrive in Loreto's capital, Iquitos, seeing them [Iquitos's "Jewish *Mestizos*"] exclusively as a people who inherited a racial and cultural mixture from their Jewish ancestors; it would be easy to simply speak about religious contradictions in order to explain their embroiled identity that oscillates between Jewish and Christian notions, between a modern and a mythical life, between magical beliefs and a profound religiosity that in the Amazon is as real as are psychoanalysts in the big cities. It would be easy to conclude that we are witnesses of the last vestiges of Jewish life in Iquitos. The temptation to arrive at this conclusion is enticing; it is the easy path. What could be the alternative to this judgment?: To reverse the roles, theirs and mine.
>
> So, with the passing of the days, I began to realize that the Iquitos "Jews" would keep me from getting a good night's sleep . . . not because of the nights that I would have to share with them as I wrote my book, but, rather because of the profound questions as to my own Jewish identity that their persistence and survival were forcing me to confront. After a few weeks, the once long and sometimes tedious Shabbat services without Hebrew songs [they only could read the Spanish translation of the prayers] were transformed into magical events every Friday evening. Isn't it remarkable that in Iquitos, a group of "madmen" still gather to celebrate Shabbat, praying to God, expecting Him to listen to their voices that attempt to rise above the loud music and laughter coming from the bar next to the ceremonial room? Isn't it a miracle that a group of old men and youngsters who never had a Jewish education still dream of

settling in the land of their ancestors? Beyond the legal, rational, halakhic, and political aspects of their circumstances, many of these people feel themselves to be a remnant of Israel, which according to the prophets, will one day be gathered in the Promised Land together with their brothers in exile. . . . [4]

Whether I now like it or not, my own identity has trespassed the boundaries of my scholarly task. Virginia Domínguez was presented with the challenge of studying a foreign people whom she eventually learned to love and to identify with; but still, they were not her people, as she notes: "After three and a half years of fairly constant research in and on Israel, I as a non-Jew felt compelled to pose the question about my emotional reaction to Israel."[5] If a non-Jewish scholar feels compelled to question her emotional reaction toward Jews, what can be expected from a Jewish scholar? Y. H. Yerushalmi argues that Jewish historians can no longer be limited to finding continuities in Jewish history: the time has come to look at ruptures and breaches. However, to do so, Yerushalmi asserts, "The modern Jewish historian must first understand the degree to which he himself is a product of rupture."[6]

I am a product of rupture, and so I would like to apply Yerushalmi's recommendation. How am I to do this? The only way I find possible to fight against my proclivity to see Jewish history as a continuing process is by recognizing that propensity. In Lima I visited a community that was almost a replica of the one to which I belonged for twenty years in Caracas; in Iquitos, I visited a community whose uncomplicated sense of identity, accompanied by a candid desire to be Jewish, swelled my sense of pride for "my people," despite the religious syncretism of the community's members. I suddenly felt vulnerable as a scholar, as these examples from my diary reveal:

> Jaime Vázquez Izquierdo feels himself to be Jewish. I feel him to be Jewish. He has that passion of knowledge, life, and curiosity that only a few Jews still maintain. He played violin for me, interpreting lullabies that his mother sang to him when he was a child. He showed me his progress in learning Hebrew; he asked me to teach him

Hebrew songs, taping them in my small tape recorder. I borrowed one of the books he wrote. . . . He is an artist, no doubt about it!

What is he doing in Iquitos? He should be in Israel among the craziest Zionists, among the last generation of dreamers of the Jewish people!

✦

Tonight I don't want to see them [Iquitos's descendants of Jews] with a scientific lens or with a scholar's microscope. I am enjoying their universe, their spiritual wealth despite their apparent poverty. There is more "purity" in their old houses with dirty water and mosquitoes than in the tidy temples and rooms of hollow homes of many Jews in big cities.

I feel tired. It has been a long, long day. The more I become involved with them, the less scientific I want to be. I promised myself that I wouldn't participate in the Shabbat service, but Don Víctor Edery blessed me as "their special guest," so I agreed to sing them a couple of Shabbat songs. They listened to me as if I were Pavarotti . . . half Pavarotti, to avoid exaggerations! . . . This time I did not fulfill my pledge of remaining distant as an observer.

The first example reveals not only how I idealized one of the members of the community, but moreover, how I romanticized the way the Jewish people used to be, especially the Zionist pioneers who built the State of Israel. In the second example, I make public a serious confession: that there were moments during which I was losing the war against my emotions, acting more like the literary writer that I am, rather than the trained scholar that I also am. This was a dangerous situation, which, in my opinion, had only one solution, absolute honesty. Only honesty can allow the researcher to face openly his or her own emotions. In the words of Virginia Domínguez: "The introspective analysis of our own reactions—of what we love and what we hate, of what intrigues us 'irrationally' and what we simply fail to understand, of what we fear in the society we study and what we fear in our feelings toward the society we study—may ironically allow us to approximate 'reality' better than the perennial attempts to maximize objectivity by minimizing subjectivity."[7]

By studying Iquitos's Jewish descendants' individual and collective experiences in the Peruvian Amazon,[8] I was able to dig into their historical consciousness,[9] and, to a certain extent, to reshape it. These inhabitants' exposure to my Jewish identity increased as I became actively involved in their community's dynamics. It was not my original intention to become a protagonist in the history I went to observe; nevertheless, like Franz Kafka's Gregor Samsa, one morning I woke up to find myself transformed into something I probably always was, but never before realized—an emotional researcher.

✦

THE RESEARCHER WHO WOKE UP
TRANSFORMED INTO A PROTAGONIST

In Iquitos, I woke up one day to realize that I was becoming a crucial player in the day-to-day drama of the community I had come to study. The academic armor that I had striven so hard to wear began to melt quickly in the heat, under the excitement of my subjects, particularly as my *Iquiteño* informants began to relate to me as a friend, and as a Jewish teacher. (Aren't we told to be friendly when we conduct oral history? Then, why are we surprised when we finally succumb to those friendships we cultivate?)

When I arrived in Iquitos I pledged to myself that I would not consciously interfere with the natural historical process taking place among the city's "Jewish *Mestizos.*" Friends in Lima warned me that Iquitos was a very amicable city and that the Jewish descendants saw every Jewish visitor as a potential rescuer. Moreover, I was told to look upon everything they told me with a skeptical eye because, although their desire to preserve a Jewish identity was admirable, they were exaggerated persons who lived in a world of fantasy. Weeks after I was told this, Jaime Vásquez Izquierdo, "the intellectual" of the *Sociedad Israelita de Iquitos*, told me that one of the idiosyncratic characteristics of Amazonian people besides *machismo* is *mitomanía*, the tendency to tell distorted stories in which the storyteller consciously lies or boasts of having done or witnessed something that other people could never have imagined. I cannot say that I was not forewarned about how easily I could be charmed by my hosts.

Just days after my arrival in Iquitos, several "Jewish *Mestizos*" began to show up in the hostel where I was staying. They asked me to explain about

Jewish religion and about Israel, to tell them why Jews so adamantly reject Jesus as the Messiah. Why was it so hard for them to go to Israel? they asked. Could I do something to help them? I succeeded in delaying all explanations: "First I must interview you, and then, you can ask me questions," I replied. At least I could carry out most of my interviews before affecting any notion of belonging to their Jewish historical consciousness and *Imaginario.*

In some cases they forgot to question me, but sometimes, when they reminded me of my pledge, I did answer whatever they asked me following the interviews. I answered their questions vaguely, because I was concerned with not modifying their beliefs, their dreams. In doing so, I was protecting the academic nature of my scholarly enterprise, but my main concern was to respect the purity of their beliefs. I found it unethical to impose my scientific rationale over their mythical-historical consciousness. What pretext could possible justify propounding "coherent" formulas to substitute for their harmonic syncretic cosmology, even though my Western mind interpreted that cosmology as a weaving of contradictory recollections? Who could assert that my "imaginary Jewishness" is more solid that theirs? I kept Mario Vargas Llosa's *The Storyteller* in my backpack, and I constantly reviewed the words of the character Saúl Zuratas, *Mascarita,* as he talked about respecting the cultures of Amazonian tribes: "But that's the way they are and we should respect them. Being that way has helped them to live in harmony with their forest for hundreds of years. Though we don't understand their beliefs and some of their customs offend us, we have no right to [culturally] kill them off."[10] (I strongly recommend reading this endnote!)

The community I studied is not an isolated group living in the Amazonian jungle; however, they too, developed a way of living in harmony for decades in that environment; therefore, I did not feel I had the right to change that way. I did my best to restrain my ethnocentric instincts, my "Messiah complex" that pushes me to help others when I am asked (and sometimes, when nobody requests it). I tried to bridle my desire to provide my eager *paisanos* with those things they needed so much: prayer books and treatises on Jewish theology; promises to talk on their behalf when I returned to Lima; my "acknowledgment," as the "thorough Jew" they saw in me, of their Judaism. One way I found to explain to them the reason for my research in Iquitos was by asking them why they thought I had come to meet them. Only those interviewees who are college students or professionals understood clearly my scholarly mission:

I think that for those [Jews] like you who come from other places, the Iquitos community is very peculiar because many of its members, including myself, have had a Catholic education that you did not have, because we live the consequences of particular social conditions and isolation, and because our parents do not really know who they are. Don't you remember that the first time we met at the office where I work you asked me how we manage to do without a rabbi? You come from a community that has a rabbi!

✦

You must see us as a people with scarce knowledge of Judaism, so I guess, [we are] a little bit exotic, but I want you to know that I feel more identification with you than with my next-door neighbors because you are Jewish. I know there are many types of Jews—Reform, Traditionalist, Orthodox Jews— so we must be another type, but, a very unusual one due to our isolation from other Jews. When you came, I learned for first time that there are Shabbat songs.[11]

Most of Iquitos's Jewish descendants interpreted my visit as a matter of studying the accomplishments of their Jewish ancestors in the Peruvian Amazon; they seemed unaware of my attempts to understand their religious and cultural identity (no matter how hard I strove to explain my mission!). Indeed, I was surprised that some of my incisive questions—such as "How can you define yourself as Jewish if you go to church and you believe in Christ?"—failed to make them realize that I was studying them. I was trying to guide them to answer my questions logically, but soon I understood (as I registered in my diary) that in the Amazon my questions were the very elements that did not make sense. Therefore, my attempt to avoid the impression that mine was a good-faith trip to help them proved unsuccessful. Most "Jewish *Mestizos*" continued to ask me questions about Judaism. Likewise, although they did not see me as a "missionary" because they have had more contact with Jews of Lima and Israel, nevertheless, the leaders of the Israelite Society asked me to organize some lectures and participate actively in the Shabbat services after they learned that I was a scholar with some knowledge of Jewish history and liturgy. After a month in Iquitos, I was already reciting Shabbat prayers every Friday evening during the services.

Gradually I began to lose control over my self-restraint. They wanted me to help, I wanted to help them: so I stopped denying my obvious desire to participate in their rituals and attempted—at least—to clearly separate my professional and personal missions. As a modern Ecclesiastes would say, "There is a time to work and a time to feel, a time to cultivate the intellect and a time to nurture the heart." Hence, I awakened one morning transformed into a protagonist on the stage of the *Sociedad Israelita de Iquitos.* In my defense I wish to emphasize that, unlike most scholars I have cited who made field-research in communities totally unrelated to their own cultural and religious backgrounds (Rabinow, Cohen, Domínguez, etc.), I was a Jew in a community of people who wanted desperately to be Jewish and were fighting to preserve their identity in the face of challenges from their own environment and the skepticism of mainstream Jewish institutions. Somehow, Iquitos's Jewish descendants were more Jewish than I was from the standpoint of their stubbornness in preserving the identity of their Jewish ancestors. Isn't it that obsession for survival that we Jews are told time and time again at school, in the synagogue, and through our traditions, the foundation of our character?

Faced with a community of "contemporary *Marranos*" fighting against total assimilation, could I, a person with a degree in Jewish studies, become merely a chronicler of the last breaths of this community? I could not; therefore, I became Dr. Herodotus Jekyll when the situation demanded it, and a Mr. Hyde-mberg when I felt sure that my involvement in the community's affairs would not undermine my academic pursuit. "There is much more to the 'field' than fieldwork," ethnographer Smadar Lavie argues, and I say the same in my defense.[12]

Of the two prayer books they possessed, Iquitos's descendants of Jews read only the Spanish version. During the first Shabbat in which I actively participated (the fourth one I attended), I sang a few prayers in Hebrew. I let them hear the *Yedid Nefesh* (Beloved Soul), the *Lekha Dodi* (a chant in which Shabbat is compared to a bride welcomed by her bridegroom, the

Jewish people), and the *Shalom Aleikhem* (a welcome to the angels who accompany the community during Shabbat). The "Jewish *Mestizos*" clapped, and I had to explain to them that these were prayers, so it was not proper to applaud. That evening, Jaime Vásquez Izquierdo, secretary of the Israelite Society and a music professor who had sung as a tenor years ago, asked me to pass by his house in order to record for him all my Shabbat repertoire of prayers, so that he could sing them every Friday. I did so, and during our music session in his little house, Don Jaime told me that it would be good if I could help him teach those songs to the others before my departure. I acceded to his request, but I told him that we would need more prayer books with the Spanish phonetics together with the Hebrew prayers and their Spanish translations. So I had to call my friends in Lima: Sandy Cassinelli, of the *Federación Sionista del Perú*, who was my partner during many of the interviews I conducted in Lima, and Rabbi Guillermo Bronstein, the man who had "prepared" the *Iquiteños* for my visit before I went to Peru. Bronstein was "my rabbi," during our telephone conversations from Miami to Lima and the perceived "Iquitos rabbi," if one asks any member of Iquitos's Israelite Society.

While we waited for a response from Lima, I wrote down in transliteration several Shabbat songs and made photocopies to hand out. During the next month, those attending the Friday services began to sing the prayers with me. Soon Jaime Vásquez Izquierdo took the leading voice and he began to sing other Hebrew songs that I recorded but were not part of the prayer book. I remember telling those I knew in Lima that the best cantor in all Peru now was an *Iquiteño*, since Jaime Vásquez Izquierdo was an opera singer with a still-powerful and melodious voice. Eventually, Sandy Cassinelli and Rabbi Bronstein sent the prayer books so that now the worshipers could follow the prayers while the officiator read them. I also taught the *Kaddish* (mourning prayer) to those members of the community who had recently lost a loved one. In the few weeks since my arrival, Shabbat had become an event that attracted more and more worshipers, and the community made me sit in the front of the "synagogue" (a site next to a bar owned by Víctor Edery) together with Jaime Vásquez Izquierdo and spiritual guide Víctor Edery. Once in a while, Don Víctor asked me to address the audience about a religious topic, as he usually did every Kabbalat Shabbat.

Now I became a "guest lecturer," and some college students in Iquitos decided to organize a series of lectures in which Dr. Ariel Segal would speak about Jewish religion, the Holocaust, and the State of Israel. (I kept telling them that technically I still was not a doctor, but they replied that in Iquitos every educated person "is a doctor.") The organization of those lectures was a failure because the university in charge of the event changed the lecture dates the same day; nevertheless, I decided to take those people who had showed up on the evening of the first lecture (most of them descendants of Jews) to the *Biblioteca Amazónica,* where my friends in the library allowed us to hold the lecture. A second class was set for the next evening in the same place. Also, one of my *paisanos* invited me to lecture about the Holocaust in the *Instituto Pedagógico de Iquitos* (Education College), and Father Joaquín García suggested that I offer a lecture during the "Tourists' Week" in Iquitos. Again, most of the audience consisted of members of the *Sociedad Israelita de Iquitos.* Gradually, every *paisano* who visited me in the hostel or invited me to chat asked me to tell him more about the Jewish people and Israel.

Another area in which my presence catalyzed change was the political sphere of the Israelite society. Before my arrival in Iquitos, the *Sociedad Israelita* had not been holding sessions due to internal divisions. Other than the weekly Shabbat services, the community had abandoned most of the activities it had organized in the past (including Rabbi Bronstein's plans for their possible *aliyah* to Israel); all this was due to a power struggle between members of the community.

When I arrived, I decided not to involve myself in that problem; however, after I became a protagonist I started to mediate between the members of the *Sociedad Israelita,* simply because I wanted to witness a session. (The last session had been held on January 29, 1995, when they discussed, among other topics, the future visit of the *"paisano* Segal, who will come to Iquitos between May and September of this year to conduct a study of the Jewish community of Iquitos."[13]) A session was summoned for July 2, 1995, during which the community would hold the elections that had been postponed since January. After the society's members agreed to summon the community, Jaime Bensimón Puyó was elected president, substituting for the society's founding president, Víctor Edery Morales, and the board of directors continued with new leaders.

Unfortunately, a crisis occurred the day before I left Iquitos: The president of the *Sociedad Israelita,* Jaime Bensimón Puyó, had suggested opening up the institution to non-Jews and transforming it into an institution in which "religious democracy" could be exercised, so that more people would donate money to repair the Israelite cemetery. Jaime Vásquez Izquierdo strongly opposed the proposition because it meant returning to the times of the *Instituto Cultural Peruano-Israelí de Iquitos,* when the religious aspect of the community was neglected. The *Sociedad Israelita* was first founded in 1909 as a Jewish institution and had to remain so, he argued. Most of the members saw no problem in Bensimón's proposal, probably because they did not understand Jaime Vásquez Izquierdo's argument on the Jewish nature of the institution: "We can open up the institution to anyone who desires to have a Jewish life, but not to mix religions in the midst of our community and adopt foreign practices. This proves to me that the president of the institution lacks clear principles for leading an institution of Jewish roots," said Vásquez.[14]

The day after this meeting, Jaime Vásquez Izquierdo and Víctor Edery accompanied me to the airport. Jaime Vásquez Izquierdo was considering quitting the society; Víctor Edery had already made the decision to hold Shabbat services in his own home and to boycott those in Bensimón's house. They told me that Bensimón quoted me when he proposed the idea of having the community embrace a "religious democracy," since I had explained in a lecture that Israel was a Jewish democratic state in which all religious groups can exercise their religions. I could not hide a smile when I listened to their account of the amazing effect that my lecture had caused in Bensimón's mind: "He is going to establish an Israel in Iquitos?" I asked jokingly. But Edery and Vásquez were very serious; they asked for my opinion, my support. Jaime Vásquez Izquierdo suggested that I write a letter to the community in which I would explain why the idea of changing the nature of the society was a big mistake. I did write a note before boarding the airplane. I endorsed Jaime Vásquez Izquierdo and Víctor Edery, in case they decided to split from the society and found their own Jewish institution, as they were hinting they might do: "You can read my opinion to the community," I told them. "But first try to solve the problem via diplomacy." Days later, in Lima, I learned that the community did split into two congregations. I wondered how much I was responsible for that event and then I wrote in my diary: "Here are two typical Jewish situations: a Jewish community splitting and me, a Jew, feeling guilty."

Once in Lima I kept receiving phone calls from Iquitos, especially from young people confused about the whole situation: Whom should they follow? Why did Jaime Vásquez Izquierdo leave the democratically elected board of directors? I called Jaime Vásquez Izquierdo to propose to him a Solomonic way out of the conflict: Eliminate the figure of the society's president and appoint Jaime Bensimón Puyó as director of patrimony in charge of the Israelite cemetery, and Víctor Edery as director of religious affairs. In this way, the functions would be split but not the community. Jaime Vásquez Izquierdo liked the idea and Víctor Edery accepted, but Jaime Bensimón Puyó's followers did not. So, in November 1995, I received a letter from Jaime Vásquez Izquierdo announcing that a new institution, the *Sociedad Israelita de Beneficiencia y Culto de Iquitos* had been founded and was functioning independently of Bensimón's *Sociedad de Beneficiencia Israelita de Iquitos*. Each congregation celebrated Shabbat services and Jewish holidays separately, although in different letters I gradually learned that Bensimón's congregation had begun to weaken. They did not have enough books, nor enough dreamers, unlike the Edery-Vásquez congregation. Then, in April 1996, I received the good news: An agreement had been reached and the community was united again.

These events relate to another episode in Iquitos in which I became a leading player: the organization of a new project to help those *Iquiteños* eager to immigrate to Israel. Rabbi Bronstein's plan had failed because neither *Iquiteños* nor *Limeños* carried out the necessary steps to achieve it. Before embarking on my journey to Iquitos, I had promised friends in Lima that I would lecture about my experiences among the Amazonian "Jewish *Mestizos*." My friends Sandy and Ricki Cassinelli organized a meeting in their home, and I told the history of the Iquitos Jews and their descendants. I described what I saw, I expressed my opinions about them, and I showed pictures and videos. Most of my listeners were impressed by the history of Iquitos's descendants of Jews and asked how could they help these people. I told them to send books and videos of movies such as *Fiddler on the Roof.* I advised them to visit the community if they traveled to Iquitos, but most importantly, I urged the leaders of the *Federación Sionista del Perú* to help those who wanted to make *aliyah*. This time, I stressed, the task should be undertaken not on a case-by-case basis, but rather, as an effort on behalf of the entire community. I proposed to present the case to Israeli immigration authorities as it had been done by other communities regarding such groups, as the case of Ethiopians and the *Bene Israel* of India attest. A few days later, I was summoned to a meeting of the Peruvian Zionist Federation.

In that meeting I presented a brief history of Iquitos's community. I was forthright about the syncretic nature of their religion, but also stressed their amazing desire to preserve their ancestors' culture. I provided the members of the *Federación Sionista del Perú* with a list of those *Iquiteños* who had expressed a wish to immigrate to Israel, as well as a list of those who were serious regarding that pursuit. I also gave them the names of those members who made a clear distinction between Christianity and Judaism and who had chosen the Jewish faith. Finally, I proposed to write to Israeli immigration authorities and to bring to their attention two reasons why this case deserved special consideration: First, because many *Iquiteños* would not be able to prove their Jewish ancestry through religious documents because they worked in trade and fluvial navigation, and so they could not register the births of their children in civil offices in Iquitos. Instead, they had to do it before public notaries of small villages and towns whose archives, in many cases, have since been lost. Many of these Jews died in the rivers and villages scattered throughout the Amazonian forest, and they were buried in those places. That is why there are few gravestones in Iquitos's Israelite cemetery. Second, because in the past, they were recognized as a "Jewish community" by the Israeli Embassy in Peru.[15]

The members of the *Federación Sionista del Perú* promised to do everything they could to help the Iquitos community. They proposed to write letters to Israeli immigration functionaries and to the ministry of immigration: one letter from *Federación Sionista*'s president Jack Silbermán, one from Rabbi Guillermo Bronstein describing his visit to the community, and one an account that I wrote as a historian, explaining why this community cannot prove its Jewish origins through religious documents. Also, a file would be sent with Alfredo Rosenzweig's and Yaacov Hasson's articles regarding the Amazonian Jews, both published in the 1960s, and copies of León Trahtemberg's chapter about Iquitos in his book about the Jews in the provinces of Peru.

One might think such a campaign of letter writing would be adequate to initiate discussion with Israeli authorities. However, Sandy Cassinelli, my indefatigable ally during my scholarly work in Lima and a persistent sympathizer of Iquitos's "Jews," told me that it would be extremely helpful if I could speak to the Israeli ambassador in Lima. I had never thought my role as a protagonist would take me so far, but one day I was there with Sandy Cassinelli, both of us sitting in front of Ambassador Joel Salpak. I told him the whole story, and I confessed that my enthusiasm to help the "Jewish" *Iquiteños* was obviously the result of my personal involvement with them. I showed him letters from the 1960s in which ambassador Netanel Lorch thanked the "Jewish community of Iquitos" for its contribution to the State of Israel during the Six-Day War. Then I repeated my memorized *petite phrase*, "a sound bite": "Why are they recognized as Jews when they send contributions to Israel and not recognized as Jews when they want to immigrate there?" Joel Salpak told us that it was not a function of an ambassador to become involved in such cases, but he surprised us with the announcement that he had already made a plan to travel to Iquitos to inaugurate an exhibition of Israeli photographs; there he would meet with the community to advise its members. He also promised to put in a good word for them if the *Federación Sionista*'s plan progressed.

Back in Miami, while I was writing my book, I received letters from some friends in Iquitos telling me that the Israeli ambassador had traveled to the Amazonian city and met with them. Also, they told me, a man named Jack Silbermán from Lima had visited them and met with those who were interested in immigrating to Israel. The division within the community made it hard for everyone to present his or her case individually, but, apparently, Jack Silbermán compiled a list of all the candidates who were interested in *aliyah*. My *Iquiteño* friend Jacobo Casique Kohn (who, today, lives in Israel) wrote a letter to me in which he said:

> . . . Jack told us that he is going to do his best to organize the trip of this Iquitos group in the next three to six months. Later we met the ambassador during the exhibition of "Natural Landscapes of Israel," inaugurated on Monday, the 11th [September 1995] in the Continental Bank where the ambassador, his wife, Jack, and the whole community gathered for some pictures. On Tuesday the

12th there was a farewell lunch for the ambassador in Víctor Edery's house, and the ambassador thanked the community. . . . He greeted everybody telling us that we will meet again, if not in Iquitos, then in Israel. That is our house where we all belong. . . .

I want to thank you, Ariel, because you have been one of the sponsors who has caused us to receive all these blessings. May God bless you with His mercy and may His peace be with you. . . .[16]

Friends in Lima told me that the Israeli ambassador was impressed with the Iquitos community, but did not promise anything. Jack Silbermán said that in six months the Zionist Federation would try to give them an answer as to how their case was progressing. He never committed the institution to guaranteeing their *aliyah.*

The history of this community still continues with threads in Iquitos, Lima, and Jerusalem. I am no longer a protagonist (well, you should not believe me at this point; now that I live in Israel, I could write another book about my continuous relationship with "Jewish *Mestizos*" who have made *aliyah,* as I did, since mid-1997[17]) but according to Jacobo Casique Kohn's letter and other friends' missives, it seems that I was the one who got the ball rolling.

Did I stray from my original aims? Yes, I did. Does this invalidate my field research? No. I would argue that my involvement also sheds light on the question of Jewish identity, which involves all of the protagonists of this history, including myself. The act of translating a life experience into a scholarly work is per se a manifestation of ethnocentrism, so I do not worry much about being labeled ethnocentric because of my paternalistic attitude toward Iquitos's descendants of Jews. Somehow, every historical study is ethnocentric, but the fact that I have exposed some instances where I learned more from my subjects than I could have taught them reduces my ethnocentric stance, I believe.

Do I have ethical questions about my participation in the dynamics of this community? Yes, I do, in the same way that I would have questioned myself if I had not participated. The only solution for a field researcher confronted with an ethically troubling situation is to be honest with oneself, and, later, during the process of writing, to be honest with the reader.

9

Conclusions: Retracing the Steps

THROUGHOUT THIS WORK I have examined how Iquitos's present day community of "Jewish *Mestizos*" exhibits a syncretic identity. In it, elements from Christianity, Judaism, and Amazonian cosmologies converge in a harmonious synthesis that its members refer to as "their Judaism." In my role as a scholar I argue that these Jewish descendants are *Marranos* because they straddle the border between Judaism and Christianity, and because they are immersed in diverse cultural and ethnic influences as a result of being isolated from the Jewish communities of the Brazilian Amazon and the Peruvian capital. However, despite their extreme isolation, the *Iquiteños*' historical mythical-consciousness and their institutional and personal discourses reveal that they feel a strong sense of connection to the Jewish people. Therefore, I have proposed several explanations why this isolated group—descended from Jewish immigrants who were drawn to the Peruvian Amazon during the rubber boom—still preserves such a remarkable sense of identification with Lima's Jewish community, with the State of Israel, and with the Jewish people.

The historian in me concludes:

The group's survival as an organized, self-proclaimed "Jewish community" is attributable to several historical factors. One decisive factor was the relatively indulgent way that Catholicism was introduced in the Peruvian Amazon in contrast to the rigid dominion exerted by the Catholic Church in Lima, which spread along the coast and in the Andes throughout the nineteenth century. The church was unable to exercise much power in the Amazonian region, whose dense jungle thwarted the efforts of Jesuit missionaries. (Nevertheless, whole cultures and ethnic groups have been wiped out by combinations of diseases and acculturation caused by missionaries during the more than one hundred years of Christian presence in the region.) Those few Jesuits who did make it to the Amazon were expelled from the Americas under order of King Charles III of Spain in 1767. This left the Spanish Amazon with practically no network of missions, nor was headway made by Augustinian priests, who arrived in the early twentieth century. The Catholic Church in Iquitos launched a series of timid attempts to extirpate pre-Colonial Amazonian beliefs, but these half-hearted efforts did little to offset the bold (and in many cases murderous) entrepreneurial dynamic imposed by adventurous European and Asian immigrants.

The combination of relaxed Catholicism and the secularized culture of thousands of newcomers, who settled in the Peruvian Amazon during the nineteenth-century rubber boom, transformed Iquitos from a small fluvial post into a bohemian city where Amazon beliefs, Catholic rituals, and parvenu values imported from Europe created a singular environment that still exerts a powerful influence on how contemporary *Iquiteños* see themselves. The rubber boom gave rise to a new social class of immigrants and local rubber lords whose customs reflected the values of the European upper classes. The descendants of those gentlemen are proud of their lineage, no matter how great is the degree of their present-day miscegenation and poverty. Their sense of belonging to an elite combined with the influence of an omnipresent, but not almighty Catholic Church, enabled the descendants of Jews to preserve a notion of distinction from the rest of the population. Most of the "Jewish *Mestizos*" are nominal Catholics, although they claim to have "Jewish blood" in their veins because of their lineage.

To understand why Lima became the point of reference for Iquitos, and therefore, why Lima's Jewish community became the focal point for Amazonian Jewish descendants, we must take into account the historical factors of progress and modernity. In the late 1920s and early 1930s, the airplane bridged the enormous geographical, political, economic, and cultural distances between the Peruvian Amazon and the coast. Once the high Andes could be crossed in a few hours, products and goods from

Lima began to reach Amazonian cities and towns. Technological advances also enhanced communications between the Andes and Lima. Newspapers in Iquitos began covering more Peruvian events instead of publishing, almost exclusively, European news and local events, as had been customary in previous years. Lima met Iquitos; Iquitos welcomed Lima when President Fernando Belaunde Terry issued the Tax Exoneration decree from the Peruvian Amazon. Jewish merchants from the capital city helped Iquitos's first generation of Jewish descendants organize themselves as a community. The "Jewish *Mestizos*" still retained vivid memories of some of their fathers' traditions. They began to familiarize themselves with the activities of Lima's Jewry through bulletins and publications. They learned about Israel through films delivered to them by the Israeli Embassy in the capital city. These films, projected in theaters or in private homes, became the *Iquiteños'* link with a living Judaism. Progress and technological advances joined Iquitos with Lima, as well as with the wider global community of Jews.

Hence, two Jewish points of reference that had formerly been abstract paradigms for the "Jewish *Mestizos*" rapidly transformed into concrete archetypes when Lima's Jews and the State of Israel, via its embassy in Lima, established contact with Iquitos's descendants of Jews. This glorious epoch in the *Iquiteños'* history would prove to be a turning point in their search for an identity.

The subsequent reintroduction of taxes in the Peruvian Amazon in the 1970s initiated further changes. Jewish *Limeños* returned to the capital city, accompanied by many traders who had settled in Iquitos, as well as native *Iquiteños* in search of a better standard of life. Some "Jewish *Mestizos*" received a cool welcome from Lima's Jewish community and they gradually lost contact with its institutions, preferring to embrace Catholicism. The socioeconomic crisis of this decade, which worsened in the 1980s with an escalation in terrorism, prompted many Jews to immigrate to other countries. Some of Iquitos's Jewish descendants, hoping to immigrate to Israel, requested aid from Israeli functionaries in Lima; however, only a few succeeded in settling in the Jewish state. They were required to prove their Jewish origin by providing religious documents or photographs of their ancestors' tombstones in Iquitos's Israelite cemetery. Israel became a longed-for alternative for young *Iquiteño* idealists, who traveled to Lima to learn something of Judaism and, once back in Iquitos, persevered against all odds in searching for their roots. The inspiration of these youngsters—and, possibly, the nostalgia of some elder descendants of Jews who still remembered their original Jewish fathers or grandfathers and who had experienced the euphoria of the 1960s—propelled the initiative to recreate 1909's *Sociedad de Beneficiencia Israelita de Iquitos*, founded by Jewish immigrants. In 1991, the revived society began its activities, this time emphasizing the institution's religious character, calling upon its leaders to familiarize members with the teachings of the Jewish religion and the practice of Jewish rites.

The occasional visit of Jewish *Limeños* and the re-establishment of communications between Iquitos's organized community and Lima's Jewish institutions encouraged the renaissance of a sui generis Jewish life among the *Mestizo* descendants of Jews. My own field research in the city and the role I played as a protagonist reinforced this group's notion of belonging to the Jewish people.

While historical factors partly account for the survival of the "Jewish" community in Iquitos, other mechanisms have enabled *Iquiteño* descendants of Jews to harmonize successfully their Jewishness with other elements of their syncretic identity. Religion is one of these mechanisms, owing to the peculiar relationship that many native Amazonian people maintain with their cosmology. In the culturally homogeneous habitat of Iquitos, individual beliefs may be different but customs are similar. Slight variations can be found in the ways that diverse Amazonian inhabitants approach God and the supernatural. Jungle spirits and souls "retracing their steps" are conceptions endorsed by the vast majority of these people, although some Amazonian dwellers attempt to present themselves (unsuccessfully, I might add) as scientifically minded individuals. In contrast, *Iquiteños* are split regarding their belief in saints, the divinity of Jesus, and other Christian doctrines. The degree to which an individual accepts these beliefs varies according to his or her acceptance of the creeds of the Roman Catholic Church or the Protestant denomination to which he or she belongs.

The religion of "Jewish *Mestizos*" combines widespread Amazonian notions of the supernatural with a strong tendency to embrace Jewish monotheism and to question the Christian Trinity. Nevertheless, most

Amazonian Jewish descendants accept Jesus as the Messiah. Religious beliefs vary according to formal instruction and exposure to the Christian sacraments, but essentially, Jewish descendants observe without excessive fervor the traditions of both religions: Christian holidays such as Christmas and Easter, local Catholic celebrations such as that dedicated to San Juan, the Jewish High Holidays, and Passover. A few attend Shabbat services every week. It is unusual to see "Jewish *Mestizos*" participating in rituals of veneration of saints, or rituals that center around penitence or religious ecstasy (except those who attend Protestant churches and are asked to repeat and sing the prayers of the pastor). Rather, the descendants of Jews gather to enjoy those Christian holidays that provide them with the opportunity to celebrate in a festive manner, albeit with religious motifs: On Christmas they dance, drink, and eat, as does everybody else in Iquitos. As one might expect, some Jewish rituals have intertwined with Christian ones; this can be observed at the burial of "Jewish *Mestizos*," at which mourners cross themselves while they recite *Kaddish* and the deceased's tombstone may very well be adorned with both a Star of David and a Cross. One also encounters remarkable juxtaposition at the weekly Shabbat services. Here, one may find oneself praying beneath a painting of the Last Supper or hear a "Jewish *Mestizo*" explain a Jewish tradition by citing the words of Jesus' disciples.

Although the "Jewish *Mestizos*" live in a culturally homogeneous city, a kind of melting-pot cosmos where it is difficult to feel part of a distinctive people, they share a sense of peoplehood based on their common origins, on their shared possession of the Israelite cemetery, and on their membership in an institution that defines them as Jews. They identify with other Jews based on their scant knowledge of the Jewish people's history, especially the Inquisition and the Holocaust, their awareness of which was heightened following the screening of the movie *Schindler's List*. They identify with events in the State of Israel, which they can witness on their TV screens or via letters from relatives who have immigrated to the "promised land." Their identity is further reinforced by the intimate vocabulary they share (words such as Shabbat, *shalom*, Torah, *Adonai*, etc.)

The "Jewish *Mestizos*" fantasize about the day when they will arrive in the Holy Land, the day when they will be fully recognized as Jews. However, there is an intellectual component to their mythical-historical consciousness that causes them to appropriate other people's traditions, beliefs, symbols, myths, and stories as their own. I have called this component the *Imaginario,* a symbolic repertoire based on reconstructions of collective notions of peoplehood. Such a collective myth impels a group to superimpose foreign archetypes and fantastic conceptions on its own historical, religious, and cultural paradigms. The youngster who explained to me that Jews do not eat pork because it was Jesus' last supper, was obviously mixing her knowledge of a historical event with the symbolic world of her religious system. This *Imaginario* can also be found in the story of the old man who claimed that Jews do not eat pork because they were once transformed into swine *(Marranos)*. In each case, the Jewish mythical-historical consciousness has been influenced by individual mechanisms of interpretation, whose foundations rest on the syncretic cosmology of those who live in the Peruvian Amazon. In some cases, this sense of identity could be attributable to a "Jewish obsession syndrome" shared by some members of this community. Although this fabricated concept would be rejected by most social scientists, I still argue that as a historian-storyteller my definition of a "Jewish syndrome" not only helps us understand the cases of some "Jewish *Mestizos,*" but also fits into scholarly categorizations. Writer Amos Oz would most likely defend my claim: "The storyteller and the scholar differ not in the way they both relate to facts, to reality, truth, certainty, but precisely in the way they relate to words."[1]

The history of the first generation of Jewish immigrants who settled in Iquitos is the story of men who sought temporary lodging in a prosperous place, where they achieved great success and became prominent leaders in the political, economic, and cultural life of the city. However, it is the history of their children and their children's children that leads us to questions of race and class as factors that determine the relationship between center and periphery in Peru. The descendants of Jews in Iquitos are *Mestizos,* so their racial features and cultural syncretism are similar to those of the vast majority of the Peruvian population. To the white Jewish community of Lima, the notion of "Jewish *Mestizos*" is perplexing and controversial: Hierarchies of race, social class, religion, and culture are too firmly entrenched. In their minds, a wide gulf exists between white descendants of Europeans and *Mestizo* descendants of mixed marriages between Europeans and Indians. Therefore, the notion of a Jew who looks like an Indian and lives in a poor house in a small city in the middle of the jungle is, at best, an exotic footnote to the official history of Peru's Jewry, as Lima sees it.

The irony is that Lima's Jewish community, confronted with the Iquitos descendants of Jews, finds itself in the same predicament that other Jewish mainstream communities in the Western world have faced with peripheral groups. What is center and what is periphery? Can not a minority of white people living in a country made up of an overwhelming *Mestizo* population be considered the periphery? Is it not the community of Iquitos that has managed to become mainstream by harmoniously blending aspects of Peruvian culture and official religion with part of their Jewish heritage? After all, when we use the concept of mainstream, we should refer to what the majority of a country's inhabitants experience.

Within a Peruvian framework, Iquitos's Jewishness is mainstream when compared to the clannishness of its counterpart: the Jewish community of Lima. However, because the debate over "Who is a Jew?" transcends national borders, it is Iquitos's community that must look to Lima as its center. One may argue that every periphery is a center and every center a periphery, depending upon the vantage point of the beholder. Iquitos's descendants of Jews are an eloquent example of this predicament because they constitute a Jewish community in the process of total assimilation in an atmosphere of near-total tolerance. We are witnessing many Jewish communities in the first stages of that process in the Western world. On the one hand, there are Orthodox Jews becoming more insular and choosing to live in their own neighborhoods in New York, Jerusalem, and Paris in order to survive in a world of freedom and acculturation. On the other hand, we know about communities that have already disappeared due to the tolerant environment of their host countries.[2] (China is the example par excellence.) In Iquitos, more than in mainstream Jewish communities, we have an instance in which we can see more dramatically the last stages of assimilation, as if Iquitos were a freeze frame in a motion-picture reel.

The efforts of the "Jewish *Mestizos*" to distinguish themselves from other ethnic groups in the culturally homogeneous milieu of Iquitos's society are doomed to failure because of the centrifugal forces of cultural blending, sameness, and syncretism in the Peruvian Amazon. These descendants of Jews are trying to exile themselves from the paradisiacal state of being part of a city where they can easily lose their sense of distinction. Only Israel offers hope for the survival of the group's Jewish identity; but once in Israel, the "Jewish *Mestizos*" confront the reality that the predominantly modern, secular inhabitants of the Jewish state do not live the traditional way of life that the "Jewish *Mestizos*" had dreamed of recapturing from their ancestors. Thus, they face the predicament of losing an essential part of their religious background, becoming Jews without faith. In this case, the concept of *Marranism*, which is usually defined as a "no-man's land between two faiths," could be extended to encompass the complex web of groups that live in a "many-man's land" between diverse faiths, cultural references, and their consequent predicaments. Although I define *Marranism* as focusing on the syncretic identity of Jewish descendants, rather than limiting the concept to the offspring of Jews forced to convert to Christianity, I only use the term to refer to those instances of religious synthesis in which Judaism becomes the main paradigm. Others may prefer to call Iquitos's descendants of Jews "confused Christians," "exotic Jews," "madmen," or any other label that they prefer. After all, like places, people, and circumstances, definitions are "center" or "periphery" according to the scholarly specialization or academic purposes of those who use them.

The drama of Iquitos's descendants of Jews, who are obligated nearly every day to prove that they are not Christians, is summed up in a joke told to me by one of my interviewees: "The *paisano* Jesus decides to return, so he appears in La Plaza de Armas of Iquitos. There, he proclaims himself to be Christ, the son of God, but because of his appearance, a policeman approaches him, grabs his arm, and demands: 'Identity Documents . . . ID, please!'"

In La Plaza de Armas of Iquitos, the meeting place for Judaism, Catholicism, and the Amazonian, Jesus, the Jewish Christian must also identify himself. Even in a remote corner of the Amazon, an individual cannot escape from humanity's overwhelming urge to catalog each specimen of its species.

APPENDIXES

Appendix 1

List of People Buried at Iquitos Israelite Cemetery

Year of Burial	Name	Age at Death	Birthplace	Source of Data
1895	Mercedes Khan de Bohabot	22	Morocco	GR
	David Erwini	~	~	GR
1896	Jayme Cohen	45	Tetuan	GR
1899	Elisa Bensadón	34	Tangier	CA
1900	Moisés Isaac Nahón	18	Tangier	GR
	Perla Levy de Bohabot	25	Tangier	GR #
1904	Semior Amselem	32	Tangier	CA
	Rubén Benjil Bendrao	21	Tangier	CA
	Santos Ausehu	~	~	RR
1908	Isaac Barcesat	41	Tangier	GR
1909	Jacobo Toledano	53	Tangier	CA
	Jaco Isaac Medina	~	~	GR
1912	Isidro Saadia Asayac	30	Larache	GR
	Charles Samuel	39	Whittersehein	CA
1915	Moisés Edery	34	Tangier	GR
1917	Rene Weill	6 months	Iquitos	GR
	Isidoro Levy (Consul of France)	39	France	GR
1918	Marcel Asayag	~	~	CA
	Rafael Mey	~	~	CA
	E. Howard Lidy	~	~	CA
1920	Salomón Barcesat	34	Tangier	GR
1921	Estercita Edery	7	Iquitos	GR
	Joseph A. Schuler	at birth	Iquitos	GR
1925	Marcos Tapiero Darmón	~	Larache	GR
	Rafael Israel	43	Malta	GR
1927	Jaime Barcesat	48	Tangier	GR
1937	David Dávila Bendayán	70	Caballococha	GR
	Beny Benzaquén	56	Boston, England	GR
1938	Tomasa Assot	~	~	RR
1939	Anita Namías Michali	~	India	GR
1941	Abrahám Edery Benoliel	50	Tangier	CA
1942	Isaac Miguel Azulay	55	~	GR

Year of Burial	Name	Age at Death	Birthplace	Source of Data
1944	Moisés Cohén Berros	75	Alentejos, Portugal	GR
	Fortunato Edery	~	~	CA #
1947	Moisés Benzaquén	75	Tangier	GR
1950	Rafael Cohén Nahón	76	Portugal	RR
1951	Fortunato Foinquinos Atías	71	Morocco	GR
1952	Abraham Bensús Benamú	72	Spain	G
1953	Samuel Bendayán	~	~	GR
1960	Perla Bendayán García	~	~	GR
1962	Alberto Edery Fimat	80	Morocco	GR
1970	Manfred Weisselberger	~	~	GR
1976	Alberto Toledano Nahón	~	~	GR
	José Weisselberger	~	Meller, Rumania	GR
1979	Amelia Ríos (widow of Bensús)	~	~	GR
1980	Lidia R. de Bendayán	~	~	GR
1990	Moisés Bendayán Casique	~	~	GR
	Nora Casandra Edery	~	~	GR
1992	Cesar Toledano Torres	~	~	GR
1992 or 1993	Lisbiño Elaluf	~	~	WT
1995	Edwin Pizarro Panduro	~	Iquitos	WT
	Alberto Edery Morales	~	Yurimaguas	WT
?	León Tapiero	1 month	Iquitos	RR
?	Naive Simy Edery	~	~	GR

There are more than fifty people buried in Iquitos's Israelite cemetery.

GR: Data registered on the gravestones and complemented, in many cases, by information from the cemetery archives.

CA: Data confirmed in the cemetery archives.

RR: Data confirmed in Alfredo Rosenzweig's records.

WT: Data confirmed by witnesses.

: On the gravestone of Perla Levy de Bohabot it is not clear whether the date is 1900 or 1906. Fortunato Edery's death is recorded in 1944, according to Rosenzweig's records, however, the Iquitos cemetery archives list the year as 1936.

APPENDIX 2

JEWS WHO SETTLED IN THE PERUVIAN AMAZON, ACCORDING TO ALFREDO ROSENZWEIG'S RECORDS

Name	Birthplace	Returned/Died	Offspring in Amazon
David Abecasis	Tangier	R Morocco	~
David Abensur	Manchester, Eng.	R England	Several children
José Abensur	Manchester, Eng.	R England	~
Moisés Abisroar	Morocco	D Ucayali River	Some daughters
Alberto Alves	~	~	~
Salomón Alves	~	~	~
Semior Anselmi	Morocco	R Morocco	~
Elías Assayac	Morocco	R Morocco	~
León Assayac	Morocco	D Iquitos	One son, Ucayali
Santos Ausehu	Tangier	D Iquitos	~
Isajar Azerrat	Morocco	D Contamana	~
Salomón Azerrat	Rabat	D Paris	~
Isaac Miguel Azulay	Morocco	D Iquitos	~
León Banasayac	Tangier	R Morocco	Two sons
Isaac Barcesat	Tangier	D Iquitos	~
Jacobo Barcesat	Tangier	R Morocco	~
Jaime Barcesat	Morocco	D Ucayali	Two sons, Contamana
Shalom Benamú	Morocco	D Yurimaguas	Many children
Samuel Benchetril	~	~	~
León Bendayán	Morocco	R Morocco	Two sons
Moisés Bendayán	Morocco	R Morocco	~
Samuel Bendayán	Morocco	R Morocco	Two children
Rubén Benjio Bendrao	Tangier	D Iquitos	~
Abraham Bensús	Morocco	D Iquitos	~
Abraham Bentislibe	~	Lived in Yavari	~
Beny Benzaquén	England	D Iquitos	Many children
David Benzaquén	Morocco	D Iquitos	~
José Benzaquén	Morocco	Lived in Yurimaguas	~
Moisés Benzaquén	Tangier	D Iquitos	~

Name	Birthplace	Returned/Died	Offspring in Amazon
Rafael Benzaquén	Morocco	Lived in Yurimaguas	~
Alex Besso	U.S.A	R New York	~
Miguel Besso	U.S.A	R New York	~
Víctor Besso	U.S.A	R New York	~
Julio Block	France	R Paris	~
Marcel Block	Alsace, France	R France	~
David Bohabot	Morocco	R Morocco	Two children
Jaime Bohabot	Morocco	R Morocco	Many children, Contamana
José Bohabot	Tangier	~	~
Salomón Bohabot	Morocco	D Iquitos	~
Geron Caen (Khan)	France	R France	One daughter
David Cazes	England	R Gibraltar	~
Benjamín Cohen	Tangier	R Tangier	~
Meir Levy Cohen	Manchester, Eng.	R England	~
Isaac Moisés Cohen	Manchester, Eng.	D Pucallpa (married Jewish woman)	~
Jaime Cohen	Tetuan	D Iquitos	~
Lázaro Cohén	Morocco	Was mayor of Pucallpa	Three daughters
León Cohen	~	~	~
Marcel Cohen	France	R France	~
Moisés Cohen	Portugal	D Caballococha	Many children
Rafael Cohen	Portugal	D Iquitos	~
Rubén Cohen	Tangier	R Tangier	~
Ramón Coriat	Tangier	R Tangier	Two children, Iquitos
Samuel Coriat	Tangier	~	~
Abraham Dahan	Rabat	R Rabat	~
Aron Dahan	Rabat	R Rabat	~
Israel Darmón	Spanish Morocco	R Morocco	~
Isaac David	Morocco	R Morocco	Children, Caballococha
David Dávila Bendayán	Tangier	D Iquitos	~
Abraham Salomón Delmar	Tangier	R Tangier	Two daughters, six children
Marcos Delmar	Morocco	~	~

Name	Birthplace	Returned/Died	Offspring in Amazon
Alberto Edery	Morocco	D Iquitos	~
David Edery	Tangier	~	~
Isaac Edery	Morocco	D Yurimaguas	~
Moisés Edery	Tangier	D Iquitos	~
David Elaluf	Casablanca	R Casablanca	One son
David Erwini	Morocco	D Iquitos	~
Moisés Farache	Tetuan	R Tetuan	~
Fortunato Foinquinos	Morocco	D Iquitos	Many sons, Contamana
Benjamín Gabay	Tangier	R Tangier	~
Lázaro García	~	~	~
Sam Harris	England	Moved to Lima	~
David Hatchwell	England	~	~
Elías Hatchwell	England	~	~
Moisés Hatchwell	England	~	~
Rene Hirsh	Alsace, France	R France	Some children
Isaac Israel	Malta	~	~
Rafael Israel	Malta	D Iquitos	~
Víctor Israel	Malta	D Lima	Children in Lima
Edmundo Khan	France	R Paris	~
Eduardo Khan	France	D Amazon River	One son
Ferdinand Khan	Paris	R Paris w/his son	~
José Khan	France	R France	~
Salvador Knaffo	Tangier	R Tangier	~
Alfredo Koblenz	Germany	D Yurimaguas	Several children
Abraham Labos	Tangier	R Tangier	~
Samuel Laredo	Morocco	Mayor of Contamana, moved to Argentina	Four children
Alberto Levi	Tangier	~	~
Isidoro Levi	France	D Iquitos	One daughter
José Levi	Morocco	R Morocco	~
León Levi	Morocco	R Morocco	Several children, Contamana
Mauricio Levi	Alsace, France	R France	One son
Moisés Levi	Morocco	~	~
Salomón Levi	Morocco	D Contamana	Several children, Lima

Name	Birthplace	Returned/Died	Offspring in Amazon
Jaime Malca	Tangier	R Tangier	~
Rafael Marache	Tangier	R Tangier	One son, Ucayali
Carlos Margui	Morocco	R Morocco	~
Jacobo Medina	Morocco	D Iquitos	~
Isidoro Mey	France	Moved to Lima	~
Jacobo Miguel	~	~	~
Abraham Nahmías	Morocco	~	~
Isaac Nahmías	Morocco	D Contamana	~
Salomón Nahmías	Tangier	R Tangier	~
Moisés Isaac Nahón	Tangier	D Iquitos	~
Abraham Pinto	Tangier	R Tangier	~
León Pinto	Tangier	~	~
Moisés Pinto	Tangier	R Tangier	~
Samuel Pinto	Tangier	R Tangier	~
León Ruach (Tentes)	Tangier	R Tangier	~
Elías Salgado	~	~	~
Charles Samuel	Alsace, France	D Iquitos	~
Isaac Sarfati	Tangier	R Tangier	~
Pierre Schuler	France	R France	~
Theodoro Schuler	Tangier	R Tangier	~
Moisés Serfati	Tangier	R Tangier	~
Isaac Suzzana	Morocco	D Contamana	~
José Tapiero	Tangier	R Tangier	~
Alberto Toledano	Tangier	R Tangier	~
Isaac Toledano	Tangier	~	~
Jacobo Toledano	Tangier	~	Six children, Iquitos
Jorge Toledano	Tangier	~	~
José Toledano	Tangier	R Tangier	One son, Iquitos
Moisés Toledano	Tangier	R Tangier	~
Alberto Weill	France	R France	~
Lucien Weill	France	~	~
Rene Weill	France	D Iquitos	~
Moisés Zrihem and Mrs. Zrihem	Morocco	R Morocco	~

Other Immigrants Who Are Not on Rosenzweig's List

Name	Birthplace	Returned/Died	Offspring in Amazon
Kalman Abramovitz	Poland/Palestine	D Lima	~
Zeev Abramovitz	~	~	Four sons, three in Lima, one in Iquitos
Jacobo Barchilón	Morocco	Married in Iquitos, 1904°	~
Sara Jacob Benchetril	Morocco	Married in Iquitos, 1908 to Moisés Bendayán°°	~
Jack Ben Gilbert	New York	Married in Iquitos, 1943 to Estrella Cohén Dávila, of the "Catholic Religion."	~
José Benoliel	~	~	~
Jaime Bensimón	Morocco	~	Five children
Antonio Bento Otero	Portugal	D Loreto	~
A. Bitton	~	~	~
Mayer Cohén Mesulán	Manchester, Eng.	~	~
Salomón Darmont	Brazil	~	~
Solomon Joseph	~	~	~
Jacobo Kohn Jacorovicht	Hungary	D Loreto	Two children
Ramón Levy Azulay	Tangier	~	~
Francisco Mesía Rosenthal	Morocco	~	Many children
Michel Polak	Paris	~	~
Gerardo Schindler	Berlin	~	One daughter
David Seinfeld	~	~	~
Salomón Tobelem	~	~	~
Herman Weisselberger	Rumania	D Lima	Children in Lima
Joseph Weisselberger	Rumania	D Iquitos	Brought his sons
Manfred Weisselberger	Rumania	D Iqutios	Three sons in Iquitos

° First marriage certificate with the word Judío in the space for religion.

°° First marriage certificate with the word Judío for both spouses in the space for religion.

Appendix 3

Members of the Israelite Society of Iquitos, in March 1992[*]

José Ríos Asayag (1); Betty, Dora Alicia, León Iván, and León Arturo Assayag Chávez (4); Clara, Krauss, and William Assayag Vidurrizaga (3); Zeev and Jorge Abramovitz (2); Ana Ruth and Luis Aspiazú Oliveira (2); Saúl Benamú Gónzales-Pavón (1); Manuel, Renata, Alicia, and Abraham Bensús (4); Miriam and Sara Bendayán Vásquez (2); Teddy and Jaime Bendayán Díaz (2); Israel Bento Mass (1); Raquel Bento Valera (1); Amalia and Jaime Bensimón Chávez (2); Elías and Ana Bensimón Rengifo (2); Ramón Coriat Pinedo (1); Armando and Arturo Coriat (2); Wálter Cenepo Eljarrat (1); M. B. and Yasmín Delgado Assayag (2); Jorge Delgado Quintero (1); Víctor Edery Morales and Diolinda López de Edery (2); Jaime, David, Sharón, Shulamit, and Julia Edery López (5); Alberto Edery Morales (1); Alberto, David, Moisés, and Raul Edery Miguel (4); Judith Edery de Grinstein (1); Ruth Edery de Winiesky (1); Malca Edery López (1); Roger Ruíz Foinquinos (1); Róger and Grace Gonzales Assayag (2); Oscar Hirsh Casanova (1); Oriel Jarama Dávila (1); Jorge Khan Ríos (1); Malca and Jorge Khan Olórtegui (2); Werner and Fernando Levy Navarro (2); Carlos Levy Londoño (1); Cayo, Alicia, Abraham, Michael, and Patricia Levy Macedo (5); Tamar Miguel (1); Esther Miguel Macías (1); Blanca Namías de Massari (1); Miranda Oliveira Aspiazú (1); Luz Marina Olórtegui (1); Omar Pérez Edery (1); Miguel Pinasco Arévalo (1); Ronald Reategui Levy (1); Cesar and Alicia Ramal Assayag (2); Víctor Ruíz Oliveira (1); César Toledano Torres (1); Mercedes Toledano de Mattos (1); Raquel Toledano de Tang (1); Jaime Vásquez Izquierdo (1); Hugo, Luis, and Sammy Weisselberger (3); Jorge Bensimón Chávez (1); Edgar Dávila Lazo (1); Carlos Abensur Macedo (1); Nicolás Levy Vidal (1); Sara Pérez Foinquinos (1); Priscila Oliveira Aspiazu (1); Ana María Aspiazú de Oliveira (1); Hugo Aspiazú Oliveira (1); Daniel Oliveira Aspiazú (1); Alfonso Arévalo Bensús (1); Jorge and Miza Bensús Dos Santos (2); Mauricio Levy Vásquez (1); Víctor M. Levy Sarabia (1); José Pinedo Levy (1); Johny Bendayán Miguel (1); García Regalado de Bendayán (1).

[*] In 1992 the society gathered the largest number of members since its establishment in 1990.

APPENDIX 4

A summary of the cases of Bene Israel *from India, Samaritans, Karaites, and* Beta Israel *of Ethiopia and their struggle to be accepted as part of the Jewish people in the State of Israel:*

The first members of *Bene Israel* to arrive in Israel after 1948 found that most rabbis questioned their Jewishness. Furthermore, this community from Bombay was not allowed to marry "authentic Jews" without undergoing nominal rituals of conversion at least. In October 1961, the Chief Rabbinical Council officially recognized the sect's members as "full Jews in every respect," although they would still be required to submit to rituals of conversion before marriage. This decision ignited the anger of the *Bene Israel,* who announced that they might seek the status of a separate community in Israel, as had the Christians, Moslems, and Druze. The rabbis' ambiguous decision generated a political turmoil that required the intervention of President Zalman Shazar, who attempted to encourage a dialogue between Orthodox authorities and members of the sect. Finally, in August 1964, the Chief Rabbinate made a concession to the *Bene Israel,* agreeing to perform conversions only on members whose Jewish antecedents were unclear at the time of their marriage application. Ultimately, this remnant of Israel became part of its mainstream counterpart.

The Samaritans claim to be descendants of the Ten Tribes of Israel deported by the Assyrians in 722 B.C.E. According to the Bible, a few subjects of the Kingdom of Israel succeeded in staying on their lands and continued to observe their traditions, but they intermarried with other peoples of the Middle East. When the descendants of the Kingdom of Judah returned from the Babylonian exile in 538 B.C.E., they isolated themselves from those who had never left the land, whom they considered to be impure (accounts of this rift can be found in the biblical books of Ezra and Nehemiah). According to Orthodox rabbis, the present-day Samaritans descend from the Cutheans, a people settled in Samaria by orders of the Assyrian king following the deportation of the Ten Tribes. The story is described in 2 Kings 17. Most scholars who have studied the history of the Samaritans agree with the group's own version of their origin. They argue that most of its current traditions were shaped centuries after the Assyrian exile. In any case, the Samaritan traditions, which still include the Passover sacrifice of the paschal lamb on Mount Gerizim, strict observance of levitical rules pertaining to cleanliness and uncleanness, and the separation of women from the rest of the household during menstruation, seem to prove their historical linkage with the ancient Hebrews.

The Samaritans also firmly reject the Oral Law (which, according to rabbinical Judaism, cannot be separated from the written Torah), accepting only the Five

Books of Moses and none of the other books of the Hebrew Bible. The Samaritans consider Mount Gerizim, near Nablus, to be their "Jerusalem." Today, the Samaritans or *Shomronim* (Observants) number only a few hundred people, who live in the autonomous Palestinian city of Nablus and in the Israelli city of Holon, adjacent to Tel Aviv. They claim not to be Jews, but, rather, Hebrews, because they are not descended from ancient Judeans, but from Israelites from the Northern Kingdom. Therefore, they are happy to be Israeli citizens, a right that was conferred upon them in 1949 when they received the immigration privileges granted by the Law of Return. The political influence of President Izhak Ben Zvi, who convinced them to intermarry with Jews, was paramount to the decision to legitimize them as "Jews" on their identity cards at a time when such definition was still legally undefined.

The Karaites were founded in the eighth century C.E. when Anan ben David, a Jewish dissenter from an Iraqi Orthodox community, separated himself and his followers from Orthodox Jews. Karaism insists on rigid, literal interpretation of biblical law and has no regard for post-biblical holidays such as Hanukkah (which commemorates the Maccabean revolt against the Seleucids), the use of *tefillin* (phylacteries), or anything belonging to the Oral Law codified in the Talmud. In medieval times the Karaites spread throughout Asia Minor, Europe, and the Middle East. The rivalry between the Karaites and Orthodox rabbis began in the early tenth century when a master of rabbinical Judaism in the Middle East, Sa'adiah Gaon, declared them heretics who should be ostracized by all good Jews. Marriage between Karaites and Orthodox Jews has been forbidden since that time.

The approximately eight to ten thousand Karaites who emigrated to Israel, mostly from Egypt during the late 1950s, were automatically included in the Law of Return. Modern Orthodox rabbis accepted them as Jews, but they did not approve of marriages between Karaites and other Jews. Initially, this did not pose a problem to the Karaites since they do not permit their members to marry rabbinical Jews (they are an endogamous community). Eventually, the government arrived at an uneasy compromise, still in effect, that authorizes the Ministry of Religious Affairs to supply Karaite rabbis with marriage and divorce certificates, so they are spared from being under the jurisdiction of the Orthodox Rabbinate. In the case of intermarriages, however, Orthodox rabbis allow Karaites to "convert" to Judaism—a strange procedure for someone who is already Jewish.

The long-standing dispute between Orthodox rabbis and Karaites continued until 1973 when the chief rabbi of the Sephardic community of Israel, Ovadia Yosef, recognized the Karaites as full-fledged Jews. This proclamation has not altered the agreement that allows the Karaites to conduct their own civil affairs.

The *Beta Israel* (the House of Israel), better known as the Ethiopian Jews or *Falasha* (landless or wanderers, as their Ethiopian neighbors called them with disdain), also rejected the Oral Law for centuries. The origins of this community remain a matter of controversy. Legends of the Ten Lost Tribes and King Menelik, son of King Solomon and the Queen of Sheba, compete with scholarly research that traces the *Beta Israel* to first-century Hebrews who isolated themselves in the Gondar region of Ethiopia, or to groups that deserted Christianity sometime during the fifteenth or sixteenth century and became a separate sect basing its traditions on the Old Testament. Other scholars, instead, argue that Jews settled in Ethiopia after the *galut* (exile) in the first century.

The *Beta Israel* were "discovered" by nineteenth-century Jewish emissaries from the philanthropic organization *Alliance Israélite Universelle,* who introduced the sect to modern Judaism. Jews such as Joseph Halévy in the nineteenth century and his pupil, Jacques Faitlovitch, in the early twentieth century, dedicated their lives to the cause of the Ethiopian Jewry. However, it was not until the 1980s that the *Beta Israel* received any substantial aid from Jews or the State of Israel, which rescued the group from starvation and civil war and brought them to their promised land in a series of airlift missions to Sudan, called "Operation Moses" (1983), "Operation Sheba or Joshua"(1985), and "Operation Solomon" (1985–1989).

The Ethiopian Jews strictly observe the laws of the written Torah, putting emphasis on rituals of purity and *kashrut.* Like the Karaites, the Ethiopian Jews do not separate meat from milk, and they celebrate all the biblical holidays, but none of the post-biblical ones, to which they were never exposed. The *Beta Israel* maintained their faith intact because they could read the sacred texts in Ge'ez, the local liturgical tongue spoken by their *kahan* (priests). Their colloquial language was Ethiopian Amharic until they arrived in Israel, where they learned to speak Hebrew.

As in the case of the Karaites, it was the same chief rabbi of Israel's Sephardic population, Ovadia Yosef, who again in 1973 issued a religious ruling recognizing immigrants from Ethiopia as Jews. Citing rabbinical opinions from more than four hundred years earlier, Ovadia Yosef stated that these people were descendants of the lost tribe of Dan. However, Shlomo Goren, chief rabbi of Israel's Ashkenazic community, expressed his doubts about this conclusion and refused to accept the *Beta Israel* Ethiopians as Jews until they underwent full conversion.

Throughout the 1970s and early 1980s, Ethiopian immigrants in Israel were required to undergo a modified conversion ceremony: ritual immersion, a declaration of accepting rabbinical law, and (in the case of men) a symbolic recircumcision. This rule, which initially was applied to all Ethiopians, was later limited to those wishing to marry, and by 1983, the demand for recircumcision was dropped. In 1985, the vast majority of the more than forty thousand members of *Beta Israel* organized demonstrations to protest the rabbinate's demand that they convert because this requirement presupposed that they were not Jews. The Ethiopians also began to marry in traditional ceremonies conducted by their own religious leaders, although such marriages had no legal status in Israel. Looking for a compromise, the Orthodox establishment appointed Rabbi David Chelouche of Netanya, a cherished supporter of the Ethiopians, as marriage registrar for the entire community; many in the Ethiopian community subsequently registered their marriages with Rabbi Chelouche, while others accepted symbolic immersion to legalize their Judaism.

APPENDIX 5

Rabbi Guillermo Bronstein's explanation of his plan for the conversion of "Jewish Mestizos" in Iquitos, as he recalled it, during an interview on June 2, 1995.

"The prerequisite of *[Iquiteños]* having to pledge to go Israel in order to be converted would avoid creating false expectations that they would be accepted as Jews in Lima, in case they decided to move there. I wrote them a letter explaining, clearly, this prerequisite, and detailing the steps for their possible conversion. Before any conversion, I had to travel to Iquitos and see if they really were learning, and not only copying [information] from the books. [I had to check] what they were studying (this after grading their exams about topics such as *kashrut* [dietary laws], Shabbat, Jewish holidays, monotheism, and *Tauharat Hamishpaha* [purity rituals for couples]. I also wanted to check their degree of observance of Jewish precepts (of course, in the framework of their remote location; however, for example, you can eat fish and vegetables in Iquitos, thus complying with kosher requirements!). Afterward, I could report to members of the Zionist Federation in Lima that these people had really progressed, and that everything was ready to call two rabbis from abroad (I guess from Chile) and establish the *bet din* [rabbinical tribunal] to carry out conversions.

"Regarding circumcisions, taking into account that the *Iquiteños* do not have the economic means to travel to Lima to be circumcised, my proposal 'was not very halakhic' [strictly concordant to Jewish law]; nevertheless, it was still halakhic. In halakhah [Jewish law], [a situation like this] is called *bediavad,* which means something that is accepted a posteriori [things that cannot be known except by examination]—in other words, an ex post facto situation, which opposes the ideal concept of halakhah, which is *lehathilah,* or a priori [things that do not require examination]. *Lehathilah,* or a priori ways are ideal because they are performed exactly as Jewish law prescribes it. Let me explain! *Lehathilah,* the ideal way halakhah should be, was to bring [to Iquitos] a Jewish doctor to perform the circumcisions. However, it was practically impossible to do that for more or less fifteen adult candidates in just a couple of days, so we had to adapt to reality . . . [to] look for a non-Jewish specialist in urology in Iquitos who could circumcise them (there are no Jewish doctors in Iquitos!). Then, before the *tevilah* [ritual bath], we would perform what it is known as *hatafat dam brit;* this means that the rabbi uses a sterilized needle to prick the glans [the head of the penis] and so spill a little drop of blood. That little drop is called *Le-shem brit milah.* When someone was already born circumcised [something which rarely happens], or someone was circumcised through a surgical procedure (and not as it is commanded in Jewish law in order to affirm the covenant between God and Israel), then this *hatafat dam brit* must be done, because that little drop of blood that is shed symbolizes the covenant . . . [even] ex post facto. (There is a controversy as to whether this *hatafat dam brit* really should be done, but in some cases it is preferable to do it.)

"There was also the issue of the *tevilah* (ritual bath for the conversion). You know that there are also some halakhic problems regarding *tevilah* if you are going to perform it in a lake. The person must not be in contact with the mud (the floor). . . . He has to be surrounded by water everywhere. So, the plan was to go to the Quistococha Lake in Iquitos, put the candidates and the rabbis in a big boat, and from the boat they [the candidates] would jump into the lake with their bathing suits on. Once in the lake, they would undress and put [the bathing suits] in the boat. They would submerge themselves three times in the water, and then they would take back their bathing suits, dress, and return to the boat. Of course, while they were submerged in the lake, they could not have rings or any object attached to their skin (this is a halakhic requirement!). Women would be in another boat with the wife of one of the [three] rabbis and do the same [procedure] without make-up or anything covering their skin.

"Certainly, when I traveled to Iquitos they did not understand the reason for so many punctilious details, but these are Jewish precepts little known by average Jews anywhere . . . except rabbis.

"Of course, this conversion would help them to go to Israel, but the ideal was that, once there, the *Iquiteños* would undergo a more rigorous conversion *[lehathilah]*, performed by Orthodox rabbis, so they would not have problems in Israel" (AT).

(Rabbi Abraham Benzaquén, of Miami's Sephardic congregation Temple Moses, helped me understand some of the concepts that Rabbi Bronstein mentioned during the interview and suggested to me that I clarify for the reader that, for Orthodox Judaism, nothing done by Reform or Conservative rabbis has legal validity from the point of view of halakhah, no matter how meticulous these rabbis' procedures are. The fact that rabbis who are not recognized as such by Israel's rabbinate carry out these conversions makes these conversions meaningless to the Orthodox establishment. Nevertheless, after listening to the tape of my interview with Rabbi Guillermo Bronstein, Rabbi Benzaquén acknowledged that the Conservative Peruvian rabbi was being very honest because he warned all the conversion candidates, the members of the *Federación Sionista del Perú,* and, myself, of the limited validity of his conversions when the "converted" person is in Israel. Rabbi Bronstein also displayed significant candor when he suggested the *Iquiteños* convert again in Israel.)

NOTES

Works frequently cited in the notes have been identified by the following abbreviations:

APAR	Archivo Personal de Alfredo Rosenzweig
AGM	Archivo General de Maynas (Registro Civil), Iquitos.
AGN	Archivo General de la Nación
CAAAP	Centro Amazónico de Antropología y Aplicación Práctica
CETA	Centro de Estudios Teológicos de la Amazonía
FSP	Federación Sionista del Perú
ICPI	Instituto Cultural Peruano-Israelí de Iquitos
IIAP	Instituto de Investigaciones de la Amazonía Peruana
ICPII	Archivo del Instituto Cultural Peruano-Israelí de Iquitos
PSJBI	Archivo de la Parroquia San Juan Bautista de Iquitos
RPL	Archivo de los Registros Públicos de (Región) Loreto
SBC1870	Archivo de la Sociedad de Beneficiencia y Culto 1870, Lima
SBII	Archivo de la Sociedad de Beneficiencia Israelita de Iquitos
SBPI	Archivo de la Sociedad de Beneficiencia Pública de Iquitos

PREFACE

1.   Virginia R. Domínguez, *People as Subject, People as Object: Selfhood and Peoplehood in Contemporary Israel* (Madison: University of Wisconsin Press, 1989), 169.

2.   Brian S. Pullan, *The Jews of Europe and the Inquisition of Venice, 1550–1670* (Totowa, N.J.: Barnes & Noble, 1983), 207. Pullan addresses what he calls "the Problem of Marranism" in the same book (pages 201–210).

For a thorough understanding of the phenomenon of *Marranism* see also David M. Gitlitz, *Secrecy and Deceit: The Religion of the Crypto-Jews* (Philadelphia: Jewish Publication Society, 1996), 100–101; Moshe Lazar, "Scorched Parchments and Tortured Memories: The 'Jewishness' of the Anussim (Crypto-Jews)" in *Cultural Encounters: The Impact of the Inquisition in Spain and the New World,* eds. Mary Elizabeth Perry and Anne J. Cruz (Berkeley: University of California Press, 1991), 176–206; Boleslao Lewin, *Los criptojudíos: Un fenómeno religioso y social* (Buenos Aires: Editorial Mila, 1987); Anita Novinsky, "Jewish Roots of Brazil" in *The Jewish Presence in Latin America,* eds. Judith Laikin Elkin and Gilbert W. Merkx (Boston: Allen & Unwin Inc., 1987), 33–44; Haim Beinart, *Conversos on Trial: The Inquisition in Ciudad Real* (Jerusalem: Magnes Press, 1981); Yosef

Hayim Yerushalmi's article "The Re-Education of the Marranos in the Seventeenth Century," in *Third Annual Rabbi Louis Feinberg Memorial Lecture in Judaic Studies* (Cincinnati: University of Cincinnati, 1980), 8–12, 479–526, as well as his book *From Spanish Court to Italian Ghetto: Isaac Cardoso, A Study in Seventeenth-Century Marranism and Jewish Apologetics* (New York: Center of Israel and Jewish Studies of Columbia University, 1966), 1–50; I. S. Révah, "Les Marranes Portugais et l'Inquisition au XVI siécle" in *Sephardi Heritage*, vol. 1, ed. Richard D. Barnett (New York: Ktav Publishing House, 1971); and Cecil Roth, "The Religion of the Marranos," in *Jewish Quarterly Review* 1, no. 22 (July 1931): 1–34.

3.　　Sara Bendayán García, interview by author, Iquitos, 29 June 1995.

　　Regarding some aspects mentioned by Mrs. Bendayán García, on Yom Kippur a ram's horn *(shofar)* is blown to symbolize the averted sacrifice of Isaac when Abraham, instead, took a ram to the altar, thus sparing the life of his son. It also symbolizes the last opening of the gates of heaven, making it easier for the worshipper to reach "God's ears" with his prayers of repentance. Only when Shabbat coincides with Yom Kippur do people say *Shabbat Shalom;* otherwise, they only say *Shana Tovah* (Happy New Year).

4.　　See David Augusto Canelo, *The Last Crypto-Jews of Portugal,* trans. Rabbi Joshua Stampfer, ed. Talmon-l'Armee (Portland, Oreg.: IJS, 1990).

5.　　Dan Ross, *Acts of Faith: A Journey to the Fringes of Jewish Identity* (New York: Schocken Books, 1984), 26.

6.　　Ibid., 26.

7.　　Canelo, *The Last Crypto-Jews of Portugal,* 67.

8.　　The cases of these groups are mentioned in the fifth chapter of this book.

9.　　See Yeremiahu Yovel, *Spinoza and Other Heretics: The Marrano of Reason* (Princeton: Princeton University Press, 1989), ix–x.

10.　The history of these crypto-Jews can be read in Canelo, *The Last Crypto-Jews of Portugal;* Ross, "The Not-So-Secret Jews of Portugal" in *Acts of Faith,* 26–51; and Joachim Prinz, *The Secret Jews* (New York: Random House, 1973), 150–183.

　　Some aspects of the religion of the original crypto-Jews that still persist in the rituals of *Marranos* can be found in Lewin, *Los criptojudíos;* Seymore B. Liebman, *Requiem por los olvidados: Los Judíos españoles en America, 1493–1825* (Madrid:

Altalena, 1984), 86–110; Novinsky, "Jewish Roots of Brazil," 33–44; and Lazar, "Scorched Parchments and Tortured Memories: The 'Jewishness' of the Anussim (Crypto-Jews), 176–206.

INTRODUCTION

1. Domínguez, *People as Subject, People as Object*, 13–4.

2. Ibid., 16.
    Regarding the technique of analyzing the role of the researcher during his or her process of researching and writing, Virginia R. Domínguez lists the following scholars and their works: Paul Rabinow, *Reflections on Fieldwork in Morocco* (Berkeley: University of California Press, 1977); Vincent Crapanzano, *Tuhami: Portrait of a Moroccan* (Chicago: University of Chicago Press, 1980); Kevin Dwyer, *Moroccan Dialogues: Anthropology in Question* (Baltimore: Johns Hopkins University Press, 1982); Vincent Crapanzano, *Waiting: The Whites of South Africa* (New York: Random House, 1985); James Clifford, "On Ethnographic Authority," *Representations* 2 (1983): 132–143; James Clifford and George E. Marcus, *Writing Culture: The Poetics and Politics of Ethnography* (Berkeley: University of California Press, 1986); Smadar Lavie, "The Poetics of Politics" in *The Frailty of Authority*, ed. M. J. Aronoff, *Political Anthropology* 5 (New Brunswick, N.J.: Transaction Books, 1986); and Michael M. J. Fischer, *Anthropology as Cultural Critique: An Experimental Moment in the Human Sciences* (Chicago: University of Chicago Press, 1986).
    Greg Dening also presents a list of scholars who have consciously blurred historical, literary, and anthropological genres, attempting to free their discourses on history "from any claim or presumption by historians or anthropologist that by our expertise we are directed to seeing history as having one form or another." Dening mentions anthropologist-historians such as Clifford Geertz, Marshal Sallings, Renato Rosaldo, Rhys Isaac, Barney Cohn, Natalie Zemon Davis, Valerio Valeri, James Boon, Richard Price, Victor Turner, Hayden White, etc. See Greg Dening's work "A Poetic for Histories: Transformations that Present the Past" in *Clio in Oceania: Toward Historical Anthropology*, ed. Aletta Biersack (Washington, D.C.: Smithsonian Institution Press, 1991), 347–380.

3. I could have written this book contextualizing in-depth the case of Iquitos's "Jewish *Mestizos*" in light of other Amazonian Jewish communities such as those ones of Belén and Manaus. However, as a historian with a limited budget for research and a clear awareness that it is impossible to embrace everything related to my topic in a book shorter than the Bible, I had to make choices. My choice was

to study this case in the context of Peruvian history, without omitting links between Iquitos's history and the history of Brazil and the Colombian Amazon.

The Jewish immigrants who lived in the Department of Loreto after the 1880s maintained affective personal and commercial links with their Brazilian-based Jewish compatriots from Morocco and other European nations, but their process of national and cultural adaptation to Peruvian paradigms was vastly different from that of the Jews in the Brazilian Amazon. Brazilian Jewish traders did not view Iquitos as a city whose Jewish population required assistance. Iquitos was a transitory commercial spot and besides, it was not part of Brazil. Statistics show that more than 50 percent of the original Jews who came to the Peruvian Amazon returned to Brazil and Europe, which suggests that Jewish traders in Iquitos did not see themselves as immigrants. However, by the 1930s, those who had stayed in Iquitos had already established links with Lima's Jews. Hence, Lima's Jewry was the principal point of reference for the generation of Jewish immigrants and their descendants in Iquitos, as documents since the early twentieth century demonstrate.

4.   Father Joaquín García, interview by author, Iquitos, 8 July 1995.

5.   I am not interested in going deeper into the controversy of whether syncretism connotes the idea of hegemony and resistance of one population's religious system over the other or whether it is simply a natural amalgamation of different cosmologies.

Some scholars define syncretism in terms of cultural resistance, studying religious synthesis in the context of colonialism and other forms of foreign domination. The controversy surrounding the use of this concept is the consequence of the meaning attributed to it by sixteenth- and seventeenth-century Protestant theologians, who used this term as a tool to call for the reconciliation of the diverse European Christian denominations. These debates, which concerned issues of doctrine and ritual, were known as the "syncretistic controversies." During the second half of the nineteenth century, "syncretism" connoted negative meanings in the study of comparative religions. Twentieth-century anthropologists introduced the term to explain the phenomenon of the religious synthesis between Christianity and native religious traditions in the New World. See A. Droogers's "Syncretism: The Problem of Definition, the Definition of the Problem" in *Dialogue and Syncretism: An Interdisciplinary Approach,* eds. J. Gort, H. Vroom, R. Fernhout, and A. Wessels (Grand Rapids, Mich.: W. B. Eerdmans Publishing Co, 1989); and Charles Stewart's "Introduction: Problematizing Syncretism" in *Syncretism/Anti-syncretism: The Politics of Religious Synthesis,* eds. Charles Stewart and Rosalind Shaw (New York: Routledge, 1994), 1–26.

6.   The Annals School was influential in opening the gates for interdisciplinary historical studies on culture, which has evolved into the study of identity as found, for
example, in Emmanuel LeRoy Ladurie, *Montaillou: The Promised Land of Error,*
trans. Barbara Bay (New York: Random House, Vintage Books, 1979). More
recently, some scholars have delved into the mental world of groupings and nations,
dealing with the notions of peoplehood, selfhood, and otherness. In Latin American
history we have works such as Jacques Lafaye, *Quetzacóatl and Guadalupe: The
Formation of Mexican National Consciousness, 1531–1813* (Chicago: University of
Chicago Press, 1974); Richard Price, *Alabi's World* (Baltimore: Johns Hopkins University Press, 1990); and Gary Gossen et al., eds., *De palabra y obra en el nuevo
mundo,* 3 vols. (Madrid: Siglo Veintiuno, 1992).

7.   John Putnam Demos defends his right as a historian to "share my own experience of knowing the common folk and common life of a distant place" in his book,
Entertaining Satan: Witchcraft and the Culture of Early New England (New York:
Oxford University Press, 1982), ix. I also will attempt to share my experience of
knowing the feelings of the subjects of my study, by incorporating their voices and
my own perplexed one, when the writing requires it.

8.   See Richard Price, *Alabi's World* (Baltimore: Johns Hopkins University Press,
1990), xix.

9.   See Gwyn Prins's essay "Oral History" in *New Perspectives on Historical Writ-
ing,* ed. Peter Burke (University Park: Pennsylvania State University Press, 1993),
114–139. Some other interesting works concerning oral history are Jan Vansina,
Oral Tradition: A Study in Historical Methodology (London: Routledge, 1966);
Michael Palmer (and other authors), "'I Haven't Anything to Say': Reflections of
Self and Community in Collecting Oral Histories" in *International Annual of Oral
History, 1990: Subjectivity and Multiculturalism in Oral History,* ed. Ronald J.
Greele (Westport, Conn.: Greenwood Press, 1992), 167–190; Robert Perks, *Oral
History: Talking About the Past* (London: The Historical Association, 1992); and
Mark Freeman, *Rewriting the Self: History, Memory, Narrative* (London: Rout-
ledge, 1993).
    There are many theoretical works regarding oral history in *The International
Journal of Oral History,* which began to be published in 1980, and the British
Journal *Oral History.*

10. After his research in Morocco, Paul Rabinow realized that under his system-
atic questioning, one of his informants, "[Ali] was taking realms of his own world
and interpreting them for an outsider. This meant that he, too, was spending more

time in this liminal, self-conscious world between cultures." See Rabinow, *Reflections on Fieldwork*, 39.

11. Among the historians who have been bridging the art of storytelling with historical methods are Demos in *Entertaining Satan;* Price in *Alabi's World;* and Guido Ruggiero in *Binding Passions: Tales of Magic, Marriage, and Power at the End of the Renaissance* (New York: Oxford University Press, 1993).

Also, Hayden White's works have been central in focusing on the problem of narrative in historiography and literary criticism. See Hayden White, *Tropics of Discourse: Essays in Cultural Criticism* (Baltimore: Johns Hopkins University Press, 1978); and *The Content of Form: Narrative Discourse and Historical Representation* (Baltimore: Johns Hopkins University Press, 1987). Also, Dominick LaCapra in his *History & Criticism* (Ithaca, N.Y.: Cornell University Press, 1985), presents an analysis of the role of narrative discourse in contemporary historical works.

12. Fritz W. Up De Graff, *Head Hunters of the Amazon: Seven Years of Exploration and Adventure* (New York: Garden City Publishing Co., Inc, 1923), 137.

13. *Judaizantes* were those New Christians and their descendants who were accused by the Inquisition of transmitting teachings from the Jewish faith, and thereby betraying their conversion to Catholicism. The name of Diego de León Pinelo can be found in records compiled by Seymour Liebman in his work *The Inquisitors and the Jews in the New World: Summaries of Procesos, 1500–1810, & Bibliographical Guide* (Coral Gables: University of Miami Press, 1975), 179.

14. Alfredo Rosenzweig is a Peruvian geologist who worked in the Peruvian Amazon during the 1940s. After an accident in which he broke one leg, he had to stay in an Iquitos hospital for some months. Hence, he met Jewish immigrants and their sons, becoming fascinated with their history. Back in Lima, in 1949 Rosenzweig wrote the first historical work about this community in his article "Judíos en la Amazonía Peruana, 1870–1949," *Maj'Shavot* (Buenos Aires) 12 (June 1967): 19–30.

Another "accidental circumstance" caused Alfredo Rosenzweig to travel to Peru while I was in Iquitos. Previously I had called him in Israel, where he now lives, and asked him for copies of the original documents he had found in the 1940s. He provided me with those documents.

During his visit to Lima my good friend Sandy Barak Cassinelli, a gifted intuitive researcher, performed an excellent interview with Alfredo Rosenzweig. A year afterward, in August 1996, I had the pleasure of meeting him personally in Haifa, Israel, where he confirmed the information he had previously provided to Sandy and myself.

15. Regarding matrifocal societies, see such works as Elizabeth Avers Jennes, "Matrifocality in Jamaica and East London" (master's thesis, George Washington University, 1973); Beverly Newbold Chiñas, *The Isthmus Zapotecs: A Matrifocal Culture of Mexico* (Fort Worth, Tex.: Harcourt Brace Jovanovich College Publishers, 1992); Nancie González Loudon, *Rethinking the Consanguineal Household and Matrifocality* (Pittsburgh: University of Pittsburgh, 1984); and Noel-Anne G. Brennan, "A Cross-Cultural Investigation of Matrifocality" (master's thesis, University of Rhode Island, 1983).

CHAPTER 1

1. The *Indigenista* movement in Peru calls for a return to Inca roots, neglecting the fact that in some areas, such as the Amazon, there were other Indian ethnic groups who were not dominated by the *Tawantinsuyo* (Inca) empire.

2. Many transpositions—already shaped by the European Christian exegetical cosmology influenced by biblical tradition, Greek and Latin antiquity, and messianic-eschatological prophecies—found an earthly and transcendental realm in the eyes of newcomers arriving in the New World.

    See such works as Peter Mason, "Imagining Worlds: Counterfact and Artifact," in *Myth and the Imaginary in the New World,* eds. Edmundo Magaña and Peter Mason, *Latin American Studies* 34 (Holland: CEDLA, Foris Publications, 1986), 43–74; Peter Hulme, *Colonial Encounters: Europe and the Native Caribbean, 1492–1797* (New York: Methuen, 1986); María Jesús Lacarra and Juan Manuel Cacho Blecua, *Lo imaginario en la conquista de America* (Zaragosa, Spain: Ediciones Oroel, 1990); Vladimir Acosta, *El continente prodigioso: Mitos e imaginario medieval en la conquista americana* (Caracas: Ediciones de la Biblioteca, Universidad Central de Venezuela, 1992); and O. R. Dathorner, *Imagining the World: Mythical Belief Versus Reality in Global Encounters* (Westport, Conn.: Bergin & Garvey, 1994).

3. No chronicler or historian has determined when and where the first dreamer uttered the word "Dorado." The legend of *El Dorado*, in all its versions, seems to have evolved from the encounter between mythical European accounts and some actual American cities filled with gold.

4. Among the most prominent scholars who discussed the Ophirite theory were Fernandes Brandâo (*Diálogos das grandezas do Brasil,* 1555; republished as *Dialogues of the Great Things of Brazil,* trans. Frederick Holden Hall, William F. Harrison, and Dorothy Winters Welker [Albuquerque: University of New Mexico

Press, 1988]); Arias Montano (*Polyglot Bible*, 1572); Gilbert Genebrard
(*Chronologia hebraeorum major*, 1578); Miguel Angel Cabello Valboa (*Miscelánea
antártica: Una historia del Perú antiguo*, 1586; republished in Lima in 1951 by
Universidad Nacional Mayor de San Marcos); and Friar Gregorio García (*Origen
de los Indios*, 1607; republished in Mexico in 1981 by Biblioteca Americano).
For a thorough account of the Ophirite theory see Acosta, *El continente prodigioso*
and J. Imbelloni, *La segunda esfinge indiana: Antiguos y nuevos aspectos de los
origenes americanos* (Buenos Aires: Librería Hachett S.A., 1956). Concerning the
Indian-Israelite theories of the American Indians, see Acosta, "Los mitos del
poblamiento de America" in *El continente prodigioso*, 331–370; Imbelloni, "Ophir,
o la indología judaica" in *La segunda esfinge indiana*, 37–46; Lee Elridge
Huddleston, *Origins of the American Indians: European Concepts, 1492–1729*
(Austin: University of Texas, Institute of Latin American Studies, 1967; and
Menasseh ben Israel, *Mikveh Israel*, ed. Henry Méchoulan (New York: Oxford
University Press, 1987).

Gradually, Europeans dismissed the biblical aura of Ophir, focusing instead on
the tangible benefits of reaching places where they could procure wealth. Gold
became an obsession for men hungry for power and property. The most desired
land sought by European navigators all around the globe was Prester John's
domain. Prester John was a mysterious Nestorian Christian king who, according to
letters spread throughout Europe during the twelfth century, was the ruler of a
golden kingdom. The search for Prester John's kingdom was soon abandoned by
European colonizers, but the essential inspiration of that myth endured for a long
time: gold, wealth, fortune.

5.   Several scholars claim that in Europe, the river discovered by Orellana was
called *Amazonas* in reference to the mythical warrior women. See Ismael López,
De París al Amazonas: Las fieras del Putumayo (Paris: Librería Paul Ollendorff,
1912), 122. According to Leonard Irving in *The Books of the Brave* (New York:
Gordian Press, 1964), many Spanish conquerors had in mind the myth of the
Amazonian warriors after listening to chivalric stories such as *Las sergas de
espladian*. Among the most famous explorers and conquerors who looked for the
Amazonian warriors were Christopher Columbus, Amerigo Vespucci, Hernán
Cortés, Walter Raleigh, and Francisco de Orellana. Encounters with those warriors were described in Friar Gaspar Carvajal's chronicles and Fernandez de
Oviedo's *Historias*. For a complete overview of the myth of the Amazonian warriors in medieval imagination and its American versions see Acosta, *Viajeros y
maravillas*, vols. 1, 2, and 3 (Caracas: Monte Avila Editores Latinoamericana,
1993); and *El continente prodigioso*, 91–124. See also Dathorner, *Imagining
the World*.

6.   The notion of an American earthly paradise would mean that Europeans were the offspring of the first inhabitants of the "not so new" New World. This radical idea was not welcomed by the Europeans, who believed themselves to be sanctified by God since ancient times.

A renowned scholar at Lima's University of San Marcos, Antonio de León Pinelo devoted many years to studying ancient cosmology and cartography in order to find an answer to the question of the origin of mankind.

7.   A brief overview of the paleoanthropology and the history of the native inhabitants of the Peruvian Amazon can be found in Jaime Regan, *Hacia la tierra sin mal: La religión del pueblo en la Amazonía* (Iquitos: CETA, 1993), 19–114; Fernando Santos, "Etnohistoria de la alta Amazonía, siglos XV–XVIII" in *Colección 500 años ediciones* 46 (Quito: ABYA-YALA-Cayembe, 1990); and Jesús Víctor San Román, *Perfiles históricos de la Amazonía peruana* (Lima: Ediciones Paulinas-CETA, 1975).

8.   In 1638, Pedro de Vaca Cadena, governor of the major Peruvian Amazon city, Santiago de Borja, authorized the Jesuits to enter a segment of the Spanish Amazon forest in order to "civilize" and Christianize this area inhabited by diverse ethnic groups. The missionaries spread quickly throughout the villages of the region of Maynas (in the northeast of what is today the Peruvian Amazon), establishing *reducciones* by attracting or transferring Indians to towns created according to the Spanish municipal structure. In this way, the Spanish crown and the Catholic Church shared the venture of colonizing part of the Amazon jungle.

Franciscan missions also were established alongside the Ucayali River (south from Maynas); from these missions the Franciscans organized excursions to Indian villages, which eventually became the basis of numerous cities spread over Peru's Amazonian jungle. While the Franciscans maintained a presence in Maynas, their missionary campaign focused its efforts in the central and southern regions of the Peruvian Amazon (the regions of Bajo Huallaga, Ucayali, etc.). The Franciscans faced continuous native revolts, which caused them to withdraw and return to their missions. Between 1746 and 1760, the revolts of José Santos Atahualpa and Runcato practically put an end to any attempt of a military or spiritual conquest of the region. See Daniel Valcarcel, *Rebeliones indígenas* (Lima: Edit P.T.C.M., 1946); Alberto Flores Galindo, *Buscando un Inca: Identidad y utopía en los Andes,* 3rd ed. (Lima: Editorial Horizonte, 1988); and Michael F. Brown and Eduardo Fernández, *War of Shadows: The Struggle for Utopia in the Peruvian Amazon* (Berkeley: University of California Press, 1991).

Historical accounts concerning the missionary crusades of Jesuits and Franciscans in the Peruvian Amazon can be found in Mario C. Ríos Zañartu, *Historia de la*

Amazonía peruana (Iquitos: Editora "El Matutino," 1995), 43–83; Regan, *Hacia la tierra sin mal*, 29–60; Francisco Figueroa, *Informes de Jesuitas en el Amazonas, 1660–1684* (Iquitos: Monumenta Amazónica CETA, 1986); Manuel Biedma, *La conquista franciscana del alto Ucayali* (Iquitos: Serie Monumenta Amazónica, CETA-IIAP, 1989); and Manuel Marzal, "Las reducciones indígenas en la Amazonía del virreynato peruano," *Amazonía peruana* (Iquitos) 10, no. 5 (March 1984): 7–45.

9.   The province of Maynas, today a province of the department of Loreto, belonged initially to the Audiencia de Quito, a royal court that functioned under the supervision of the viceroy or governor-general of Nueva Granada. After Requena's request, Maynas became an area under the jurisdiction of the viceroy of Lima.

10.   The year of foundation of Iquitos is a matter of controversy. There are three versions of the actual establishment of the city in the years 1840, 1842, and the accepted date in which *Iquiteños* officially celebrate the foundation of the city, January 5, 1864. See Ríos Zañartu, *Historia de la Amazonía peruana*, 92.

11.   Brazil opposed a policy of free navigation of the Amazon River by foreign ships until 1851, when, persuaded by North American diplomats, it agreed to open its rivers to universal trade. In July of 1853, the Brazilian steamship *Marajo* navigated through Iquitos to Nauta, thus initiating the era of steam navigation in the Amazon. The opening of the Amazon River and its tributaries to free trade presented moments of tension, which explain the urge of governments to accelerate the building of shipyards and naval factories at that time. Matters of "national security" and "defense of the sovereignty" were involved in the Peruvian, Brazilian, Ecuadorian, and Colombian discourses of that era. A brief description of the diplomatic struggle on the rights to free navigation along the Amazon and its adjacent rivers can be found in López, *De París al Amazonas*.

12.   The way this capitalist system worked in each stratum of the chain—foreign companies, local lords, commercial houses, overseers, laborers—is described in detail by José A. Flores Marín, *La explotación del caucho en la selva* (Lima: CONCYTEC, 1987); and Guido Pennano, *La economía del caucho* (Iquitos: Serie Debate Amazónico, CETA, CONCYTEC, 1987).
       Both works also present an analysis of the rubber boom's socioeconomic impact on the region and its present repercussions. For literature in English see Barbara Weinstein, *The Amazon Rubber Boom, 1850–1926* (Stanford: Stanford University Press, 1983).

13.   In this segment I paraphrased Father Joaquín García's arguments supporting his claim of a "Second Industrial Revolution" during the rubber boom of the late

nineteenth century. (Father Joaquín García, interview by author, Iquitos, 8 July 1995).

14. The amount of elastic rubber exported to Europe and the United States from 1884 to 1905 increased from 540,529 kilograms to 2,492,896.

See Hildebrando Fuentes, *Loreto: Apuntes geográficos, históricos, estadísticos, políticos y sociales* (Lima: Imprenta de la Revista, 1908), 297.

15. Casement's investigation shed light on the participation of British investors and wardens from Barbados who were assigned to the task of hunting down potential runaway Indians, all of them suspected executors of bloody crimes in the Putumayo area controlled by Julio C. Arana and his colleagues of the Peruvian Rubber Company.

Julio Arana was a Peruvian businessman who went to Iquitos from San Martin as soon as he heard the first news of a rubber boom in the low jungle. He purchased a huge area between Putumayo and Caquetá, territories in dispute with Colombia, and associated with other rubber lords of the area, including English entrepreneurs, establishing the Peruvian Amazon Company. In his domain, Indians were forced to work under unendurable conditions; they were mistreated and even murdered. The terrible massacre of Indians in the Putumayo was denounced to Iquitos authorities, but Arana's fortune silenced everyone. He became mayor of Iquitos in 1902 and president of the Commercial Chamber in 1903. In 1913, the British consul in the city, Sir Roger Casement, presented a document to the British government absolving all the British citizens involved in the killings of Putumayo despite published accounts of this massacre that were written by an adventurer who witnessed the harassment of the Indians. For a thorough description of those crimes see Walter E. Hardenburg, *The Putumayo, The Devil's Paradise: Travels in the Peruvian Amazon Region and an Account of the Atrocities Committed Upon the Indians Therein* (London: T. F. Unwin, 1912). Another famous rich man of the Amazon, Carlos Fermín Fitzcarrald, established a rubber empire in today's departments of Ucayali and Madre de Dios, and also is blamed for having led a company of murderers against the Mashco natives. Werner Herzog's film *Fitzcarraldo* (1982) presents the bohemian nature of this rubber baron, who dreamed of building an opera theater in Iquitos superior to the one in Manaus. Although the film focuses on his bohemian personality (neglecting the view of historians who portray Fitzcarrald as a cool-blooded entrepreneur), it is an excellent visual source for learning about the life of Iquitos and Manaus bohemians and the fate of Amazonian Indians in the rubber woodlands.

See also Wade Davis, *One River: Explorations and Discoveries in the Amazon Rain Forest* (New York: Simon & Schuster, 1996), 237–240.

16. José Eustasio Rivera's novel *La vorágine,* published in 1924, describes with intense imagery the contrast between *caucheros* life in the jungle and the city, as well as the corrupt nature of the political accomplices of the rubber lord. See José Eustasio Rivera, *La vóragine* (Bogotá: Arango Editores, 1989), 285. A historical background to this novel can be seen in Vicente Pérez Silva, *Raíces históricas de la vóragine* (Bogotá: Buena Semilla, 1988).

Among the commercial houses established by the immigrants were the firms Wesche y Cia; Kahn & Polack; Luis F. Morey; Marius, Levy & Schuler; David Cazés; Adolfo Morey y Cía; Rocha Hnos; Cecilio Hernández e Hijos; Magne y Cía; Julio C. Arana; V. Israel y Cía; José Santos Cruz; Guillermo Shermuley; etc. See Fuentes, *Loreto,* 29–30.

17. Roger Rumrrill and Pierre de Zutter, *Amazonía y capitalismo: Los condenados de la selva* (Lima: Editorial Horizonte, 1976), 20.

18. For example, in today's International Social Center, there is a commemorative plaque recreating the document signed by the founders of that institution, called then *Club de los Trece:*

October 16, 1913:

Gathered in the "London Bar" we declare that:

Due to the moral collapse of this place, realizing the total abandonment that some individuals have undergone, who know the exquisite wines of Champagne, and convinced as we are, of our incomparable virtues, we, survivors of the defeat, have decided to establish a gathering center.

Safeguarded behind a formidable ham [pork] and forgetting all worldly preoccupations, one of the strong men proposed to denominate this center: Cercle Des Treize (AT).

The members of this society were Luis Savel, Raoul De Kaldember, Pascual Inecco, Roberto Roch, Alfredo Belmann, Marcel Joseph, Rene Hirsh, Ernest Hoffmann, Jerome Levy, Solomon Joseph, Pierre Schuler, Clement Roch, Pascual Ansobordo."

(Commemorative plaque of the foundation of the *Club de los Trece* in the Club Social Internacional, 6 October 1913).

Peru encouraged, as did most Latin American nations, the immigration of European newcomers to their soils. In 1868 President José Balta issued a decree offering protection, aid, and lands to native Peruvians and foreigners who wished to settle alongside the Amazon and its adjacent rivers; in 1872, President Manuel Pardo established the Society of European Immigration to promote this type of migration. In the 1880s and 1890s the central government of Peru provided free lands to any person who requested them. In 1899 President Andrés Cáceres bestowed upon the Peruvian Corporation Limited a concession in the Perené jungle of two million hectares. This agreement, signed in exchange for an exoneration of Peru's external debt, marked the beginning of British and foreign investments in the Amazon.

A summary of these migratory policies can be found in San Román, *Perfiles históricos de la Amazonía peruana*, 122–132, and Carlos Larrabure I. Correa, *Colección de leyes, decretos, resoluciones y otros documentos oficiales referentes al departamento de Loreto* (Lima: Imp. de "La Opinión Pública," 1905). For analytical works regarding specific types of immigration to the Peruvian Amazon in the late nineteenth century, see Isabelle Lausent-Herrera, "Los inmigrantes chinos en la Amazonía peruana" in *Primer seminario sobre poblaciones inmigratorias, 1986*, vol. 2, eds. Amelia Morimoto and José Carlos Luciano (Lima: CONCYTEC, 1988), 109–126; and Martha Achung Rodríguez, "Poblamiento de la Amazonía desde el siglo XIX hasta 1940," *Shupihui* (Iquitos) 37, no. 11 (1986): 7–28.

The history of the Perené Colony is by itself a testimony to the harsh conditions that native Amazonian people underwent in their region under the hegemonic rule of foreign investors. See Manuel Manrique, *La Peruvian Corporation en la selva central del Perú* (Lima: Centro de Investigaciones y Promoción de la Amazonía, 1982) and Frederica Barclay, *La colonia del Perené: Capital Inglés y economía cafetalera en la configuración de la región de Chanchamayo* (Iquitos: CETA, 1987).

19.   Joseph Orton Kerbey, *The Land of To-morrow: A Newspaper Exploration Up the Amazon and Over the Andes to the California of South America* (New York: W. F. Brainard Publisher, 1906), 113.

20.   See Avencio Villarejo, *Así es la selva* (Iquitos: CETA, 1988), 133.

21.   The Department of Loreto exported 2,349,395 kilograms of rubber in 1913 and the production decreased to 1,570,188 kilograms by 1914 when World War I began. In 1914 the price of rubber fell in international markets because of the excessive production of the product. England imported rubber from its Far Eastern colonies, whose prices were very low. (From 1913 to 1914 rubber exports from the Amazon to England decreased from 62 percent to 49 percent.) For detailed statistics of the decline of the rubber economy in the Amazonian region see Flores Marín, *La explotación del caucho* and Pennano, *La economía del caucho*.

22.   After the rubber boom the main commercial houses of Iquitos traded *tagua* (vegetable ivory utilized for manufacturing buttons, taken from the palm tree

yarina), *balata* (plastic rubber tree whose wood was utilized in the building industry), *barbasco* or *cube* (for fumigation), *leche caspi* (latex for production of gum), woods, and the skin of wild animals such as caiman, big cats, and snakes.

For a detailed explanation and statistics of the extraction of these products, see Ríos Zañartu, *Historia de la Amazonía peruana*, 126–130.

23. The accounts of Henry Warren Kelly, the U.S. vice-consul to Peru in Iquitos, written in the 1930s and 1940s, depict a changing city with wealthy people yearning for the days when they were even richer: "Social life centered in the clubs, the Plaza de Armas [main square], and the cinemas. The most select clubs in town were the Club Social Iquitos, the Centro Internacional, and the Casino Militar. Membership in the Casino was limited to officers of the Peruvian Army, Navy, and Air Corps. Of the two civilian clubs, the Cloob [*sic*] Social Iquitos was, by all odds, the most fashionable. Its membership boasted the four hundred—every merchant, politician, professional man, and military and civilian official of consequence. Admission was freely granted to foreigners on the same modest basis that applied to Peruvian members—ten soles per month ($1.50)."

See Henry Warren Kelly, *Dancing Diplomats* (Albuquerque: University of New Mexico Press, 1950), 88–89.

24. James Ramsey Ullman, *The Other Side of the Mountain: An Escape to the Amazon* (New York: Carrick & Evans, 1938), 242.

25. The most significant of these revolts was that led by Captain Guillermo Cervantes in 1921. This quixotic character, together with members of his brigade, took power on August 25, proclaiming an anti-centralist doctrine supported by many people who had been victims of Lima's abandonment. Cervantes seized the Peruvian and London Bank, taking from it all the deposits in pounds sterling and distributing money among unpaid public functionaries and military men. Another revolutionary decree ordered the printing of fifty thousand gold pounds of cash with his picture on it (the so-called *billetes cervantinos*) and forced the entire population to utilize this form of currency. Those who refused to do so were fined or punished by his troops. The revolution lasted six months until it was crushed after many difficult battles by President Leguía's soldiers from Lima.

Other important revolts ocurred in 1956 (Merino's revolt), in 1957 (riots in Iquitos's movie theaters), and in 1968 (the bus and taxi drivers riots).

For details about the causes, descriptions, and sequels of these revolts see Ríos Zañartu, *Historia de la Amazonía peruana*, 143–156. José Barletti Pasquale analyzes the character of these revolts in "Luchas autonómicas anticentralistas," *Kanatari* (Iquitos), vol. 11, (17 April, 1994): 9–11.

26. Father José María Arroyo, interview by author, Iquitos, 14 June 1995.

27. Professor of Economy Genaro García argues that there has always been a total lack of knowledge of the Amazonian region by the different central governments of Peru. He claims that "all the policies applied in the Peruvian Amazon have been the product of circumstantial episodes and not of a clear view of what Peru wants to do in this place." (Professor Genaro García, interview by author, Iquitos, 26 June 1995).

Oscar A. Gómez Perea's report, "La política tributaria en la región del Amazonas," presented in a seminar held in Iquitos in 1988, provides a historical overview of taxation in Loreto and Iquitos, with emphasis on the 156000 Law of Tax Exoneration. Genaro García's unpublished work, "Veinticinco años de economía regional" focuses on Iquitos's socioeconomic situation in the last quarter of the twentieth century.

28. See Brian Kelly and Mark London's work, *Amazon* (San Diego: Harcourt Brace Jovanovich Publishers, 1983).

29. Historian José Barletti Pasquale, interview by author, Iquitos, 27 July 1995.

30. See Mario Vargas Llosa's *Pantaleón y las Visitadoras* (Barcelona: Editorial Seix Barral, 1973).

31. Ullman, *The Other Side of the Mountain*, 242.

32. Father Joaquín García, interview by author, Iquitos, 8 July 1995.

33. Marlene Dobkin de Ríos asserts that these social classes are constituted by racially different typologies of people: the white educated high class, the *trigueños* or lighter *Mestizos* of the middle classes, and the poor *cholos* or dark-skinned urbanized Indians who seek the status of *Mestizos* but still are considered uncivilized Indians by whites and *Mestizos*. However, I did not find that these racial categories played an important role in the way *Iquiteños* interact with each other in the 1990s. See Marlene Dobkin de Ríos, *Visionary Vine: Hallucinogenic Healing in the Peruvian Amazon* (Prospect Heights, Ill.: Waveland Press, Inc., 1984), 49–65.

34. Ibid., 58.

35. Ullman, *The Other Side of the Mountain*, 242.

CHAPTER 2

1. Although a picture of *Diego* de León Pinelo, dean of San Marcos University of Lima (the one listed by the Inquisition), hangs on the wall of the main hallway of the school, the historian and principal of the school, Professor León Trahtemberg, explains that the school's name was selected to honor *Antonio* de León Pinelo, "Jew" *(Marrano),* professor, scholar, and dean of Universidad Nacional Mayor de San Marcos in the seventeenth century. See León Trahtemberg's work *Los Judíos de Lima y las provincias del Perú* (Lima: UIP, 1989), 42. The León Pinelo family name was selected due to a policy of the Peruvian governments of the 1940s that forbade schools to adopt the names of non-Peruvian personalities. Therefore, the first principal of the *Colegio León Pinelo* opted for the name of a famous Peruvian who—he believed—had observed Jewish traditions in secrecy.

But . . . who was honored: Diego or Antonio? *Limeño* Jews do not agree on the answer to this question.

2. Rafael Rodríguez, an amateur historian, related to me a detailed history of the Peruvian Conquest during the age of Pizarro, defining it as a religious civil war between Pizarro's Old Christian allies and de Almagro's New Christian band. He also pointed out that the Jews of Celendín, in Cajamarca, erected a sculpture honoring the "Jew" Diego de Almagro. Another famous conqueror who could have been crypto-Jewish is Sebastián de Benálcazar.

Seymour Liebman refers to Celendín in his *Requiem por los olvidados,* 177. The physical aspect of many inhabitants of this city, white people with green eyes, has ignited the curiosity of scholars and inquisitive people, such as some colleagues of Liebman, who told him how Celendín was founded by Portuguese Jews who gradually lost their religious beliefs, but still practice endogamy like their ancestors.

3. The association of Portuguese and Jews, popularized after 1580, is a product of Spain's annexation of the kingdom of Portugal, bringing back to its domain descendants of Jews who had established themselves in that nation after the 1492 edict ordering the expulsion of the Jews from Spain. Four years later, King Manuel the Fortunate agreed to cleanse his kingdom of Jews in order to marry the daughter of Ferdinand and Isabella of Spain. The Portuguese king was reluctant to do so, but nevertheless he announced the edict expelling the Jews from Portugal by the end of October 1497.

In the ten-month period that Jews could leave Portugal, King Manuel conducted a campaign of massive conversion (especially of children, who were taken to be raised by Christian families). Many Jews were forcibly baptized. In this way they became nominally New Christian, even though most maintained their devotion to their Jewish faith: "The forced conversion of Jews allowed King Manuel to say to the Catholic kings that there were no more Jews in Portugal, and yet, allowed Portugal to continue counting on the ability and strength of the work of the Jews." See Canelo, *The Last Crypto-Jews of Portugal*, 23.

In 1580, when they were again made subjects of Spain, many Portuguese New Christians obtained visas to travel to Spanish dependencies. Hence, until the eighteenth century, those who observed Mosaic law in the Americas were called "Portuguese" and "Jew" interchangeably.

4.   See Charles Henry Lea, *The Inquisition in the Spanish Dependencies*, rev. ed. (London: Macmillan & Co., Ltd., 1992); José Toribio Medina, *Historia del tribunal de la Inquisición de Lima, 1569–1820* (Santiago de Chile: Fondo Histórico y Bibliográfico J. T. Medina, 1956); and Seymour Liebman's two works: *The Inquisitors and the Jews in the New World* and *Requiem por los olvidados*.

5.   Cecil Roth, *A History of the Marranos* (Philadelphia: Jewish Publication Society of America, 1941), 279.

6.   Cecil Roth describes this martyr's defiance toward his inquisitors: Maldonado da Silva "wrote with ink made from charcoal, and pens cut out of a chicken-bone with a knife fashioned from a nail, long treatises vindicating his attitude [in defense of Judaism]." (Ibid.,164–165).

7.   The case of Francisco Maldonado da Silva is studied in detail by Gunter Böhm in his *Historia de los Judíos en Chile* (Santiago de Chile: Editorial Andrés Bello, 1984). It also has been fictionalized in Marcos Aguinis's historical novel *La gesta del Marrano* (Barcelona: Ed Planeta, 1991). For basic literature about *Marranos* in the Americas, see classic works by Seymour Liebman, Boleslao Lewin, Gunter Böhm, Anita Novinsky, and Stanley Hordes.

8.   Provisional statutes of the San Martín government 10/08/1821; constitutions of 1823, 1826, 1828, 1834, 1839, 1856. In all codes before the 1839 constitution the state forbade the practice of non-Catholic religions until it was specified that other religions could not be practiced publicly. The 1929 constitution eliminated the prohibition to practice other religions, although the state kept protecting the official one: Roman Apostolic Catholicism.

Although Peruvian constitutions did not allow the public practice of non-Catholic religions, there were other articles highlighting the right of every citizen to freedom of opinions and beliefs. These laws forbade the harassment of any person due to his or her ideas.

9. See Mario C. Vásquez, "Inmigración y mestizaje en el siglo XIX en el Perú" in *Race and Class in Latin America,* ed. Magnus Mörner (New York: Columbia University Press, 1970), 73; and León Trahtemberg's chapter, "La inmigración extranjera al Peru y su status legal (1821–1930)" in *La inmigración Judía al Perú, 1848–1948: Una historia documentada de la inmigración de los Judíos de habla Alemana* (Lima: UIP, 1987), 31–41.

10. In the 1860s, Peru attempted to establish agricultural colonies for European immigrants in emulation of the North American and Argentinian experiences, but these efforts proved to be unsuccessful. In contrast, concessions to bring Asian immigrants thrived.

11. Between 1849 and 1874 more than 80,000 Chinese came to Peru, and later, at the beginning of the twentieth century, President Augusto Leguía encouraged contracts and conditions for massive migrations of Japanese laborers to Peru. (Approximately forty thousand Japanese immigrants arrived in the nation between 1900 and 1930.) Despite alluring offers to white immigrants to settle in the prosperous country, including such national efforts as the establishment of the Society of European Immigration in 1872, Peru failed to attract the great wave of European immigrants who flooded the shores of the Americas in the nineteenth century.

Compared to the massive influx of newcomers to the United States (approximately ten million immigrants between 1860 and 1890, and many more immigrants afterwards), Brazil (where the rate of immigration was approximately 112,500 people annually between 1891 and 1900, and half-a-million between 1911 and 1913), and Argentina (three million European immigrants between 1817 and 1914), the flow of European immigrants to Peru was so modest that almost no historian has provided statistics of this migration.

Jorge Basadre, in his classic *Historia de la República del Perú* (Lima: Editorial Universitaria S.A., 1968) limits his emphasis to the Asian migration to Peru because it is "the only one of large scale in the country." Marrion Wilcox, author of "Immigration to Latin America" in *The Encyclopedia of Latin America,* eds. Marrion Wilcox and George Edwin Rines (New York: Encyclopedia Americana Corporation, 1917), provides numbers of European migratory currents in almost all Latin American countries, but in the case of Peru he only mentions the importance of Chinese, Japanese, and black immigrants. Furthermore, Juan de Arona, author of *La inmigración en el Perú* (Lima: Academia Diplomática del Perú, 1971), does not provide numbers of immigrants who came to that nation during the nineteenth century, but instead, presents a table of the countries of origin of immigrants living in Peru in the 1970s, including 11,185 Japanese, 8,779 Chinese, and only around 25,000 Europeans, mainly from Spain, Italy, and Germany.

12. Records of Lima's Jewish community list Max Bromberg as the first Jew to marry a Catholic Peruvian lady—Isabel Lazurtegui—on 16 April 1865. Many other single Jewish men followed him, some of whom, by the way, were also members of the *"Club Germanía."*

Examples of these certificates are reproduced by Trahtemberg in *La inmigración Judía al Perú*, 79–81.

13. Cited by Gunter Böhm in *Judíos en el Perú durante el siglo XIX* (Santiago de Chile: Universidad de Chile, 1985), 57–58.

14. In 1875 they acquired a lot from the North American Jewish contractor Enrique Meiggs, the prominent entrepreneur hired by President Nicolás de Pierola to extend railroads throughout Peru. This lot of land, the Baquijano Jewish cemetery, is still the only common graveyard for Lima's Jewry.

15. The society accomplished most of its tasks. In 1882 the first births (including those previous to the date of the society's foundation) and marriages were transcribed in a book of records from documents registered in Peruvian civil offices. A year later, the Jewish community began to list death certificates of deceased members in their own files. The society built, developed, and later expanded the Jewish cemetery; they made deals with the French society that owned the *Maison Santé* hospital in order to provide medical assistance to Jewish members; and in other cases, such as the need for old people's asylums, they requested help from other immigrant societies or foreign individuals with influence on health centers and beneficence institutions guaranteeing the right to lodge their members through regular payments made by the *Sociedad Israelita*.

16. Segismund Jacobi and his brother Eduard were among the first Jews to arrive in Peru in the twentieth century. Both worked as stockbrokers representing the Rothschilds' house in Lima.

17. Germany was the cradle of the Reform movement. The philosophy of *Wissenschaft des Judentums*—the scientific study of Jewish history and religious literature—was shared by most of the enlightened German Jews, who gradually conducted a predominantly secular life, disregarding many of the Orthodox traditions of their ancestors.

18. Thanks to Rafael Rodríguez's assistance, I obtained in the *Archivo General de la Nación* in Lima fifteen records of Jews who enrolled as new immigrants. All of them worked in commerce, registering their professions under different labels

such as *comerciante, mercachifle, vendedor de mercancías, empleado de comercio,* and *"contador."* An important aspect of these documents is the way some Jewish immigrants were registered as Israelites, as they were registered in Iquitos in most cases. In documents where they are cataloged as Israelites, it is not clear what their native country is. For detailed information concerning names, countries of origin, and activities of Jews in Lima and the Peruvian provinces, see Trahtemberg's books *La inmigración Judía al Perú* and *Los Judíos de Lima.*

19. In most of the Latin American nations, the early Jewish communities presented similar patterns of organization. For example, in Cuba there were three congregations co-existing: English-speaking North Americans, Yiddish-speaking *Ashkenazim,* and French and Ladino-speaking *Sephardim.* See Robert M. Levine, *Tropical Diaspora: The Jewish Experience in Cuba* (Gainsville: University Press of Florida, 1993). For overviews of the organization of Jewish communities in Latin America see Judith Laikin Elkin, *Jews of the Latin American Republics* (Chapel Hill: University of North Carolina Press, 1980) and *The Jewish Presence in Latin America,* eds. Judith Laikin Elkin and Gilbert W. Merkx (Boston: Allen & Unwin Inc., 1987).

20. Since President Sánchez Cerro's administration from 1930 to 1933, when he was murdered, the successive governments of Oscar Benavides (1933–1939) and Manuel Prado (1939–1945) enacted laws that guaranteed a minimum of native workers in each commercial and industrial enterprise.

A thorough overview of the political and legal policies of Peru concerning immigrants from the 1930s to 1960s can be found in León Trahtemberg's "Consideraciones políticas y legales hacia la inmigración Judía al Perú desde 1930," in *La inmigración Judía al Perú,* 159–176. These types of protectionist laws were also enacted in other Latin American countries, such as Argentina and Brazil. An example of this type of legislation is the Cuban "Law of 50 Percent" enacted in the early 1930s, which required that half of the workers of every firm had to be Cuban born. See Levine, *Tropical Diaspora,* 52–59. Regarding immigration history and legislation in other Latin American countries, see Haim Avni's works *Argentina y la historia de la inmigración Judía, 1810–1950* (Buenos Aires: Editorial Universitaria Magnes and Universidad Hebrea de Jerusalem, AMIA, 1983), and *Mexico: Immigration and Refuge* (Washington, D.C.: Woodrow Wilson International Center for Scholars, 1989). See also Jeffrey H. Lesser, *Welcoming the Undesirables: Brazil and the Jewish Question* (Berkeley: University of California Press, 1995).

21. The policy of President Manuel Prado's government, which maintained an alliance between Peru and the United States, led the South American country to

adopt measures against citizens of Germany, Japan, and Italy. Control and deportations of some unwelcome foreigners were carried out, the main industries were nationalized, and immigration was hermetically closed. Paradoxically, German Jewish refugees suffered the consequences of this anti-Axis policy, and Jewish international organizations such as J.O.I.N.T (The American Jewish Joint Distribution Committee in the U.S.) and H.I.C.E.M. (Jewish International Agency in Paris), as well as Jewish Peruvian institutions such as the *Comité de Protección a los Inmigrantes Israelitas del Perú* (founded in 1935), struggled to provide economic aid to newcomers and put political pressure on Peruvian authorities to receive Jewish refugees. Lima's Jewish community spared some German Jews from deportation through legal actions that distinguished these Jews from other German immigrants and transacted visas for Jews who came from and to Bolivia.

The Jewish community of Arequipa opened a branch of the *Comité de Protección a los Inmigrantes Israelitas del Perú* in order to facilitate financial and political aid to Jewish immigrants. Some Jews requested a provisional visa to stay for a short period of time in the city of Puno, promising to leave as soon they could find another country willing to receive them. Many did leave, but others went to Lima and managed to stay thanks to the negligence of Peruvian authorities or the diplomatic efforts of Jews in the capital city.

22. In the 1940s and 1950s the *Unión Israelita* suffered internal divisions that led to the establishment of two separate synagogues, *Knesset Israel* and *Adat Israel*. In the 1990s the Ashkenazic Jews share again the same synagogue but divisions have arisen among the three congregations, especially the *Unión Israelita* and the Sephardic Society regarding the *Sociedad Israelita 1870*. There are two houses for elderly people, and in 1994 a circumstantial episode led the Orthodox rabbis of the Sephardic and Ashkenazic congregations to separate their burial society from that of the Conservative congregation "1870."

23. The *Alliance Israélite Universelle* (AIU) was founded by British and French Jews in order to "ameliorate the poverty and cultural backwardness of Afro-Asian Jewry." The Western European Jews would educate these Jews in the French language, the lingua franca of the day in North Africa. For a review of the AIU in Morocco, see Michael Laskier, *The Alliance Israélite Universelle and the Jewish Communities of Morocco, 1862–1962* (Albany: SUNY Press, 1983).

24. Bibliography concerning the history of Moroccan Jews is extensive. Most of these works are in French or Hebrew; for example, Donath Bensimon, *Evolution du judaisme marocain sous le Protectorat Francais* (Paris: Mouton, 1968); Abraham I. Laredo, *Les noms de Juifs du Maroc: essai d'onomastique judeo-marocai* (Madrid:

Instituto Arias Montano, 1978); and a classic work in Hebrew by Shlomo Deshen, *The Mellah Society: Jewish Community Life in Sherifian Morocco,* trans. Shlomo Deshen (Chicago: University of Chicago Press, 1989). The recent interest of North American scholars in Sephardic studies has produced some books about Judaism in Morocco such as that of Mitchell M. Serels, *A History of the Jews of Tangier in the Nineteenth and Twentieth Centuries* (New York: Sepher-Hermon Press, 1991); and Michael Laskier, *North African Jewry in the Twentieth Century: The Jews of Morocco, Tunisia and Algeria* (New York: New York University Press, 1994). An analysis of the reasons that led Jewish Moroccans to emigrate to the Americas can be found in Susan Gilson Miller's "Kippur on the Amazon: Jewish Emigration from Northern Morocco in the Late Nineteenth Century" in *Sephardi and Middle Eastern Jewries: History and Culture in the Modern Era,* ed. Harvey E. Goldberg (Bloomington: Indiana University Press, 1996), 190–209.

25. Sephardic Jews had viewed Brazil as a haven since the seventeenth century, when northeastern Brazil became a colony of the Protestant Dutch empire. A number of Sephardic Jews left the seventeenth-century site of religious tolerance par excellence, Amsterdam, to go to Dutch Brazil, where they were joined by crypto-Jews coming from Portuguese Catholic Brazil, who began to practice openly their Judaism in that tolerant harbor. The *Tzur Israel* congregation, founded in 1637 in the Brazilian province of Recife, became the first Jewish community in the Americas. When Portugal reconquered this area in 1654, many Jews returned together with the colonizers to Amsterdam and the Dutch Caribbean islands. Approximately twenty-three families went to New Amsterdam, a Dutch colony later conceded to England and renamed New York.

26. In the twentieth century, the Jews in Manaus were more successful than those of Iquitos in adapting to the shift from a rubber economy to one based on other resources. Many Brazilian Jews struggled to maintain productive enterprises in the Amazonian region, based on other regional products such as wood, skins, and oil, and their first- and second-generation descendants became part of the dominant entrepreneurial class when the major English, German, and French companies stopped exploiting those products in Brazil. A number of Jewish entrepreneurs established industries to process natural products of the Amazon and branched into other sectors of the economy, such as the wood and oil industries. In addition, Brazil experienced a second rubber boom following the 1942 signing of the Washington Agreements with the United States, whose purpose was to create the *Banco da Borracha* with North American capital bestowing a small percentage of the exploitation of *borracha silvestre* [raw rubber] to the state.

Some Jews in the Brazilian Amazon established petroleum companies (I. B. Sabbá was the owner of the Manaus oil refinery Ganso Azul) and industries to process the rubber and transform it in other products. These factors ensured a steadier monetary flow for Jewish businessmen and enabled the Amazonian Jewish communities of Brazil to continue to thrive well through this decade.

Not only were the Jews in the Brazilian Amazon blessed with more favorable economic conditions, they also enjoyed quick and easy communications with coastal cities because there were no mountains between the two regions. In many cases, businessmen's wives lived in the northeastern cities of Brazil (many of them were also Moroccan Jews). The children stayed with the fathers until they completed their high school studies and joined their commercial and industrial ventures to become their successors. Jewish life also developed in the Amazon itself: they had some professors from the *Alliance Israélite Universelle;* they made their homes in cities like Bélem do Pará and Porto Velho; rabbis and performers of the circumcision rite settled in the region; and they had synagogues. Eventually the Jews of the Brazilian Amazon established a solid community in Manaus led by the Israelite Committee of the Amazon, with a synagogue, *Beth Jacob,* a Jewish club, and most of the other Jewish organizations that regularly exist in large cities. As of the 1990s, Manaus is home to approximately 600 Jewish souls, who are intermarrying and assimilating quickly into the society at large, although they claim that "the Christians are the ones who assimilate into Judaism" as a consequence of these marriages. Bélem boasts a community of approximately 250 Jewish families.

For an overview of Jewish entrepreneurs in Manaus, Bélem do Pará, and other Amazonian cities of Brazil, see Samuel Benchimol, "Judeus no ciclo da borracha: Trabalho apresentado no Primeiro Encontro Brasileiro de Estudos Judaicos da Universidade do Rio de Janeiro no período de 24 a 26 de Outubro de 1994" (Manaus, Brazil: Amazonas, 1994). Regarding the organization of Jewish communities in the Brazilian Amazon see David Finkelstein, "After 400 Years, Brazil's Jews Face an Uncertain Future," *The Jewish Monthly* (December 1994): 39–42. Also see the April 1984 edition of the Brazilian *Shalom* magazine: "A descuberta da Amazònia: A aventura dos Judeus marroquinos que desbravan o norte do país" (April 1984): 6–27.

27. Susan Gilson Miller discusses the profound changes that occurred in the lives of families and Jewish communities of Morocco, due to the economic aid received by those who went to the Americas. She also analyzes the social changes that these Jewish communities underwent with the return of many of these émigrés, who challenged the religious and hierarchical dynamics of "old Jewish aristocrats" and rabbis. See Miller's "Kippur on the Amazon," 190–209.

28. According to Rosenzweig, "Judíos en la Amazonía Peruana, 1870–1949," 19–30, and Trahtemberg's chapter about Jews in Iquitos in his book *Los Judíos de Lima*, 183–194, in 1895 some Jews purchased from the Public Beneficence of Iquitos a burial site from the general cemetery administrated by that institution. I strove to find the document of this transaction in the files of the Public Beneficence of Iquitos, only to learn in an unexpected twist that this could not be possible for one simple reason: the Public Beneficence of Iquitos was founded on November 13, 1898, three years after the first dates impressed in the oldest gravestones of the Jewish cemetery. This "discovery" urged me to find out who were the owners and the sellers of this lot, so I went to the Property Records Office of Iquitos where I found in one of the earliest books of reports a record indicating that the Public Beneficence acquired the parcels of today's general cemetery on November 12, 1904 from a private owner, Antonio Joaquín de Campos Henríquez (*RPL*, vol. 2).

However, a *paisano* in Iquitos insisted that he once had the 1895 acquisition document of the Jewish cemetery but that he had lost it. Most of the "Jewish *Mestizos*" blamed the Public Beneficence of Iquitos of hiding the original property document because it attempted to expand the general cemetery in 1990 through demolishing the Jewish parcel. The idea of demolishing the Israelite cemetery was disproved when Father Joaquín García included the cemetery in a list of historical monuments and national patrimonies.

According to my findings, I only can argue with certainty that the Jewish cemetery was built before the modern Christian one, whose land belonged to a particular owner. This fact makes me assume that in 1895, when the Jews acquired the lot to bury their people, most likely they bought it from a particular landlord (possibly the same Campos Henríquez) and probably through an oral agreement, as many transactions were carried out in the area. Of course, a written proof of this acquisition would be a welcomed confirmation of my theory.

29. Among the Jews who moved from Yurimaguas to Iquitos were Alberto and Isaac Edery and their families, Abraham and Anita Nahmías, Elías Hatchwell and his son David, Solomon Joseph, Gustavo Khan Meza, and the Tapiero, Amiel, Bento, Benzaquén, Benamú, and Farache families. Most of these names would become important in the commercial life of Iquitos at the beginning of the twentieth century, but a few of these family members stayed in Yurimaguas, where they became public figures. Shalom Benamú, for example, was elected mayor of Yurimaguas for five years (1927, 1928, 1930, 1931, 1932), following in the footsteps of his *paisano*.

During his trip to Iquitos in 1948–1949, geologist Alfredo Rosenzweig obtained a list of 138 Jewish immigrants who lived in the Peruvian Amazon

between 1890 and 1912. Ninety-two came from Morocco, the majority of them
from Tangier, including the Pinto, Toledano, Cohén, Barcesat, Benzaquén, Aser-
rat, Edery, Bohabot, Coriat, and Sarfati families. Twenty-three of those on his list
came from France (most of them from Alsace), including Kahan, Weill, Schuler,
and Block. The rest of the Jews came from England (Cohen, Abensur, Hatchwell,
etc.), the United States (the Besso brothers), Malta (the brothers Isaac, Rafael,
and Víctor Israel), and a handful of Jews came from Germany.

This list of names was based on Rosenzweig's documentation of Jews buried
in the Israelite cemetery, the members of the 1909 *Sociedad Israelita de Iquitos,*
and oral testimonies that he gathered in 1949. I have found in property and parish
records of Iquitos names that are not mentioned in Rosenzweig's article, including
the numerous descendants of Francisco Mesía's son, Toribio, who fathered at least
a dozen children in the Peruvian Amazon. Alfredo Rosenzweig is the only person
who has attempted to provide an approximation of the number of Jewish immigrants in the Peruvian Amazon, a task that must be acknowledged. Initially, I was
planing to provide my own statistics but I gave up this idea after realizing that
many Jews who lived most of the time navigating rivers or in the jungle did not
register their names in Iquitos and that the records for those who may have registered in other towns are now lost. (See Appendix 2).

See also Rosenzweig, "Judíos en la Amazonía Peruana, 1870–1949,"19–30.

30. Mauro Coblentz Lazo, interview by author, Iquitos, 20 July 1995. Mauro
Coblentz Lazo brought a dictionary to the interview to show me the origin of his
family name: Koblentz is the name of a German town. It is common to find Jewish
surnames whose origins are the names of European cities and towns.

31. Saúl Benamú Gónzales-Pavón, interview by author, Iquitos, 15 June 1995.

32. Sofía Ruiz del Aguila, interview by author, Iquitos, 11 June 1995. The reference to cutting the back of a cock's neck, which Doña Sofía obviously found
"weird," can be found in the Talmud. It specifies that Jews must perform a sacrifice before Yom Kippur. The sacrificed cock is given to poor people as a way of
doing a good deed before atonement. It is called the *Kappara* (root of the word
Kippur), and today this tradition has been adapted to modern practices; some Jews
bless a symbolic amount of money and later give it to charity.

33. Among the most important commercial houses run by Jews between 1902 and
1910 were: Abensur y Cia; Farache Hermanos Import/Export; Khan and Polak;
Benasayag, Toledano i Cia; Pinto Hermanos; Barsesat & Edery; Marius Levy &
Schuler; Nahón & Gabai; Toledano & Delmar; A. Bitton y Cia; Cohen & Toledano;

Khan y Cia; Magni & Edery; Benzaquén & Toledano; Elaluf i Cia; Ederi & Delmar; Nahón y Serfati; Israel y Cía.

Property records of that time provide us with some clues about how the Jews of Iquitos ran their businesses; many Jews who founded import/export companies in Iquitos either lived in Europe and sent representatives to manage their businesses or they spent most of their time out of Iquitos. In some cases these companies were run by a single family while in other cases two or more Jews associated for business purposes. Records listing the names of employees and representatives of these commercial houses show that owners tended to hire other Jews (often from their native countries). There are only a few cases of Jewish-Gentile associations. Most of the companies had a short life. This, in turn, caused former competitors to associate with one another to form new commercial houses.

34. Fuentes, *Loreto,* 29–30.

35. The original report in Spanish is in the *Enciclopedia Judaica Castellana,* ed. Eduardo Winfeld (México: n.p., 1950), 430–31. The English translation can be found in Serels, *A History of the Jews of Tangier,* 176.

36. Ibid., 176.

37. Alfredo Rosenzweig, interview by Sandy Barak Cassinelli, Lima, 7 July 1995.

38. Juan E. Coriat, *El hombre del Amazonas: Ensayo monográfico de Loreto* (Lima: Librería Coriat, 1943), 13.

39. References to Salomón Casés's coup against the Iquitos governor can be found in Up De Graff, *Head Hunters of the Amazon,* 139–140. (In the English version of this book the name of Salomón Casés is written as "Solomon Casas.")

40. These numbers are provided by Rosenzweig in "Judíos en la Amazonía Peruana, 1870–1949," 19–30.

41. With the collapse of the rubber economy, Víctor Israel, the Maltese Jew, owner of the commercial house Israel y Cía and one of the richest men of Iquitos, expressed his sorrow for the decline of the good life in Iquitos: "'The situation is very bad,' sighed Don Víctor from behind his massive ledger. 'Why, do you know that Iquitos, in spite of its large Chinese colony, is the only city in the Republic that can't claim a single *chifa* [Chinese restaurant]! When the *Chinos* won't touch it, you may be certain the situation is tough!'"

This account by Henry Warren Kelly, the U.S. vice-consul of Peru in Iquitos, written in the 1930s and 1940s, depicts a changing city with wealthy people yearning for the days when they were even richer.

See Kelly's *Dancing Diplomats*, 22.

42. Founders of the *Sociedad Israelita de Beneficiencia de Iquitos* in 1909: Víctor Israel; Abraham Edery Fimat; Samuel Laredo; Lázaro García; Isaac Toledano; Lucien Weill; Benjamín Gabay; Jacobo A. Toledano; Moisés Zrihem; Jacob Miguel; Moisés Bendayán; David Zrihem; Alberto Alvez; León Bendayán; Salomón Cohén; Moisés A. Bendayán; León Pinto; Rafael Marache; Abraham Nahmías; Jaime Barsesat; Jorge Toledano; Salomón Alvez; Moisés Serfaty; León Cohén; A. H. Toledano; Fortunato Foinquinos; Elías Salgado; Marcos Delmar; Salomón Coriat; Isaac Israel; León Benasayac; David Abecasis; Abraham Delmar; Carlos Margui; E. Hatchwell; David Cazés; Samuel Coriat; David Elaluf; Salomón Azor.

This first meeting was held in the house of the Pinto brothers to submit for debate the statutes presented by the commission.

This information is based on a document annexed to the 6 November 1945 act of reestablishment and registration of the Israelite Society in the Public Records of Iquitos (*RPL,* Part no. 372, 1945).

43. In the 1928 document, the Israelite Society's board of directors ratified in their session of 19 December 1927 the statutes set during the meeting of 9 January 1909. The board of directors was confirmed by Víctor Israel, Sam Harris, José Toledano, Moisés Benzaquén, Salomón Azerrad, David Ederi, Miguel Besso, and José Tapiero.

44. *RPL,* Part no. 372, 1945.

45. According to Víctor Israel's stepdaughter, Josefa Pizarro Vásquez (who claims to be a descendant of Francisco Pizarro), Víctor Israel received baptism and confirmation during his wedding with her mother, Josefa Vásquez Cordova in Lima: "He was profoundly Christian but he never ate pork, or fish without scales; he fasted on Yom Kippur, and prayed in Hebrew and Latin. He was a man of faith in both religions." (Josefa Pizarro Vásquez, interview by author, Lima, 7 August 1995.) Víctor Israel, founder of the Israelite Society of Iquitos, is ironically buried in the Christian cemetery *El Angel* in Lima, as he requested before his death.

46. Some "Jewish *Mestizos*" believe that Salomón Azerrad took those documents with him when he went to Brazil, where he passed away. According to a couple of my informants in Iquitos, Azerrad spent the last years of his life in Manaus; there-

fore, I wrote letters to institutions of the Jewish community of that city requesting information about those documents, but I did not receive answers.

CHAPTER 3

1.   Mario Vargas Llosa, *The Storyteller,* trans. Helen Lane (New York: Penguin Books, 1990), 100.

2.   Dobkin de Ríos, *Visionary Vine,* 49.

3.   Ronald Reategui Levy, interview by author, Iquitos, 19 June 1995.

4.   Joseph Orton Kerbey, the United States consul in Pará, Brazil, visited Iquitos in the first decade of the twentieth century, and described in detail the corrupt behavior of most secular priests who lived in that city: "Some of the churches in these interiors which do not have the oversight of the bishops, are often controlled by unscrupulous priests who make no effort to correct the existing evils, and the people have become accustomed to the conditions." See Kerbey, *The Land of To-morrow,* 116.

5.   Father García asserts that "state and church had a common discourse about civilization and barbarism that it is still latent in the current Latin American thought." (Father Joaquín García, interview by author, Iquitos, 8 July 1995).

6.   Historian José Barletti Pasquale, interview by author, Iquitos, 27 July 1995.

7.   "This place [Iquitos] was dominated by rubber lords and their foreign benefactors, so they were happy to have priests who allowed them to do whatever they wanted. . . . They [these priests] did not see, did not hear and shut up. . . . (Historian José Barletti Pasquale, interview by author, Iquitos, 27 July 1995.)

8.   "Secular priests challenged the missionaries: 'Iquitos is not an uncivilized place. Then, go through the rivers to the jungle!'"(Father Joaquín García, interview by author, Iquitos, 8 July 1995.)

9.   A brief description of Julio Arana's responsibilities on the Putumayo crimes can be seen in chapter 1, endnote 15.

10.   The 1903 city census prepared by the *subprefecto* (vice-governor) of the province, Benito E. Lores, yielded these numbers of immigrants: 8,896 Peruvians,

95 Spaniards, 80 Brazilians, 74 Asians, 64 Portuguese, 52 Italians, 38 Germans, 36 Moroccans, 33 French, 24 Ecuadorians, 14 Colombians, 14 British, 5 North Americans, and 4 Russians. See Fuentes, *Loreto,* 246.

11. The Protestant movements that arrived in the Peruvian Amazon are the Christian Alliance (1923), Adventists (1927), Baptist Evangelicals (1942), Witness of J (1955), Assembly of God (1965), and three millenarian groups that have found a fertile "paradise" in the Amazonian region: The Mormons (1966), *Los Hermanos de la Cruz* (1971), and *La Iglesia Israelita* (1986).

12. *"Los Hermanos de la Cruz,* founded in 1963 by Francisco Da Cruz in Brazil, and *La Iglesia Israelita,* established in the Peruvian Andes in 1968 by Ezequiel Atacusi, consider their leaders to be "messiahs" who eventually will lead their followers to the Amazon, their promised land, the last refuge on earth where believers of both sects will stay during the end of time.

    The followers of *La Iglesia Israelita* look for political power in Lima and in the whole nation—Atacusi has run as presidential candidate in two national elections." (Anthropologist Javier Neyra, interview by author, Iquitos, 20 July 1995).

    For a more detailed account of these two religious movements in the Peruvian Amazon see Javier Neyra, *Los que llegaron después: Estudio del impacto cultural de las denominaciones religiosas no Católicas en Iquitos* (Iquitos: CETA, 1992), 189–204 and Regan, *Hacia la tierra sin mal,* 337–370.

13. Father Joaquín García, interview by author, Iquitos, 8 July 1995.

14. Dobkin de Ríos, *Visionary Vine,* 7–8.

15. Father Joaquín García, interview by author, Iquitos, 8 July 1995.

16. Ibid.

17. Father José María Arroyo, interview by author, Iquitos, 14 June 1995.

18. The belief in *El Señor de los Milagros* has its origins in Lima, where a miraculous image has been worshiped in the church of *Las Nazarenas* since 1651. This belief has spread throughout Peru, turning the image into a national religious symbol.

19. Anthropologist Javier Neyra, interview by author, Iquitos, 20 July 1995.

20. Father Joaquín García, interview by author, Iquitos, 8 July 1995.

21. See Dobkin de Ríos's analysis of family life in the urban slum of Belén in Iquitos in *Visionary Vine*, 58–65.

22. Regan, *Hacía la tierra sin mal*, 101.

23. Professor José Barletti Pasquale explains how the Catholic Church dealt with this problem: "One can read the reports of fathers Uriarte and Moroni condemning polygamy, but they never could control it. Here [in the Amazon] the people have unbridled passions; they go astray. . . . The same Pope Pious X wrote how the people here felt caught in a natural and wild environment that unbinds passions. . . . The church attempts to impose a minimum of social control through the sacraments, and rituals, but its power only is visible in the cultural sphere. The power of the church does not reflect itself in the daily life of people." (Historian José Barletti Pasquale, interview by author Iquitos, 27 July 1995.)

24. Regan, *Hacia la tierra sin mal*, 104.

25. Ibid., 141, 145, and 196.

26. Vargas Llosa, *The Storyteller*, 101.

27. The quotations are taken from John Vincent's work *Disraeli* (Oxford: Oxford University Press, 1992).

28. Oswald Rufeisen, or Brother Daniel, was a Jew who managed to escape the Nazis by taking shelter in a convent where he lived for eighteen months dressed as a nun. He became interested in Catholic theology, converted to Christianity in 1942, and decided in 1945 to join the Carmelite Order of monks in Poland, becoming Brother Daniel. In 1959 he settled in Israel, where he requested to be registered as a citizen of Christian religion and Jewish nationality, provoking a national debate concerning the Law of Return and the question of who is a Jew. See Oscar Kraines, *The Impossible Dilemma: Who Is a Jew in the State of Israel?* (New York: Bloch Publishing Company, 1976), 22.

29. Jean-Marie Lustiger recalls when he made the decision to convert to Catholicism: "It was not a political rationale. I never thought that I was negating my Jewish identity. Just the opposite! I saw Christ as Israel's messiah, and I believed that there were Christians who loved Judaism" (AT). See *Jean-Marie Lustiger: La elección de*

Dios (Barcelona: Editorial Planeta, 1989), 39. The book is the transcription of an interview with Lustiger, carried out by Jean-Louis Missika and Dominique Wolton.

30. See Elaine Marks, *Marrano as Metaphor: The Jewish Presence in French Writing* (New York: Columbia University Press, 1996), 129–130.

31. Ibid., 133.
    I do not share Elaine Marks's use of the concept of *Marranism*—and more-over—of crypto-Judaism (which implies secrecy) for the case of acculturated Jews.

32. Dr. Frank C. Stuart, professor of British and Renaissance history at the University of Miami, suggested that it would be interesting to compare the religion of the "Jewish *Mestizos*" with that of the early Christians during the first and second centuries C.E., not only because of the blending of Jewish and Christian motifs, but also because of the fluid way the early Christians combined practices and beliefs from the two faiths.

33. Alfredo Rosenzweig, interview by Sandy Barak Cassinelli, Lima, 7 July 1995.

34. Víctor Edery Morales, interview by author, Iquitos, 7 July 1995.

35. Saúl Benamú Gónzales-Pavón, interview by author, Iquitos, 15 June 1995.

36. In Iquitos's parish records of the *Iglesia Matriz*, the names of the children and grandchildren of prominent Jewish immigrants are registered in the book of baptisms, among them, last names such as Israel, Toledano, Kahan, Cohen, etc.

    An example that illustrates the frequency of baptisms among descendants of Jews in Iquitos can be found in the list of the board of directors of the Peruvian-Israeli Cultural Institute founded in 1966. Out of eleven members seven were baptized, including the president Werner Levy Navarro and the vice-president Willy Benzaquén Nájar. Practically all members of today's Israelite Society of Iquitos were baptized and the majority were married in the church.

37. Eva Moreno Rodríguez de Abramovitz, interview by author, Iquitos, 22 June 22, 1995; Luis Weisselberger Vílchez, interview by author, Iquitos, 6 July 1995; Elizabeth Kohn Casique, interview by author, Iquitos, 25 June 1995; Werner Levy Navarro, interview by author, Iquitos, 17 June 1995; and Sara Bendayán García, interview by author, Iquitos, 29, June 1995.

38. Marco Mesía Rodríguez, interview by author, Iquitos, 18 June 1995.

39. Jorge Abramovitz Rodríguez, interview by author, Iquitos, 22 June 1995; Sara Bendayán Tello, interview by author, Iquitos, 29 June 1995; and Cecilia Weill Quiroz, interview by author, Iquitos, 26 June 1995.

40. Fernando Levy Martínez, interview by author, Iquitos, 17 June 1995; Teddy Bendayán Díaz, interview by author, Iquitos, 20 June 1995; Alicia Assayag Chávez, interview by author, Iquitos, 12 June 1995; and Pedro Reategui Panduro, interview by author, Iquitos, 17 June 1995.

41. Becky Ríos Bensimón, interview by author, Iquitos, 14 July 1995.

42. Israel Bento Mass, interview by author, Iquitos, 7 July 1995; and León Delmar Ruiz, interview by author, Iquitos, 4 July 1995.

43. Saúl Benamú Gónzales-Pavón, interview by author, Iquitos, 15 June 1995; Becky Ríos Bensimón, interview by author, Iquitos, 14 July 1995; and Israel Bento Mass, interview by author, Iquitos, 7 July 1995.

44. Father José María Arroyo, interview by author, Iquitos, 14 June 1995.

45. This information was confirmed by Ana Mesía Velasco's daughter, Judith Velasco Mesía, who lives in Lima.

46. While I was in Iquitos, I had the opportunity to witness the *Shloshim,* a ceremony performed in the cemetery thirty days after a person's death. It was thirty days after Víctor Edery Morales's brother's death, so the widow and two sons of Alberto Edery Morales came from Lima to Iquitos to read the mourning prayer, the *Kaddish,* to honor their father.

47. Luz Lazo Nahmías, interview by author, Iquitos, 27 June 1995; Heysen Casique Kohn, interview by author, Iquitos, 25 June 1995; and Ramón Coriat, interview by author, Iquitos, 12 July 1995.

48. Fernando Levy Martínez, interview by author, Iquitos, 17 June 1995; Víctor Edery Morales, interview by author, Iquitos, 7 July 1995; Luis Coblentz Pérez, interview by author, Iquitos, 26 July 1995; León Delmar Ruiz, interview by author, Iquitos, 4 July 1995; Sara Bendayán García, interview by author, Iquitos, 29 June 1995; Kelly Mesía Costa, interview by author, Iquitos, 18 June 1995; Jaime

Bensimón Puyó, interview by author, Iquitos, 11 June 1995; and Edgar Dávila Lazo, interview by author, Iquitos, 12 July 1995.

49. *SBII*, 14 October 1991.

50. Jaime Vásquez Izquierdo, interview by author, Iquitos, 10 June 1995.

51. On 2 July 1995, while I was in Iquitos, the Israelite Society of Iquitos held elections to select a new board of directors. After four years as president of the society, Víctor Edery Morales was defeated by Jaime Bensimón Puyó, but he remained to fulfill the role of spiritual guide in the community.

In a session held on 30 July, the new president, Jaime Bensimón Puyó proposed to open the society to any sympathizer who wished to join them, changing the name of the institution to the Cultural Israelite Society, so that "members of other religions could belong to the society." This caused a vigorous reaction from Jaime Vásquez Izquierdo, who explained that the goal of the society was to spread "Jewish life" among its members.

Most of the society members scarcely understood the debate and thought that indeed, it was a good idea to recruit more people to get more money and, thereby, repair the Israelite cemetery and organize more activities. Jaime Vásquez Izquierdo wrote a letter to me in Miami explaining that he quit the society because "the people simply do not understand what the society is for." Together with Víctor Edery Morales, Vásquez Izquierdo founded a new institution, the Beneficence and Religious Israelite Society, and its members were meeting in Víctor Edery Morales's home for the Shabbat service.

In the last letter I received from members who continue to meet at Jaime Bensimón Puyó's home, they tell me that they do not understand Jaime Vásquez Izquierdo's reasons for his resigning and they do not know what to do.

It seems that this division is causing Bensimón's group to fade, and some youngsters are approaching Edery Morales and Vásquez Izquierdo's party.

52. Viviana Toledano, interview by author, Iquitos, 11 June 1995.

53. Fernando Levy Martínez, interview by author, Iquitos, 17 June 1995; Enrique Mesía Ochoa, interview by author, Iquitos, 22 June 1995; Sara Bendayán García, interview by author, Iquitos, 29 June 1995; and León Delmar Ruiz, interview by author, Iquitos, 4 July 1995.

54. Becky Ríos Bensimón, interview by author, Iquitos, 14 July 1995; Víctor Edery Morales, interview by author, Iquitos, 15 June 1995; León Delmar Ruiz,

interview by author, Iquitos, 4 July 1995; and Cecilia Weill Quiroz, interview by author, Iquitos, 26 June 1995.

CHAPTER 4

1.   In his book *Conversion to Judaism: From the Biblical Period to the Present,* Joseph R. Rosenbloom claims that during the biblical times there were frequent cases of intermarriage. The author also emphasizes cases of massive conversions to Judaism such as the Adiabenans in Asia Minor during the first century C.E., the Khazzars in the tenth century, and other communities. See Joseph R. Rosenbloom, *Conversion to Judaism: From the Biblical Period to the Present* (Cincinnati: Hebrew Union College Press, 1978).

2.   The control of social and sexual behaviors is an issue extensively analyzed by Michel Foucault in two works: *Discipline and Punishment: The Birth of the Prison* (New York: Random House, 1979) and *The History of Sexuality* (New York: Pantheon Books, 1978). It is also explored in Antonio Gramsci, *Letters from the Prison* (New York: Harper Colophon Edition, 1975).

Disciples of the Annals School have also produced several works on the study of the deliberate or instinctive control that European elites and institutions exercised over popular culture in modern early Europe, controlling bodies and symbolic meanings that led to modern notions of urbanity, manners, morality, and property. See, for example, James Augustus St. John, *The History of the Manners and Customs of Ancient Greece* (Port Washington, N.Y.: Kennikat Press, 1971); Giulia Calvi, *Histories of a Plague Year: The Social and the Imaginary in Baroque Florence* (Berkeley: University of California Press, 1984); Robert Muchembled, *Popular Culture and Elite Culture in France 1400–1750* (Baton Rouge: Louisiana State University Press, 1985); Ruggiero, *Binding Passions;* and Marjorie Morgan, *Manners, Morals, and Class in England, 1774–1858* (New York: Macmillian Press, 1994).

Obviously, these mechanisms of social control were (and are) also applied beyond European borders, as the case of the Roman Catholic Church in Latin America attests.

3.   With the exception of the North American Jewry, the Jews in the rest of the continent tended to be very conservative and clannish, avoiding too much involvement in public life. This pattern of behavior has undergone slight changes in the 1980s and 1990s with the emergence of democratic governments encouraging Jews to participate in the political scenery of their countries.

In Peru, for example, several Jewish functionaries have participated in the last two governments, including Efraím Goldemberg, who served as prime minister for president Alberto Fujimori, an evangelist, and son of Japanese immigrants. Certainly in the 1990s, the trend of members of minorities participating in politics indicates dramatic changes.

For a theoretical panorama of trends in how Latin American Jews have adapted and assimilated to their societies, see Judith Laikin Elkin, "The Evolution of the Latin American-Jewish Communities: Retrospect and Prospect," in *The Jewish Presence in Latin America*, ed. Judith Laikin Elkin and Gilbert W. Merkx (Boston: Allen & Unwin Inc., 1987) 309–324; and Robert M. Levine, "Adaptive Strategies of Jews in Latin America," (Ibid.), 71–84.

4.   These categorizations could be compared to those proposed by Benedict Anderson, who developed a system for analyzing the identity of "imagined communities." Ethnicity determined by halakhah (having a Jewish mother) would be the equivalent of Anderson's "dynastic realm," in which a group of people shares the awareness of being members of a family or descendants of common ancestors. The practice of rituals can be paralleled with Anderson's "religious community" in which the knowledge of a "sacred" language is necessary in order to feel part of a nation (or at least, in the case of Jewish rituals, to be able to read Hebrew while performing those rituals). The Jewish identification with a common history and annual events can be likened to Anderson's "apprehension of time," which provides a conception of temporality in which cosmology and history blend.

See Benedict Anderson, *Imagined Communities: Reflections on the Origin and Spread of Nationalism* (New York and London: Verso, 1991), 9–36.

5.   Michel Radzinky's speech is quoted in Trahtemberg's work, *Los Judíos de Lima*, 74.

6.   Ibid., 75.

7.   Alain Finkielkraut, *The Imaginary Jew*, trans. Kevin O'Neill and David Suchoff (Lincoln: University of Nebraska Press, 1994), 15.

8.   Several old Jews remember Brener as an excellent spiritual guide, a very knowledgeable rabbi, but too fond of money. Several raise questions about what determined his decisions. The schism that shook the Ashkenazic congregation in 1942 when a group of Orthodox *Ashkenazim* accused Brener of using his position for personal gain shows the controversial nature of the first Orthodox rabbi in Lima.

9.   In Iquitos the case of the Abramovitz children is well remembered. In 1959 Benjamín Samolsky paid Brener's travel expenses and services to perform the circumcision of his son Simón in his Iquitos home. Zeev Abramovitz took advantage of the rabbi's presence to ask him to circumcise two of his children, ages four and five. The mother of those children, Eva Moreno Rodríguez de Abramovitz, recalls the "famous" *brit milah:* "When my older kid was circumcised, I went out with Pepe, my younger one, to avoid having him see that [circumcision]. Both of them suffered a lot and finally we had to take them to the hospital. . . . The rabbi stayed in the Weisselbergers' house and he saw some of our hens in the yard and he asked my husband to give him a few as a gift, so he took the hens." (Eva Moreno Rodríguez de Abramovitz, interview by author, Iquitos, 22 June 1995.)

Eva Barak remembers her husband, Simón, who accompanied the rabbi as he came down from the airplane "holding four hens by their tied legs." (Eva and Simón Barak, interview by author, Lima, 25 May 1995.) Simón Samolsky also remembers the "famous" *brit* of the Abramovitz brothers, who were circumcised without anesthesia because the rabbi had to leave quickly.

Mr. Aaron Goldemberg recalls how the Jews of Arequipa used to tell a joke about Brener: "He came to circumcise one or two of our children and he ended up making circumcisions on the Arab kids too." (Aaron Goldemberg, interview by author, Lima, 29 May 1995.)

Beyond being anecdotes, these testimonies reveal that circumcisions were a way of making a living rather than a "mission" for this rabbi. These were meaningful rituals for the fathers who employed the services of the rabbi, but these circumcisions did not validate the Judaism of those children, who later went to Lima to be recognized as Jews. Simón Samolsky believes that "these were moral, rather than legal validations of a Judaism felt by those fathers who married non-Jewish women. It was an opportunity to materialize in an emotional way the sense of Judaism that these fathers felt regarding their non-Jewish sons." (Simón Samolsky, interview by author, Lima, 5 June 1995.)

10.   In the novel *The Fragmented Life of Don Jacobo Lerner,* Isaac Goldemberg fictionalizes a situation in which the religious and political authorities of Lima ignore Jewish law. In one chapter Miriam Abramovitz goes to the Israelite cemetery to visit her husband's gravestone only to find out that he was buried in the rear of the graveyard because he committed suicide (a deed that obligates Jews not to bury the deceased inside the Jewish cemetery). The widow complains: "I asked Moisés why the grave wasn't with the others and he put his hand on my shoulder and said, 'Don't worry, Miriam, you know how the rabbi is; we'll see after some time goes by.'" See Isaac Goldemberg, *The Fragmented Life of Don Jacobo Lerner,* trans. Robert S. Picciotto (New York: Persea Books, 1976), 66.

Some time goes by and on page 119 of the novel we read in one of the Chronicles of 1930–1931: "A religious ceremony is held at the Jewish cemetery of Bellavista, in which a tablet is placed on the tomb of Daniel Abramowitz, who had died on October 17, 1930. Mr. Abramowitz had been an active member of the community. His widow donates fifty *soles* to the coffers of the Hebrew Union." (Ibid.), 119.

Any similarity with real facts is pure coincidence.

11. I restrain from providing the name of the person I am quoting to avoid controversies that might affect some people in Lima's Jewish community.

One of the Orthodox rabbis of Lima explained to me halakhic details related to cases Lima's rabbis have tackled in their congregations. The topic is very complex and full of rabbinical considerations that belong to the domain of Jewish Law and exceptional situations. It is enough to say that based on halakhah, the Orthodox rabbis of Lima have been able to cope with questionable aspects of their congregations' Jewishness when decisions were made by prior rabbis, but now, Orthodox rabbis are less flexible when it comes to current cases of conversions and recognizing the Judaism of individuals and groups.

12. What distinguishes Latin American Jewish communities from those in North America is the weak presence of Conservative or Reform Judaism in their midst. Even in Argentina and Chile, where Conservative congregations have some independence from the mainstream Orthodox trend, there is no full consciousness of the possibility of assuming a challenging stance vis-á-vis Orthodoxy.

In Lima, as in many other Latin American cities, it is very hard to convert non-Jews to Judaism. The Orthodox rabbis rarely perform conversions while the Conservative congregation, led by Rabbi Guillermo Bronstein since 1985, requires two years of study before testing candidates. Afterwards, the ritual is carried out in Chile in the presence of two other Conservative rabbis (according to Jewish Law, there must be a rabbinical tribunal of at least three practicing Jews in order to convert).

Although Orthodox rabbis are very strict, according to some Jews there have been occasions on which they relax conditions when requested to by prominent men of the community, especially in issues related to burying their relatives in the Israelite cemetery or registering their children in the Jewish school. These type of stories repeat themselves in almost all Latin American Jewish communities.

For a discussion of the religious pattern in Latin American communities, see Elkin's two works, "The Evolution of the Latin American-Jewish Communities: Retrospect and Prospect" in *The Jewish Presence in Latin America*, 309–324; and *Jews of the Latin American Republics* (Chapel Hill: University of North Carolina Press, 1980).

13. León Trahtemberg, interview by author, Lima, 10 August 1995.

Conservative and Reform rabbis in the United States maintain a more personal relationship with their congregations, serving as ethical leaders who perform professional and social functions. Rather than legitimizing the Jewishness of their congregations, modern synagogues attempt to create a sense of community among their members for whom style is more important than content; therefore, argues Eugene B. Borowitz, "we do not really care how much Torah he [the rabbi] knows and teaches as long as he dignifies us in public—particularly when there are guests present." See Eugene B. Borowitz, *The Masks Jews Wear: The Self-Deceptions of American Jewry* (New York: Sh'ma, 1980), 177.

14. In the words of anthropologist Virginia Domínguez: "The thing about rituals we notice the most is that we notice them." Domínguez, *People as Subject, People as Object*, 42.

15. Rafael Rodríguez, interview by author, Lima, 22 May 1995.

For statistics concerning the recent number of children of mixed marriages, based on the studies of students of the "León Pinelo" School, see Trahtemberg's work *Demografía Judía del Perú* (Lima: Ort-Perú, 1988), 37–41.

16. Borowitz, *The Masks Jews Wear*, 16.

17. Finkielkraut, *The Imaginary Jew*, 38.

18. Goldemberg, *The Fragmented Life*, 22–23.

19. Borowitz, *The Masks Jews Wear*, 66.

20. León Trahtemberg, interview by author, Lima, 15 August 1995.

21. Finkielkraut, *The Imaginary Jew*, 45.

22. Borowitz, *The Masks Jews Wear*, 217.

23. This categorical statement was written by the president of the Institute in a draft of the statutes presented to its members in the session of 13 February 1968, more than a year after the institution was established. The final draft of the institution's statutes expresses the non-religious character of this association in milder language. The statutes enumerate the goals of the association, emphasizing its social and cultural nature, its aim to encourage relations with other Jewish communities of the world and the State of Israel, and its desire to "extend among its

members general culture, and especially, the Jewish tradition and history."
(Statutes of the *ICPII*, written by its president, Werner Levy Navarro. There is no
date indicated on the document.)

24. Domínguez, *People as Subject, People as Object,* 189.

25. Letter from Werner Levy Navarro, president of the *Instituto Cultural Peruano-
Israelí de Iquitos* to Mr. S. B.Yeshaya, president of the Institute of Cultural Relations Between Israel-Latin America, Spain, and Portugal. (*ICPII*, 30 April 1967.)

26. Luis Weisselberger Vílchez, interview by author, Iquitos, 6 July 1995; Manfred Weisselberger Meléndez, interview by author, Iquitos, 6 July 1995; Fernando
Levy Martínez, interview by author, Iquitos, 17 June 1995; Luis Coblentz Pérez,
interview by author, Iquitos, 26 July 1995; and Teddy Bendayán Díaz, interview by
author, Iquitos, 20 June 1995.

27. Teddy Bendayán Díaz, interview by author, Iquitos, 20 June 1995; and Cecilia
Weill Quiroz, interview by author, Iquitos, 26 June 1995.

28. Edgar Dávila Lazo, interview by author, Iquitos, 12 July 1995.

29. Salomón Abensur Boria, interview by author, Iquitos, 22 July 1995.

30. Father José María Arroyo, interview by author, Iquitos, 14 June 1995.
    The case of the brothers Jorge and Néstor Cárdenas Regra reveals this pas-
sion for tracing one's ancestors. Before 13 July 1995, Nestor's last name was Cárdenas Murrieta, but through a judicial process in a civil court he *"adicionó
judicialmente"* (added judicially) his last name, changing it to Cárdenas Regra. The
request was introduced in court on 25 June 1995, and finally was issued on 10 July,
so that now Néstor Cárdenas's last name and the last name of his three children is
Cárdenas Regra, honoring the surname of a great-grandmother who, they claim,
was Jewish. Jorge Cárdenas also requested that his second last name be changed.
Both families made *aliyah* in 1998.
    Another interesting aspect of this case is that the brothers have searched in
Iquitos and other Amazonian cities for people with obviously Jewish last names to
teach them about their origins. It was the brothers Cárdenas Regra who told Heysen and Jacobo Casique Kohn that the name Kohn was Jewish; this piece of information ignited the two youngsters' search for their Jewish roots.
    According to the Cárdenas Regra brothers, all Spanish last names whose
meanings refer to nature mask the identities of Jewish *Conversos* forced to

become Christians in the Iberian Peninsula. They gave me these examples: Delmar, Parra, Flores, Prado, Ríos, Villamar, and Peña.

31. León Delmar Ruiz, interview by author, Iquitos, 4 July 1995.

32. Statutes of the *Sociedad de Beneficiencia Israelita de Iquitos,* Article 2 *(SBII).*

33. Ibid., Article 3 *(SBII).*

34. *SBII,* 16 November 1991.

35. Salomón Abensur Boria, interview by author, Iquitos, 22 July 1995; Enrique Mesía Ochoa, interview by author, Iquitos, 22 June 1995; and Luis Weisselberger Vílchez, interview by author, Iquitos, 6 July 1995.

36. León Delmar Ruiz, interview by author, Iquitos, 4 July 1995.

37. Pedro Reategui Panduro, interview by author, Iquitos, 17 June 1995; and Alicia Assayag Chávez, interview by author, Iquitos, 12 June 1995.
    I found that several descendant of Jews in Iquitos have read Leon Uris's novel *Exodus* and that the book has become the source of inspiration. I also was amazed that the whole family of Sammy Weisselberger had read both novels of a not-so-known Israeli author, Amos Kolleck: *Don't Ask Me If I Love* and *She Brought the War.*

38. They asked me to lecture to them about the Holocaust, and so I did in the *Biblioteca Amazónica.* They also asked me to teach them two songs from the movie soundtrack: one is the *Yiddish* children's song, *"Oifn Pripichek"* ("By the Fireside") and the other is Israel's national anthem *"Hatikvah"* ("Hope"), which the older members remembered from the 1950s and 1960s.

39. Werner Levy Navarro, interview by author, Iquitos, 17 June 1995; and Kelly Mesía Costa, interview by author, Iquitos, 18 June 1995.

40. Pedro Reategui Panduro, interview by author, Iquitos, 17 June 1995; and Sara Bendayán García, interview by author, Iquitos, 29 June 1995.

41. Portocarrero Vargas's letter addressed to the Superior Court of the Department of Loreto (Iquitos, 7 April 1967), as well as the answer of Mr. Jorge Noriega Vargas representing the Superior Court (Iquitos, 20 June 1967), is kept in the archives of the *Sociedad de Beneficiencia Israelita de Iquitos.*

CHAPTER 5

1.   Rabbinical Judaism vs. Karaites since the eighth century, Rationalists vs. Kabbalists in the Middle Ages, Hassidim vs. Mitnagdim in the eighteenth century, Orthodox vs. Conservative and Reform Judaism in the twentieth century. See *Great Schisms in Jewish History,* eds. Raphael Jaspe and Stanley M. Wagner (New York: Ktav Publishing House, 1981).

2.   For literature concerning the history and philosophy of Orthodox, Conservative, Reform, and Reconstructionist Judaism see works such as Nathan Glezer, *American Judaism* (Chicago: University of Chicago Press, 1972); Marshall Sklare, *Conservative Judaism: An American Religious Movement* (New York: Schocken Books, Inc., 1972); Marc Lee Raphael, *Profiles in American Judaism: The Reform, Conservative, Orthodox and Reconstrucionist Traditions in Historical Perspective* (San Francisco: Harper & Row, 1984); and Gilbert S. Rosenthal, *Contemporary Judaism: Patterns of Survival* (New York: Human Sciences Press, 1986), etc.

3.   To avoid the collapse of the government, which abandonment by the National Religious Party would precipitate, Ben-Gurion dealt with the problem creatively. He called upon forty-five internationally prominent Jewish scholars, religious leaders, and legal philosophers to give their opinions on questions regarding registration of children born of mixed marriages. These consultants were asked to keep in mind Israel's policy of freedom of religion, its commitment to encourage mass immigration of Jews, especially those from hostile countries, and its linkage with Diaspora Jews. Ben-Gurion's government never defined "Who is a Jew?" but his strategy of consultations allowed him to postpone answering this intricate political, legal, and religious question, so the Orthodox Chief Rabbinate and the Supreme Court made decisions based on particular cases.

Since the Supreme Court passed the amendment, controversy has switched to the meaning of the word "conversion." The Reform, Conservative, and Reconstructionist movements still oppose this decision because it excludes many North American Jews converted by their rabbis. These conversions are not accepted as "kosher" (properly performed) because these movements do not follow the strict Orthodox interpretation of halakhah. The question "Who is a Jew?" is an ongoing controversy whose legal, religious, political, and philosophical aspects are too complex to analyze in this work. In November 1995, Israel's Supreme Court determined that Conservative and Reform rabbis must be accepted in the country's religious courts. Orthodox political parties have played a major role in Israel's parliamentary system. The Labor Party and the Likud Party have relied upon religious parties to form coalitions in order to obtain the sixty-one seats in the

Knesset, thereby forming governments. Of course, these parties must comply with some religious exigencies, a situation that gives Orthodox Judaism an overwhelming influence over matters of state.

Among the works that analyze the influence of religious parties on Israeli politics are Robert Owen Freedman, *Israel in the Begin Era* (New York: Prager, 1982); Charles Liebman and Eliezer Don-Yehiya, *Civil Religion in Israel: Traditional Judaism and Political Culture in the Jewish State* (Berkeley: University of California Press, 1983); Daniel J. Elazar, *Kinship and Consent: The Jewish Political Tradition and Its Contemporary Uses* (Washington, D.C.: University Press of America, 1983); Sol Roth, *Halakha and Politics: The Jewish Idea of the State* (New York: Ktav Publishing House, 1988); Menachem Mor, *Jewish Sects, Religious Movements, and Political Parties: Proceedings of the Third Annual Symposium of the Philp M. and Ethel Klutznick Chair in Jewish Civilization* (Omaha, NE: Creighton University Press, 1990); and Eva Etzioni-Halevy, "The Religion Elite Connection and Some Problems of Israeli Democracy," in *Government and Opposition* 4, no. 29 (Autumn 1994), 477–495.

4.   The Israeli system of recording the religious status of its citizens does not imply any discriminatory policy; rather, it has been a necessary record-keeping device to assure that assistance is provided to those who qualify according to the Law of Return. This law reflects what Israel has meant to the Jews over centuries of exile—an ancient homeland to which every Jew has the right to return. Although non-Jewish immigrants are welcome to become Israeli citizens, they are not considered among those returning from exile. Thus, religion is registered on the identity cards of Israelis because matters of status, such as marriage and divorce, are under the authority of various religious courts: Jewish, Moslem, Druze, Christian, etc.

The complexity of the relations between secular and religious institutions of the State of Israel in civil cases requires an exhaustive study of many works related to the question of "Who is a Jew?" The literature is extensive. I will recommend some books and articles, such as Ben Halpern, *The Idea of the Jewish State* (Cambridge: Harvard University Press, 1969); Kraines, *The Impossible Dilemma*; S. Z. Abramov, *Perpetual Dilemma: Jewish Religion in the Jewish State* (Rutherford, N.J.: Fairleigh Dickenson University Press, 1976); David Biale, "The Real Issue Behind Who-Is-A-Jew," *Tikkun* 4, no. 4 (July–August 1989): 82–87; Edward Norden, "Behind 'Who Is a Jew': A Letter from Jerusalem," *Commentary* 4, no. 87 (April 1989): 21–34; Domínguez, *People as Subject, People as Object*, 153–188; and Uri Huppert, Joni Marra, and Linda MacMonagle, "The Israeli Law of Return," *Free Inquiry* 3, no. 12 (Summer 1992): 28–32.

5.   An excellent review of specific cases of individuals and groups dealing with the legal, political, and religious ranges of being regarded as Jews in Israel can be found in Kraines, *The Impossible Dilemma.*

6.   The literature concerning all these groups and their struggles to be recognized as Jews by the Orthodox establishment of Israel and mainstream Jewish communities is very diverse. Izhak Ben Zvi, *The Exiled and the Redeemed* (Philadelphia: Jewish Publication Society, 1957), provides a thorough account of the history and struggles of groups such as the Samaritans (103–109), the Karaites (129–137), and the Himyarite and Ethiopian Jews (251–255), among other minority Jewish groups from Africa and Arab countries. Ben Zvi not only was a scholar devoted to the Israeli society, but also served as president of Israel in the late 1950s. Ben Zvi's research and continuous contacts with these communities led to the establishment of the Ben-Zvi Institute of the Hebrew University for the study of Jewish communities in the Near and Middle East.

Another work that surveys the history and struggles of peripheral groups attempting to be recognized as Jews is Ross, *Acts of Faith.* In this book the reader can find interesting accounts regarding the *Bene Israel* Jews from India (193–213), Samaritans (99–119), Karaites (120–142), and Ethiopian Jews (143–166).

Short descriptions of each of these groups can be found in the *Encyclopedia Judaica* (Jerusalem: Keter Publishing House Ltd., 1972). The literature of each community is too large to cite here, especially the case of the Ethiopian Jews, whose ongoing history in Israel appeals to many scholars of ethnic studies. I will just mention three works on this community that I consider to be very enlightening: David Kaplan, *The Falashas: The Forgotten Jews of Ethiopia* (New York: Schocken Books, 1985); Steven Kaplan, *The Beta Israel (Falasha) in Ethiopia: From Earliest Times to the Twentieth Century* (New York: New York University Press, 1992); and Steve Kaplan and Ruth Westheimer, *Surviving Salvation: The Ethiopian Jewish Family in Transition* (New York: New York University Press, 1992).

I also have relied on some newspapers and magazine articles in order to update the status of these groups in today's Israel.

7.   Concerning Jewish immigration from Russia to Israel, see Andrew Bilski's article "Exodus to the Promised Land: Soviet Immigrate to Israel," *Maclean's* 16, no. 103 (16 April 1990): 25–26; Richard Z. Chesnoff, "The New Exodus: A Huge Influx of Soviet Jews Is Already Transforming Israel," *U.S. News & World Report* 18, no. 180 (7 May 1990): 45–48; and Theodoro Stanger, "Strangers in Their Midst: An Exodus with an Unexpected Surprise: Not All of Israel's New Soviet Immigrants Are Jewish," *Newsweek* 14, no. 117 (8 April 1991): 50–52.

8.   The State of Israel has not recognized as Jews the American Black Israelites in Dimona, and a few families of *Chuetas* from Majorca, who returned to their birthland in the early 1970s after refusing to convert to Judaism. A concise summary of the case of the American Black Israelites in Israel can be seen in Kraines, *The Impossible Dilemma,* 74–76. See also Jesse Nemerofsky, "The Black Hebrews," *Society* 1, no. 32 (November 1994): 72; and Bernard J. Wolfson, "The Soul of Judaism," *Emerge* 10, no. 6 (September 1995): 42–46.

The case of the *Chuetas* from Majorca is analyzed by Raphael Patai in "The Chuetas of Majorca," *Midstream* (Spring 1962): 59–68; and by Ross in *Acts of Faith,* 52–66. Joachim Prinz also deals with the *Chuetas* of Majorca and other Crypto-Jewish sects derived from Christian Spain and Portugal in *The Secret Jews* (New York: Random House, 1973).

9.   See Fritz Becker, "The New Jews of San Nicandro," *Commentary* (April 1948): 346–349; and Phinn Lapide, "San Nicandro's New Jews in Israel," *Commentary* (September 1951): 246–251.

10.   Seymour Liebman, "The Mestizo Jews of Mexico," *American Jewish Historical Society* 19 (1967): 144–174.

11.   Patai discovered that there were two dissimilar "Jewish" groups in Mexico, both of whom considered themselves "Jewish Indians." One group, *La Iglesia de Dios,* was apparently founded by missionaries from the United States who went to Mexico to proselytize for the American Church of God in the early 1900s. This group observed biblical Jewish holidays, asserting that they knew about them because they were descended from the Ten Lost Tribes. At the same time, *La Iglesia de Dios* also believed that Jesus was God and the Messiah. Eventually—they claimed—all Jews would accept that truth. The other "Indian Jewish" group identified by Patai had settled in Venta Prieta and were heirs of a group that split from *La Iglesia de Dios* in the 1930s.

Bibliography on the *"Mestizo* Jews" of Mexico can be found in Raphael Patai, "The Jewish Indians of Mexico" and "Venta Prieta Revisited" in *On Jewish Folklore* (Detroit: Wayne State University Press, 1983), 447–475 and 476–492; Liebman, "The Mestizo Jews of Mexico," 144–174; and Ross, *Acts of Faith,* 1–25.

12.   Liebman, "The Mestizo Jews of Mexico," 166.

13.   Ibid.

14.   Patai, *On Jewish Folklore,* 469.

15. In the 1980s Rabbi Eliahu Avihail founded *Amishav,* an association that searches for descendants of the Ten Lost Tribes around the world. Although Rabbi Avichail knew that the Venta Prieta congregation was not a remnant of Israel, he decided to help this group convert to Judaism after sending emissaries who confirmed how serious these Mexicans were about adopting the Jewish faith.

Amishav has been following the cases of millions of people who claim to be descendants of the Lost Tribes, including the *Patanim* from Pakistan and Afghanistan. In the 1990s Rabbi Avichail himself organized the *aliyah* of fifty-seven people from Manipur, a state on India's border with Burma, who went immediately to a trailer park in the West Bank settlement of Quiryat Arba. These people from India claim that they are descendants of the lost tribe of Manasseh.

A North American organization known as *Kulanu* (All of Us), which is affiliated with the Israel-based *Amishav,* also traces descendants of the Ten Lost Tribes, as well as the progeny of *Marranos* around the world. Recently, *Kulanu* has been demanding that Israel recognize the *Orits,* an Ethiopian group alleged to be linked to the *Beta Israel* community. *Kulanu* also supports those descendants of Spanish and Portuguese Jews who were "lost" when they settled in the New World and who declare their determination to return to Judaism.

The campaigns of *Amishav* and *Kulanu,* committed to helping lost Jewish communities, have helped reawaken the controversy of "Who is a Jew?" Israeli politicians have begun to contemplate the possibility of amending or even repealing the Law of Return. The "discovery" of large numbers of potential new Jews claiming descent from ancient Jews has some intellectuals and politicians in Israel worried about the specter of the country's gates being opened to millions of additional foreigners with similar claims.

See Clide Haberman's article "Lost Tribe Has Israelis Pondering Law of Return," *New York Times* (6 October 1994), sec. 3, p. 1.

Other groups claiming descent from the Lost Tribes are the Black Jews of Venda, a territory situated between the southern border of Zimbabwe and the northeastern corner of the Transvaal. The Black Jews of Venda share common beliefs with the Ethiopian Jews regarding their origin, among them, the possibility of having descended from the lost tribe of Dan. The Lemba "Jews" who live in South Africa, primarily in the black township of Soweto, also claim to be related to the Venda and Ethiopian Jews. They keep kosher, circumcise their young, separate milk and meat, and observe the biblical laws of purity. Their tribal symbol is the Star of David with an elephant inside it.

Some Japanese groups, including a few members of the Makuya community, believe themselves to be descendants of the lost tribe of Zebulun. Also, the Mormons and the Rastafarians of Jamaica consider themselves descendants of Lost Tribes. Descriptions of these groups can be found in Tudor Parfitt, *The Thirteenth*

Gate: Travels Among the Lost Tribes of Israel (Bethesda, Md.: Adler & Adler Publishers Inc., 1987), 88–119 and 149–164. Regarding the Mormons and the Rastafarians, see Henry Mayhew, *The Mormons, or Latter-Day Saints: A Contemporary History* (London: Office of National Illustrated Library, 1851), which includes Joseph Smith's *Book of Mormons.* See also Leonard Barrett, *The Rastafarians: Sounds of Cultural Dissonance* (Boston: Beacon Press, 1988).

16.   Demetrio Guerra Torres's personal memoirs added to his request to immigrate to Israel, addressed to Israeli functionaries of immigration. (*FSP,* Lima, 1986),

17.   David and Niela Kiperstok, interview by author, Lima, 26 May 1995.

18.   While I was in Lima I had the opportunity to interview Hernán Valderrama, a member of this congregation, the day before he departed to Israel to join some of his children.

19.   In Israel data about the *Bene Moshe* case can be requested from the *Amishav* organization. Of course, anybody interested in learning this story from its own protagonists can find them in the West Bank settlement of Eilon More. My sources concerning *Bene Moshe* come from letters and forms related to some members of the congregation (including Segundo Villanueva and Demetrio Guerra). These documents are kept in the archives of the *Federación Sionista del Perú* in Lima. In October 1994, I also received a letter from Luis Aguilar Marín, one of the members of this congregation who still lives in Peru, in which he kindly described to me the "Brief History of the Community *Bene Moshe.*" The interviews with David and Niela Kiperstok (Lima, 26 May 1995) and Hernán Valderrama (Lima, 7 August 1995) are also part of my documentation concerning this case.

Rabbi Eliahu Avichail only wrote a few pages about this case in "Seekers of Judaism in Peru: *Bene Moshe,*" in *The Tribes of Israel* (Jerusalem: Agudat Amishav, 1990), 174–176.

There are also a few newspaper articles that covered this story. For example Herb Keinon, "Extraordinary New Jews," *Jerusalem Post* (9 March 1990): 9, and another article by the same journalist, which mentions the immigration of fifty members of *Bene Moshe,* who had stayed in their agricultural settlement in the Peruvian Amazon and finally joined their compatriots in Eilon More in 1991: "Amazon Jungle Community May Come: More Peruvian Olim Arrive in Eilon More," *Jerusalem Post* (16 August 1991): 3.

20.   Roth, *A History of the Marranos,* 29.

21. David M. Gitlitz analyzes in detail the religion of the crypto-Jews, arguing that most crypto-Jews in Spain, Portugal, and the colonies "who continued to think of themselves primarily as Jews clung to five basic principles that constituted the essence of their Jewishness: (1) God is one; (2) the Messiah has not come, but is coming; (3) belief in the Law of Moses is a prerequisite for individual salvation; (4) observance is required in addition to belief; and (5) Judaism is the preferred religion." See Gitlitz, *Secrecy and Deceit*, 100–101.

Some aspects of the religion of the *Marranos* can be found in Roth, "The Religion of the Marranos," 1–34; Lewin, *Los criptojudíos;* Liebman, *Requiem por los olvidados,* 86–110; Novinsky, "Jewish Roots of Brazil," 33–44; and Lazar "Scorched Parchments and Tortured Memories: The 'Jewishness' of the Anussim (Crypto-Jews)," 176–206.

For analyses of the phenomena of *Marranism* in Europe see footnote 2 in the preface.

22. According to Liebman the discovery of such actions originated massive arrests in Peru. See Liebman, *Requiem por los olvidados,* 88.

23. Such groups identifying themselves with the Jewish people have been variously denominated according to different concepts. Scholar Dan Ross calls them "groups on the fringes of Jewish identity," and Virginia Domínguez defines them as "Jews in limbo." See Ross, *Acts of Faith,* and Domínguez, *People as Subject, People as Object.*

24. Erik Cohen, *Seker HaMiyutim Be Israel* (Jerusalem: Hebrew University Asian and African Studies Institute-Truman Institute, 1972).

Regarding modern-day *Marranos* see the work of Stanley Hordes, "The Inquisition and the Crypto-Jewish Community in Colonial New Spain and New Mexico" in *Cultural Encounters: The Impact of the Inquisition in Spain and the New World,* eds. Mary Elizabeth Perry and Anne J. Cruz (Berkeley: University of California Press, 1991), 207–217; and Hordes's recent articles about the *Marranos* of New Mexico. See also Steven Almond, "Their Judaism Was/Is A Secret," *Echoes of Sepharad* 2 (October 1991): 26–28; Howard G. Chua-Eoan, "Plight of the Conversos," *Time Magazine,* 4 March 1991; Elaine DeRosa's article, "Marranos of New Mexico," *The Jerusalem Post* (23 April 1991); and Patricia Giniger Snyder, "America's Secret Jews: Hispanic Marranos Emerge from Centuries in Hiding," *Jewish Monthly* (October 1991): 26–30 and 38.

Also, Helio Daniel Cordero, founder of the Society of Marranic Studies in São Paulo, argues that 10 percent of 150 million inhabitants of Brazil have *Marrano*

ancestors: "Perhaps 500,000 have maintained Jewish practices over the generations. . . . Of those people, 8,000 to 10,000 want to formally shed their Christian
identity and become Jewish again." See Bill Broadway, "Claiming A Lost Past:
After Centuries as Christians, Brazilian, Ethiopian Groups Seek to Reconnect
With Judaism," *Washington Post* (26 November 1994) sec. C, p. 7.

Another article dealing with the topic of potential Brazilian *Marranos* is
William R. Long, "Jews Rewriting Brazil's History in Own Image; Millions May
Have Ancestors Who Fled Portugal During Inquisition," *Los Angeles Times* (26
January 1993) sec. 2, p. 1.

25. Ross, *Acts of Faith,* 81. Literature regarding the Mashhadis can also be found
in Ben Zvi, *The Exiled and the Redeemed,* 93–99; Joseph Schetman, "The Remarkable Marranos of Meshed," *Jewish Heritage* (Fall 1960): 24–30; Raphael Patai,
"Marriage Among the Marranos of Meshed" (Hebrew, with English summary),
Edoth, no. 2 (1946–47): 165–192, and 311–314; and Ross, *Acts of Faith,* 67–82.

26. The news of Shabbatai Zevi's conversion to Islam in 1666—after the Sultan of
Turkey and his court gave him the choice of conversion or death—greatly disap-
pointed his followers, but some interpreted his apostasy as a sign of the pre-
Messianic era, which was to be characterized by a suffering Messiah forced to
convert to Islam without rejecting his Jewish traditions. Hence, the Torah had to
be practiced in secret until Shabbatai Zevi would return to inaugurate the Messianic age.

During four centuries, the Döhnme Jews observed Jewish holidays while
adopting Islamic religious customs and habits. This dual identity had severe repercussions. In Salonika, they were seen as Moslems by Jews and Jews by Moslems.
By the 1960s members of this group still lived in Turkey, but most of them had not
reidentified themselves with the Jewish people.

The existence of Döhnme *Marranos* still waiting for Shabbatai Zevi in the
twentieth century reveals the intensity of the mass hysteria caused by this character
of the 1600s. A small number of Shabbatean groups survived, especially in Salonika,
Izmir, and Istanbul, after the false Messiah's death, the Döhnme *Marranos* being
the most devoted followers. There were also secret Shabbateans in Italy, Germany,
and Poland. Jacob Frank (1726–1791), a Polish Jew who spent some years in
Turkey, presented himself as the spiritual heir and reincarnation of Shabbatai Zevi,
igniting the anger of rabbis who condemned his group's orgiastic rites. Frank's followers were converted to Catholicism between 1756 and 1760 as encouraged by
Polish Catholic priests, who promised to respect their belief in Shabbatai Zevi.

For analysis of the Shabbatean phenomenon among the Jews and the
Döhnme *Marranos,* see Ben Zvi, *The Exiled and the Redeemed,* 110–128;

Gershom Scholem, "The Crypto-Jewish Sect of the Döhnmeh (Shabbateans) in Turkey," in *The Messianic Idea in Judaism and Other Essays* (New York: Schocken Books, 1971), 142–166; and Ross, *Acts of Faith*, 83–98. There is a vast literature on Shabbatai Zevi, the false Messiah; for example, Gershom Scholem, *Shabbatai Zevi: The Mystical Messiah, 1626–1676* (Princeton: Princeton University Press, Bollingen Series 93, 1973); and Stephen Sharot, *Messianism, Mysticism and Magic: A Sociological Analysis of Jewish Religious Movements* (Chapel Hill: University of North Carolina Press, 1982).

27. Ross, *Acts of Faith*, 93.

28. There are no records of the exact numbers of Iquitos's descendants of Jews who have settled in Israel. This is because the bureaucratic process involved in applying for the Law of Return is carried out in Lima, where the files of all Peruvian Jews who went to Israel are not open for research without the permission of each applicant.

The cases I know of immigrants from Iquitos were described to me by the families of those who are today in Israel and by some functionaries of Lima's Jewish institutions.

CHAPTER 6

1. See *Enciclopedia Judaica Castellana,* ed. Eduardo Winfeld, 430–431; Rosenzweig, "Judíos en la Amazonía Peruana, 1870–1949;" and Trahtemberg, *Los Judíos de Lima,* 1893; Böhm, *Judíos en el Perú,* 98–105; and Trahtemberg, *Los Judíos de Lima,* 183–194.

2. C. Gamarra, "Los Judíos en el Departamento de Loreto," *Nosotros* (Lima) 14 (February 1932): 17–18.

Also, in the 1930s, the magazine *La voz israelita* published a list of Jews in Iquitos: Salomón Azerrat, Elías Hatchwell, José Toledano, Isidoro Mey, Solomon Joseph, Moisés Benzaquén, Sam Harris, Mayer Cohen, Marcos Delmar, David Edery and Alfredo Nuñez. The article, filed by León Trahtemberg, is not dated, but according to its content it can be placed sometime between 1930 and 1940. The source from which this information is based is an article without precise date (maybe 1934) published in *La voz israelita* and quoted by Trahtemberg in *Los Judíos de Lima,* 188.

3. *Nosotros* (Lima) 26 (March 1934): 5.

4.   On 16 September 1940, the Amazonian Jews delivered 200 *soles;* on 23 March 1944, they sent 16,700 *soles oro;* on 27 March 1945, the community contributed 14,050 *soles oro;* and they later added another 2,000 *soles oro* in May to buy cloth for these immigrants. The last contribution was registered in September 1946, when the *Sociedad Israelita de Iquitos* sent 6,944 *soles oro* to J.O.I.N.T. (Jewish Organization for Immigrants), 2,472 *soles oro* for W.I.Z.O. (Zionist Women Organization), and 2,472 *soles oro* for *Keren Kayemet Le-Yisrael* (Forestation Fund of Israel).

5.   Letter from Salomón Azerrad and Rafael Toledano, president and general secretary respectively of the *Sociedad de Beneficienica Israelita de Iquitos,* to Jacobo Franco, president of the *Asociación de Sociedades Israelitas del Perú* (Iquitos, 17 July 1944). The contents of the letter reveal Salomón Azerrad's and Rafael Toledano's interest in obtaining any kind of official recognition of their Israelite Society in Lima, in order to register their association in public records of Iquitos. This matter is addressed in chapter 2.

6.   The Amazonian delegation was represented by one *Iquiteño,* Víctor Israel, and two *Limeños* who had established temporarily in Iquitos, Lázaro Fogiel and Mauricio Gleiser.

7.   Benjamín Samolsky, the most prosperous Jewish merchant in Iquitos during the 1940s and 1950s, had married Venus Edery Morales, the daughter of Moroccan immigrant Alberto (Abraham) Edery Fimat and his native Amazonian wife Trinidad Morales. He decided to pay Rabbi Moisés Brener for his airplane expenses and his services as *mohel* so the rabbi could perform the circumcision of his son Simón in his residence in Iquitos.

Regarding León Trahtemberg's account of Rabbi Brener's visit to Iquitos, the scholar does not mention the source of this description; however, he told me that he had read about it in an article from one of the several Jewish magazines edited in Lima during the 1940s. See Trahtemberg, *Los Judíos de Lima,* 189. One of the author's interviewees, Blanca Cohen de Blumen, also described Rabbi Brener's visit to Iquitos as an "almost mythical event," but as she emphasized to me: "Don't take me too seriously because I was only a seven-year-old girl watching for the first time a rabbi, a man with a big black hat and black beard, reciting some prayers during the circumcision of Sarita's [Samolsky] brother." (Blanca Cohen de Blumen, interview by author, Lima, 25 May 1995.)

8.   Rosenzweig, "Judíos en la Amazonía Peruana, 1870–1949," 19–30.

9.   *El Oriente* (Iquitos) (20 December 1966): 1.

10. Rubén Braidman represented the *Instituto Cultural Peruano-Israelí de Lima,* Dr. Salomón Pardo was the emissary of Lima's Sephardic congregation (considered to be the most fitting association to sponsor any effort made by Iquitos's descendants of Sephardic Jews), and Professor Yaacov Hasson, director of a human rights office in Lima and cultural agent of the Israeli embassy, was the representative of the Israeli ambassador in Lima.

On 9 December 1966, Salomón Pardo presented a written description of the Lima delegation's trip to Iquitos to members of the *Sociedad de Beneficiencia Israelita Sefardita* and the *Instituto Cultural Peruano-Israelí de Lima.* Attached to this report was an article written by Yaacov Hasson, which was eventually published in a Jewish Latin American journal (*FSP,* 8 December 1966). See Yaacov Hasson, "Iquitos: Alma Judía en la Amazonía peruana," *Comunidades Judías de Latín América* (1972–75), 367–373.

11. Menu for the cocktail party in the *Hotel de Turistas (ICPII,* 18 November 1966).

12. Report of Salomón Pardo, vice-president of the *Sociedad de Beneficiencia Israelita Sefardita,* addressed to members of the institution and to members of the *Instituto Cultural Peruano-Israelí de Lima,* regarding the trip to Iquitos made by three delegates of Lima's Jewish community (*FSP,* Lima, 8 December 1966).

13. An account of this lecture can be found in Hebraica Sport Club's bulletin *Hebraica* (Lima) 4, (1 December 1966): 1.

14. By August 1970, Hasson had sent ninety books to the *Instituto Cultural Peruano-Israelí de Iquitos* (ICPI), mostly concerning Israel's history and struggle for survival. The books received by the vice-president of the ICPI reveal an exaggerated emphasis on literature concerning Zionism, Israel, and anti-Semitism, compared to books regarding Jewish history and religion.

Different letters in the archives of the ICPI attest to a fluent communication between the new institute and diverse Jewish organizations in Lima from December 1967 to September 1969.

15. In a letter sent by Werner Levy Navarro to the Israeli ambassador in Lima, Netanel Lorch, dated 15 March 1967, the president of ICPI confesses that many members of the community had a difficult time understanding the lecturer due to their scarce knowledge of Israel's history. Werner Levy Navarro requested again that a teacher of Jewish history stay with them for a period of time, and asked the ambassador to personally help find an institution that could help them finance the

teacher's stay in the city. (Letter from Werner Levy to the Israeli ambassador in Lima, *ICPII*, 15 March 1967.)

16. *ICPII*, 30 November 1966.

17. Letter from Jaime Gomberoff, president of the *Asociación de Sociedades del Perú*, to the *Instituto Cultural Peruano-Israelí de Iquitos* (*ICPII*, 12 January 1968).
     The two engineers who traveled to assess the state of Iquitos's Israelite ceme-tery were Jacobo Kapilivsky and Hugo Lamp.

18. According to a letter sent by Werner Levy Navarro to S. B. Yeshaya, president of the *Instituto Central de Relaciones Culturales Israel-Iberoamerica, España and Portugal* in Jerusalem, the Iquitos association (ICPI) included 180 Jews from approximately 70 families (*ICPII*, 23 February 1967).
     On 18 January 1967, the board of directors decided to invite Salomón Tobelem, Joaquín Abensur, and Alberto Toledano Nahón, three "prominent" Jews, to integrate themselves with, and to collaborate (a subtle euphemism for money contribution!) with the institution. Three months later, they sent another letter to Alberto Toledano Nahón, relaying the news that he had been granted the designa-tion *socio benemérito* (meritorious member) of the institution. In the letter, the not-so-subtle president and vice-president of ICPI requested that the *socio bene-mérito* make a donation to the association (*ICPII*, 15 March 1967).

19. Letter from Werner Levy Navarro, president of ICPII, to the Israeli ambas-sador Netanel Lorch (*ICPII*, 8 June 1967). Letter from Netanel Lorch to Werner Levy Navarro thanking the Iquitos community for its financial contributions dur-ing the period of the Six-Day War (*ICPII*, 12 June 1967).

20. *ICPII*, 13 December 1967. This letter was finally sent to Israeli ambassador Moshe Yuval on 2 January 1968. In my text, I have respected the way they refer to the Israeli leaders with the title of Doctor.

21. Jaime Vásquez Izquierdo recalls how Jacobo Goldstein, a Jewish *Limeño* who came to Iquitos during the wave of migration to the tax-free Peruvian Amazon in the 1960s, insisted on the importance of building a synagogue. He offered to put up 25 percent of the money for that purpose, but the board of directors consid-ered the project too expensive for the community's economic means. Then, Jacobo Goldstein offered to provide 50 percent of the money, "but the nice man could not convince the others to pay the other 50 percent. Can you imagine how different

things might had been if we had had a synagogue in the 1960s?" (Jaime Vásquez Izquierdo, interview by author, Iquitos, 10 June 1995.)

The only member who sent his two sons for free to the *Colegio León Pinelo* was Werner Levy Navarro. According to the first president of the *Instituto Cultural Peruano-Israelí de Iquitos,* the principal of the school during the 1965–1968 period, Dr. Eliahu Kehati, invited all the children of members of Iquitos's association to study in the Jewish educational center. (Werner Levy Navarro, interview by author, Iquitos, 17 June 1995.) However, Willy Benzaquén Nájar, vice-president of the ICPI, does not recall any such letter of invitation from Dr. Kehati. Willy Benzaquén Nájar was vice-president when Werner Levy Navarro supposedly received this offer, so "it is extremely weird that I do not recall anything about that!" (Willy Benzaquén Nájar, interview by author, Lima, 4 August 1995.)

In letters from the ICPII to Jewish institutions in Lima there are frequent requests to have teachers sent to Iquitos; however, I found no document attesting to Werner Levy Navarro's statement that an official message from the *Colegio León Pinelo* was mailed to the ICPII.

22. The list of candidates applying for *aliyah* was sent to Lima, attached to the list of members of the *Instituto Cultural Peruano-Israelí de Iquitos* on 8 August 1970. Names such as Henry and Ronald Ruiz Vidurrizaga, Walter García Reategui, Astenia Lozano Ruiz, and Carmen Arevalo de Chávez appear next to others such as Nancy and Virgilio Bensimón Rengifo, Moisés Bendayán Acosta, Julio Cohén Tello, and Carlos Benamú Panduro.

I learned that Carlos Benamú Panduro and the Bensimón's siblings went to Israel. The person in charge of *aliyah* in Iquitos was Roger Foinquinos Ruiz, member of ICPI *(FSP and ICPII).*

23. Willy Benzaquén Nájar, interview by author, Lima, 4 August 1995.

24. Jaime Vásquez Izquierdo, interview by author, Iquitos, 10 June 1995.

25. Willy Benzaquén Nájar, interview by author, Lima, 4 August 1995.

26. Report of Salomón Pardo to members of the institution and to members of the *Instituto Cultural Peruano-Israelí de Lima (FSP,* Lima, 8 December 1966).

27. Hasson, "Iquitos: Alma Judía en la Amazonía Peruana," 368.

28. In the 1980s three sons of Víctor Edery Morales and Diolinda de Edery returned from Israel; two daughters married Jews in Israel and later moved to

Montreal and Miami. Since the late 1980s, any descendant of Jews wishing to celebrate the High Holidays in the Edery Morales's home has been able to do so, in the company of the couple's daughters and their respective Jewish husbands, who visit the Amazonian city twice a year to conduct these religious ceremonies.

29. Ronald Benzaquén Pinedo, interview by author, Lima, 6 August 1995.

30. Ibid.
     Roger Foinquinos Ruiz played an important role in Iquitos during the 1970s and 1980s. He drew up lists of sympathizers of Israel who wanted to make *aliyah*. Traveling often to Lima, Foinquinos brought back to Iquitos books and bulletins concerning the Jewish community to his "Jewish" *paisanos*. In addition, he took care of the maintenance of the Israelite cemetery, even after the ICPI was dissolved.

31. Ibid.

32. Different interviews with *Iquiteño* Jews (May, June, July, and August 1995).
     In the last testimony, it is relevant to clarify that the person who told me this story believes that the issue of circumcision was the obstacle to burying suspected non-Jews in a Jewish cemetery, but the rabbi's criteria was based on the fact that the deceased himself was not the son of a Jewish mother. Circumcision does not make a person Jewish; rather, it is only one of many requirements for conversion!

33. Statistics of 1985 showed that from a total of 446 families in which one of the parents was not Jewish, only 18 percent sent their children to the Jewish school. From a sample of the 112 children of these mixed marriages, only 16 students were accepted in the school, while 23 shifted to other schools, and 73 of these families sent their children to private schools because they preferred to do so. In the 1980s, the number of mixed marriages in Lima was estimated to be more than 25 percent of the Jewish population.
     Non-official estimation of families that send their children to the *Colegio León Pinelo* as of July, 1988:

Types of Families	%
Type A: Requires financial aid from the Jewish community for basic subsistence.	12
Type B: Can hardly save. Requires fellowships or discounts from the Jewish school.	23
Type C: Middle class.	35
Type D: Upper class.	20
Type E: Belong to wealthiest layers of the population.	10

These statistics are based on families of children who studied in the *Colegio León Pinelo* in 1988.

Trahtemberg, *Demografía Judía del Perú*, 13–15 and 114.

34. Professor León Trahtemberg argues that, like most Latin American communities, Lima's Jewry also presents a form of Jewish exhibitionism caused by the sudden "crossing over" from poverty to wealth experienced by the generation of the immigrants: "This led to the universal phenomenon of the nouveau riche, which became automatically pretentious," adds Trahtemberg, "and also, of having been a people denied lands, a people without rights to be involved in political issues or to study in universities during centuries of hostilities against the Jews, which suddenly changed in the mid-twentieth century. Jews were allowed to apply skills that they acquired as a consequence of their migratory movements, [as a consequence] of their need to develop economic expertise in order to survive, so there were Jewish doctors, Jewish bankers. . . . All these factors have also led to an overestimation of the Jewish intelligence." (León Trahtemberg, interview by author, Lima, 10 August 1995.)

35. Between 1975 and 1984, 15 percent of those students who graduated from the *Colegio León Pinelo* immigrated to Israel, 14 percent to the United States, and 10 percent to other countries. Trahtemberg, *Demografía Judía del Perú*, 55.

36. Letter from Ronald Reategui Levy to different functionaries of the *Federación Sionista del Perú* on 28 September 1985; 27 September 1986; 8 January 1987; 26 March 1987; 19 February 1989; 10 August 1984; and December 1990 *(FSP)*.

37. Debora Frank recalls: "[The Peruvian Zionist Federation] had little relationship with Iquitos, but it was more or less constant (even before I began to work for the Jewish community in 1987). They wrote from time to time, but it was too difficult for them to communicate with Lima because the telephone, the fax, and the bureaucracy made it too expensive for them." (Debora Frank, interview by author, Lima, 1 June 1995.)

38. Jaime Vásquez Izquierdo, interview by author, Iquitos, 10 June 1995. Víctor Edery Morales and Roger Foinquinos Ruiz confirmed this story.

39. This idea was proposed by Debora Frank to Ronald Reategui Levy in a letter dated 6 December 1990.

40. *SBII*, 11 April 1991.

41. The minutes of the session following Rabbi Bronstein's visit (22 April 1991) do not mention the rabbi's suggestions; instead, the minutes focus on the ceremonies organized for the distinguished visitor.

42. This is mentioned several times in different documents, but the first reference can be found in the *SBII*'s records of 29 April 1991.

43. *SBII*, 17 June 1991.

44. The *Sociedad de Beneficiencia Israelita de Iquitos* summarized Dror Fogel's speech in a letter addressed to Debora Frank, written on 3 August 1991 (*SBII* and *FSP*).

45. Jaime Vásquez Izquierdo, interview by author, Iquitos, 10 June 1995; Víctor Edery Morales and Yared Edery López, interview by author, Iquitos, 16 July 1995.
    After his visit to the Peruvian Amazon, Fogel told a Sephardic congregation in New York about the Iquitos "Jews." On 16 September 1991, Víctor Edery Morales received a phone call from New York announcing that a delegation of members of that community, including rabbis, would come to Iquitos in the near future. This promise never materialized.

46. Records regarding Dror Fogel and Víctor Edery Morales's communications with this Sephardic community in New York can be found in the minutes of the *SBII* sessions on 12 August 1991 and 16 September 1991. The radio interview with *Kol Yisrael* is briefly mentioned in the session of 30 September 1991.

47. *SBII*, 14 October 1991.

48. Debora Frank, interview by author, Lima, 1 June 1995.

49. Statutes of the *Sociedad de Beneficiencia Israelita de Iquitos* (*SBII*, 31 August 1991).

50. Informe Comunidad de Iquitos presented by Debora Frank to the *Federación Sionista del Perú* in January 1992 (*FSP*).

51. *FSP* (Ibid).

52. *FSP* (Ibid).

53. Ronald Reategui Levy, interview by author, Iquitos, 19 June 1995.

54. Fernando Levy Martínez, interview by author, Iquitos, 17 June 1995.

55. Records of an extraordinary session held by the SBII to honor Dr. Yuval Metzer, Israeli ambassador to Peru (*SBII*, 9 February 1992).

56. On 19 March 1992, the *Sociedad Israelita* asked a Jewish *Limeño* who had returned to the capital city to rent them his house in Iquitos so they could use it as synagogue; however, things suddenly seemed to be working out when, a few weeks later, Luis Elaluf Prado, a member of the Iquitos society, offered to donate land to build a synagogue in San Antonio's *Pueblo Joven* (shanty town). Unfortunately, Elaluf never delivered what he had promised.

    Letter from Víctor Edery Morales to Adam Polak, Iquitos, 19 March 1992. Other letters registered in the *SBII* (25 April 1992), and letter from Víctor Edery Morales to Luis Elaluf Prado (*SBII*, 27 April 1992).

57. Letter from the *Sociedad Israelita de Beneficiencia de Iquitos* to Rabbi Guillermo Bronstein (*SBII* and *SBC1870*, 6 January 1993).

58. Letter from Rabbi Guillermo Bronstein to the *Sociedad Israelita de Beneficiencia de Iquitos* (*SBC1870*, 18 February 1993).

59. Letter from Rabbi Bronstein to the *Sociedad de Beneficiencia Israelita de Iquitos* (*SBC1870*, 2 June 1993).

60. Letter of 16 August 1993 from Salomón Lerner, president of the *Federación Sionista del Perú*, to Marcos Brujis, requesting the purchase of some books of Jewish history and religion. In a letter written on 13 October 1993, Salomón Lerner informed Rabbi Bronstein that the books had already been sent to Iquitos (*FSP*).

61. *SBII*, 10 July 1994.

62. *SBII*, 29 January 1995.

63. The board of directors of the *Sociedad de Beneficiencia Israelita de Iquitos* elected Jaime Bensimón Puyó as president and Kelly Mesía Costa as vice-president (*SBII*, 2 July 1995).

    I witnessed this session. A letter, dated 13 July 1995, announced the selection of this new board of directors and was sent to Jewish institutions in Lima (*SBII*).

CHAPTER 7

1.   When candidate Alberto Fujimori went to the second electoral round against writer Mario Vargas Llosa, some despairing members of the ruling classes proclaimed that Peru was not ready to have a first generation Peruvian as president. This and other xenophobic and racist sentiments became more frequent when the polls showed Fujimori's increasing popularity and of course, once he won the elections. Literature about the Fujimori phenomenon and about Peru's complex and subtle racial tensions can be found in Julio Ortega's "A Vote for Equality: Election of Alberto Fujimori in Peru," *World Press Review* 38, no. 37 (August 1990): 38–39; Jeffrey Klaiber, "Fujimori: Race and Religion in Peru," *America* 6, no. 163 (8 September 1990): 133–135; Jose María Salcedo, *Tsunami Fujimori* (Lima: Arte & Comunicación, La Republica, 1990); and Luis Jochamowitz, *Ciudadano Fujimori: La construcción de un político* (Lima: PEISA, 1993).

2.   Bibliography regarding the question of race in some Latin American nations during the late nineteenth century and early twentieth century can be found in Magnus Mörner's essay "Renacimiento del indio y el mestizaje revaluado" in *La mezcla de razas en la historia de America Latina,* ed. Magnus Mörner (Buenos Aires: Paidos, 1969), 135–145; as well as in his book *Race and Class in Latin America* (New York: Columbia University Press, 1970); and in *The Idea of Race in Latin Amercia, 1870–1940,* ed. Richard Graham (Austin: Institute of Latin American Studies of University of Texas Press, 1990).

3.   The "champion" Latin American theorist of "the virtues of hybridism" was the Mexican José Vasconcelos, who considered *Mestizos,* specifically the Mexican *Mestizos,* to be the representatives of the "cosmic race," a superior type of man who blended the best of different races. See José Vasconcelos, *La raza cósmica* (París: Misión de la Raza Iberoamericana, Agencia Mundial de Librería, 1925), and the work of José Vasconcelos and Manuel Gamio, *Aspects of Mexican Civilization* (Chicago: University of Chicago Press, 1926). Vasconcelos's thesis parallels Gilberto Freyre's argument of a Luso-Brazilian model miscegenation in his *Casa grande e senzala* (Rio de Janeiro: José Olympio, 1933). This work was translated into English as *Masters and Slaves* by Samuel Putnam (New York: Knopf, 1956).

4.   See Hildebrando Castro Pozo's *El ayllu al Cooperativismo Socialista* (Lima: Librería Editorial J. Mejía Baca, 1969). *Indigenista* thinkers such as Luis E. Valcárcel, Gamaliel Churata, and Ezequiel Uriola influenced socialist leaders such as José Carlos Mariategui and Luis Raul Haya de la Torre, who incorporated *Indigenista* motifs into their political thinkings and discourses. See Francois Chevalier,

"Official *Indigenismo* in Peru in 1920: Origins, Significance, and Socioeconomic Scope," in Mörner, *Race and Class in Latin America,* 184–198; Manuel Aquezolo Castro, *La pólemica del indigenismo* (Lima: Mosca Azul Editores, 1976); and José Tamayo Herrera, *El indigenismo limeño: "La sierra" y "amauta": Similutides y diferencias, 1926–1930* (Lima: Facultad de Ciencias Humanas, Universidad de Lima, 1988). Regarding Mariategui's and Haya de la Torre's *Indigenista* ideals see Felipe Cossio del Pomar, *Haya de la torre: El indoamericano* (Mexico D.F.: Editorial America, 1939); and Kinichiro Harada's essay "Mariategui: Una confluencia del indigenismo y el marxismo" in *Mariategui y las ciencias sociales,* ed. Manfred Kossok (Lima: Biblioteca Amauta, 1982).

5.   See Flores Galindo, *Buscando un Inca,* 259. Regarding racism in modern Peru see José Varallanos, *El cholo y Perú: Introducción al estudio sociológico de un hombre y un pueblo mestizo y su destino cultural* (Buenos Aires: Impr. López, 1962); Amalia Mendoza Arroyo, *Cuestión de piel: Testimonios de racismo en el Perú* (Lima: ADEC & ATC, 1993); and the important work of Gonzalo Portocarrero Maisch, *Racismo y mestizaje* (Lima: Sur Casa de Estudios del Socialismo, 1993).

6.   See Flores Galindo, *Buscando un Inca,* and Portocarrero Maisch, *Racismo y mestizaje.*

7.   Census of the Province of Lima, 26 June 1908, in *"Dirección de salubridad pública,"* (Lima: Imprenta de la Opinión Nacional, 1915).

8.   See Gamarra, "Los Judíos del Departamento de Loreto," 17–18.

9.   Ibid., 18.

10. Ibid., 18.

11. Report of Salomón Pardo, vice-president of the *Sociedad de Beneficiencia Israelita Sefardita,* addressed to the members of its institution and to the members of the *Instituto Cultural Peruano-Israelí de Lima,* regarding the trip made by three delegates of Lima's Jewish community to Iquitos (*APAR,* Lima, 8 December 1966, 3).

12. Ibid., 4.

13. In the archives of the San Juan Parish office in Iquitos, I found a number of certificates enumerating marriages performed in the San Juan church—specifically

those marriages of members of the *Instituto Cultural Peruano-Israelí de Iquitos* board of directors. For instance, file 242 notes the marriage of president Werner Levy Navarro to Elva Martínez; and file 487 records the marriage of vice-president Willy Benzaquén Nájar to Olga Emilia Montani Young *(PSJBI).*

14. Hasson, "Iquitos: Alma Judía en la Amazonía Peruana," 369.

15. *Nuestro Mundo* (Lima), (May 1976): 10.

16. Oscar Hirsh, interview by author, Iquitos, 30 June 1995.

17. Informe Comunidad de Iquitos presented by Debora Frank to the *Federación Sionista del Perú,* on January 1992 *(FSP).*

18. Finkielkraut, *The Imaginary Jew.*

19. Beny Weisselberger, interview by author, Lima, 25 May 1995.

20. Víctor Edery Morales, interview by author, Iquitos, 16 July 1995.

21. Víctor Jr. and Yared Edery López, interview by author, 6 July 1995. Apparently, according to Víctor Edery Morales's daughter (the one who went to the program), Dror Fogel participated in the radio program and was the one who suggested broadcasting an interview with Iquitos immigrants (in Israel) and *Iquiteños* from the Amazon.

22. Although official Peruvian discourse regarding *el pueblo* (the people) proclaims the ideal of a racially mixed nation, the discourse of ordinary people in the streets still reveals high levels of prejudice among whites and *Mestizos,* among inhabitants of different regions *(Costeños, Cholos, Charapas),* among native Peruvians, and among descendants of immigrants.

Some works that analyze Peru's racial tendencies are Mendoza Arroyo, *Cuestión de piel,* and Maisch, *Racismo y mestizaje.* Jochamovitz's book, *Ciudadano Fujimori,* provides interesting insights into the role that Fujimori's Asian origin played in his gaining political support from Peruvian *Mestizos* during the presidential elections of 1990.

23. The Baghdadi descendants of Iraqi Jews who live in Bombay accuse the isolated members of *Bene Israel* of being totally assimilated into the Hindu society as

well as being poor, uneducated, and backward with "no pure Jewish blood flowing in the veins."

Literature about the relationship between Baghdadi Jews and *Bene Israel* of India can be found in Parfitt, "The Tribes in India" in *The Thirteenth Gate*, 36–67; Ross, *Acts of Faith*, 193–213; and Sadok Masliyah, "The Bene Israel and the Baghdadis: Two Indian Jewish Communities in Conflict," *Judaism: A Quarterly Journal of Jewish Life and Thought* 3, no. 43 (Summer 1994): 279–294. For a thorough analysis of Jewish identity in India, see Nathan Katz and Ellen S. Goldberg, *The Last Jews of Cochin: Jewish Identity in Hindu India* (Columbia: University of South Carolina Press, 1993).

24. Accounts of how Shanghai Jews struggled to help descendants of Kaifeng Jews are recorded in Michael Pollak, *Mandarins, Jews, and Missionaries: The Jewish Experience in the Chinese Empire* (Philadelphia: Jewish Publication Society, 1980).

25. I will not provide the name of this interviewee in order to protect him from those who might be furious at his honest opinion, Lima, July 1995.

26. Sara Bendayán García, interview by author, Iquitos, 29 June 1995.

27. Ramón Coriat, interview by author, Iquitos, 12 July 1995.

28. Becky Ríos Bensimón, twenty-four years old, interview by author, Iquitos, 14 July 1995; Edgar Dávila Lazo, thirty years old, interview by author, Iquitos, 12 July 1995; Marco Mesía Rodríguez, twenty-five years old, interview by author, Iquitos, 18 June 1995; and Pedro Reategui Panduro, twenty-three years old, interview by author, Iquitos, 17 June 1995.

29. *SBII*, 16 November 1991.

30. Letter from Alicia Assayag Chávez to Sandy Barak Cassinelli (*FSP*, 23 February 1993, 2–3).

31. Salomón Abensur Boria, interview by author, Iquitos, 22 July 1995. Several interviewes expressed similar views concerning hard-working Jews and Israelis who "well deserved their wealth."

32. Mauro Coblentz Lazo, interview by author, Iquitos, 20 July 1995; Luis Weisselberger, interview by author, Iquitos, 6 July 1995; Pedro Coblentz, interview by

author, Iquitos, 26 July 1995; Víctor Edery Morales, interview by author, Iquitos, 16 July 1995.

33. Wilson Benzaquén, interview by author, Lima, 29 May 1995; and Simón Samolsky, interview by author, Lima, 5 June 1995.

34. See Jeffrey Klaiber, "Fujimori: Race and Religion in Peru."

35. Jonathan D. Hill, "Myth and History" and Terence Turner, "Ethno-Ethno History: Myth and History in Native South American Representations of Contact with Western Society" in *Rethinking History and Myth: Indigenous South American Perspectives on the Past,* ed. Jonathan D. Hill (Chicago: University of Illinois Press, 1988), 1–17 and 235–281.

36. Letter from Ronald Reategui Levy to Jack Drassinower, Santa María de Nieva (border between Peru and Ecuador), (*FSP,* 10 November 1986).

37. Letter from Ronald Reategui Levy to Jack Drassinower, Santa María de Nieva (*FSP,* September 1987).

38. Letter from Ronald Reategui Levy to Jack Drassinower, Iquitos (*FSP,* 26 March 1988).

39. Ronald Reategui Levy, interview by author, Iquitos, 19 June 1995.

40. Letter from Sandy Barak Cassinelli to Abraham Azancot (*FSP,* 23 June 1993).

41. Letter from Elías Assayag to Alicia Assayag Chávez, Manaus (*FSP,* 4 August 1993).

42. *FSP,* 23 February 1993.

43. Alicia Assayag Chávez, interview by author, Iquitos, 12 June 1995.

44. Letter from Father Ramón Lourido to Father Joaquín García, Tangier (*CETA,* Iquitos, 18 February 1994).

45. Letter from Sandy Cassinelli to Abraham Azancot, Lima (*FSP,* 19 January 1995).

46. Amos Oz, "The Real Cause of My Grandmother's Death," in *Israel, Palestine and Peace* (New York: Harcourt Brace & Company, 1995), 27.

47. Although I provide my own definition of *Imaginario,* it is important to mention different scholars who have developed their own interpretations of this concept in recent historiography; for example, Jaques Le Goff's ideas in *L'imaginaire médiéval,* which has been translated into English as *The Medieval Imagination* (Chicago and London: University of Chicago Press, 1988); Serge Gruzinsky in *La Colonisation de l'imaginaire (The Conquest of Mexico),* (Cambridge: Polity Press, 1993); and Acosta in *El continente prodigioso.*

These three works discuss different concepts of the term "Imaginary," viewing it as a historical category rather than a psychological or sociological one. Most of the historians who have started to incorporate the term into their scientific vocabulary prefer not to define it, but merely to apply it. (That is why the term *Imaginaire*/Imaginary is omited or changed to "Imagination" in the English translations).

48. My definition of *Imaginario* approaches Maurice Halbwachs's argument of how collective memory is a process of reconstruction of the past according to the social frameworks to which we belong and the social imagination that we require. In the *Legendary Topography of the Gospels of the Holy Land,* published in 1941, Halbwachs proposed the theory that in medieval times Christianity developed a collective memory of the life of Jesus based on superimposed European notions of the holy land: "shrines of Judaism were re-identified and reshaped to conform to Christian conceptions." See Patrick H. Hutton, *History as an Art of Memory* (Hanover: University Press of New England, University of Vermont, 1993), 80.

49. Enrique Mesía Ochoa, interview by author, Iquitos, 22 June 1995.

50. Pedro Reategui Panduro, during a Shabbat service, Iquitos, 23 June 1995.

CHAPTER 8

1. During a lecture that I gave in the Department of History of the University of Miami, my colleague Cristina Merthens pointed out how I constantly interchanged expressions such as "the Jewish *Mestizos,*" "the Iquitos Jews," "my *paisanos,*" "they," "we," "our people," and so on, indicating the interesting multivocality of my own Jewish being. She proposed that I think about it, and this chapter is part of a conscious effort to explain the switching stances of my schizophrenic Jewish identity.

2. The technique of including oneself in the recounting of historical events was initiated by literary writers such as George Orwell in his personal recollections of the Spanish civil war, *Homage to Catalonia* (New York: Brace, Harcourt, 1952);

Arthur Koestler in his narratives of World War II, *Scum of the Earth* (London: V. Gollancz Limited, 1941); and in his accounts on the Spanish civil war, *Dialogue with Death* (New York: Macmillian, 1942); Stefan Zweig in his classic autobiography, *The World of Yesterday* (New York: Viking Press, 1943); and other authors. Later, some professional historians began to adopt the autobiographical style. For example, John Lukacs presented a modern history of the Cold War in his work *Confessions of an Original Sinner* (New York: Ticknor & Fields, 1990).

Scholars' recognition of the closeness of the imaginative worlds of history and fiction has led to an increasing use of the "I" voice in historical writings. This "I" voice allows the researcher to recognize himself or herself in others' discourses and to present a confessional, self-reflective account in which the author discovers his or her own cultural identity by attempting to comprehend the subjects of the study. Two of the boldest works in which the researcher's voice is as important as that of his or her informants are Rabinow's *Reflections on Fieldwork* and Lavie's *The Poetics of Military Occupation*.

Rabinow presents almost a novel about a researcher and his friends/informants as they engage in a "contest of participation" during the dialectic process of fieldwork. Smadar Lavie offers a remarkably emotional study of Bedouins, in which her involvement leads her to assume two authorial voices: one, the scholarly voice called "the anthropologist," and the other, the ordinary woman called Smadar. Lavie notes: "Sometimes in the text, Smadar and the anthropologist converse with each other. At times the anthropologist instructs Smadar how to conduct herself and her research to optimize the rate of data return, but at other times, Smadar has to remind the anthropologist that there is much more to the 'field' than fieldwork." See Lavie's *The Poetics of Military Occupation*, 38.

3.   I especially recommend the reading of Domínguez's *People as Subject, People as Object,* an excellent work in which the scholar succeeds in presenting the discourse and the constitution of peoplehood in Israel while keeping the reader aware of the process of objectification that she, as a scholar, is compelled to practice.

This type of Bertolt Brecht technique applied to history (in which the actor-scholar reminds the audience that he is an actor playing a role) has been used in such historical works as Clifford Geertz's *The Social History of an Indonesian Town* (Cambridge: M.I.T. Press, 1965). In this work the scholar includes reflexive notes that he wrote during meetings with the people of Modjokerto, Indonesia. Geertz has also merged anthropology and history. In his 1972 essay "Deep Play: Notes on the Balinese Cockfight" in *Rethinking Popular Culture: Contemporary Perspectives in Cultural Studies*, eds. Chandra Mukerji and Michael Schudson (Oxford: University of California Press, 1991), Geertz not only questions himself as observer, but moreover, questions his observed subjects.

Similarly, in *Siaya: The Historical Anthropology of an African Landscape* (Athens: Ohio University Press, 1989), anthropologists David William Cohen and E. S. Atieno Odhiambo attempt to bring together the vision of the ethnographer and the vision of the Luo-speaking peoples of western Kenya. Cohen and Odhiambo emphasize the voices of their subjects but include their own questioning voices out of an awareness that any discourse over the nature of the "other" proceeds outside the "other."

Among theoretical works that focus on the role of intrusive scholars during their field research see George W. Stocking's two works, *Observers Observed: Essays on Ethnographic Fieldwork* (Madison: University of Wisconsin Press, 1983), and *The Ethnographist Magic and Other Essays in the History of Anthropology* (Madison: University of Winsconsin Press, 1992); Marcus and Fischer, *Anthropology as Cultural Critique;* James Clifford and George E. Marcus, *Writing Culture: The Poetics and Politics of Ethnography; A School of American Research Advanced Seminar* (Berkeley: University of California Press, 1986); Clifford Geertz, *Work and Lives: The Anthropologist as Author* (Palo Alto: Standford University Press, 1988); and John Van Maanen, *Tales of the Field: On Writing Ethnography* (Chicago: University of Chicago Press, 1988).

4.   Excerpts from my notes: "Iquitos: Viaje al fondo de mí identidad Judía," written in Miami in October 1995.

5.   Domínguez, *People as Subject, People as Object,* 15.

6.   Yosef Hayim Yerushalmi, *Zakhor: Jewish History and Jewish Memory* (Seattle: University of Washington Press, 1982), 101.

7.   Domínguez, *People as Subject, People as Object,* 13–14.

8.   In their work *Jewish Memories,* Lucette Valensi and Nathan Wachtel present recollections of life stories of Jewish interviewees who were asked to recall their birthlands; thus, individual memory made itself multiple, a collective memory within each person "speaking of him(her)self, spoke of 'us' and 'ours.'" See Valensi and Wachtel, *Jewish Memories,* 2.

9.   Y. H. Yerushalmi defines historical consciousness "not as a social metaphor but a social reality transmitted and sustained through the conscious efforts and institutions of the group." See Yerushalmi, *Zakhor,* 101.

10.   Vargas Llosa, *The Storyteller,* 26.

An anthropologist and friend who has lived in the Amazon and read the draft of this book wrote from New York, criticizing my frequent allusions in this work to Mario Vargas Llosa's novel *The Storyteller.* He claims: ". . . the medium is the message—or rather, with Mario Vargas Llosa as a medium, the message is one of paternalism, condescension, elitism, etc., regardless of the man's words. Here is a guy who spends most of his time in London and Madrid and for whom Lima is too 'déclassé.' You can find many fine authors who have interesting things to say about indigenous peoples and their relationship to the Amazonian ecosystem without having to resort to Vargas Llosa. Even better would be to quote the indigenous [people] themselves. I know you think that *The Storyteller* is particularly germane to your work because it is about a Jew going native. As a Jew who has 'gone native' on more than a few occasions, I still advise you to drop it; Mario Vargas Llosa has nothing interesting or original to say" (New York, 10 February 1997).

I did not want to "drop" Vargas Llosa and his *Storyteller.* This work explores so many of my own feelings of awe and discovery in Iquitos that the idea of pruning my text of references to it is almost painful. Perhaps because *The Storyteller* produces such a powerful effect on Jews, my friend himself added in his letter: "I had a strong emotional relation to your work: confusion and consternation! It's actually very ironic that I am a Jew who wants to be an Indian, and many of the Iquitos Jews are practically the opposite! To me, Jewish identity has always been an extremely heavy and painful thing. As a secular Jew, with no religious education, I never turned to the religion for solace or to compensate for what I felt to be the negative aspects of my Jewishness. Edery and company [the "Jewish *Mestizos*"] are particularly fascinating in terms of their attachment to roots that I would prefer to not even have, but somehow cannot get rid of" (Ibid).

What can I say to my friend? I just hope that one day his Jewishness will become a joyful heritage instead of a heavy burden, and I tell him not to rely exclusively on the solace of the religion he may profess as an anthropologist. Maybe, then, he will come to terms with Vargas Llosa and everybody else will seem contradictory, so long as we are honest with ourselves.

11. Marco Mesía Rodríguez, interview by author, Iquitos, 18 June 1995; and Pedro Reategui Panduro, interview by author, Iquitos, 17 June 1995.

12. Lavie, *The Poetics of Military Occupation,* 38.

13. Minutes of the *Sociedad de Beneficiencia Israelita de Iquitos* (*SBII*, 29 January 1995).

14. Letter from Jaime Vásquez Izquierdo to Jaime Bensimón Puyó announcing his decision to quit as secreatry of the *Sociedad de Beneficiencia Israelita de Iquitos,* 24 August 1995. Jaime Vásquez mailed me a copy of this letter to Miami.

15. On August 1995, I wrote a report for the *Federación Sionista del Perú* explaining with details these arguments.

16. Letter from Jacobo Kohn Jacorovicht to Ariel Segal (Iquitos, 13 September 1995).

17. In 1997, the family of Sara Bendayán Tello, daughter of Moisés Bendayán Casique, immigrated to Israel. Once there, Sara, her husband, Denis Tello, and their three children, Moshe, Sarita, and Alejandro, met Sara's sister, Miriam Bendayán Vásquez, who had been living in Israel since 1992. Also, three siblings from the family Casique Kohn (Linda, Heysen, and Jacobo) made *aliyah.* At the time this book was written, the first family was living in Beer Sheba and son Moshe had a Bar Mitzvah at the *Kotel* (Wailing Wall); Linda was studying in Haifa and Jacobo and Heysen were studying in Tiberias. Of course, this historian-protagonist continued to help them once in a while when they asked him to do so.

CHAPTER 9

1. Oz, "The Real Cause of My Grandmother's Death," 33.

2. I find it important to reproduce excerpts from two letters that I received from friends who read parts of the draft of this book. Isaac Nahón, a Jewish Venezuelan scholar who now lives in Montreal wrote me:

"I feel that your investigation, although it focuses on the history of a small group of "lost" Jews in the Peruvian Amazon, can shed light on the problem of whether or not what seems an incoherent Judaism has to be necessarily excluded from Judaism . . . for me, a central problem faced by the Jewish people and [the State of] Israel.

"As you point out in your work, this tension between particularism and universalism is the great question that Judaism will have to answer nowadays. How to balance these two tendencies that are not necessarily excluded from one another? There are those who say that this tension can be resolved by enhancing particularism (the most radical Orthodoxy). Other Jews think that we must be a universal people, and they assimilate [to their country's environment]. Others live on the frontier of identity, like your *paisanos.* They sway from here to there, but they surely do it with a logic of their own. I think that we, most of the Jews, are living on that frontier, like acrobats trying not to fall." (Letter from Isaac Nahón to Ariel Segal, Montreal, 22 November 1997.)

Another friend of mine (I have my reasons for omiting his name), a non-Jewish Peruvian profoundly linked to Lima's Jewish community, confided to me:

"Since a year ago I have being asking myself why Jews do not publicize their nice traditions: to promote to others the celebration of Passover, of Hanukkah, etc. I have realized that *goyim* [gentiles] are very interested in learning about that beautiful and human side, the exemplary face of Judaism. Up until today, I have not gotten a satisfactory answer to my question. The only reason I could think of seems to be the principle of exclusion: Judaism for the Jews. Don't ask me about what is mine, because I am not interested in learning about what is yours. Zionism was an energetic force that trespassed the tendencies of ostracism. There was opposition to it, but [Zionists] succeeded in gathering Jews who for one hundred years joined to pursue a common and ample ideal, [they were people] attuned with the [reality that was happening in the] world. I believe that if Judaism fails to find new, powerful ideas, in tune with our epoch, and it falls into the trap of ostracism, Judaism will transform into an anachronistic tyranny—such as what Islam is today for many of its followers—a culture that was [and is], a sarcophagus." (Lima, 7 February 1996.)

GLOSSARY

Aliyah (Hebrew): Literally means "ascending" or "going up." The word is commonly used to refer to immigrating to Israel.

Ashkenazi(c) (plural, *Ashkenazim*): Jews who trace their ancestors to Germany or to northern, central, or eastern Europe.

Audiencia (Spanish): The highest royal court and consultative council in colonial Spanish America.

Ayaymama (regional Peruvian): Bird of the Amazon region whose crying is reminiscent of the wail of an orphan calling its mother.

Bar Mitzvah (Hebrew): Ceremonies at which young men accept the obligation to obey the commandments of Jewish Law.

Brit Milah (Hebrew): Circumcision ceremony by which a Jewish male enters the covenant between God and the Jewish people.

Bufeo (regional Peruvian): Amazonian dolphin.

Bufeo Colorado (regional Peruvian): Colored dolphin of the Amazon River, which may transform itself into a bearded white man in order to kidnap young ladies.

Cauchero (Spanish): "Rubber man." Generic term to refer to those who were dedicated to the rubber business. Although the term has been generically applied to all individuals involved in rubber exploitation (including rubber barons, their partners, and employees), it usually refers to adventurous men who worked in the jungle extracting latex from rubber trees.

Charapa (regional Peruvian): Native inhabitant of the Peruvian Amazon. The term comes from the name of a specific turtle and is sometimes used with a racial connotation to refer to a "slow" person from the jungle.

Chibolito (regional Peruvian): Kid, young person.

Cholo (regional Peruvian): A *Mestizo* who comes from the Peruvian Andes. Sometimes it is used with a racial connotation to refer to an ordinary, plain person.

Chullachaqui (regional Peruvian): Spirit of the jungle that assumes a human appearance and misleads people until they get lost in the jungle.

Conversos (Spanish): Jews forced to convert to Christianity by agents of the Inquisition. They were also called New Christians although not all New Christians are descended from Jews.

Convivencia (regional Peruvian): Concubine or mistress, depending on the context of the man's discourse.

Costeño (regional Peruvian): Inhabitant of the Peruvian coastal area.

Crypto-Jews (Secret Jews): *Conversos* and their descendants who behaved according to Christianity in public places, performing all the Catholic Church's rituals, while still practicing the Mosaic Law and believing in the Jewish faith in the secrecy of their homes.

Encomendero (Spanish): A person who received an *encomienda,* a tribute in Spanish America through which Spaniards received Indians as an entrustment to protect and to Christianize, for which, in return, Spaniards could demand tribute, including labor.

Guano: High-quality fertilizer that became Peru's most important export between 1840 and 1880.

Gaucho (Spanish): The "cowboy" of the Pampas, the Argentinean hinterland.

Halakhic: From the Hebrew "halakhah," Jewish Law comprised of the written and oral Torah (Pentateuch).

Hanukkah (Hebrew): Holiday in which the Jews commemorate the rebellion of the Macabbeans against the Seleucids, and the restoration and purification of the Jerusalem Temple.

Ḥazzan (Hebrew): Cantor.

High Holidays: Rosh Hashanah and Yom Kippur.

Indigenismo, Indigenista (Spanish): Movement that calls for a return to pre-Columbian values and the defense of the rights of Indian tribes that still exist throughout Latin America.

Iquiteño (Spanish): Inhabitant of Iquitos.

Kabbalat Shabbat (Hebrew): The eve of Shabbat; the Friday evening service to "welcome" the Shabbat.

Kasher, Kosher, Kashrut (Yiddish and Hebrew): Literally "fitness"; term describing the Orthodox Jewish requirements for ritually fit foods that persons and things must meet.

Limeño (Spanish): Inhabitant of Lima.

Maligno (regional Peruvian): A bad spirit from the Amazon jungle, a bad *Tunchi*.

Marranos (Spanish): Derogatory name (meaning swine) for *Conversos* utilized by the majority of the common people in Spain and Portugal. In Inquisitorial records those accused of "Judaizing" were called *Conversos*, "those of the nation" (the Jewish one), or heretical New Christians. In the Americas the *Marranos* were called *Portuguese* after the compulsory massive conversions of Portuguese Jews ordered by King Don Manuel in 1496. The term *Marrano* has been adopted in modern historiography to refer to *Conversos* and their offspring. *Marranism* implies a whole range of stands toward the Jewish faith, from those individuals who had totally adopted Christianity to those who secretly kept Jewish rituals (crypto-Jews). In Jewish communities *Marranos* were called *anusim*, meaning "the compelled" or "the raped ones." Those *Marranos* whose ancestors willingly converted to Christianity were called *meshumadim*.

Mercachifle (Spanish): Peddler, vendor.

Mestizo (Spanish): Descendant of mixed parentage. Usually it refers to a European-Indian mixture.

Mestizaje (Spanish): Miscegenation, hybridization. Modern historiography utilizes the term, implying a biological as well as a cultural and religious mixture.

Mohel (Hebrew): Person trained to perform ritual circumcisions.

New Christians: Term used in the Iberian Peninsula since the time of the Inquisition to distinguish Christians of "pure blood," or descendants of families of long "Christian lineage," from descendants of recent non-Christians converted to Christianity.

Paisano (Spanish): Compatriot, countryman, fellow man.

Patrón (regional Peruvian): Employee of the rubber barons. *Patrones* supervised the work of Indians in the jungle while their bosses remained most of the time in Amazonian cities.

Patronato (Spanish): System through which the Catholic Church gave to the nineteenth-century Latin American states the right to control ecclesiastical issues.

Pesaḥ (Hebrew): Passover.

Prefecto (Spanish): Governor.

Prefecturas (Spanish): Administrative regions.

Prelatura (Spanish): Region under ecclesiastical jurisdiction. It has higher hierarchical status than a *Vicariato*.

Quechua: Language of the native Andean inhabitants of Peru, which was then adopted by the Incas who conquered them. In today's Bolivia, the native language is Aymara.

Real Cédula (Spanish): Royal edict from Spanish monarch.

Regatón (Spanish): Trader who traveled through the rivers bringing merchandise from the cities to villages in the jungle, exchanging it for native products. During the rubber boom period, the *regatones* hired from commercial houses steamships, navigation equipment, and goods to trade to Indians in exchange for *bolas de caucho* (rubber balls); but the role of the *regatón* in the economic rubber system diminished when the most powerful rubber lords assigned their own crews and *patrónes* (overseers) to exploit the Indians.

Reducciones (Spanish): Resettlement program to cluster scattered native peoples into Hispanic-style towns; the resettled villages.

Rosh Hashanah (Hebrew): Jewish New Year.

Seringueiro (Portuguese): Brazilian rubber tapper.

Sephardi(c) (Plural, *Sephardim*): Derived from the Hebrew word "*Sepharad,*" for Spain. A Jew descended from members of the Jewish communities of Spain or Portugal and driven out by the Inquisition, particularly during the fifteenth century. The word today describes the Jews who resided thereafter in the Mediterranean countries, North Africa, and the Middle East.

Serrano (Spanish): Inhabitant of the Peruvian Andes.

Shabbat (Hebrew): Jewish seventh day hallowed by God after the creation. It runs from Friday evening to Saturday evening.

Shabbes Goy (Yiddish): Non-Jewish person whose services are requested during Shabbat in order to accomplish some tasks forbidden according to halakhah.

Shaman: Wise man of an Indian tribe. Healer, prophet, religious leader.

Shema (Hebrew): The statement of the unity of God.

Shohet (Hebrew): Person trained to supervise the kashrut of meat. He slaughters the live stock.

Tanakh (Hebrew): The Old Testament, the Hebrew Bible. TANAKH stands for Torah, Nevi'im, and Kethuvim, the three parts of the Hebrew Bible.

Tawantinsuyo (regional Peruvian): Inca Empire.

Tunchi (regional Peruvian): Birds of the Amazon whose shrieking cry makes Amazonian people see them as jungle spirits.

Vicariato (Spanish): Region under ecclesiastical jurisdiction.

Viracocha (regional Peruvian): One of the gods worshiped by the Incas, whom they associated with the Spanish conquerors.

Yacunamas (regional Peruvian): River spirits.

Yacurunas (regional Peruvian): The river's mother, represented by the figure of a serpent.

Yom Kippur (Hebrew): Day of Atonement. One of the holiest holidays of the Jewish people.

BIBLIOGRAPHY

PERSONAL LITERATURE OF THE PERIOD

Benchimol, Samuel. *Amazônia: Um Pouco-Antes E Além-Depois*. Manaus, Brazil: Coleção Amazoniana 1, Editora Umberto Calderaro, 1977.

Coriat, Juan E. *El hombre del Amazonas: Ensayo monográfico de Loreto*. Lima: Librería Coriat, 1943.

Fuentes, Hildebrando. *Loreto: Apuntes geográficos, históricos, estadísticos, políticos y sociales*. Lima: Imprenta de la Revista, 1908.

Hasson, Yaacov. "Iquitos: Alma Judía en la Amazonía Peruana." *Comunidades Judías de Latin América* 1972–75: 367–373.

Kelly, Henry Warren. *Dancing Diplomats*. Albuquerque: University of New Mexico Press, 1950.

Kerbey, Joseph Orton. *The Land of To-morrow: A Newspaper Exploration Up the Amazon and Over the Andes to the California of South America*. New York: W. F. Brainard Publisher, 1906.

López, Ismael. *De París al Amazonas: Las fieras del Putumayo*. Paris: Librería Paul Ollendorff, 1912.

Lorch, Netanel. *Hanahar Haloheshet: Al haPeru VeIsrael*. Jerusalem: Misrad Habitahon. 1969.

Ullman, James Ramsey. *The Other Side of the Mountain: An Escape to the Amazon*. New York: Carrick & Evans, 1938.

Up De Graff, Fritz W. *Head Hunters of the Amazon: Seven Years of Exploration and Adventure*. New York: Garden City Publishing Co., Inc., 1923.

Vásquez Izquierdo, Jaime. *Cordero de Dios (I)*. Iquitos: CONCYTEC, Bufeo Colorado Editores, 1989.

_____. *Cordero de Dios (II)*. Iquitos: CONCYTEC, Bufeo Colorado Editores, 1991.

ANTHOLOGIES

Acosta, Vladimir. *Viajeros y maravillas*. Vols. 1, 2, and 3. Caracas: Monte Avila Editores Latinoamericana, 1993.

Correa, Carlos Larrabure I. *Colección de leyes, decretos, resoluciones y otros documentos oficiales referentes al departamento de Loreto*. Lima: Imp. de "La Opinión Pública," 1905.

Encyclopedia Judaica. Jerusalem: Keter Publishing House Ltd., 1972.

Gossen, Gary, et al. *De palabra y obra en el nuevo mundo*. 3 vols. Madrid: Siglo Veintiuno, 1992.

Liebman, Seymour B. *The Inquisitors and the Jews in the New World: Summaries of Procesos, 1500–1810 & Bibliographic Guide.* Coral Gables: University of Miami Press, 1975.

Winfeld, Eduardo, ed. *Enciclopedia Judaica Castellana.* México: n.p., 1950.

SECONDARY SOURCES

Abramov, S. Z. *Perpetual Dilemma: Jewish Religion in the Jewish State.* Rutherford, N.J.: Fairleigh Dickenson University Press, 1976.

Achung Rodríguez, Martha. "Poblamiento de la Amazonía desde el siglo XIX hasta 1940." *Shupihui* (Iquitos) 37, no. 11 (1986): 7–28.

Acosta, Vladimir. *El continente prodigioso: Mitos e imaginario medieval en la conquista americana.* Caracas: Ediciones de la Biblioteca, Universidad Central de Venezuela, 1992.

Allen, Barbara. "Story in Oral History: Clues to Historical Consciousness." *Journal of American History* 2, no. 79 (September 1992): 606–611.

Anderson, Benedict. *Imagined Communities: Reflections on the Origin and Spread of Nationalism.* New York: Verso, 1983.

Aviahail, Eliahu (Rabbi), *The Tribes of Israel.* Jerusalem: Agudat Amishav, 1990.

Barclay, Frederica. *La colonia del Perené: Capital Inglés y economía cafetalera en la configuración de la región de Chanchamayo.* Iquitos: CETA, 1987.

Barletti Pasquale, José. "Luchas autonómicas anticentralistas." *Kanatari* (Iquitos), vol. 11 (April 17, 1994): 9–11.

Basadre, Jorge. *Historia de la República del Perú.* Lima: Editorial Universitaria S.A., 1968.

Beinart, Haim. *Conversos on Trial: The Inquisition in Ciudad Real.* Jerusalem: Magnes Press, 1981.

Ben Zvi, Izhak. *The Exiled and the Redeemed.* Philadelphia: Jewish Publication Society of America, 1957.

Biedma, Manuel. *La conquista franciscana del alto Ucayali.* Iquitos: Serie Monumenta Amazónica, CETA-IIAP, 1989.

Böhm, Gunter. *Judíos en el Perú durante el siglo XIX.* Santiago de Chile: Universidad de Chile, 1985.

Borowitz, Eugene B. *The Masks Jews Wear: The Self-Deceptions of American Jewry.* New York: Sh'ma, 1980.

Brown, Michael F. and Eduardo Fernández. *War of Shadows: The Struggle for Utopia in the Peruvian Amazon.* Berkeley: University of California Press, 1991.

Bushnell, David and Macaulay Neill. *The Emergence of Latin America in the Nineteenth Century.* New York: Oxford University Press, 1988.

Canelo, David Augusto. *The Last Crypto-Jews of Portugal.* Trans. Rabbi Joshua Stampfer. Ed. Talmon-l'Armee. Portland Oreg.: IJS, 1990

Cohen, David William, and E. S. Atieno Odhiambo. *Siaya: The Historical Anthropology of an African Landscape.* Athens: Ohio University Press, 1989.

Cohen, Erik. *Seker HaMiyutim Be Israel*. Jerusalem: Hebrew University Asian and African Studies Institute-Truman Institute, 1972.

Correa, Carlos Larrabure I. *Colección de leyes, decretos, resoluciones y otros documentos oficiales referentes al departamento de Loreto*. Lima: Imp. de "La Opinión Pública," 1905.

Dathorner, O. R. *Imagining the World: Mythical Belief Versus Reality in Global Encounters*. Westport, Conn.: Bergin & Garvey, 1994.

Davis, Wade. *One River: Explorations and Discoveries in the Amazon Rain Forest*. New York: Simon & Schuster, 1996.

de Arona, Juan. *La inmigración en el Perú*. Lima: Academia Diplomática del Perú, 1971.

Demos, John Putnam. *Entertaining Satan: Witchcraft and the Culture of Early New England*. New York: Oxford University Press, 1982.

Dening, Greg. *Islands and Beaches: Discourse on a Silent Land, Marquesas, 1774–1880*. Honolulu: University Press of Hawaii, 1980.

_____. "A Poetic for Histories: Transformations that Present the Past." In *Clio in Oceania: Toward Historical Anthropology*. Ed. Aletta Biersack. Washington D.C.: Smithsonian Institution Press, 1991.

Deshen, Shlomo, trans. *The Mellah Society: Jewish Community Life in Sherifian Morocco*. Chicago: University of Chicago Press, 1989.

Dobkin de Ríos, Marlene. *Amazon Healer: The Life and Times of an Urban Shaman*. Fullerton: California State University, Prims-Unity, 1992.

_____. *Visionary Vine: Hallucinogenic Healing in the Peruvian Amazon*. Prospect Heights, Ill.: Waveland Press, Inc., 1984.

Dobyns, Henry F. and Paul L. Doughty. *Peru: A Cultural History*. New York: Oxford University Press, 1976.

Domínguez, Virginia R. *People as Subject, People as Object: Selfhood and Peoplehood in Contemporary Israel*. Madison: University of Wisconsin Press, 1989.

Elkin, Judith Laikin. "The Evolution of the Latin American-Jewish Communities: Retrospect and Prospect." In *The Jewish Presence in Latin America*. Ed. Judith Laikin Elkin and Gilbert W. Merkx. Boston: Allen & Unwin Inc., 1987.

_____. *Jews of the Latin American Republics*. Chapel Hill: University of North Carolina Press, 1980.

Figueroa, Francisco. *Informes de Jesuitas en el Amazonas, 1660–1684*. Iquitos: Monumenta Amazónica CETA, 1986.

Finkielkraut, Alain. *The Imaginary Jew*. Trans. Kevin O'Neill and David Suchoff. Lincoln: University of Nebraska Press, 1994.

Flores Galindo, Alberto. *Buscando un Inca: Identidad y utopía en los Andes*. 3rd ed. Lima: Editorial Horizonte, 1988.

Flores Marín, José A. *La explotación del caucho en la selva*. Lima: CONCYTEC, 1987.

Freeman, Mark. *Rewriting the Self: History, Memory, Narrative*. London: Routledge, 1993.

Freilich, Alicia. *Cláper*. Caracas: Planeta, 1987.

García Sánchez, Joaquín. "Iquitos: Una isla blanca en el mar verde." In *Selva Musical*. Iquitos: Edición Fica, 1982.

Geertz, Clifford. "Deep Play: Notes on the Balinese Cockfight." In *Rethinking Popular Culture: Contemporary Perspectives in Cultural Studies*. Ed. Chandra Mukerji and Michael Schudson. Oxford: University of California Press, 1991.

_____. *The Social History of an Indonesian Town*. Cambridge: M.I.T. Press, 1965.

_____. *Work and Lives: The Anthropologist as Author*. Palo Alto: Standford University Press, 1988.

Gitlitz, David M. *Secrecy and Deceit: The Religion of the Crypto-Jews*. Philadelphia: Jewish Publication Society, 1996.

Goldemberg, Isaac. *The Fragmented Life of Don Jacobo Lerner*. Trans. Robert S. Picciotto. New York: Persea Books, 1976.

Graham, Richard. *The Idea of Race in Latin Amercia, 1870–1940*. Austin: Institute of Latin American Studies of University of Texas Press, 1990.

Halbwachs, Maurice. *The Collective Memory*. Trans. Francis J. Ditter and Vida Yazdi Ditter. New York: Harper & Row, 1980.

Halpern, Ben. *The Idea of the Jewish State*. Cambridge: Harvard University Press, 1969.

Hardenburg, Walter E. *The Putumayo, The Devil's Paradise: Travels in the Peruvian Amazon Region and an Account of the Atrocities Committed Upon the Indians Therein*. London: T. F. Unwin, 1912.

Hill, Jonathan D. "Myth and History." In *Rethinking History and Myth: Indigenous South American Perspectives on the Past*. Ed. Jonathan D. Hill. Chicago: University of Illinois Press, 1988.

Hordes, Stanley. "The Crypto-Jewish Community of New Spain, 1620–1819: A Collective Biography," Ph.D. diss., Tulane University, 1980.

_____. "The Inquisition and the Crypto-Jewish Community in Colonial New Spain and New Mexico." In *Cultural Encounters: The Impact of the Inquisition in Spain and the New World*. Ed. Mary Elizabeth Perry and Anne J. Cruz. Berkeley: University of California Press, 1991.

Hulme, Peter. *Colonial Encounters: Europe and the Native Caribbean, 1492–1797*. New York: Methuen, 1986.

Huppert, Uri, Joni Marra, and Linda MacMonagle. "The Israeli Law of Return." *Free Inquiry* 3, no. 12, (Summer 1992): 28–32.

Hutton, Patrick H. *History as an Art of Memory*. Hanover: University Press of New England, University of Vermont, 1993.

Kaplan, Steven. *The Beta Israel (Falasha) in Ethiopia: From Earliest Times to the Twentieth Century*. New York: New York University Press, 1992.

Katz, Nathan and Ellen S. Goldberg. *The Last Jews of Cochin: Jewish Identity in Hindu India*. Columbia: University of South Carolina Press, 1993.

Kelly, Brian and Mark London. *Amazon*. San Diego: Harcourt Brace Jovanovich Publishers, 1983.

Kraines, Oscar. *The Impossible Dilemma: Who Is A Jew in the State of Israel?* New York: Bloch Publishing Company, 1976.

Lacarra, María Jesús and Juan Manuel Cacho Blecua. *Lo Imaginario en la conquista de America*. Zaragosa, Spain: Ediciones Oroel, 1990.

Lafaye, Jacques. *Quetzacóatl and Guadalupe: The Formation of Mexican National Consciousness, 1531–1813*. Chicago: University of Chicago Press, 1974.

Laskier, Michael. *The Alliance Israélite Universelle and the Jewish Communities of Morocco, 1862–1962*. Albany: SUNY Press, 1983.

_____. *North African Jewry in the Twentieth Century: The Jews of Morocco, Tunisia and Algeria*. New York: New York University Press, 1994.

Lausent-Herrera, Isabelle. "Los inmigrantes chinos en la Amazonía peruana." In *Primer seminario sobre poblaciones inmigratorias, 1986*. Vol. 2. Ed. Amelia Morimoto and José Carlos Luciano. Lima: CONCYTEC, 1988.

Lavie, Smadar. *The Poetics of Military Occupation: Mzeina Allegories of Bedouin Identity Under Israeli and Egyptian Rule*. Berkeley: University of California Press, 1990.

Lazar, Moshe. "Scorched Parchments and Tortured Memories: The 'Jewishness' of the Anussim (Crypto-Jews)." In *Cultural Encounters: The Impact of the Inquisition in Spain and the New World*. Ed. Mary Elizabeth Perry and Anne J. Cruz. Berkeley: University of California Press, 1991.

Lea, Henry Charles. *The Inquisition in the Spanish Dependencies*. Rev. ed. London: Macmillan and Company, Ltd., 1992.

Le Goff, Jacques. *History and Memory*. Trans. Steven Rendall and Elizabeth Claman. New York: Columbia University Press, 1992.

León Pinelo, Antonio de. *El Paraíso en el Nuevo Mundo: Comentario Apologético, Historia Natural y Peregrina de las Indias Occidentales Islas de Tierra Firme del Mar Oceano (1645–1650)*. Ed. Porras Barrenechea. Lima: Comité del IV Centenario del Descubrimiento del Amazonas, 1943.

Levine, Robert M. "Adaptive Strategies of Jews in Latin America." In *The Jewish Presence in Latin America*. Ed. Judith Laikin Elkin and Gilbert W. Merkx. Boston: Allen & Unwin Inc., 1987.

Lewin, Boleslao. *Los criptojudíos: Un fenómeno religioso y social*. Buenos Aires: Editorial Mila, 1987.

Liebman, Charles and Eliezer Don-Yehiya. *Civil Religion in Israel: Traditional Judaism and Political Culture in the Jewish State*. Berkeley: University of California Press, 1983.

Liebman, Seymour B. "The Mestizo Jews of Mexico." *American Jewish Historical Society* 19 (1967): 144–174.

_____. *Requiem por los olvidados: Los Judíos españoles en America 1493–1825*. Madrid: Altalena, 1984.

Lukacs, John. *Historical Consciousness: The Remembered Past*. New York: Harper & Row Publishers, 1968.

Manrique, Manuel. *La Peruvian Corporation en la selva central del Perú*. Lima: Centro de Investigaciones y Promoción de la Amazonía, 1982.

Marazzani Mindreau, Emilio. *1870–1970: Cien Años de Vida Judía en el Perú*. Lima: Sociedad Israelita 1870, 1970.

Marks, Elaine. *Marrano as Metaphor: The Jewish Presence in French Writing*. New York: Columbia University Press, 1996.

Marzal, Manuel. "Las reducciones indígenas en la Amazonía del virreynato peruano." *Amazonía peruana* (Iquitos) 10, no. 5 (March 1984): 7–45.

Mason, Peter. "Imagining Worlds: Counterfact and Artifact." In *Myth and the Imaginary in the New World*. Ed. Edmundo Magaña and Peter Mason. *Latin American Studies* 34. Holland: CEDLA, Foris Publications, 1986: 43–74.

Merkx, Gilbert W. "Jewish Studies as a Subject of Latin American Studies." In *The Jewish Presence in Latin America*. Ed. Judith Laikin Elkin and Gilbert W. Merkx. Boston: Allen & Unwin Inc., 1987.

Miller, Susan Gilson. "Kippur on the Amazon: Jewish Emigration from Northern Morocco in the Late Nineteenth Century." In *Sephardi and Middle Eastern Jewries: History and Culture in the Modern Era*. Ed. Harvey E. Goldberg. Bloomington: Indiana University Press, 1996.

Mor, Menachem. *Jewish Sects, Religious Movements, and Political Parties: Proceedings of the Third Annual Symposium of the Philip M. and Ethel Klutznick Chair in Jewish Civilization*. Omaha: Creighton University Press, 1990.

Mörner, Magnus, ed. *Race and Class in Latin America*. New York: Columbia University Press, 1970.

Neusner, Jacob. *Judaism and Its Social Metaphors: Israel in the History of Jewish Thought*. New York: Cambridge University Press, 1989.

Neyra, Javier. *Los que llegaron después: Estudio del impacto cultural de las denominaciones religiosas no Católicas en Iquitos*. Iquitos: CETA, 1992.

Novinsky, Anita. *Inquisicão: Inventarios de Ben Confiscados a Cristãos Novos: Fontes para a História de Portugal e do Brasil (Brasil-Século XVIII)*. Rio de Janeiro: Imprensa Nacional, Casa da Moeda, Livraria Camões, 1976.

_____. "Jewish Roots of Brazil." In *The Jewish Presence in Latin America*. Ed. Judith Laikin Elkin and Gilbert W. Merkx. Boston: Allen & Unwin, Inc., 1987.

Parfitt, Tudor. *The Thirteenth Gate: Travels Among the Lost Tribes of Israel*. Bethesda, Md.: Adler & Adler Publishers Inc., 1987.

Patai, Raphael. "The Jewish Indians of Mexico." In *On Jewish Folklore*. Detroit: Wayne University Press, 1983.

_____. "Venta Prieta Revisited." In *On Jewish Folklore*. Detroit: Wayne State University Press, 1983.

Paz, Octavio. *The Labyrinth of Solitude*. Trans. Lysander Kemp, Yara Milos, and Rachel Phillips Belash. New York: Grove Press, 1985.

Pennano, Guido. *La economía del caucho*. Iquitos: Serie Debate Amazónico, CETA, CONCYTEC, 1987.

Perks, Robert. *Oral History: Talking About the Past*. London: The Historical Association, 1992.

Portocarrero Maish, Gonzalo. *Racismo y mestizaje*. Lima: Sur Casa de Estudios del Socialismo, 1993.

Price, Richard. *Alabi's World*. Baltimore: Johns Hopkins University Press, 1990.

Prins, Gwyn. "Oral History." In *New Perspectives on Historical Writing*. Ed. Peter Burke. University Park: Pennsylvania State University Press, 1993).

Prinz, Joachim. *The Secret Jews*. New York: Random House, 1973.

Pullan, Brian S. *The Jews of Europe and the Inquisition of Venice, 1550–1670*. Totowa, N.J.: Barnes & Noble, 1983.

Rabinow, Paul. *Reflections on Fieldwork in Morocco*. Berkeley: University of California Press, 1977.

Regan, Jaime. *Hacia la tierra sin mal: La religión del pueblo en la Amazonía*. Iquitos: CETA, 1993.

Ríos Zañartu, Mario C. *Historia de la Amazonía peruana*. Iquitos: Editora "El Matutino," 1995.

Rosenbloom, Joseph R. *Conversion to Judaism: From the Biblical Period to the Present*. Cincinnati: Hebrew Union College, 1978.

Rosenzweig, Alfredo. "Judíos en la Amazonía Peruana, 1870–1949." *Maj'Shavot* (Buenos Aires) 12 (June 1967): 19–30.

Ross, Dan. *Acts of Faith: A Journey to the Fringes of Jewish Identity*. New York: Schocken Books, 1984.

Roth, Cecil. *A History of the Marranos*. Philadelphia: Jewish Publication Society of America, 1941.

_____. "The Religion of the Marranos." *Jewish Quarterly Review* 1, no. 22 (July 1931): 1–34.

Roth, Sol. *Halakha and Politics: The Jewish Idea of the State*. New York: Ktav Publishing House, 1988.

Ruggiero, Guido. *Binding Passions: Tales of Magic, Marriage, and Power at the End of the Renaissance*. New York: Oxford University Press, 1993.

Rumrrill, Roger and Pierre de Zutter. *Amazonía y capitalismo: Los condenados de la selva*. Lima: Editorial Horizonte, 1976.

San Román, Jesús Víctor. *Perfiles históricos de la Amazonía peruana*. Lima: Ediciones Paulina-CETA, 1975.

Santos, Fernando. "Etnohistoria de la alta Amazonía, siglos XV–XVIII." In *Colección 500 años ediciones* 46. Quito: ABYA-YALA-Cayembe, 1990.

Serels, Mitchell M. *A History of the Jews of Tangier in the Nineteenth and Twentieth Centuries*. New York: Sepher-Hermon Press, 1991.

Stocking, George W. *Observers Observed: Essays on Ethnographic Fieldwork*. Madison: University of Wisconsin Press, 1983.

Toribio Medina, José. *Historia del tribunal de la Inquisición de Lima, 1569–1820*. Santiago de Chile: Fondo Histórico y Bibliográfico J. T. Medina, 1956.

Trahtemberg, León. *Demografía Judía del Perú*. Lima: Ort-Perú, 1988.

_____. *La inmigración Judía al Perú, 1848–1948: Una historia documentada de la inmigración de los Judíos de habla Alemana*. Lima: UIP, 1987.

_____. *Los Judíos de Lima y las provincias del Perú*. Lima: UIP, 1989.

Turner, Terence. "Ethno-Ethno History: Myth and History in Native South American Representations of Contact with Western Society." In *Rethinking History and Myth: Indigenous South American Perspectives on the Past*. Ed. Jonathan D. Hill. Chicago: University of Illinois Press, 1988.

Valcarcel, Daniel. *Rebeliones indígenas*. Lima: Edit P.T.C.M., 1946.

Valensi, Lucette and Nathan Wachtel. *Jewish Memories*. Trans. Barabara Harshav. Berkeley: University of California Press, 1991.

Van Maanen, John. *Tales of the Field: On Writing Ethnography*. Chicago: University of Chicago Press, 1988.

Vansina, Jan. *Oral Tradition: A Study in Historical Methodology*. London: Routledge, 1966.

Vargas Llosa, Mario. *Pantaleón y las Visitadoras*. Barcelona: Editorial Seix Barral, 1973.

_____. *The Storyteller*. Trans. Helen Lane. New York: Penguin Books, 1990.

Vargas Ugarte, Rubén. *El Episcopado en los Tiempos de la Emancipación Sudamericana (1809–1830)*. Buenos Aires: Impr. de Amorrortul, 1932.

Villarejo, Avencio. *Así es la selva*. Iquitos: CETA, 1988.

Weinstein, Barbara. *The Amazon Rubber Boom, 1850–1926*. Stanford: Stanford University Press, 1983.

Witnitzer, Arnold. *Jews in Colonial Brazil*. New York: Columbia University Press, 1960.

Yerushalmi, Yosef Hayim. *From Spanish Court to Italian Ghetto: Isaac Cardoso, A Study in Seventeenth-Century Marranism and Jewish Apologetics*. New York: Center of Israel and Jewish Studies of Columbia University, 1966.

_____. "The Re-Education of Marranos in the Seventeenth Century." In *Third Annual Rabbi Louis Feinberg Memorial Lecture in Judaic Studies*. Cincinnati: University of Cincinnati, 1980.

_____. *Zakhor: Jewish History and Jewish Memory*. Seattle: University of Washington Press, 1982.

Yovel, Yeremiahu. *Spinoza and Other Heretics: The Marrano of Reason*. Princeton: Princeton University Press, 1989.

INDEX

People with compound Spanish surnames are
indexed according to their second surname

photographs